Colonialism, Antisemitism, and Germans of
Jewish Descent in Imperial Germany

For a complete list of titles, please see www.press.umich.edu

Colonialism, Antisemitism, and Germans of Jewish Descent in Imperial Germany

CHRISTIAN S. DAVIS

The University of Michigan Press
Ann Arbor

Published in the United States of America by
The University of Michigan Press
Manufactured in the United States of America
⊚ Printed on acid-free paper

2015   2014   2013   2012   4   3   2   1

A CIP catalog record for this book is available from the British Library.

Library of Congress Cataloging-in-Publication Data

Davis, Christian S., 1974–
    Colonialism, antisemitism, and Germans of Jewish descent in imperial Germany / Christian S. Davis.
        p. cm. — (Social history, popular culture, and politics in Germany)
    Includes bibliographical references and index.
    ISBN 978-0-472-11797-0 (cloth : alk. paper) — ISBN 978-0-472-02780-4 (e-book)
    1. Antisemitism—Germany—History—19th century.
    2. Antisemitism—Germany—History—20th century.
    3. Germany—Colonies—Administration—History.
    4. Germany—Colonies—Officials and employees—Biography.
    5. Germany—Politics and government—1871–1918.   6. Dernburg, Bernhard, 1865–1937.   I. Title.
    DS146.G4D38   2011
    305.892'404309034—dc23   2011028332

For Michelle, Lilly, and Jasper

Acknowledgments

This project began as a dissertation at Rutgers University, and it was Omer Bartov who, in a research seminar, first pointed me toward German colonialism. I want to thank him for his initial guidance and also for his efforts in supporting and promoting my research since then. My other committee members, Michael Adas, Matt Matsuda, and Isabel V. Hull, provided helpful critiques of this project during its earlier incarnation. More recently, I benefited from advice and feedback from the editors of the *Leo Baeck Institute Year Book,* who published an early and abbreviated version of chapter 4 in their journal, as well as from Geoff Eley and the readers for the University of Michigan Press. Before the project began, my interests in ethnic nationalism in Central Europe and, more specifically, German antisemitism were encouraged by my mentors in the MA history program at the University of Georgia, Athens, chief among them John Haag and John Morrow, Jr.

Over the years, I received financial assistance for this work from a number of institutions and organizations. The German Academic Exchange Service provided funding that helped pay for an extended stay in Germany. I received additional support from the German Historical Institute, the American Historical Association, and Salem College as well as from the Claudia Clark-Rebecca Gershenson-Megan McClintock Memorial Fund of the History Department of Rutgers, the State University of New Jersey–New Brunswick. Toward the end, I benefited greatly from financial support in the form of research and travel grants from the College of Charleston. I owe a heartfelt debt of gratitude to the history department as a whole and to certain members in particular: to Lee Drago, who assisted me with my book proposal, and to the department chair during my stay, Bill Olejniczak, whose generosity and kindness made my time at the College of Charleston such an enjoyable experience. I also want to thank Michael Galgano and the history department at James Madison University, who, in the final stage of the project, provided me with the space and equipment that I needed.

In addition, I want to acknowledge family and friends. My wonderful parents, Ronald and Patricia Davis, provided moral and financial support that made this work possible. What is more, my father, a professor emeritus of history at California State University, Northridge, gave crucial feedback on this project at its various stages, as did my sister, Stacey Davis, a professor of history at Evergreen State College. My good friend, Gabriel Clinton, has likewise been a constant source of encouragement. Finally, I want to thank my loving wife, Michelle Maraffi, and my two children, Lilly and Jasper. Michelle has shown remarkable resilience over the years. She was the breadwinner of the family while I worked on the PhD, and she provided the lion's share of the childcare for Lilly and Jasper, especially as the book neared completion. During the long hours that I spent in archives, in libraries, and at my office at school, working on the project, she cared for our children with admirable strength and wisdom. Moreover, her faith in me kept me going when the combined tasks of research, writing, and teaching seemed overwhelming. I also owe much to Lilly and Jasper with their endless supplies of smiles, kisses, and hugs. This book is dedicated to Michelle and my children.

Contents

Introduction: Colonialism, Antisemitism, and Germans of Jewish Descent

On March 14, 1896, the Social Democratic daily *Vorwärts: Berliner Volks-blatt* printed an unsigned, front-page commentary on an important event that occurred in the Reichstag the preceding day. On March 13, the Social Democratic leader August Bebel vehemently denounced the colonial official Carl Peters for his alleged brutality against Africans in 1891 and 1892 while serving as an imperial commissioner in German East Africa. According to Bebel, Peters married an African girl in accordance with local tradition but executed her along with her lover, one of Peters's male African servants, upon discovering her infidelity. *Vorwärts* claimed that the revelations exposed on the floor of the Reichstag amounted to "a black day for German 'colonial policy.'" The article compares Peters to Menelik II, the Ethiopian emperor whose forces had tortured to death hundreds of Italian soldiers and their *askari*[1] troops following the recent battle at Adwa.[2] In explaining Peters's actions, *Vorwärts* stated that the two executed Africans were in fact substitutes for the real targets of his rage. "Germany has not succumbed to an African Menelik," the newspaper proclaimed. Germany "has found its Menelik in a German—in a 'truly Teutonic man,' an enraged 'Aryan,' who wishes to destroy all Jews, but, for a lack of Jews over there in Africa, shoots Negroes dead like sparrows and hangs Negro girls for his own pleasure after they have satisfied his desires."

---

1. From Arabic, meaning "soldier," used to denote European-led African infantries in northern and eastern Africa.

2. On March 1, 1895, an Ethiopian force of 100,000 annihilated a much smaller Italian army of 20,000 (including *askaris*) at Adwa (Thomas Pakenham, *The Scramble for Africa: White Man's Conquest of the Dark Continent from 1876 to 1912* [New York: Avon Books, 1991], 471–82).

Vorwärts characterized Peters as "the classic representative of German colonial policy."[3]

The suggestion made by *Vorwärts* that Carl Peters substituted Africans for Jews as the targets of his murderous rage is both interesting and remarkable. Writing at a time when physical violence against Jews was rare within Germany and when the horrors of the Holocaust could not have been imagined, the article's author anticipated Hannah Arendt's idea of a link between radical antisemitism and the brutalities of the colonial project. In her 1951 book, *The Origins of Totalitarianism,* Arendt argued that the colonial experience in Africa during the age of high imperialism laid the ideological groundwork for the Holocaust by radicalizing European racism, imbuing it with genocidal possibilities, and propagating a racial consciousness throughout European society. Arendt claimed that colonialism also engendered the techniques of racial domination later used by the Nazis, saying that it was in Africa where Europeans learned "how peoples could be converted into races and how, simply by taking the initiative in this process, one might push one's own people into the position of the master race."[4] Like Arendt, the *Vorwärts* article recognizes a dynamic

---

3. "Ein schwarzer Tag," *Vorwärts: Berliner Volksblatt,* March 14, 1896. Carl Peters was one of the most active and important early members of imperial Germany's colonial movement. He founded the Society for German Colonization in 1884, which organized treaty-signing expeditions to east Africa, laying the foundations of the future German colony. Peters led several expeditions himself, and he became a well-known and popular spokesman for the colonial cause. The government appointed him as one of three imperial commissioners of German East Africa in 1891, and it was while serving in this capacity on the slopes of Mt. Kilimanjaro that the events discussed in the Reichstag in March 1896 are alleged to have taken place. Although Peters admitted to having had sexual relations with African women, he denied marrying the African girl or ordering the executions out of jealousy. An official investigation determined that Peters had lied about the incident to his superiors, and a disciplinary court charged him with filing false reports. He was dismissed from his post following this conviction (Martin Reuss, "The Disgrace and Fall of Carl Peters: Morality, Politics, and *Staatsräson* in the Time of Wilhelm II," *Central European History* 14 [1981]: 110–41; Jonathon Glassman, *Feasts and Riots: Revelry, Rebellion, and Popular Consciousness on the Swahili Coast, 1856–1888* [Portsmouth: Heinemann, 1995], 184, 195; Juhani Koponen, *Development for Exploitation: German Colonial Policies in Mainland Tanzania, 1884–1914* [Helsinki: Finnish Historical Society, 1995], 69–84).

4. Hannah Arendt, *The Origins of Totalitarianism* (San Diego: Harcourt Brace, 1979), 206. Arendt received a doctoral degree in philosophy from the University of Heidelberg in 1928. A Jew, she fled Germany for Paris in 1933 and immigrated to the United States in 1941. She joined the faculty at the University of Chicago from 1963 to 1967 and afterward the New School for Social Research in New York City. Arendt's interests as a political theorist centered on political action, participatory freedom, and the division between the public and private spheres of life. Her reputation as a historical analyst of totalitarianism has increased in recent years due to a renewed interest in *Origins.*

link between colonialism and antisemitism, but reverses, in a sense, Arendt's thesis. The article implies that antisemitism influenced the actions and attitudes of colonialists toward Africans. From this perspective, Africa served as a stage for the acting out of violent, well-entrenched, and substantially developed antisemitic fantasies.

This study investigates the connections between antisemitism and colonialism in imperial Germany from approximately 1884 to 1914. It examines the significant involvement with and investment in colonialism of dedicated antisemites—individual actors as well as the major antisemitic political parties and extraparliamentary organizations of the day—studying modern German antisemitism in the context of Germany's colonial racial states. My work is influenced by Arendt's idea of a link between colonialism during the age of high imperialism and the type of racial thinking that structured National Socialism later on, but I depart from Arendt in my emphasis and interpretation. Unlike Arendt, I focus on the reciprocal dimensions of the relationship between colonialism and antisemitism, arguing that the antisemitic and colonialist movements of the *Kaiserreich* era impinged upon each other in meaningful ways. I also insist on the fundamentally contradictory nature of the relationship, showing how colonialism worked both for and against the new racial antisemitism.

The example and experience of colonial racial states both influenced and reinforced racialist points of view in antisemitic circles while giving antisemites new platforms on which to propagate ideas of racial hierarchies to the broader public. At the same time, colonialism actually undermined one of the central arguments of racial antisemites against the Jews—that they were biologically incapable of true German patriotism—by providing public examples of German Jews and Germans of Jewish descent working on behalf of colonial empire. In addition, by creating discursive spaces in politics and society for the articulation and refinement of radical racist ideas, colonialism enabled antisemites to help shape colonizing discourses that, though directed at colonial subjects abroad, eventually encompassed the main tenets of the new racial antisemitism. What is more, hardened antisemites were hands-on participants in the project of creating colonial empire and, as such, influenced colonialism's character at important stages in its development. In short, this book explores the varied and complex implications that colonial empire had for the domestic antisemitic movement, while revealing how antisemitic actors and imaginations affected the colonial project in real ways.

A central part of this story concerns the participation in colonialism of

Germans of Jewish descent. Men designated as "Jewish" by their peers played prominent roles in Germany's colonial project, as administrators, financiers, publicists, and political and extraparliamentary advocates. Both the leader of the Colonial Division of the Foreign Office from 1890 to 1896, Paul Kayser, and his successor, Bernhard Dernburg—who ran the Colonial Division and then the newly independent Colonial Office from 1906 to 1910—had one or more Jewish parents. The Jewish ancestry of these and other important colonial actors—like the explorer Emin Pasha—was public knowledge, but this did not stop them from winning varying degrees of popular acclaim. Dernburg and Emin Pasha even became heroes to the procolonial public, lauded as champions of colonialism. This book studies the ramifications that this had for the antisemitic movement: how the participation of Germans of Jewish descent in a patriotic project of empire building informed by ideologies of racial domination affected an antisemitic movement that increasingly painted Jews as threatening racial aliens. It is only by examining the phenomenon of "Jewish" involvement in colonialism, and the reactions to this from the procolonial public and among dedicated antisemites, that the true complexity of the interrelationship of colonialism and antisemitism during the *Kaiserreich* era can be ascertained.[5]

Historians have recently shown a renewed interest in imperial Germany's colonial history, driven in part by new, sometimes critical attention paid to Arendt's hypothesis of a link between the spirit and policies of National Socialism and the colonial imperialism of a slightly earlier age. The conventional wisdom that viewed imperial Germany's short-lived colonial empire as relatively unimportant has given way to increased interest in its domestic ramifications and attention to its effects on colonized populations. A controversial new "continuity thesis" has arisen, driven by historians who highlight what they see as the colonial antecedents of National Socialist ideas about race and space and of Nazi actions and attitudes in Eastern Europe during the Second World War.[6] Other new work explores

---

5. The term *antisemitic community* will be used to designate the broad spectrum of individuals and organizations in imperial Germany whose heightened concern over the Jewish Question distinguished them from a broader public that, by 1900 if not before, shared many of the antisemites' own prejudices. This included individuals who read or wrote for antisemitic publications as well as the leadership and rank and file of political parties and extraparliamentary organizations for whom an antisemitic outlook was—implicitly or explicitly—a central part of their overall philosophy.

6. Jürgen Zimmerer, "Colonialism and the Holocaust: Towards an Archeology of Genocide," *Genocide and Settler Society: Frontier Violence and Stolen Indigenous Children in Australian History,* edited by A. Dirk Moses (New York: Berghahn Books. 2004), 49–76; Ben-

colonialism's effects on contemporary German culture and self-awareness, illustrating how colonialism made itself felt in everything from Wilhelminian consumerism and advertising, to ideas about citizenship and national belonging, to working-class reading habits, to right-wing feminist aspirations.[7] Recent attention has been paid as well to colonial violence, especially that of Southwest Africa, which witnessed a German-imposed genocide in 1904.[8] Some historians have also begun to interpret German control

---

jamin Madley, "From Africa to Auschwitz: How German South West Africa Incubated Ideas and Methods Adopted and Developed by the Nazis in Eastern Europe," *European History Quarterly* 35 (2005): 429–64; Zimmerer, "The Birth of the *Ostland* out of the Spirit of Colonialism: A Postcolonial Perspective on the Nazi Policy of Conquest and Extermination," *Patterns of Prejudice* 39 (2005): 197–219. Also see A. Dirk Moses, "Empire, Colony, Genocide: Keywords and the Philosophy of History," in *Empire, Colony, Genocide: Conquest, Occupation, and Subaltern Resistance in World History,* ed. A. Dirk Moses (New York: Berghahn Books, 2008), 3–54; David Furber and Wendy Lower, "Colonialism and Genocide in Nazi-Occupied Poland and Ukraine," in *Empire, Colony, Genocide,* 372–402; and Helmut Walser Smith, *The Continuities of German History: Nation, Religion, and Race across the Long Nineteenth Century* (Cambridge: Cambridge University Press, 2008), 167–210.

7. Some of the most interesting work to appear since the late 1990s includes Susanne Zantop, *Colonial Fantasies: Conquest, Family, and Nation in Precolonial Germany, 1770–1870* (Durham: Duke University Press, 1997); Sara Friedrichsmeyer, Sara Lennox, and Susanne Zantop, eds., *The Imperialist Imagination: German Colonialism and Its Legacy* (Ann Arbor: University of Michigan Press, 1998); Pascal Grosse, *Kolonialismus, Eugenik und bürgerliche Gesellschaft in Deutschland, 1850–1918* (Frankfurt am Main: Campus Verlag, 2000); Lora Wildenthal, *German Women for Empire, 1884–1945* (Durham: Duke University Press, 2001); Andrew Zimmerman, *Anthropology and Antihumanism in Imperial Germany* (Chicago: University of Chicago Press, 2001); Jürgen Zimmerer, *Deutsche Herrschaft über Afrikaner: Staatlicher Machtanspruch und Wirklichkeit im kolonialen Namibia* (Münster: Lit Verlag, 2002); Birthe Kundrus, ed., *Phantasiereiche: Zur Kulturgeschichte des deutschen Kolonialismus* (Frankfurt am Main: Campus Verlag, 2003); Arne Perras, *Carl Peters and German Imperialism, 1856–1918: A Political Biography* (Oxford: Oxford University Press, 2004); Patricia Mazón and Reinhild Steingröver, eds., *Not so Plain as Black and White: Afro-German Culture and History, 1890–2000* (Rochester: University of Rochester Press, 2005); Eric Ames, Marcia Klotz, and Lora Wildenthal, eds., *Germany's Colonial Pasts* (Lincoln: University of Nebraska Press, 2005); Erik Grimmer-Solem, "The Professors' Africa: Economists, the Elections of 1907, and the Legitimation of German Imperialism," *German History* 25 (2007): 313–47; Helmut Walser Smith, *The Continuities of German History: Nation, Religion, and Race across the Long Nineteenth Century* (Cambridge: Cambridge University Press, 2008).

8. Isabel V. Hull, *Absolute Destruction: Military Culture and the Practices of War in Imperial Germany* (Ithaca: Cornell University Press, 2005); Thoralf Klein and Frank Schumacher, eds., *Kolonialkriege: Militärische Gewalt im Zeichen des Imperialismus* (Hamburg: HIS Verlag, 2006); George Steinmetz, *The Devil's Handwriting: Precoloniality and the German Colonial State in Qingdao, Samoa, and Southwest Africa* (Chicago: University of Chicago Press, 2007); Jürgen Zimmerer and Joachim Zeller, eds., *Genocide in German South-West Africa: The Colonial War of 1904–1908 and Its Aftermath,* trans. E. J. Neather (Monmouth, Wales: Merlin Press, 2008).

over Polish Prussia during the *Kaiserreich* period in colonial terms, speaking of a continental colonial empire in addition to an overseas one.[9]

The new scholarship—which I examine in greater detail later in the Introduction—offers much that is rich and revealing. It broadens our understanding of colonialism's place in the narrative of modern German history, reintegrating it after a long period of relative neglect. It offers little or no perspective, however, on the actual practical interrelationship of the contemporaneous colonial and antisemitic movements of the *Kaiserreich* era. As a result, it fails to recognize the reciprocal dynamic at work between colonialism and antisemitism. What is more, the current historiography fails to reflect on the involvement of those Germans of Jewish descent who, while themselves the targets of racial hatred, participated at the highest levels in the creation and maintenance of overseas colonial racial states.

By investigating the participation of, and collaboration among, antisemites, German Jews, and Germans of Jewish descent in imperial Germany's colonial project, my work moves the discussion of the domestic effects of German colonialism in new directions, with ramifications for our evolving understanding of the relationship between Wilhelminian colonialism and the National Socialist age. It does so by examining the actual experiences with and perceptions of colonialism of the men and women who, decades before the implementation of the Holocaust, developed and propagated its driving motor: racial antisemitism. Furthermore, by closely examining the contemporaneous involvement in German colonizing efforts of antisemites and individuals of Jewish descent, my study expands our understanding of the pressures and complexities of life in imperial Germany for those who suffered the vicious barbs of antisemitic hatred, even as it illuminates the peculiar character of this cooperation.

---

9. Dieter Gosewinkel, *Einbürgern und Ausschließen: Die Nationalisierung der Staatsangehörigkeit vom deutschen Bund bis zur Bundesrepublik Deutschland* (Göttingen: Vandenhoeck und Ruprecht, 2003); Philipp Ther, "Imperial instead of National History: Positioning Modern German History on the Map of European Empires," in *Imperial Rule,* ed. Alexei Miller and Alfred J. Rieber (Budapest: Central European University Press, 2004), 47–68; Kristin Kopp, "Constructing Racial Difference in Colonial Poland," in *Germany's Colonial Pasts,* ed. Eric Ames, Marcia Klotz, and Lora Wildenthal (Lincoln: University of Nebraska Press, 2005), 76 96; Sebastian Conrad, *Globalisierung und Nation im Deutschen Kaiserreich* (Munich: C. H. Beck, 2006).

The era of German colonialism spanned approximately thirty-five of imperial Germany's forty-seven years, lasting from 1884 until the victors of the First World War stripped Germany of its colonial possessions in early 1919. The geographical land holdings of the German colonies encompassed much of today's nations of Togo, Cameroon, Tanzania, and Namibia, plus several islands in the South Pacific and a small region in China, a total area many times the size of Germany's European territory. Until recently, scholars of modern Germany and European imperialism tended to marginalize the history of German colonialism, and they did so for several reasons. First, imperial Germany entered the quest for overseas empire late in the game and, as a result, was a colonial power for a much shorter time than Britain and France. Second, Germany's colonies failed to meet desired economic expectations, costing more to maintain than the profits earned back in trade.[10] Finally, the colonies never became important destinations for German immigration. Only Southwest Africa (Namibia) approached the status of a settler colony, with a white population of about 14,000 by the eve of the Great War. This number was minuscule compared with the flood of immigrants that left Germany for the Americas during the same period. By 1913, the German colonies had less than 25,000 white residents.

Although historians traditionally questioned the relevance of German colonialism to developments internal to the Wilhelminian Reich, they have long recognized its devastating impact on indigenous populations.[11] Like all colonial endeavors during the age of high imperialism, German colonialism was marked by remarkable violence. Unlike elsewhere, however, the idea of a "civilizing mission" did not mitigate the brutalities of colonial rule in the German colonies. While British and French administrators took the "civilizing mission" seriously, believing that they had a responsibility to uplift and assimilate the colonized, German poli-

---

10. Exceptions were Togo, which yielded a trade surplus, and Samoa, which also turned a profit.

11. Fritz F. Müller, *Kolonien unter der Peitsche* (Berlin: Rütten und Loening, 1962); Horst Drechsler, *"Let Us Die Fighting": The Struggle of the Herero and Nama against German Imperialism, 1884–1915* (London: Zed Press, 1966); Helmut Bley, *South-West Africa under German Rule* (Evanston: Northwestern University Press, 1971); Juhani Koponen, *Development for Exploitation;* Johnathan Glassman, *Feasts and Riots: Revelry, Rebellion, and Popular Consciousness on the Swahili Coast, 1856–1888* (Portsmouth: Heinemann, 1995); Robert J. Gordon and Stuart Sholto Douglas, *The Bushman Myth: The Making of a Namibian Underclass,* 2nd ed. (Boulder: Westview Press, 2000).

cymakers and colonial enthusiasts were much more open about the exploitative nature of the colonial project.[12] Although talk of a "white man's burden" was not absent from German colonialism, German administrators and financiers typically rationalized their actions by referring to the principle of national self-interest, viewing colonialism solely as an economic venture.

The violent nature of German colonialism emerges most clearly in the history of the conquest and rule of German East and Southwest Africa. The first was Germany's largest colony, measuring some 384,180 square miles, and it also contained the greatest number of indigenous people, estimated at about three million when the Germans arrived.[13] Major colonial-era exports from East Africa consisted of coffee, cotton, and sisal—grown on white-owned plantations and also by indigenous farmers—as well as copal and rubber retrieved from the hinterland. German Southwest Africa was almost as large but contained a much smaller indigenous population, numbering only in the hundreds of thousands. An arid climate precluded the possibility of cash crop plantations but encouraged white settler immigration because the area was free from the diseases that plagued Togo, Cameroon, and East Africa. The conditions of German rule engendered lengthy wars in both colonies beginning in 1904 and 1905, as indigenes rebelled against the oppressive German system. Germany crushed these rebellions with extreme brutality and, in their aftermath, consolidated its control by erecting even harsher systems of racial domination.

The suppression of the 1904 uprisings in Southwest Africa was especially brutal, with devastating aftereffects for the native populations. When the German government first extended its protection to German commercial interests in the area in 1884, the territory contained about 80,000 Herero and 20,000 Nama, ethnic groups living in the colony's central and southern regions.[14] During the early stages of the Herero and Nama Wars,

---

12. For a discussion of the civilizing mission in British and French colonial theory and practice, see Michael Adas, *Machines as the Measure of Men: Science, Technology, and Ideologies of Western Dominance* (Ithaca: Cornell University Press, 1989); Alice L. Conklin, *A Mission to Civilize: The Republican Idea of Empire in France and West Africa, 1895–1930* (Stanford: Stanford University Press, 1997); Harald Fischer-Tiné and Michael Mann, eds., *Colonialism as Civilizing Mission: Cultural Ideology in British India* (London: Anthem Press, 2004).

13. The German Reich in Europe was only 208,780 square miles.

14. German Southwest Africa contained a third large ethnic group, the Ovambo, who numbered about 100,000. The Ovambo lived in very hot areas in the far north, effectively beyond German control during the colonial era.

the German military commander General von Trotha pursued what amounted to a policy of genocide. Trotha had a long history of suppressing colonial uprisings—having fought earlier revolts in East Africa and in China against the Boxer Rebellion—and he interpreted the Herero revolt as a race war. His military tactics decimated the Herero as a people, resulting in what historians now interpret as the first genocide of the twentieth century. By the conflict's end, Herero and Nama numbers had shrunk by approximately 80 and 50 percent, respectively. Most of the destruction resulted from military actions—against women and children as well as men—but Germans also eliminated large numbers of captives through deliberate policies of deprivation. Systematic deprivation led to the deaths of all but 193 of about 3,500 individuals at the infamous concentration camp on Shark Island, run from 1905 to 1907.[15]

German East Africa experienced its own massive uprising in 1905, and indigenous groups also suffered heavily under German reprisals. Although the colony's much larger population meant that German military actions did not have the same staggering effect as they did in Southwest Africa, the loss of life was even greater. The German government estimated that 75,000 rebels died during the so-called Maji-Maji rebellion. Historians argue for a much higher number—between 250,000 and 300,000—and insist that a majority were noncombatants who died from starvation and disease as the result of German scorched-earth tactics.[16]

The uprisings that occurred in both colonies were revolts against the specific nature of German colonialism. Although policies differed from colony to colony, and personnel changes often altered the character of colonial governance, German rule generally entailed the harsh subjugation of indigenous populations and their exploitation for the benefit of the colonizing nation.[17] In German Southwest Africa, the government deliberately expropriated African property and impoverished indigenous groups to create a mobile labor force for white farmers and the state. The administration impounded Herero livestock that crossed into Crown territory during the 1880s and 1890s and provoked small uprisings to justify the seizure of indigenous property. From 1884 to 1902, Herero cattle herds

---

15. Madley, "From Africa to Auschwitz," 447.

16. Koponen, *Development for Exploitation,* 597.

17. In *The Devil's Handwriting,* George Steinmetz examines the effects that changes in personnel had on colonial policies.

dwindled from several hundred thousand to barely fifty thousand animals, while the herds of a few hundred German settlers increased exponentially.

The government in East Africa compelled indigenes to labor on colonial projects and enterprises. Although the government officially rejected coercion, coercion was defined so narrowly during the first decades of German rule that only the most blatant forms of forced labor were prohibited. As a result, forced labor—sometimes paid, sometimes not—became an important part of everyday life in colonial East Africa. For years, white employers in the colony also enjoyed an unrestricted right to inflict corporal punishment. This resulted in such brutal conditions for workers on white-owned plantations that Britain banned the further exportation of laborers from India and Singapore to German East Africa in 1894, and China followed suit soon after.[18] The situation deteriorated to such an extent that the Colonial Division of the Foreign Office felt compelled to issue decrees in 1896 regulating the use of corporal punishment.

In Southwest Africa, forced impoverishment through the expropriation of wealth and resources was not the worst aspect of German rule. Herero leaders were outraged by German colonial policies that deprived their people of political and social rights, reducing them to a state of virtual dependency, and this was the principal reason given by these leaders for the 1904 uprisings. For example, the government subjected indigenes in Southwest Africa to special jurisdiction under "Native Law." This denied them the constitutional protections enjoyed by German citizens, subjected them to special punishments, and established a dual legal system, effectively creating a racial hierarchy. Unequal treatment before the law infuriated indigenous leaders and was accompanied by the racism of German settlers, which increased over time. The first generation of settlers cultivated good relations with the Africans, but beginning in the late 1890s, newly arriving immigrants rejected the idea of African humanity and acted like members of a conquering race.[19]

---

18. Britain banned the exportation of laborers from Singapore after sixty-five workers from the island died during a two-year stretch on a German tobacco plantation (Koponen, 338).

19. A petition defending corporal punishment sent by settlers to the Colonial Division of the Foreign Office in 1900 exemplifies this racist mind-set. "From time immemorial our natives have grown used to laziness, brutality, and stupidity," it states. "The dirtier they are, the more they feel at ease. Any white man who has lived among natives finds it almost impossible to regard them as human beings at all in any European sense" (Helmut Bley, *Namibia under German Rule,* trans. Hugh Ridley [Hamburg: LIT Verlag], 97).

The situation in both colonies only worsened following the defeat of the Herero, Nama, and Maji-Maji uprisings. The exploitation and subjugation of indigenous groups intensified, especially in Southwest Africa, where the government seized the remaining land and cattle of rebel groups following the outbreak of violence. After the war, government dicta forced most Southwest African blacks to carry passes as well as proof of employment and prohibited them from living together in groups of more than ten families, a measure designed to weaken the unity of the "tribes." In East Africa, instances of flogging skyrocketed following the Maji-Maji uprising. The increase occurred despite new regulations from Berlin limiting even further the right of white employers to inflict corporal punishment.[20]

From the perspective of policymakers, however, the aftermath of the uprisings heralded a new beginning. This was because German colonialism had suffered one problem after another in the years leading up to the rebellions. After an initial burst of enthusiasm in the 1880s, public support for colonialism fell. German businesses shied away from investing in the colonies, and political opposition in the Reichstag stymied colonial funding. Colonial scandals emerged with distressing regularity as stories about the sadism of individual German officers—like the explorer Carl Peters—appeared back home, horrifying the public's more sensitive members. The critics of colonialism on the political Left and Center attacked the colonial office for its bureaucratic inefficiency and criticized certain policies, like the granting of monopolistic privileges in the colonies to a handful of large British and German concession companies. The Herero, Nama, and Maji-Maji uprisings initially exacerbated domestic discontent, but they also galvanized extraparliamentary procolonial forces and generated a new interest in colonialism among the general public. In September 1906, the German chancellor appointed a new director to head the Colonial Division of the Foreign Office, charged with setting the colonial project back on track. Elevated to the position of state secretary in 1907, Bernhard Dernburg took advantage of the new, pacified state of affairs in German Africa. He instituted important reforms that brought the concession companies under control, increased private investment, and set the stage for financial independence for the colonies.[21]

---

20. Müller, *Kolonien unter der Peitsche,* 114.

21. Werner Schiefel, *Bernhard Dernburg, 1865–1937: Kolonialpolitiker und Bankier im wilhelminischen Deutschland* (Zurich: Atlantis Verlag, 1974); Thaddeus Sunseri, "The *Baumwollfrage:* Cotton Colonialism in German East Africa," *Central European History* 34 (2001): 31–51.

Antisemitism as a modern political movement emerged in Germany a few years before the acquisition of the colonies. The first mass-based political party with an overtly antisemitic platform came into being at the end of the 1870s. A petition drive conducted by several well-known antisemites in 1880 attached an extraordinary 225,000 signatures to a statement demanding the exclusion of Jews from government offices and from employment in public schools, plus the limitation of Jewish immigration into the Reich. The following decade witnessed the formation of many more antisemitic political parties. Unlike the first political antisemites, members of these newer organizations embraced racial antisemitism. They rejected the older interpretation of Jewry as a religious community, arguing instead that the Jews were a race apart.[22]

This antisemitic movement of the *Kaiserreich* era peaked during the early 1890s. At the beginning of the decade, five members of the antisemitic parties were elected to the Reichstag. Two years later, the powerful Conservative Party became the first mainstream political organization to insert an antisemitic statement into its platform.[23] The antisemitic parties (not counting the Conservatives) scored an even larger success in 1893, gaining sixteen seats in parliament, and for a few years, their deputies voted en bloc. The elected antisemites compared Jews to cholera germs from the floor of the Reichstag, denounced them as the enemies of the German people, and advocated the revocation of Jewish civil rights. Radicals even called for the Jews' physical destruction. At the same time that policies of racial subjugation were being implemented in the colonies, antisemites demanded that Jews lose their citizenship and essentially be treated like colonized people.[24]

Following their electoral successes in the early 1890s, however, the antisemites saw their political fortunes decline. From 1896 to 1903, the antise-

---

22. Peter Pulzer, *The Rise of Political Anti-Semitism in Germany and Austria* (New York: John Wiley and Sons, Inc., 1964); Jacob Katz, *From Prejudice to Destruction: Anti-Semitism, 1700–1933* (Cambridge: Harvard University Press, 1980); Klaus P. Fischer, *The History of an Obsession: German Judeophobia and the Holocaust* (New York: Continuum, 2001).

23. The statement reads: "We fight the multifarious and obtrusive Jewish influence that decomposes our people's life. We demand Christian authority and Christian teachers for Christian pupils" (Paul W. Massing, *Rehearsal for Destruction: A Study of Political Anti-Semitism in Imperial Germany* [New York: Harper and Brothers, 1949], 66).

24. The 1890 program of the antisemitic German Social Party demanded the "nullification of the civil rights laws" for Jews and the "placement of Jews under a special alien law," the "Jew Law" (George Bernstein, "Anti-Semitism in Imperial Germany, 1871–1914: Selected Documents" [EdD diss., Teachers College, Columbia University, 1973], 376).

mitic parties lost seats in the Reichstag, and their membership shrank. Although mild antisemitism remained politically acceptable—and even spread to other mainstream parties—the virulent antisemitism of earlier years became a political liability, and public acts of antisemitic violence declined.[25] Part of the reason for this turn of events was the disappearance of the first generation of charismatic antisemitic leaders through death or retirement. In addition, a series of international crises, beginning with the Boer War in 1899, distracted the public from the so-called Jewish problem.[26] Events like the Herero, Nama, and Maji-Maji uprisings focused public attention on racial conflicts outside of, rather than within, the European borders of the German empire.

Antisemites did maintain seats in the Reichstag. The antisemitic political parties even increased their representation to seventeen deputies in the elections of 1907, riding a wave of public nationalism sparked by the fighting in the colonies. Yet the antisemitic deputies were no longer capable of independent action in parliament, unlike during the 1890s. In order to attract an electorate, they were forced to lighten their antisemitic rhetoric and focus on other issues, like the threat of socialism and the colonial project. This change prompted August Bebel to remark in 1906 that antisemitism had "no prospect of ever exercising a decisive influence on political and social life in Germany."[27] From the turn of the century to the end of the First World War, antisemitism in Eastern European countries like Russia appeared to many German Jews as a much greater problem than the weak antisemitic movement at home.[28]

Nevertheless, antisemitism profoundly affected the Jews of the *Kaiserreich,* and the events of the 1880s and 1890s seemed quite threatening at the time. Antisemitic riots erupted repeatedly in Germany during this period, proving that the *Kaiserreich* was not immune to the violent emotions that brought significant death and destruction to the Jewish communities of the

---

25. For a discussion of antisemitism within the National Liberal Party, see Eric Kurlander, *The Price of Exclusion: Ethnicity, National Identity, and the Decline of German Liberalism, 1898–1933* (New York: Berghahn Books, 2006).

26. These included the Russo-Japanese War, the naval arms race with Britain, and the First and Second Moroccan Crises.

27. Pulzer, *Rise of Political Anti-Semitism,* 197. Original quote taken from August Bebel, *Sozialdemokratie und Antisemitismus,* 38.

28. Violent pogroms erupted in Russia in 1903, 1905, and 1906, and reports of the tsar's complicity outraged Western Jews. Jews in Russia also suffered legal discrimination long after Jews in Germany and Austria received legal equality (Albert S. Lindemann, *Esau's Tears: Modern Anti-Semitism and the Rise of the Jews* [Cambridge: Cambridge University Press, 1997], 290–305).

Russian Empire.[29] In addition, the rapid growth of the political antisemitic movement and its early successes raised the specter, however improbable, of a reversal of Jewish emancipation, and the psychological repercussions of these events continued to be felt long after the immediate threat was gone.[30] As a result, Zionism became increasingly popular after 1900 with young German Jews who were disillusioned by the strength of domestic antisemitism and disenchanted with the promises of emancipation. The 1890s witnessed the rise of Jewish defense organizations and the proliferation of Jewish fraternities and associations, events also tied to the antisemites' temporary political triumphs.[31] Zionism and the defense movement did not end when the political fortunes of the antisemitic movement declined.

What is more, the racist dimension of the new antisemitism challenged the idea of assimilation and, with it, the prospect of total acceptance in Gentile society. Even before emancipation, Jews had enthusiastically embraced German culture, enamored with the humanism and cosmopolitan spirit of the eighteenth-century German Enlightenment.[32] Assimilation proceeded apace after the granting of complete legal equality in 1871, as Jews merged into the German middle class, actively participating in the cultural life of the new nation. The expression *deutsche Staatsbürger jüdischen Glaubens,* meaning German citizens of the Jewish faith, encapsulated the self-image of an increasing number of Jews who saw themselves as loyal members of the state, different from Gentiles only in religious matters. Yet the new antisemitism challenged this self-perception by defining Jewishness as a matter of race rather than faith. Although this definition remained highly controversial, racial antisemites succeeded in

---

29. Christhard Hoffmann, Werner Bergmann, and Helmut Walser Smith, eds., *Exclusionary Violence: Antisemitic Riots in Modern German History* (Ann Arbor: University of Michigan Press, 2002); Helmut Walser Smith, *The Butcher's Tale: Murder and Anti-Semitism in a German Town* (New York: W. W. Norton, 2002).

30. Although German unification in 1871 brought legal emancipation to all Jewish citizens, barriers to full equality remained. Baptism, for example, was usually a prerequisite for positions in the upper echelons of the civil service, including the officer corps of the Prussian army (Fischer, *History of an Obsession,* 101).

31. The Central Association of German Citizens of Jewish Faith (*Central Verein deutscher Staatsbürger jüdischen Glaubens*) came into being in 1893 after the Conservative Party incorporated an explicitly antisemitic statement into its party platform. The association used the courts to prosecute antisemitic slander, and it claimed 100,000 members by 1903. It published the newspaper *Im deutschen Reich.*

32. Jehuda Reinharz and Walter Schatzberg, eds., *The Jewish Response to German Culture: From the Enlightenment to the Second World War* (Hanover: University Press of New England, 1985).

focusing attention on Jewish difference, seeding doubts about the possibility of Jews ever becoming fully Germanized. Conversion to Christianity became a tacit requirement for advancement in government and in some private professions, and converted Jews found it nearly impossible to penetrate the officer corp of the German army.[33] Paradoxically, antisemitic prejudices in public and private life continued to spread following the electoral reversals of the antisemitic political parties; negative perceptions of Jews became widespread, finding voice even within the ostensibly "anti-anti-semitic" Social Democratic Party.[34]

German science reminded Jews of their alleged difference as well. The question of the location, origin, and character of Jewish difference fairly obsessed the German scientific community, and German ethnologists and physical anthropologists focused on Jews to a much greater extent than their counterparts in other countries.[35] Statistical studies of Jewish anatomy and alleged Jewish pathologies filled the scientific literature by 1900. A consensus failed to emerge concerning the exact nature of Jewish difference or on other popular questions such as the existence of one or more Jewish racial types, but the notion persisted that Jews were somehow physically and psychologically unique. Since many Jews were themselves scientists, academics, and doctors, German Jews were quite aware of the scientific discourses that focused on Jewish minds and bodies.

Historians have reevaluated the importance of German colonialism. Scholars in both Europe and the United States have successfully challenged what was once conventional wisdom: the idea best expressed by Lewis H. Gann that "German colonialism was of but marginal importance to the Wilhelminian Reich."[36] They have done so by moving beyond economic and immigration issues to consider colonialism's effects on German self-perception and on developments in German culture, drawing in part

---

33. Lindemann, *Esau's Tears,* 103–25, 319–54.

34. Lars Fischer, *The Socialist Response to Antisemitism in Imperial Germany* (Cambridge: Cambridge University Press, 2007).

35. John M. Efron, *Defenders of the Race: Jewish Doctors and Race Science in Fin-de-Siècle Europe* (New Haven: Yale University Press, 1994); Sander Gilman, *The Jew's Body* (New York: Routledge, 1991). A few notable nineteenth-century British scientists and thinkers did write about Jews (like Robert Knox, Francis Galton, and Joseph Jacobs), but most British physical anthropologists focused on Africans.

36. Lewis H. Gann, "Marginal Colonialism: The German Case," in *Germans in the Tropics: Essays in German Colonial History,* ed. Arthur J. Knoll and Lewis H. Gann (New York: Greenwood Press, 1987), 15.

upon Edward Said's ideas about the existence of a European imperialist mentality and demonstrating their applicability to Germany.[37]

In the late 1990s, important work by Susanne Zantop, Nina Berman, Sara Friedrichsmeyer, Tina Campt, and others explored the creation and ramifications of a German "imperialist imagination," finding that a deeply embedded colonial mind-set influenced narratives about German identity both before, during, and after the existence of overseas empire.[38] Lora Wildenthal introduced gender issues into the discussion in 2001 by examining the projection of fantasies of feminist liberation on the colonial project in her book *German Women for Empire,* showing how women both cooperated and competed with men in the colonial movement, using colonialism as a means to engage and shape discourses about gender and race.[39] Since then, a spate of historians have entered the debate, documenting how, in the words of Edward Ross Dickinson, "living in a state with colonial dependencies shaped the consciousness of Germans in important ways."[40] From advertising to anthropology to adventure fiction to middle-class magazines, and in many other spheres, colonialism made itself felt in German culture and identity formation.[41] Some historians, mindful of Said's important work, have also looked back to Hannah Arendt and have taken on the task of exploring the relationship between National Socialism and an earlier colonialism structured by racial domination.

Initially, however, Arendt's theories about colonialism generated interest but little follow-up research. When *The Origins of Totalitarianism* first appeared, most historians appreciated Arendt's comparison of Nazism with Stalinism.[42] Her idea that colonialism in Africa produced a new type of racism and totalitarian methods of rule received much less attention, and scholarly works supporting her theories did not appear until

---

37. Edward W. Said, *Orientalism* (New York: Vintage Books); *Culture and Imperialism* (London: Chatto and Windus, 1993).

38. Friedrichsmeyer, Lennox, and Zantop, eds., *The Imperialist Imagination;* Zantop, *Colonial Fantasies.*

39. Wildenthal, *German Women for Empire.*

40. Edward Ross Dickinson, "The German Empire: An Empire?", *History Workshop Journal* 66 (2008): 131.

41. In addition to the scholarship referenced above, see John Phillip Short, "Everyman's Colonial Library: Imperialism and Working-Class Readers in Leipzig, 1890–1914," *German History* 21 (2003): 445–75; Sandra Maß, *Weiße Helden, schwarze Krieger: Zur Geschichte kolonialer Männlichkeit in Deutschland, 1918–1964* (Cologne: Böhlau, 2006); Matthew Fitzpatrick, "Narrating Empire: *Die Gartenlaube* and Germany's Nineteenth-Century Liberal Expansionism," *German Studies Review* 30 (2007): 97–120.

42. In *Origins,* Arendt classified the National Socialist and Stalinist regimes as, essentially, different versions of the same totalitarian model of government.

the late 1960s. One of the first was Helmut Bley's *South-West Africa under German Rule.* Bley insisted that conditions in the colony suggest that "the seeds of totalitarianism can be found in the period of colonial rule in Africa."[43] According to Bley, German Southwest Africa experienced a period of incomparable colonial extremism after 1904, during which the indigenous inhabitants lost their lands, cattle, and lives in what can only be called a policy of genocide. Those surviving became little more than the "'servants'" of whites.[44] Bley noted that Africans retained some economic initiative in Germany's other colonies, and white regimes elsewhere did not attempt to eliminate traditional forms of social organization. Southwest African officials went farther than anyone else in creating what Bley called "the psychological guarantees for colonial rule" and consequently the "racial, social, and bureaucratic predisposition to totalitarianism."[45]

A handful of studies from the 1980s also support Arendt's ideas without mentioning Arendt directly. Roger Chickering's *We Men Who Feel Most German: A Cultural Study of the Pan-German League, 1886–1914* and Woodruff D. Smith's *The Ideological Origins of Nazi Imperialism* both contend that colonial imperialism radicalized the German Right during the Wilhelminian era, imbuing it with an aggressively imperialist worldview that anticipated aspects of National Socialism.[46] Smith detailed how procolonial groups "developed and enunciated" the concept of *Lebensraum* that the Nazis later adopted.[47] Smith also discussed the role that colonial fiction played in popularizing a Nazi-like racial imperialism. The historian Joachim Warmbold made similar observations several years later. In *Germania in Africa: Germany's Colonial Literature,* Warmbold noted that "the Third Reich would doubtlessly have been several ideas poorer" without the contributions of certain colonial authors.[48] German writers of colonial literature were advocating the elimination of so-called inferior races long before the Holocaust.[49]

---

43. Helmut Bley, *Namibia under German Rule,* trans. Hugh Ridley (Hamburg: LIT Verlag, 1996), 224. This is a more recent edition of Bley's original 1971 book, but under a slightly different title.

44. Ibid., xvii.

45. Ibid., 223–24.

46. Roger Chickering, *We Men Who Feel Most German: A Cultural Study of the Pan-German League, 1886–1914* (Boston: George Allen and Unwin, 1984); Woodruff D. Smith, *The Ideological Origins of Nazi Imperialism* (New York: Oxford University Press, 1986).

47. Smith, 95.

48. Joachim Warmbold, *Germania in Africa: Germany's Colonial Literature* (New York: Peter Lang, 1989), 125–26.

49. Ibid., 127.

From here, the discussion moved to the popularization of racist discourses of exclusion in Wilhelminian society and politics. Important works appeared in and around the late 1990s tying this phenomenon to Germany's overseas colonies. In her 1997 essay "Zwischen Vernunft und Gefühl," Cornelia Essner examined the controversy that colonial antimiscegenation laws sparked in the Reichstag in 1912, when a parliamentary debate over their legality took place. Revealing that even deputies on the political Left expressed discomfort with miscegenation, Essner argued that colonialism caused "the penetration of new racist positions into politics" by making matters like "race-mixing" affairs of the state.[50] Helmut Walser Smith came to a similar conclusion in his own examinations of parliamentary deliberations over colonial matters involving issues of race.[51] He, too, found a proliferation of racial thinking "across the political spectrum": conservative deputies adopted a new "ideologically driven, future-oriented racism" when voicing support for the antimiscegenation laws of 1912, and Social Democrats voiced discomfort with miscegenation despite having ridiculed in earlier years talk of mixed races.[52] This argument—that the racialization of the German sense of self dates to the *Kaiserreich* and was tied to overseas colonialism—gained added momentum in 2000 with the appearance of Pascal Grosse's study of German eugenics. Grosse argued that concerns in the colonies over race mixing filtered back to the metropole, influencing eugenic discourses at home in important ways. As with Essner and Smith, the implication is that colonialism strengthened the idea that Germany was a community based on race.[53]

Pascal Grosse denied a causal relationship between colonialism and the Third Reich.[54] But his work contributed to a revived discussion about the ways in which colonialism prefigured the ideological content, violent temperament, and genocidal policies of National Socialism. In 2003, Enzo Traverso published *The Origins of Nazi Violence,* where he gave weight to

---

50. Cornelia Essner, "Zwischen Vernunft und Gefühl: Die Reichstagsdebatten von 1912 um koloniale 'Rassenmischehe' und 'Sexualität,'" *Zeitschrift für Geschichtswissenschaft* 45, no. 6 (1997): 503–19.

51. Helmut Walser Smith, "The Talk of Genocide, the Rhetoric of Miscegenation: Notes on Debates in the German Reichstag Concerning Southwest Africa, 1904–1914," in *The Imperialist Imagination,* ed. Friedrichsmeyer, Lennox, and Zantop, 107–23.

52. Ibid., 118, 121.

53. Grosse, *Kolonialismus.*

54. Grosse, "What Does German Colonialism Have to Do with National Socialism? A Conceptual Framework," in *Germany's Colonial Pasts,* ed. Ames, Klotz, and Wildenthal, 115–34.

the theory and practice of racial domination developed in Africa during the age of high imperialism.[55] Since then, Jürgen Zimmerer and Benjamin Madley took the lead in making the argument that colonialism birthed not only important ideological concepts for the Nazis—like the notion of *Lebensraum*—but also methods of rule as well as models of racially motivated mass annihilation.[56] Arguing that the Nazi occupation of Eastern Europe was, in fact, a type of colonialism, both authors delineated the similarities between Nazi actions and attitudes in the eastern theaters of war and the situation in the overseas colonies. From the creation of racialized legal systems, to the use of concentration camps, to the attempted annihilation of an entire ethnic group, the experiences in the German colonies modeled, they claimed, what would later occur in many Nazi-occupied regions in more radicalized forms and on much larger scales. Zimmerer put special emphasis on the Herero genocide, insisting that "this breaking of the ultimate taboo" made the Holocaust "imaginable."[57] Both authors recounted the ways in which the colonial experience was passed down to later generations: through novels, textbooks, and films, but also through personal connections—individuals who bridged both eras, transmitting their colonial *Weltanschauung* to the Weimar, and then the National Socialist, age.[58]

In the past few years, there has been a backlash against this kind of thinking—or what has been called the new "continuity thesis"—with very recent work questioning the relevance of overseas colonialism to the Na-

---

55. Enzo Traverso, *The Origins of Nazi Violence,* trans. Janet Lloyd (New York: New Press, 2003). Traverso argued that the deeper roots of Nazi violence lay in colonial Africa. His discussion of the connection is too general and speculative, however, to significantly advance our understanding of the dynamics of the relationship.

56. Zimmerer, "Colonialism and the Holocaust"; Zimmerer, "The Birth of the *Ostland*"; Madley, "From Africa to Auschwitz."

57. Zimmerer, "War, Concentration Camps, and Genocide in South-West Africa: The First German Genocide," in *Genocide in German South-West Africa,* ed. Zimmerer and Zeller, 59–60.

58. Benjamin Madley identified Hermann Göring, Franz Ritter von Epp, and Eugen Fischer as three important "conduits through which colonial ideas and methods were transferred from German South West Africa to the leadership of the Third Reich" (Madley, 450). Göring's father, Heinrich, had served as the first *Reichskommissar* for German Southwest Africa; von Epp took part as a soldier in the Herero genocide; and Fischer developed theories about racial mixing while studying Herero and Nama children in the colony's concentration camps. Von Epp led an army battalion after the First World War and in this capacity, had close relationships with future Nazi leaders who served under him, including Rudolf Hess, Gregor Strasser, Walther Schultze, and Ernst Röhm. Fischer became the head of the Kaiser Wilhelm Institute for Anthropology, Human Heredity, and Eugenics in 1927, which later trained SS doctors, including Josef Mengele.

tional Socialist experience. Historians Matthew Fitzpatrick, Birthe Kundrus, Robert Gerwarth, and Stephan Malinowski highlight what they see as crucial differences between *Kaiserreich*-era colonialism and the actions and attitudes of the Nazi government.[59] They point out that warfare in the German colonies was about crushing rebellions, giving it a very different logic than the racially motivated violence in Nazi-occupied Eastern Europe—often an "end in itself"—even if race was used to define the targets in both cases.[60] They argue that the guiding principle behind the creation of the Nazi racial state was the preservation of racial purity against the threat of pollution, while administrators in the German colonies used racial categories as a strategy of rule over ethnically dissimilar populations. Those authors who downplay the importance of the colonial era in explaining National Socialism also point out that Britain and France maintained their democratic traditions despite colonial experiences similar to Germany's. They note that the British had their own colonial massacres and concentration camps and that violent racial-thinking pervaded the European colonial universe in the late nineteenth and early twentieth centuries. Kundrus, Gerwarth, Malinowski, and others suggest that the trauma of 1914 to 1923—in particular, the German defeat in the First World War—is much more important in understanding National Socialism than the history of German colonialism.[61]

This recent work does not reestablish, however, the older conventional wisdom that colonialism was "of but marginal importance" to *Kaiserreich* Germany.[62] In fact, the degree to which the colonies influenced Wilhelminian culture is becoming constantly clearer, as new scholarship on topics as diverse as consumerism, postcards, the women's movement, travel literature, eugenics, and election campaigns reveals the myriad ways in which

---

59. Matthew P. Fitzpatrick, "The Pre-History of the Holocaust? The *Sonderweg* and *Historikerstreit* Debates and the Abject Colonial Past," *Central European History* 41 (2008): 477–503; Birthe Kundrus, "Continuities, Parallels, Receptions: Reflections on the 'Colonization' of National Socialism," *Journal of Namibian Studies* 4 (2008): 25–46; Robert Gerwarth and Stephan Malinowski, "Hannah Arendt's Ghosts: Reflections on the Disputable Path from Windhoeck to Auschwitz," *Central European History* 42 (2009): 279–300.

60. Gerwarth and Malinowski, "Hannah Arendt's Ghosts," 293.

61. Pascal Grosse, too, argues for the importance of the First World War in explaining why postwar Germany took a different path than colonial powers like Britain and France. He sees the premature ending of Germany's empire as decisive, insisting that this is what radicalized German racist fantasies of colonial domination. See "What Does German Colonialism Have to Do with National Socialism? A Conceptual Framework."

62. Gann, *Rulers of German Africa,* 15.

overseas colonialism affected how contemporary Germans viewed them-selves and the world around them.[63] Those scholars who strip the colonial period of any real explanatory power for what came after 1933 do not deny these influences, only that the Wilhelminian era contained the important prehistory of National Socialism. They locate the prehistory instead in the crisis-producing years immediately before and after the foundation of the Weimar Republic.[64]

But in arguing this—and in emphasizing only the differences between National Socialist actions and attitudes and past colonialism—they fore-shorten their gaze, becoming, to borrow a phrase, "chronologically my-opic" in a way that obscures the deeper historical roots of the Nazis' radi-cal racial antisemitism and its eventual normalization.[65] Their almost ahistorical view of National Socialism dismisses the real influences that the colonial project had on shaping, propagating, and popularizing a danger-ous racial thinking, one that, though colonial, could only have facilitated the rise and public acceptance of Nazi racialism. This work sides, there-fore, with the proponents of the new "continuity thesis" who give weight to Germany's colonial experiences when explaining the Third Reich. And yet, this study shows that the relationship between colonialism and radical racial antisemitism was considerably more ambiguous during the *Kaiser-reich* era than proponents of the new "continuity thesis" imagine. I argue that colonialism benefited the contemporaneous antisemitic cause at the same time that it partly undermined it.

This book explores the relationship between antisemitism and colonialism during the Wilhelminian period in four main chapters. The first, "Anti-semitism, Colonialism, and Colonial Violence," examines the contribu-tions to, and perceptions of, overseas colonialism by hardened antisemites:

---

63. Erik Grimmer-Solem, "The Professors' Africa"; Medardus Brehl, "'The drama was played out on the dark stage of the sandveldt': The Destruction of Herero and Nama in Ger-man (Popular) Literature," in *Genocide in German South-West Africa,* 100–112; "Forum: The German Colonial Imagination," *German History* 26 (2008): 251–71; Volker Langbehn, ed., *German Colonialism, Visual Culture, and Modern Memory* (New York: Routledge, 2009); Michael Perraudin and Jürgen Zimmerer, eds., *German Colonialism and National Identity* (New York: Routledge, 2009).

64. Isabel V. Hull takes an intermediate position. In *Absolute Destruction,* she identifies a German military culture geared to absolute solutions already in existence during the Wil-helminian age. But she rejects the hypothesis that annihilationist thinking emerged out of the colonial experience, denying colonialism the explanatory power for National Socialism at-tributed it by Jürgen Zimmerer, Benjamin Madley, and others.

65. Smith, *The Continuities of German History,* 3.

men and women who distinguished themselves against a backdrop of widespread social and cultural antisemitism by virtue of the centrality of antisemitism to their worldviews; the intensity of their hatred of Jews; or their commitment to, involvement with, and promotion of the antisemitic cause. The chapter documents a significant convergence in the memberships of the contemporaneous antisemitic and colonial movements, revealing that antisemites who believed in political solutions to the so-called Jewish Question enthusiastically supported overseas colonialism even as they criticized the pace of colonial development and specific colonial policies. Antisemites who shunned active politicking were divided, with some numbering among the colonies' most ardent and active supporters, and others remaining skeptical. Chapter 1 also explores the antisemitic ethos of on-the-ground colonial actors, paying special attention to the activists and agents tied to the violent Carl Peters. It argues that these colonial antisemites numbered among the most articulate early proponents and active practitioners of a brutal colonizing *Weltanschauung,* one that justified brutality as an appropriate and proportional response to the inhumanity of the colonized Other.

Chapter 2, "The Meeting of Jews and Africans in the German Imagination," illustrates how Jews and black Africans came to occupy comparable positions in German thinking through their radical Othering, a process that predated the acquisition of overseas colonies but peaked in the final decade and a half of colonial empire. Special attention is paid to the demonization of black Africans after the outbreak of the Herero uprising in 1904, when the nationalist and colonial presses increasingly portrayed blacks in ways that paralleled the most outrageous depictions of Jews by racial antisemites: as an unchanging devilish antirace, completely un-Christian and malicious to the core, without any redeeming qualities found in representations of other colonial subjects. The chapter then examines how images of blacks and Jews merged not just across but also within the antisemitic and colonial movements. Antisemites increasingly linked Jews with blacks, attributing to them nearly identical characteristics and ascribing "Negro components" to the Jewish bloodline, intimating the need for colonial solutions to the perceived Jewish problem. At the same time, German jurists looked to defunct Prussian antisemitic legislation when debating the legality of discriminatory laws against black Africans, and colonialists attributed Jewish backgrounds and behavioral traits to the leaders of indigenous uprisings.

The third chapter, "Jews, Germans of Jewish Descent, and German

Colonialism," focuses on the first two decades of empire, examining the roles played in colonial empire by Germans identified as Jewish by their peers. It concentrates on Emin Pasha and Paul Kayser, using their stories to elucidate the complex ramifications that "Jewish" participation in colonialism had for the antisemitic movement as well as for the German-Jewish individuals involved. For the latter, it furnished patriotic credentials that did not, however, immunize them from antisemitic attacks, and it divided antisemites between their proponents and detractors. Chapter 3 also examines the positions that colonial actors of Jewish descent took on so-called native policy, to see if the targets of antisemitic hatred had more liberal attitudes toward race than was normal at the time. Particular attention is given to Kayser, who headed the colonial bureaucracy during the zenith of the political influence of the antisemitic political parties.

Chapter 4, "Colonial Director Bernhard Dernburg: A 'Jew' with 'German Spirit'?," delves deeper into the peculiar nature of the participation in colonialism of individuals of Jewish descent by focusing on Bernhard Dernburg. Although widely perceived to be a liberal Jew because of his family background, Dernburg became tremendously popular with the pro-colonial public, gaining a reputation as a fighting champion of colonialism and a model of German manliness. His popularity even extended to many antisemites, generating discord within the movement about the degree to which one's ideological orientation could counteract one's Jewish ancestry. Support for Dernburg among antisemites led to the ironic situation where some of the state secretary's most vocal advocates in parliament came from the representatives of the antisemitic political parties. At the same time, antisemitic jabs and references to his Jewish heritage came largely from critics of colonialism on the political Left and Center, where the strongest opponents of political antisemitism could be found.

The aim of this book is to elucidate a relationship between imperial Germany's colonial and antisemitic movements that was contradictory and complex. Research tying the racialization of the German sense of self to the acquisition of overseas colonies would seem to suggest that colonialism necessarily advanced the domestic agenda of antisemites who championed the new racial thinking in order to expel Jews from the community of the German ethnic nation. Yet the experiences of Dernburg and others show that colonialism gave rise to a new identity, the white colonizer, in which both "Jews" and "Gentiles" could partake. As such, it could serve as a vehicle for inclusion for precisely those members of the body politic who had the most to lose from the racialization of the German sense of self encouraged by the creation of colonial racial states. Colonialism also generated discord within the antisemitic movement, not only over the participation of "Jews," but also over the purpose and benefits of overseas colonies, given the existence of a vocal minority of antisemites who were colonial skeptics.

At the same time, colonialism benefited the antisemitic movement in certain ways. Most antisemites were united in their procolonial sentiments, not a small thing for a movement riddled with divisions. By championing the colonies, antisemitic politicians also found common cause with mainstream political parties and organizations, something that translated into electoral victories in 1907. More important, however, is the fact that colonialism gave weight to a key component of racial antisemitism by reifying for the public the reality and importance of race. In addition, the hardening of discourses about black Africans after 1904 familiarized procolonial Germans with a logic and rhetoric that closely approximated the thinking of antisemitic extremists on the Jewish Question. The popularization of a colonial philosophy of racially motivated violence, one structured by a similar logic of justification as that which informed calls to preemptive action against the Jews, did the same. Procolonial antisemites at times encouraged these developments, harnessing colonialism to the cause of the most violently minded type of racial antisemitism.

CHAPTER I

Antisemitism, Colonialism, and Colonial Violence

The German colonial empire came into being on April 24, 1884. On that day, the German consul at Cape Town received a telegram from Chancellor Otto von Bismarck in Berlin, proclaiming that the government had taken under its protection areas in southwestern Africa purchased from local notables by a German tobacco merchant. Bismarck extended government protection to German commercial interests in Togo and Cameroon several months later, dispatching a gunboat to the region. Early the next year, he offered similar guarantees to the German East Africa Company, an organization founded by Carl Peters, which claimed large areas off the coast of Zanzibar. Antisemites back in Germany who had long supported the idea of empire celebrated these developments. One antisemitic newspaper in Berlin stated in May, "We would be extraordinarily happy if the German flag suddenly fluttered on the coast of Africa and are convinced that England and France would reckon silently with this *fait accompli,* albeit with envious eyes."[1] Months later, the newspaper insisted that "every German patriot" would greet "with open joy" the acquisition of colonies.[2]

This chapter initiates the investigation into the relationship between colonialism and antisemitism. It argues that colonialism and antisemitism often went hand in hand during the imperial era, as did antisemitism and radical colonial violence. First, the chapter examines how dedicated antisemites perceived German colonizing efforts; after outlining the history of the modern antisemitic movement, it explores the attitudes toward colo-

---

1. "Weltlage," *Staatsbürger-Zeitung,* May 25, 1884. The *Staatsbürger-Zeitung* was one of the longest-running antisemitic dailies in Germany, founded in 1865 and lasting through the *Kaiserreich* era. The antisemitic journalist Wilhelm Bruhn assumed control of the editorship in the late 1890s.

2. "Angra Pequena," *Staatsbürger-Zeitung,* June 12, 1884.

nialism among movement members, looking at stay-at-home antisemites of different stripes. The chapter shows that antisemitic politicians, ideologues, and the antisemitic press energetically engaged in the public debate about colonialism's objectives, means, and costs, infusing the antisemitic movement with a colonial consciousness, with majority opinion strongly backing the colonial project. Second, the chapter details the penetration of antisemitism into the ranks of on-the-ground colonial actors. It illustrates how men and women imbued with a strong antisemitic *Weltanschauung* not only helped to create and administer the new colonial empire but also infused it with an ethos of racially justified violence. The evidence presented here shows that the colonial and antisemitic movements of the imperial era were deeply intertwined and affected one another.

The rise of the modern German antisemitic movement roughly coincided with the creation of Germany's colonial empire. The late 1870s witnessed the formation of Adolf Stöcker's Christian Social Workers' Party, the first antisemitic party with a national agenda and aspirations to the Reichstag. The petition drive of 1880 spurred the creation of several more antisemitic political parties later that same year, such as the short-lived Social Reich Party in Berlin and the more successful German Reform Party in Dresden, both rivals to Stöcker's organization. New antisemitic political parties continued to appear throughout the following decade. In 1889, the German Social Party emerged in Bochum (Westphalia), and Erfurt (Saxony) became the home of the newly formed Antisemitic People's Party in 1890. The 1880s and 1890s also witnessed the creation of an antisemitic press, replete with both weeklies and dailies. Some of the antisemitic newspapers founded during this time survived into the Nazi era.[3]

The economic crash of 1873 helped make the new phenomenon of political antisemitism possible. The crash ruined thousands of small investors, and the ensuing depression generated a widespread discontent with the policies and theories of economic liberalism, a discontent that ideologues were able to channel into antisemitism. For years, antisemites had insisted that the gradual emancipation of Germany's Jews since Napoleonic times was largely responsible for the emergence of the modern economy of mobile capital, free enterprise, and market speculation. Artisans, merchants, peasant farmers, civil servants, and small entrepreneurs—

---

3. These include the *Deutsche Zeitung* (Berlin, 1896–1934), the *Deutsche Tageszeitung* (Berlin, 1894–1934), and the *Tägliche Rundschau* (Berlin, 1881–1937). The antisemitic *Hammer* magazine (Leipzig, 1902–40) was also long-running.

the group that constituted Germany's *Mittelstand*—were susceptible to this anticapitalist and anti-Jewish rhetoric even before 1873, fearing as they did the abstract world of high finance and the impersonal exchange of capital and commodities that threatened to engulf their more easily comprehensible traditional economy. The crash and the ensuing depression exacerbated their anticapitalist and antiliberal tendencies. It made them even more receptive to the antisemites, who took their complaints about the evils of modern capitalism seriously but, unlike the Social Democrats, did not advocate the overthrow of the traditional social order or relegate the *Mittelstand* to the dustbin of history.[4]

The antisemitic parties that emerged in the immediate years before and after the acquisition of the colonies did so with *Mittelstand* support, and they commonly proposed social and economic reforms to benefit those hurt by the new free-market economy. The resurrection of antiusury laws, taxes on stock exchange operations, the creation of compulsory trade corporations to regulate apprenticeships and represent workers' interests, legislation on standard working hours, the abolition of female and child labor, and restrictions on certain forms of trade, like door-to-door selling and itinerant markets, were common demands in the programs of the antisemitic political parties. The different parties also shared similar grievances against the Jews. The image of the Jew as a heartless market speculator and as the usurious purveyor of the new economic system that impoverished German workers and ruined the *Mittelstand* appealed to antisemites of all stripes. So too did the idea that Jews were unduly represented in positions of power and had, in this way, forced economic liberalism onto German society. The different antisemitic parties hoped to end Jewish immigration and prohibit Jews from public office. They explicitly linked this antisemitic program to their crusade against the evils of big business, high finance, and the unregulated free market.[5]

Beyond these basic ideological stances, which also included an extreme nationalism, the different segments of the new political antisemitic movement were extremely disunited. The most significant split developed

---

4. The term *Mittelstand* refers to the German lower middle class, or petty bourgeoisie, consisting of clerical workers, educational functionaries, small retailers, sales personnel, and bank clerks, as well as those groups mentioned above.

5. The Antisemites Petition of 1880 attacked "the existing laws which give priority to capitalist interests and which were formed under Jewish influence," and it denounced Jewish wealth as arising from "usury, market speculation, [and] banks and bonds" (quoted in George Bernstein, "Anti-Semitism in Imperial Germany, 1871–1914: Selected Documents" [EdD diss., Teachers College, Columbia University, 1973], 368).

between the Christian Social Party and the various antisemitic political organizations that followed it. Adolf Stöcker, a Lutheran pastor who founded the Christian Socials in 1878, became a fixture of Berlin high society during the 1870s and 1880s after being appointed in 1874 as the Imperial Court Chaplain. Stöcker created the Christian Socials to organize a mass movement of the Right that would, through economic and social reform, tie the lower classes to the conservative Junkers and reconcile working Germans with the authority of the Christian State.[6] Stöcker and the Christian Socials stressed the power and importance of Christian religiosity and, accordingly, viewed the Jewish Question as a matter of religion and ethics rather than race. Although the Jews supposedly represented everything that threatened the traditional German-Christian state, genuine conversion would, from the Christian Social perspective, eliminate the danger, and civic equality should accompany one's acceptance of the Christian faith.

Stöcker's devotion to Christianity and the conservative Junkers, and his refutation of the idea of a Jewish race, differentiated him from the leaders of the antisemitic political parties founded during the 1880s.[7] These newer organizations (like the German Social Party) repeated many of Stöcker's demands for economic and social reform, but their relationships with the Conservative Party—the party of the Junkers—were more ambiguous: cooperative at some times and hostile at others. Also, Christianity did not greatly influence their political philosophies, and some of their more radical spokesmen even rejected the Christian faith. Most important, these new parties espoused racial antisemitism. From this perspective, the Jews were not merely the agents of a corrupting materialism and economic liberalism that threatened to undermine traditional values and an older way of life; they were also the instruments of racial degeneration, poisoning the German racial stock through intermarriage. These attitudes inclined the representatives of the newer parties to accept more radical solutions to the so-called Jewish Question. The German Social Party, for example, demanded the "nullification of the civil rights laws" and the re-

---

6. Stöcker removed the word *Workers* from his party's name in 1881 once he realized that the *Mittelstand,* and not the workers, formed his popular base. For more on Stöcker, see Paul W. Massing, *Rehearsal for Destruction: A Study of Political Anti-Semitism in Imperial Germany* (New York: Harper and Brothers, 1949). This still contains one of the most detailed discussions of him.

7. Stöcker was not always consistent on the racial issue, however, and he sometimes used language that resembled that of the racial antisemites (D. A. Jeremy Telman, "Adolf Stoecker: Anti-Semite with a Christian Mission," *Jewish History* 9 [1995]: 93–112).

duction of German Jews to the status of resident aliens.[8] In contrast, Stöcker regarded Jewish emancipation as a "fact" and did not attempt to undo it, even though he also advocated restrictions on Jews, like limiting the number of Jewish judges and removing Jewish teachers from primary schools.[9]

In addition to the divide between the racial and religious antisemites, the racial antisemites were also split among themselves. Though united in their racial approach to the Jewish Question, they were separated into left and right wings with different attitudes toward parliamentary democracy. The founder of the German Social Party, the aristocrat and former army officer Max Hugo Liebermann von Sonnenberg, was antidemocratic.[10] The founder of the German Social Antisemitic People's Party, Otto Böckel,[11] was quite the opposite and supported extending the equal franchise into Prussia.[12] When both Böckel and Liebermann von Sonnenberg were elected to the Reichstag in 1890, the latter refused to join the antisemitic *Fraktion* (group) that Böckel formed with four other parliamentary deputies from his People's Party.

The racial antisemites were also divided into moderate and radical factions within the individual parties. For example, the more moderate rank-and-file German Socials disapproved of the untraditional religiosity of some of their leaders. This dissent eventually forced one of the party's founders, Theodor Fritsch, to leave his post as the publisher of the *Deutsch-Soziale Blätter,* most likely due to his attacks on the Old Testa-

---

8. Quoted in Bernstein, "Anti-Semitism in Imperial Germany," 376.

9. Peter Pulzer, *The Rise of Political Antisemitism in Germany and Austria* (New York: John Wiley and Sons, 1964), 101.

10. Liebermann von Sonnenberg, born in 1848 into a landless Junker family, served in the Prussian army during the Franco-Prussian War of 1870–71. He left the armed services in 1880 as a first lieutenant and soon became involved in antisemitic politics in Berlin. Liebermann von Sonnenberg despised political liberalism and regarded parliament as "the source of all evil" (Pulzer, *Rise of Political Anti-Semitism,* 95; Richard S. Levy, *The Downfall of the Anti-Semitic Political Parties in Imperial Germany* [New Haven: Yale University Press, 1975], 24–26).

11. Otto Böckel, born in Frankfurt in 1859, was a pioneering figure of the antisemitic movement. Playing on the fears of indebted peasant farmers in Hesse who suffered from imports of cheap foreign grain, Böckel was elected to the Reichstag in 1887 as a member of his own independent antisemitic party. Böckel's influence in the movement did not last past the mid-1890s, when he made a series of political missteps, like refusing to join forces with the German Socials (Levy, *Downfall,* 104–5; Albert S. Lindemann, *Esau's Tears: Modern Anti-Semitism and the Rise of the Jews* [Cambridge: Cambridge University Press, 1997], 152–55).

12. The Prussian system, with its three voting classes, gave wealthy voters a disproportionate amount of electoral power.

ment and his rejection of the Jewish roots of Christianity.[13] Fritsch turned his back on party politics and founded his own "unpolitical" periodical and organizations.[14] His actions demonstrated yet another important rift within the racists' camp, this time between the radical "idealists" who despaired of party politics and the entire governmental process as hopelessly "Jewified" and those willing to work within the existing political system. The former—whose ranks included the antisemitic ideologue and publisher Friedrich Lange—expressed what historian Paul W. Massing classifies as a type of "nihilistic pessimism."[15] They avoided political activity, arguing that Germany's problems were too deep-seated to be solved through conventional political means. These revolutionaries confined their activities to publishing antisemitic literature and to forming small, elitist, antisemitic organizations whose members contemplated a future transformation of German politics, culture, and society in conformation with what they deemed to be the true German spirit.

This lack of cohesion prevented the antisemitic parties from becoming a major political force during the Wilhelminian era. Their representatives in the Reichstag failed to overturn Jewish emancipation or even to pass overtly antisemitic legislation. Furthermore, ideological differences split their votes on most issues, and the major antisemitic parliamentary factions managed to unite into a single party for only six short years. From this perspective, the new antisemitic movement that began with the Christian Socials in the late 1870s was a political failure.[16]

This is not to say that the antisemitic movement left no mark on German politics or society. In the first place, the politicking of the antisemitic political parties made antisemitism part of everyday political life. The fact that the antisemitic movement enjoyed continuous representation in the

---

13. Andreas Herzog, "Theodor Fritschs Zeitschrift *Hammer* und der Aufbau des 'Reichs-Hammerbundes' als Instrumente der antisemitischen völkischen Reformbewegung (1902–1914)," in *Das bewegte Buch. Buchwesen und soziale, nationale und kulturelle Bewegungen um 1900,* ed. Mark Lehmstedt and Andreas Herzog (Weisbaden: Harrassowitz Verlag, 1999), 155.

14. Reginald H. Phelps identifies Fritsch as "probably the most significant figure of German antisemitism before the Nazis" ("'Before Hitler Came': Thule Society and Germanen Orden," *Journal of Modern History* 35, no. 3 [1963]: 247). Fritsch was a prolific writer and proponent of "scientific" racism, and he helped organize secretive antisemitic organizations whose members contributed to the radical right-wing movements of the postwar era. Adolf Hitler and other prominent Nazis sent telegrams and letters of condolence to Fritsch's *Hammer* magazine upon Fritsch's death in 1933 (Alexander Volland, "Theodor Fritsch [1852–1933] und die Zeitschrift 'Hammer'" [PhD diss., Johannes Gutenberg-Universität, 1993], 16).

15. Massing, *Rehearsal for Destruction,* 78.

16. Levy argues this point in *Downfall.*

Reichstag following Adolf Stöcker's election in 1881 clearly indicates that antisemitism had a place in German electoral politics, at least when linked to platforms stressing social and economic reform. The antisemitic political movement also achieved a level of respectability, and it managed for a time to win partial support from within some of the better established political parties: when antisemitic parliamentary deputies introduced a bill in 1894 to restrict the immigration into Germany of Eastern European Jews, they drew support from Conservative Party and Reichspartei members.[17] In later years, both the National Liberal and Progressive Parties, reviled by the antisemites as thoroughly "Jewified," allied themselves with antisemitic candidates when politically convenient.

The antisemites also succeeded in using the Reichstag as a pulpit to air their accusations against the Jews before the entire nation. As a result of the 1893 national elections, which gave the antisemitic parties a quarter-million votes and increased their seats in parliament from six to sixteen, the antisemites gained the right to submit bills and demand representation on parliamentary committees.[18] Over the next five years, the newly formed German Social Reform Party, an amalgamation of the German Socials and German Reformers, introduced a series of antisemitic legislative bills that sparked several major debates within the Reichstag over the Jewish Question. The antisemites also frequently inserted antisemitic asides, and sometimes lengthy digressions, into their vocal contributions to legislative discussions on seemingly unrelated matters, such as taxation and colonial policy. The injection of antisemitic orations into political dialogues within the nation's highest legislative body undoubtedly helped legitimate antisemitic fantasies for segments of the observing German public. It elevated to the national stage the antisemitic delusions and paranoia that had already become at the local level "part of the warp and woof of everyday life."[19]

In the mid-1890s, the antisemites' parliamentary influence on, and independence from, the major political parties in the Reichstag declined.

---

17. The Reichspartei, also known as the Free Conservative Party, contained both landowners and industrialists, while the Conservative Party catered more exclusively to the interests of the aristocracy and landed property (Gordon A. Craig, *Germany, 1866–1945* [New York: Oxford University Press, 1980], 62).

18. A party needed fifteen seats before it was allowed to submit bills and demand representation on committees.

19. H. Smith, *Butcher's Tale,* 22. Smith argues that the tendency to focus on antisemitic ideologues, organizations, and politics hampers an understanding of how antisemitic prejudices played out at the local level and figured into "everyday life." Smith breaks from this pattern in *The Butcher's Tale* by studying antisemitism as a social phenomenon, a prejudice propagated through rumors and spurred by private malice and jealousy.

The political antisemites lost several seats in 1898, and the German Social
Reformers split into two rival parties in 1900. Yet the antisemites had
something of a revival in 1907. As a result of the so-called Hottentot election that year, during which colonial issues featured prominently, the
Christian Socials and the reconstituted German Social and German Reform Parties won a total of seventeen seats in parliament, which they
maintained until 1912.[20] Although the antisemites submitted no antisemitic legislation during this time, their numbers ensured that their
voices continued to be heard in the Reichstag. Antisemitic deputies participated frequently in parliamentary debates over colonial policy. Following the 1907 Reichstag elections, members of the German Social and
German Reform Parties emerged as some of the most vocal proponents of
reform in colonial matters.

The antisemitic movement was, in general, quite receptive to the concept of
colonies. This support did not extend to all members, and different factions had different opinions on specific colonial issues. Nevertheless, support for the colonial project, mixed with criticism of certain colonial policies, characterized the attitudes of most important antisemitic leaders
during the colonial era, many of whom were also members of the extraparliamentary, procolonial pressure group, the Pan-German League.[21] The
major antisemitic political parties endorsed colonialism quite explicitly.
Ernst Henrici's short-lived Social Reich Party, created in 1880 to challenge
Stöcker's leadership of the new political antisemitism, called for an active
colonial policy in addition to social reform and anti-Jewish measures, and
it was the first political party to advocate overseas colonialism.[22] The
longer-lasting and more successful German Reform Party, based in Dresden, also embraced colonial empire. The inaugural issue of its party organ,
the *Deutsche Wacht,* identified an "externally powerful and feared, and an
internally united and firmly organized, state" as "the prerequisite for all re-

---

20. *Hottentot* is a pejorative term used by Europeans to describe pastoralists who speak
Khoi in southern Africa.

21. Founded in the early 1890s, the Pan-German League differed from other procolonial
organizations by the extent of its purview. While the German Society for Colonization concerned itself with the colonies, the Pan-German League supported "German ethnic aspirations" worldwide, both in Europe and overseas (Roger Chickering, *We Men Who Feel Most
German: A Cultural Study of the Pan-German League, 1886–1914* [Boston: George Allen and
Unwin, 1984], 49). Despite its small membership—18,000 by 1914—the league enjoyed considerable political influence and had an ability to mobilize public opinion.

22. Levy, *Downfall,* 23. The Social Reich Party crumbled after failing to win electoral support outside of Berlin during the parliamentary elections of 1881.

forms aimed at the social welfare of the entire people and the furtherance of the material, ethical, and spiritual life of a nation." Accordingly, the *Wacht* pledged the party's support for both "the preservation and strengthening of our military potential" and "German colonial policy."[23] Liebermann von Sonnenberg's German Social Party backed colonialism as well, advocating in its party program of 1890 "an active and purposeful colonial policy aimed at the acquisition of trade and farmer colonies."[24] This procolonial attitude was reflected in much of the antisemitic press, in newspapers both connected to and independent from the antisemitic parties.

Most antisemites who supported the colonial project were motivated by both conventional patriotism and ethnic-national beliefs. The idea that Germany needed a colonial empire in order to maintain its great-power status and compete economically with rival European states coexisted in the antisemites' *Weltanschauung* with a powerful conviction that colonies were also needed to promote the health and preserve the racial and cultural unity of the German people. Most procolonial antisemites therefore subscribed to a mixture of what historian Woodruff D. Smith identifies as the two competing imperialist ideologies of the Wilhelminian era: economic imperialism, sometimes called *Weltpolitik,* and migrationist colonialism, which Smith denotes in *The Ideological Origins of Nazi Imperialism* with the anachronism *Lebensraum*. According to Smith, the first envisioned a worldwide foreign policy aimed at protecting and promoting Germany's industrial economy. Its proponents assigned government an important role in planning the nation's economic development, and they valued the colonies for their potential benefits as markets or sources of raw materials for German industry. Advocates of *Lebensraum* were less concerned with the material benefits that colonialism might bring. For them, the colonies were important first and foremost as settlement areas where German immigrants would maintain their cultural and linguistic ties to the homeland, unlike in the United States, where such ties quickly dissipated. They saw the spread of the German *Volk* across the globe, undiluted by foreign influences, as necessary if Germans were to successfully compete on the

---

23. "Was wir wollen," *Deutsche Wacht: Wochenschrift für nationales Deutschtum und sociale Reform,* April 5, 1887. The German Reform Party began in Dresden in 1881. It succeeded on the local level during the early 1880s, then faded, but was revived in 1889 under the combined leadership of Oswald Zimmermann and Otto Böckel. The GRP won four of the five seats awarded to antisemites in the parliamentary election of 1890, and then eleven out of sixteen seats in 1893. It merged with the German Social Party in 1894 to form the German Social Reform Party, but split off in 1900 (Levy, *Downfall,* 100–101).

24. Quoted in Bernstein, "Anti-Semitism in Imperial Germany," 376.

world stage with other ethnic communities.[25] Antisemites of different stripes subscribed to the two imperialist ideologies to different degrees, but most borrowed from both in order to construct the strongest possible argument for the acquisition, and then retention, of the colonies.

The German Social Party adopted this strategy. By advocating within their party program "the acquisition of trade and farmer colonies," the German Socials expressed the ambitions of the advocates of both the *Weltpolitik* and *Lebensraum* ideologies. Accordingly, the party's organ, the *Deutsch-Soziale Blätter,* explicitly linked economic imperialism with settler colonialism when making the case within its pages for the possession of colonies overseas. Without settlements abroad, the argument ran, Germany's "excess population" would continue to flow into foreign states, thereby strengthening its "economic enemies." The *Blätter* reasoned that settlement colonies would prevent this from happening by creating a destination within Reich territories for German immigrants, while at the same time allowing Germany to mimic British mercantilism by creating its own exclusive foreign markets.[26] The German Social point man on colonial matters in the legislature, Reichstag deputy Wilhelm Lattmann, likewise borrowed from both imperialist ideologies. He emphasized the potential economic advantages of colonial possessions while also arguing the necessity of large German settlements within the colonies. Lattmann argued that both the working class and the *Mittelstand* would benefit immensely from a sensible colonial policy, which he defined as "the creation of export markets and the expansion over there of production, in order to secure for us an importation of goods that we either don't produce, or don't produce in sufficient quantity."[27] He also insisted that "the farmer, the settler, and the German peasantry abroad must form the backbone of our colonies."[28] This outlook differentiated him from staunch *Weltpolitiker* who opposed colonial settlements and championed instead the model of the large company-owned plantation.

The German Reformers had a similar perspective on colonialism. Like the German Socials, the Reformers identified the colonies as potential

---

25. W. Smith, *Ideological Origins,* 52–111.

26. "Südwestafrika und die Sozialdemokratie—Rothäute und Schwarzhäute," *Deutsch-Soziale Blätter,* November 12, 1904.

27. *Stenographische Berichte über die Verhandlungen des Reichstags* (hereafter *Sten. Ber.*) XII/I/125, March 18, 1908, 4084. Lattmann was born in 1864 and studied law in Tübingen and Göttingen. He served as a district court judge in the town of Schmalkalden in central Germany and was elected to the Reichstag in 1903.

28. *Sten. Ber.* XII/II/76, April 30, 1910, 2790.

exporters of raw materials and importers of German goods, as well as targets for German immigration. Likewise, party members elected to parliament championed both positions before the legislative body. In his capacity as a Reichstag deputy beginning in 1890, party member Ludwig Werner advocated the development of small farm settlements in German Africa in order to relieve Germany's "surplus population,"[29] but he also insisted that the success of the large cotton plantations was something "to which all must subscribe who intend to take the blossoming of the colonies seriously and wish to make Germany independent from foreign countries."[30] The party's leader, Oswald Zimmermann, held out the additional hope that colonialism could blunt the threat posed by Social Democracy, if only it were pursued properly. While a deputy in the Reichstag during the 1890s, Zimmermann advocated "colonial policy on a larger scale" and insisted that "in no way can we reach a solution to the social question without a sufficient colonial policy."[31] Zimmermann envisioned sending Germany's unemployed to the African colonies, and he claimed that such a program, if applied to the *Mittelstand,* would help prevent its proletarianization.[32]

Of the major antisemitic political parties, only the Christian Socials departed from the strategy of drawing heavily upon both the *Weltpolitik* and *Lebensraum* ideologies. Unlike the German Reformers and the German Socials, the Christian Socials identified the "civilizing mission" in the form of spreading Christianity as the most important reason for pursuing colonies. The proselytizing impulse was clearly a significant motivating force for Adolf Stöcker's own support for the colonial project, because when he interceded in debates in the Reichstag on colonial matters in his capacity as a parliamentary deputy, he almost always did so to promote missionary activity. Throughout his parliamentary career, Stöcker championed the causes connected with the colonial missions, like the movement to

---

29. *Sten. Ber.* XII/I/125, March 18, 1908, 4086. Ludwig Werner (1885–1935) was one of five antisemites elected to the Reichstag in 1890, and he retained his seat for much of the rest of the *Kaiserreich* era. Werner sat on the German Reform Party's central committee (Levy, *Downfall,* 55).

30. *Sten. Ber.* XII/I/216, March 1, 1909, 7228. The somewhat fanciful idea that the colonies could liberate German industry from its dependence on foreign exports of raw materials, like American cotton, was also popular with members of the more mainstream procolonial organizations, like the German Colonial Society.

31. *Sten. Ber.* IX/II/9, November 30, 1893, 179. Zimmermann, born in 1859 as the son of a Prussian official, was a literary critic and poet before entering antisemitic politics. He founded the *Deutsche Wacht* in 1887 as a mouthpiece for his movement against the Jews and social democracy (Wilhelm Kretzer, "Unsere Abgeordneten," *Reichsgeldmonopol,* July 19, 1890).

32. *Sten. Ber.* IX/IV/6, December 12, 1895, 85.

abolish the liquor trade and the battle against the spread of Islam in the colonies. Stöcker advanced several resolutions concerning these issues during the late 1880s and early 1890s, including a proposal urging the government to create zones of influence exclusive to individual denominations within the colonies.

As with the German Socials and German Reformers, however, conventional patriotism and an appreciation of some of the goals of *Weltpolitik* also motivated the Christian Socials in their support for overseas colonialism. Along with Ludwig Werner, Stöcker believed that tropical colonies might liberate German industry from its reliance on foreign imports of raw materials, which he claimed would strengthen Germany's hand, internationally.[33] In addition, Stöcker made it quite clear during his career in the Reichstag that he considered the pursuit of a successful colonial policy to be a matter of national prestige. Speaking before the Reichstag in December 1904 following the outbreak of the Herero uprising, Stöcker insisted that Germans needed to pursue a colonial policy "even if we don't want to," because "all the large powers carry out a *Weltpolitik*" and "we must surely desire to take part in the European concert."[34]

Support for colonialism did not, however, entail an unquestioning acceptance by political antisemites of the government's colonial policies. In fact, until the suppression of the Herero and Nama uprisings in 1907, the antisemitic Reichstag deputies sharply criticized the slow pace of colonial development and condemned a number of official actions, such as the government's exchange of Zanzibar and other islands along the coast of German East Africa for Helgoland in 1890.[35] Antisemitic deputies contested colonial measures that contradicted their vision of sensible colonial policy. Despite their support for some of the goals of *Weltpolitik,* they rejected with particular vehemence policies that favored big businesses at the expense of colonial settlers or that provided what they considered excessive remuneration to colonial land, mining, and railroad companies.

And yet, anger over certain official actions did not prevent antisemites from siding with the government in defense of colonialism when it appeared in danger. Such a crisis emerged in January 1904 with the outbreak of the Herero uprising in German Southwest Africa. The colonial admin-

---

33. *Sten. Ber.* XI/I/108, December 9, 1904, 3453.

34. Ibid., 3453.

35. The small North Sea island had strategic value for the German navy (Hajo Holborn, *A History of Modern Germany, 1840–1945* [Princeton: Princeton University Press, 1982], 304).

istration was caught completely off-guard by the rebellion, which killed over a hundred German settlers and soldiers in the first few weeks. After a brief period of national unity, when even the Social Democrats did not oppose sending reinforcement troops to the colony, criticism of the government mounted as colonial critics accused it of implementing flawed colonial policies. The parliamentary representatives of the antisemitic political parties joined other nationalists in censuring the critics, demanding a patriotic front "as long as the bloody battle over there has not ended."[36]

Another crisis broke out in 1906, when a number of scandals erupted in rapid succession concerning German Africa. Reports about atrocities committed by individual officials against African indigenes coincided with revelations about the granting of fantastic monopolistic privileges by the government to large companies doing business in the colonies. These disclosures motivated the Catholic Center Party to unite with the Social Democrats at the year's end to vote down the government's request for a supplementary appropriation of funds to maintain the contemporary fighting force of eight thousand men in Southwest Africa needed to continue the war with the Nama.[37] The antisemites criticized the business monopolies but attacked the allegations of atrocities committed against indigenous people brought forth by deputies from the Left and Center as sensationalistic and out of bounds.[38] The parliamentary representatives of the German Social, Christian Social, and German Reform Parties sided with the government toward the end of 1906 in voting to approve the re-

---

36. *Sten. Ber.* XI/I/107, December 7, 1904, 3424. The speaker was Oswald Zimmermann.

37. The Catholic Center Party supported colonialism as a means to spread Christianity. Revelations about the mistreatment and murder of Africans, government inefficiency, and the business monopolies angered Center Party leaders, leading to the stalemate in 1906. The Social Democrats saw colonialism as perpetuating capitalism, and so they opposed colonialism in theory. In practice, however, patriotism motivated many Social Democrats to support the idea of colonies (George Dunlap Crothers, "The German Elections of 1907" [PhD diss., Columbia University, 1941]; Klaus Epstein, "Erzberger and the German Colonial Scandals, 1905–1910," *English Historical Review* 74 [1959]: 637–63; Erik Grimmer-Solem, "The Professors' Africa: Economists, the Elections of 1907, and the Legitimation of German Imperialism," *German History* 25 [2007]: 313–47).

38. See Lattmann, *Sten. Ber.* XI/II/130, November 30, 1906, 4017; Werner, *Sten. Ber.* XI/II/133, December 4, 1906, 4125. Some accusations were truly horrific, such as the mutilation of black prisoners, the drowning of black children, and sadistic executions. The government acknowledged the veracity of some of these stories. In December 1906, it admitted that a colonial officer in west Africa had executed three black "highwaymen" with a cannon after tying them to a tree, as alleged by colonial critics in the Reichstag (*Sten. Ber.* XI/II/133, December 4, 1906, 4145).

quested funds. This was not enough to pass the supplementary appropria-
tions, but it proved that the antisemites' commitment to colonialism survived their disappointment over specific colonial policies.[39]

Many of the most visible procolonial political antisemites were also members of the Pan-German League. According to Mildred S. Wertheimer, 15
percent of the league's membership came from the antisemitic political
parties, and these members included the abovementioned Liebermann von
Sonnenberg, Wilhelm Lattmann, Ludwig Werner, and Oswald Zimmermann, among others.[40] The involvement of the political antisemites in
colonialism therefore exceeded their work in the Reichstag and entered the
realm of extraparliamentary pressure group activity. The political antisemites were not, however, leaders in the league. These men also had little
to do with the actual creation of the colonial empire, and for the most part,
they lacked direct, personal connections with the colonies. Their most important actions on behalf of German colonialism were largely limited to
their vocal agitation in its defense within the Reichstag and to the common
cause they made with other colonial advocates in supporting the government's budgets for the colonies.

To find the most direct and active connection between the antisemitic
movement and the colonial cause, we must look beyond the movement's
political wing to the radical idealists. As we shall see below, support for the
colonial project was actually more uncertain among idealists (or revolutionary antisemites) who avoided conventional politicking than among the
members of the antisemitic political parties. Indeed, the few outspoken antisemitic critics of the very idea of colonial empire came from the movement's radical revolutionary wing, whose members occasionally doubted
the benefits of colonialism and freely noted its drawbacks. It was also
within the radical "unpolitical" wing, however, that some of the most ardent and fanatical advocates of colonialism with the strongest direct connections to it could be found, people who had a hand in founding German
colonies. The most important individual of this sort was the publisher and
former schoolteacher Friedrich Lange, a doctor of philosophy from
Goslar who helped organize the initial treaty-signing expeditions to east

---

39. Chancellor Bülow used the defeat of the supplementary funding bill as an excuse to
dissolve the Reichstag. Progovernment parties increased their representation in the ensuing
election, winning 216 out of 397 seats (Epstein, "Erzberger," 659–61).

40. Mildred S. Wertheimer, *The Pan-German League, 1890–1914* (New York: Columbia
University, 1924), 133.

Africa in the 1880s before becoming one of the leading ideologues of revolutionary antisemitism in Germany. Other revolutionary antisemites directly involved in colonialism included the fanatic Bernhard Förster and his wife, Elisabeth Förster-Nietzsche, who together established an "Aryan" settlement colony in central Paraguay during the mid-1880s. The following pages examine Lange's contributions to both the antisemitic and colonial movements at length, before briefly reviewing the Försters' own, less successful, colonizing endeavors. This precedes an examination of the more critical perspectives on colonialism held by other revolutionary antisemites, those who lacked Lange's confidence in the advantages of colonies.

Friedrich Lange was a very influential and prolific figure in the antisemitic movement of the imperial era. In one historian's view, had Lange been born slightly later, he would likely have "outdone a Streicher or a Goebbels" as a propagandist for the Nazis.[41] This comment belies the fact that Lange's talent for engaging in the pseudoscientific, antisemitic talk of the day was largely confined to the written rather than the spoken word. Unlike his contemporary Adolf Stöcker, Lange was not a mesmerizing speaker, but was best known for publishing—and writing for—the fiercely antisemitic Berliner daily the *Deutsche Zeitung,* which he founded in 1896 and directed until 1912. The newspaper, along with its weekly edition, the *Deutsche Welt,* operated as a fount of antisemitic hatred, though Lange tried to differentiate it from the supposedly less refined antisemitic newspapers that filled the literary landscape. He also founded the small and exclusive antisemitic organization, the *Deutschbund,* which represented an important part of the "intellectual" wing of the antisemitic movement. As a founding member of the colonial movement as well, he associated for a brief period with Carl Peters. Lange's antisemitism and procolonial sentiments formed part of a complex and violent *Weltanschauung* that focused on racial conflict and glorified war and territorial expansion.

This *Weltanschauung* encompassed a burning hatred of Jews. Like most of the political antisemites, Lange identified the Jewish people as members of a threatening foreign race, possessing significantly un-German racial characteristics. He advocated revoking Jewish civil rights and, in language tinged with hints of violence, spoke of the need for *Räumungsarbeit,* or "cleansing work" against the Jews, something he admitted "many irk-

---

41. Fritz Ferdinand Müller, *Deutschland—Zanzibar—Ostafrika: Geschichte einer deutschen Kolonialeroberung, 1884–1890* (Berlin: Rütten und Loening, 1959), 99.

some and delicate nerves may find unpleasant, and that may also disturb incorrigible dreamers in their illusions of humanity."[42] Although Lange shared similar goals with the political antisemites regarding the Jewish Question, he nevertheless remained aloof from the political parties. He condemned what he characterized as the "demagogical character" of their leaders, and he insisted that by railing against Jewish wealth and by fueling sensational rumors of ritual murders and other fantastical Jewish depravities, the political antisemites appealed "to the lowest instincts" of the German people, thereby debasing the "holy war" against the Jews that Lange himself was leading.[43] Throughout his career as an antisemitic ideologue and publicist, Lange sharply criticized the politicians and the politically oriented antisemitic press for what he termed their *"nur-Antisemitismus,"* or their program of pure antisemitism. He accused them of forgetting that "antisemitism must only be one element, and not at all the most important, of a much wider and higher national *Weltanschauung* and politics." In Lange's opinion, this "national *Weltanschauung*" dictated the restructuring of German culture, society, and national life in conformation with German "racial instincts," and subjugating the Jews was but a single step to this end. Accordingly, Lange attempted to make his *Deutsche Zeitung* an alternative voice in the antisemitic community, one dedicated to the moral regeneration of the German people, thereby advancing a positive program in contrast to the simpleminded Jew-hatred of other periodicals.

Lange's support for colonialism was a natural outgrowth of his militant Social Darwinism and his veneration of physical combat. One of the many accusations that Lange made over the years against the Jews was that, by striving for "eternal peace" on earth, Jews disparaged military prowess and worked to estrange the Germans from their own "innate bellicosity." Far from being a sin, bellicosity was in fact a virtue. According to Lange, military prowess kept a people young, and eternal peace would only tranquilize the "powerful ebullitions" of the German blood that stimulated what was noble within the German spirit.[44] In addition to venerating warfare for its rejuvenating and ennobling effects, Lange also celebrated it as the appropriate medium—in his words, the "bloody test"—for determining the hierarchy among the different "Aryan" peoples.[45] Combined

---

42. Friedrich Lange, *Reines Deutschtum: Grundzüge einer nationalen Weltanschauung* (Berlin: Verlag von Alexander Duncker, 1904), 91.
43. Ibid., 92–93.
44. Ibid., 158.
45. Ibid., 236.

with a belief that colonies engendered strong national economies and, as "coaling stations" in distant lands, promoted the expansion of European power and influence abroad, Lange's fantasies about conflict and international and interracial competition fueled his belief in the necessity of a colonial empire.[46]

This conviction likely motivated Lange to join Germany's colonial movement in its formative years. In April 1884, while working as the editor of a Berlin newspaper, the *Tägliche Rundschau*, Lange became a member of the executive committee of the Society for German Colonization, an organization created by Carl Peters to seize the initiative in procolonial agitation from the preexisting Colonial Association.[47] The thirty-two-year-old Lange quickly ascended to a position of influence within the society. While serving on its executive committee, he sided with a faction that envisioned Africa rather than South America as the proper target of the group's colonial endeavors. It was through Lange's machinations in April and May 1884—a period when Peters was largely absent, having left Berlin for Hanover to work on his *Habilitation* thesis in history—that the Africa faction wrested control from those members who pushed for settlement activity in Argentina.

During the summer of 1884, Lange worked with Peters and other members of the Africa faction to raise a total of 65,000 marks for a proposed expedition of three society members—including Peters—to establish an "independent German agricultural and trading colony" in Angola.[48] When, several weeks before the departure date, the German Foreign Office declared the proposed area of exploration to be under Portugal's control, Lange helped persuade a reluctant Peters to accept the Usagara region of East Africa as a substitute destination. The expedition went ahead, and during Peters's absence, Lange wrote optimistic articles for the German press defending the venture. Peters returned to Berlin in early

---

46. Ibid., 286.

47. The German Colonial Association was founded at the end of 1883 by a group of intellectuals, politicians, and small businessmen for the purpose of pressuring the government to extend national protection to German trading stations located overseas and, in this way, to create the preconditions for colonial empire. The association's founders did not intend to actively partake in the actual exploration and creation of colonies. For this reason, more energetic and ambitious men like Peters formed the Society for German Colonization (Richard Victor Pierard, "The German Colonial Society, 1882–1914" [PhD diss., Graduate College of the State University of Iowa, 1964], 13–50).

48. Johannes Wagner, *Deutsch-Ostafrika. Geschichte der Gesellschaft für deutsche Kolonisation und der Deutsch-Ostafrikanische Gesellschaft nach den amtlichen Quellen* (Berlin: Engelhardt, 1886), 16.

February the following year, claiming to have made ten treaties with East African "sultans" that assigned control of 140,000 square kilometers of land to the society. The society then relinquished its claimed rights over these territories to a newly formed business organization, the German East Africa Company (or DOAG, short for the Deutsch-Ostafrikanishe Gesellschaft), whose directorate of four initially contained both Lange and Peters. In late February, Chancellor Bismarck signed an imperial charter giving government protection to the DOAG's territories, effectively birthing the new German East Africa colony.[49]

Despite Lange's important contributions to the DOAG and the Society for German Colonization, his involvement with the two organizations was surprisingly brief.[50] Antagonism between Lange and Peters, fueled in part by the incompatibility of their personalities, but also by disagreements over the future direction of the DOAG, led to Lange's resignation from the directorate at the end of 1885 and his disassociation from the company. Disparaging remarks that he made in later years about the Society for German Colonization's successor, the German Colonial Society, suggest that he eventually distanced himself from the organized colonial movement overall.[51] Yet his alienation from the society and the DOAG did not entail his estrangement from the colonial cause. Lange continued to champion colonialism in the pages of the *Tägliche Rundschau,* and after he left the newspaper in 1895, he used the *Deutsche Zeitung* to air his Social Darwinist *Weltanschauung* and both his antisemitic and procolonial beliefs. During the 1890s, Lange also cultivated an increasingly close relationship with the fanatically procolonial Pan-German League. An influential member of the league, Baron Georg von Stössel, provided the initial financial backing for the *Deutsche Zeitung.* In addition, Lange's elitist, antisemitic organization, the *Deutschbund,* incorporated within its ranks an increasing number of league members over the years, so much so that the

49. Pierard, "German Colonial Society," 58–62, 66–69; Müller, *Deutschland-Zanziber-Ostafrika,* 144; Juhani Koponen, *Development for Exploitation: German Colonial Policies in Mainland Tanzania, 1884–1914* (Helsinki: Finnish Historical Society, 1995), 51–85.

50. Lange's associates later remembered him as an extremely influential figure in the society. According to Joachim Graf von Pfeil, one of the society's leading personalities, Lange was the organization's resident "politician . . . the only one among us who possessed a general knowledge of the contemporary political situation . . . to him goes the credit for bringing the Society to life mentally" (Müller, *Deutschland-Zanziber-Ostafrika,* 100).

51. In 1904, Lange accused the German Colonial Society of being under "the inept leadership of retired generals and privy councillors" and of "sinking back more and more into the anemic condition and indecisiveness of the garrulous old Colonial Association" (*Reines Deutschtum,* 285).

Deutschbund's ten-man national directorate contained six Pan-Germans in 1913.[52]

The cross-membership between the *Deutschbund* and the league is not surprising, given their shared philosophies. Founded by Lange in 1894 as "a nursery and proving ground for all natural germinations of our German essence," the *Deutschbund,* like the league, embraced *völkisch* nationalism, practicing what amounted to a near-religious worship of German culture and ethnicity.[53] Both the league and the *Deutschbund* advocated an aggressive foreign policy aimed at creating a German-dominated Europe and pressed for settler colonies in the name of procuring more *Lebensraum* for the German people. Contrary to more mainstream procolonial organizations like the German Colonial Society, they did not limit their ambitions to territories overseas but called for expansion both within and without the European continent, in the former instance, looking to the east.

These similarities in outlook were accompanied by important differences. Unlike the league, the *Deutschbund* avoided political action, and it restricted its size by making membership by invitation only. *Deutschbund* members also tended to avoid the type of active agitation necessary to drum up support for their philosophy of *völkisch* nationalism among the general public, preferring instead to concentrate on cultivating their own inner "Germanness." The Pan-Germans, on the other hand, used the political system as one route among many to influence government policy. League members elected to parliament like Ernst Hasse, who headed the organization until 1908, pressed the league's agenda within the legislative body. In addition, the league aspired to be a mass organization. To this end, league chapters proselytized constantly, using mass meetings, demonstrations, public lectures, and tours, and organizing charitable activities to attract attention to their cause with the aim of conversion. By 1900, the league's membership was approximately 21,000 strong, while, at the same time, the *Deutschbund* only had 800 members divided into thirty-five "communities."[54] Finally, the two groups differed in terms of their antisemitism. While the league evolved over time into a de facto antisemitic organization, embracing racial antisemitism with increasing fervor after 1901, racial antisemitism lay at the heart of the *Deutschbund's Weltanschauung* from the

---

52. Chickering, *We Men Who,* 241.

53. Lange, *Reines Deutschtum,* 354.

54. Lange, *Reines Deutschtum,* 352; Chickering, *We Men Who,* 323. The *Deutschbund* grew to 1,534 members by 1914 (Uwe Puschner, *Die völkische Bewegung im wilhelminischen Kaiserreich: Sprache, Rasse, Religion* [Darmstadt: Wissenschaftliche Buchgesellschaft, 2001], 384).

very beginning. The *Deutschbund*'s founding charter prohibited individuals with "Jewish blood" from joining, and it enjoined members to "ward off the detrimental influence of Jewry from ourselves and our people."[55]

Although not identical, the two organizations' ideologies were nevertheless close enough to explain the significant overlap in their memberships. Not only did important league members create *Deutschbund* "communities," but *Deutschbund* members also founded, sustained, and directed league chapters in multiple towns and cities. The cross-membership of the *Deutschbund* and the league, as well as the presence within the latter's ranks of leading antisemitic politicians, contributed to the penetration of racial antisemitism into the league's *Weltanschauung* after the turn of the century. This was arguably Lange's most significant legacy, given the central role that the Pan-German League played in the last decade of the *Kaiserreich* in propagating racial theories.[56]

Friedrich Lange's involvement with the Society for German Colonization, and the close relationship between Lange's *Deutschbund* organization and the Pan-German League, are important examples of how radical antisemitism intersected with colonialism during the imperial era. Lange was both a mystic and a revolutionary. His purview surpassed civil rights, labor laws, and tax codes to encompass what he called the "inborn idealism" of the German people, and his program for a "national rebirth" included such radical proposals as substituting "German" for "Christian" values and encouraging the gradual withering away of Christianity. Even so, like procolonialists, he was also concerned with more earthy, practical matters, like strengthening Germany's national economy and increasing the international power and prestige of the German people. These latter concerns were pivotal in generating his support for the colonial movement, and they motivated his opposition in 1884 to the idea of creating a German settlement within a preexisting South American republic, because he believed this would sacrifice the "German-national character" of the future colony.[57] Lange's mysticism and his preoccupation with what he described as the German soul, German ideals, and German moral instincts did not,

---

55. Lange, *Reines Deutschtum,* 353.

56. According to Chickering, Heinrich Class created a *Deutschbund* "community" in Mainz in 1894 and afterward led it into the Pan-German League. Class succeeded Ernst Hasse as the leader of the league in 1908. Chickering also writes that the board of officers for the Pan-German League chapters in Darmstadt, Gotha, Jena, Kassel, Bochum, and Meiningen were, by 1910, controlled by men who belonged to *Deutschbund* "communities" (Chickering, *We Men Who,* 236, 241).

57. Lange, *Reines Deutschtum,* 263.

therefore, preclude an interest in the material world. His militant Social Darwinism and veneration of international conflict and ethnic-national competition motivated Lange to attempt to augment, through colonial possessions, the power that the German state and ethnic nation projected outward toward other peoples.

Lange's attitude did not, however, typify the outlook of all procolonial antisemitic idealists. A concern for inborn German "ideals" and an obsession with preserving what was supposedly genuine and unadulterated within the German spirit motivated some antisemites to concentrate solely on the imagined spiritual, cultural, and racial benefits of colonialism and, in so doing, to attempt the very type of colonial project that Lange rejected. Such was the case with Bernhard Förster, a Berlin schoolteacher who helped organize the Antisemites' Petition of 1880, and his wife, Elisabeth Förster-Nietzsche, the sister of Friedrich Nietzsche. Like Lange, Bernhard and Elisabeth were revolutionary antisemites; after the Antisemites' Petition failed, Bernhard Förster became convinced of the futility of using conventional politics to solve Germany's problems, which he defined as the corruption of German culture through Jewish capitalism. Like Lange again, the Försters identified a successful colonial project as crucial to the future of the German people, but their ideas of colonialism differed significantly. Förster was not interested in colonization as a means to strengthen the economic and military capabilities of the German nation-state. Rather, colonies were meant to serve as isolated breeding grounds for purebred Aryans. Such colonies would achieve the "preservation of human culture" and the "purification and rebirth of the human race."[58] They would remain separate and independent from a Germany that, in Forster's view, had degenerated into a "step-fatherland" through the Jews' deleterious influences.[59]

Approximately half a year after attending the Dresden International Antisemitic Congress in September 1882, Bernhard Förster left for South America to find a location for his future colony, eventually settling on an isolated spot in central Paraguay. With the help of Elisabeth, whom he married in 1885, he spent several years raising funds for his venture and attempting to win the moral support of his hero, Richard Wagner, another

---

58. Bernhard Förster, *Deutsche Colonien in dem oberen Laplata-Gebiete mit besonderer Berücksichtigung von Paraguay. Ergebnisse eingehender Prüfungen, praktischer Arbeiten und Reisen, 1883–1885* (Naumburg, 1886), 221.

59. Ben Macintyre, *Forgotten Fatherland: The Search for Elisabeth Nietzsche* (New York: Farrar Straus Giroux, 1992), 111.

important member of the "unpolitical" antisemitic scene. In the winter of 1886, the Försters and fourteen German families—mostly peasants from Saxony—set sail for Nueva Germania, which Bernhard now referred to as a potential new Fatherland, one free from Jewish influences. The entire venture fell apart, however, within two years, plagued by financial difficulties. Bernhard committed suicide in Paraguay in 1889, and Elisabeth returned to Germany several years later, publicly scandalized by the accusations of disgruntled Nueva Germania colonists who accused the Försters of misleading them about the harsh reality of life in Paraguay. Although Bernhard Förster did not significantly affect the course of German colonialism, National Socialists later hailed him as a martyr to the colonial cause and one of their intellectual forefathers. In 1934, Adolf Hitler sent a package of German soil to San Bernardino, Paraguay, to be spread upon Bernhard's grave.[60]

Other revolutionary antisemites also viewed settlement colonies primarily as a means to achieve racial rebirth and cultural purification. In 1909, racial antisemites and *völkisch* nationalists formed an organization called the *Siedelungs-Gesellschaft Heimland* and purchased 117 hectares of land in Ostprignitz, northwest of Berlin, for settlement purposes.[61] In 1912, supporters of the antisemitic ideologue Willibald Hentschel began drawing up plans for a breeding colony to be located in either Canada or Argentina.[62] Bernhard Förster, Hentschel's supporters, and the participants in the *Heimland* colony all came from the same milieu of culturally disaffected malcontents who interpreted the rise of modern society as a sign of the racial and spiritual degeneration of the German people. Their efforts at "colonization" were born largely from despair. Unlike Lange and the political antisemites, they did not mean for their colonies to augment the military and economic power and prestige of the German nation-state, but to purify and reenergize the German race and spirit.

---

60. Ibid., 193.

61. The radical antisemitic publisher Theodor Fritsch sat on the *Heimland*'s board of trustees. Potential *Heimland* settlers had to prove their Aryan heritage to be accepted into the colony, and a dozen people lived and worked there by early 1910. The experiment suffered from an imbalance between the sexes—only three settlers were women—and also from financial problems (Puschner, *Die völkische Bewegung*, 195–201).

62. Hentschel was a biologist who preached the need for "planned breeding" in order to revitalize the Aryan race. He proposed creating a breeding colony, consisting of 1,000 women and 100 men, where marriages would only last the length of pregnancy. Hentschel's ideas were controversial even within the revolutionary wing of the antisemitic movement. His followers never succeeded in establishing such a colony (Puschner, *Die völkische Bewegung*, 188–95).

The divide between Lange and the Försters over the proper form and purpose of colonialism was not the only important difference within the revolutionary wing of the antisemitic movement concerning colonies. Certain segments were simply unimpressed by the official colonial project. They saw the government's colonizing endeavors as failing to address the erosion of traditional German culture, the degeneration of the German racial stock through the incursion of foreign elements, and the alienation of the German people from their supposedly inborn sensibilities. Highly critical of the modern, capitalist, industrialized economy, these radical antisemites attacked any concessions in colonial matters to the interests of big business and industry. Concerned to the point of paranoia about racial intermixing, they also sharply condemned the potential dangers that the colonial venture posed to German racial purity.

This ambivalence toward colonialism by a segment of Germany's revolutionary antisemites can be seen most clearly in the pages of Theodor Fritsch's *Hammer* magazine. Although Fritsch was connected for a time to the political wing of the antisemitic movement, his radical views on religion and other matters eventually forced him from the German Social Party.[63] From 1902 until his death in 1933, Fritsch devoted much of his energy to publishing the *Hammer* from Leipzig, which espoused a combination of "scientific" racial antisemitism and *völkisch* nationalism that presaged the National Socialists' own beliefs. Presenting himself as a leader of the intellectual wing of the antisemitic movement, Fritsch disparaged the rabble-rousing tactics of antisemitic agitators who, in his estimation, lacked the intellectual depth and spiritual profundity required for a genuine understanding of the Jewish Question.[64] In his magazine, which appeared twice a month, Fritsch advanced a holistic program for the national revival of the German people, discussing everything from art and literature to educational reform and racial hygiene. *Hammer* readers across Germany formed themselves into local groups, called *Hammer* communities—resembling to an extent the chapters of the *Deutschbund*—and these joined together in 1910 into the *Reichs-Hammerbund*, which quickly became one of the most prolific purveyors of antisemitic literature in Germany.[65] In ad-

---

63. Fritsch supported Hentschel's controversial plan to establish a breeding colony.

64. Theodor Fritsch, "Antisemit?—oder Judenschimpfer?" *Hammer: Blätter für deutschen Sinn* 3 (1904): 542–45.

65. The *Reichs-Hammerbund* distributed over two million antisemitic pamphlets in 1912 and 1913. The readership of the *Hammer* magazine was much smaller. Fritsch claimed 3,000 subscribers in 1905 and 85,000 by the beginning of the First World War (Herzog, "Theodor Fritschs Zietschrift," 167, 159).

dition to writing for and running the *Hammer,* Fritsch authored numerous antisemitic tracts, which he published himself and distributed widely. A number of these appeared in consolidated form in 1907 under the title *Handbuch der Judenfrage,* and no less a prominent Nazi than Julius Streicher claimed that the *Handbuch* inspired his own antisemitism.[66]

Although colonial matters did not feature prominently within the pages of the *Hammer,* occasional letters from readers and short, often anonymous, annotations (presumably from the editor), as well as a few articles, appeared in response to the major colonial issues of the day from 1904 to 1914. Most contributors disapproved of the government's colonial policies and doubted the value of a colonial empire that appeared to promote individual material gain while ignoring the greater needs of the German people. These sentiments found voice in the article "Volkstum und Imperialismus," published in April 1904. A lecturer in history at Munich's Technical University, Dr. Albrecht Wirth wrote the piece at a time when colonial matters were coming to the forefront of the national consciousness. The Herero uprising in Southwest Africa was only a few months old and was generating intense criticism across the political spectrum of the government's "native policies."[67] Wirth did not mention the uprising but criticized the overall course and character of German colonialism for neglecting the spiritual needs of the German people. His article exemplifies the disquiet felt by a segment of the revolutionary wing of the antisemitic movement over the direction that German colonialism had taken.

Wirth acknowledged the divide within the community of *Hammer* readers over the merits of overseas colonies. Citing the abovementioned Willibald Hentschel as an example, Wirth stated that "there are good friends of the fatherland (like Hentschel) who bear ill will toward imperialism and condemn all world politics." According to Wirth, these critics identified the "world politics" of medieval German emperors as having had "only one result: that unlimited, heroic, German blood was spilled uselessly on Italian and Syrian soil." From this perspective, "increasing the *Volkskraft,* putting one's own house in order, governing well in the homeland as the guardian of pious traditions, the custodian of inherited prosperity, and a model for the rising generation . . . is worth more than the

66. Volland, "Theodor Fritschs," 17–18.

67. Criticisms reflected political ideologies. Critics on the political Left claimed that the governor of Southwest Africa, Theodor Leutwein, had provoked the uprising by treating the Herero and Nama too severely. Critics on the political right accused the governor of excessive leniency and interpreted the revolt as the consequence of perceived German weakness by indigenous peoples.

eternal thirst for the new and wandering aimlessly in the world . . . where morals and manners slacken . . . and where the lofty example is quickly lost in the whirl of life." In Wirth's estimation, opponents of imperialism also feared the "centralization of government" and the "dangerous increase in the rights of the crown" that might accompany an enhancement of Germany's international power. These individuals believed that "power will only be achieved at the cost of freedom."[68]

For Wirth, however, the real problem with contemporary imperialism was something else, namely, the propensity of "world politics" to perpetuate rather than alleviate the evils of the modern, capitalist, industrialized economy. "What use is it to you to have obtained the entire world," Wirth asked in an implicit criticism of Germany's contemporary imperialist policies, "if you incur damage to your soul? What good is the toughest and most relentless of power politics if, in the end, a people's higher goal, spiritual and bodily perfection, isn't furthered through it? Human art," Wirth continued, "is a creation of noble nature, Herder has already said. But it is impossible to see something noble in the growing industrialization of Germany, in the increasing darkening and dirtying of our life's air, in the mechanization, brutalization, and modern enslavement of factory workers. We must therefore reject not only the nebulous utopia of the socialists, but also all world and power politics that only emanate from the industrial idea." Unlike with Hentschel, Wirth's dissatisfaction with the colonial project did not entail an outright rejection of empire but of *Weltpolitik* and the accompanying policies that, in his mind, funneled the benefits of colonialism to a small group of privileged people. In their place, Wirth advocated migrationist colonialism to relieve what he saw as Germany's excessive overpopulation: "The situation is not helped with new market-sources for our industry in foreign lands, with tropical colonies where only a few dozen white entrepreneurs acquire fortunes . . . [or] with new trade treaties. . . . Only land and land again can help us, new soil for the thronging millions of our excess people." According to Wirth, this would "check the enervation and weakening of our *Volks-Kraft,*" and only such an imperialism, one that "increases our inner, as opposed to our outer, riches," was justifiable. Wirth ended his article on a note of despair. Reminding his audience that industrial production and trade were not ends in themselves, but means toward the "elevation" of the "individual and the entire nationality," Wirth stated that the achievement of this goal would necessitate "a

---

68. Dr. A. Wirth, "Volkstum und Imperialismus," *Hammer: Blätter für deutschen Sinn* 3 (1904): 151.

complete alteration of our policies," something that he thought would never occur: "I say it with painful certainty that for the present, there is not the slightest prospect, to be sure, that this will happen."[69]

Wirth's characterization of the colonial empire as essentially an exercise in greed that privileged the selfish desires of the few over the needs of the many, and his pessimism concerning the prospect of reform both in colonial matters and in German life, generally, typified most commentaries that appeared in the *Hammer* concerning the German colonies. Although almost all supporters of colonialism shared this negativity in the years before Bernhard Dernburg's reforming policies, it was almost never moderated in the *Hammer* by the same sort of impassioned defense of the idea of colonialism that mitigated criticisms elsewhere. For example, the *Deutsch-Soziale Blätter* harshly criticized government policy in German Southwest Africa after the outbreak of the Herero uprising. It printed several long articles in 1904 denouncing Governor Leutwein's supposed leniency toward the Africans. It also attacked the government for having privileged the interests of large, often foreign-owned, land and mining companies.[70] Nevertheless, the *Blätter* still defended the idea of colonialism. Approximately one month after printing a stinging indictment of Leutwein, it published a long front-page article discussing Southwest Africa's merits as a colony and outlining the rationale for colonial possessions.[71] The *Deutsche Welt* (the weekly edition of the *Deutsche Zeitung*) followed suit. Several weeks after it published a harsh critique in 1904 of government policy in Southwest Africa, the *Deutsche Welt* ran a piece emphasizing the dire need for colonies. It claimed that degeneration through excessive urbanization threatened the German race if it failed to plant its "excess people" in "outer territories."[72]

By contrast, the *Hammer* editors let stand unchallenged the anticolonial comments of a contributor whose letter appeared in September 1904:

---

69. Ibid., 151–52.

70. "Zur Verschlimmerung in Südwest-Afrika," *Deutsch-Soziale Blätter*, October 19, 1904; "Unsere Kolonien," *Deutsch-Soziale Blätter*, December 31, 1904.

71. "Südwestafrika und die Sozialdemokratie—Rothäute und Schwarzhäute," *Deutsch-Soziale Blätter*, November 12, 1904; "Südwestafrika und die Sozialdemokratie—Rothäute und Schwarzhäute," *Deutsch-Soziale Blätter*, November 15, 1904. The *Deutsch-Soziale Blätter* argued in these articles that colonies were needed as destinations for German immigrants and markets for German exports.

72. Fr. Henkel, "Der Hereroaufstand. Entweder—oder!" *Deutsche Welt*, July 31, 1904; F. Eichler, "Im Kampf um die Weltmachtungstellung," *Deutsche Welt*, August 14, 1904. Eichler also argued that Germany needed colonies to free itself from its dependence on food imports from foreign countries.

"if today a good friend entered my room and said he wanted to settle in our colonies, I would immediately send for a doctor and have him examined for sunstroke."[73] Although two years later, the *Hammer* did balance a letter extremely critical of colonialism with one much more positive,[74] no rejoinder was made to a contributor who, shaken by his encounters with Africans in German cities, suggested in 1908 that the colonies had come at too great a price, namely, Germany's "negroization."[75] This remained the last word on the colonies in the *Hammer* for almost two years, as it was that long before the magazine again discussed colonial matters.

The *Hammer*'s attitude toward the colonial project reflects the "cultural despair" that informed the worldview of many nonpolitical antisemites who saw the corrupting effects of modernity and capitalism as pervading all areas of German life and society.[76] In addition to making the *Hammer*'s assessment of German colonialism more consistently negative than that of other colonial critics, this attitude also contributed to a perspective that was in some ways more objective, which again put the magazine at odds with more ardently procolonial antisemites. In its initial reaction to the Herero revolt printed in the form of an anonymous note at the back of a February issue, for example, the *Hammer* abstained from denouncing the Hereros for their supposed treachery and barbarism, the common response in the mainstream, right-wing German press. It attacked instead the unscrupulous business practices of colonial Germans vis-à-vis indigenous Africans, going so far as to identify the notoriously exploitative credit system used by European traders as the root cause of the Herero uprising.[77] "That the Hereros don't consider the credit system and the system of forced exchange to be a desirable cultural achievement," the *Hammer* proclaimed, "is something we can't really hold against them."[78]

---

73. Hans Heinrich von Schwießel, "Kolonial-Dummheiten," *Hammer: Blätter für deutschen Sinn* 3 (1904): 400.

74. The first letter disparages Germany's colonies as the leftover "crumbs" of the African continent and recommends "inner" rather than "outer" colonization. The second defends the need for overseas colonialism and paints a much rosier picture of German Africa (J. H., "Innere oder äußere Kolonisation?" *Hammer: Blätter für deutschen Sinn* 5 [1906]: 723; H. R., "Zur Kolonial-Frage," *Hammer: Blätter für deutschen Sinn* 6 [1907]: 186–88).

75. Alb. Grimpen, "Die Negerfrage in Deutschland," *Hammer: Blätter für deutschen Sinn* 7 (1908): 147.

76. Fritz Stern, *The Politics of Cultural Despair: A Study in the Rise of the Germanic Ideology* (Berkeley: University of California Press, 1974).

77. European traders commonly overcharged Africans for their goods by as much as 100 percent. They seized cattle and other livestock as payment for materials that they often forced upon their indigenous "customers."

78. "Zum Herero-Aufstand," *Hammer: Blätter für deutschen Sinn* 3 (1904): 71.

The magazine reiterated this criticism several months later in an anonymous lead article, where it stated that "the careless collection of debt claims and the appropriation of cattle and landed property essentially caused the Hereros' rebellion."[79] These statements contrast markedly with the political antisemites' public responses to the Herero uprising, which typically laid the blame squarely on the Africans. Only a few days after the revolt began, Liebermann von Sonnenberg insinuated before the assembled Reichstag that the Hereros rebelled in order to return to their former life of "theft, robbery, and murder."[80] Later that year, von Sonnenberg's newspaper, the *Deutsch-Soziale Blätter,* reprinted a long article from the weekly journal, *Der Deutsche,* that characterizes the Southwestern Africans as "wicked capitalists," quite the reverse of the *Hammer's* portrayal of the Herero as the victims of dishonest European businessmen who cheated them out of their land and property.[81]

The *Hammer's* critical outlook also led it to censure the government's conduct of the war in Southwest Africa. In a note printed in November 1904, the paper characterized German military tactics as "hopeless" and complained in another that General von Trotha's destruction of the Herero's cattle herds incurred great hardships for the colony.[82] This, too, put the *Hammer* at odds with the leader of the German Socials, because at about the same time, Liebermann von Sonnenberg indicated his appreciation of Trotha while speaking before parliament.[83] When state secretary Bernhard Dernburg criticized Trotha's military campaign several years later, blaming the paucity of the indigenous workforce in Southwest Africa on Trotha's actions, the *Deutsch-Soziale Blätter* called Dernburg's remarks "tactless" and printed the general's written response to Dernburg's charges.[84]

79. "Ueberraschungen," *Hammer: Blätter für deutschen Sinn* 3 (1904): 170.

80. *Sten. Ber.* XI/I/14, January 19, 1904, 370. In his speech, Libermann von Sonnenberg read from a letter by a German who had recently lived in Southwest Africa.

81. "Zur Verschlimmerung in Südwest-Afrika," *Deutsch-Soziale Blätter,* October 19, 1904. Taken from an article in *Der Deutsche* by Adolf Stein. Discussing the vices of the Herero and Nama, Stein wrote: "The brown gentlemen are wicked capitalists who exploit their women as work animals and, according to reactionary concepts of property, even trade them like wares."

82. "Aussichten im Herero-Lande," *Hammer: Blätter für deutschen Sinn* 3 (1904): 503; "Südwest-Afrika," *Hammer: Blätter für deutschen Sinn* 3 (1904): 552. The Herero lost a large percentage of their cattle in 1904 when General von Trotha pushed them into the Omaheke sandveld.

83. *Sten. Ber.* XI/I/106, December 6, 1904, 3403.

84. "'De richtige Taktus,'" *Deutsch-Soziale Blätter,* March 3, 1909; H. Teut., "Deutsche Kolonialpolitik, *Deutsch-Soziale Blätter,* February 6, 1909.

German antisemites were not, therefore, unanimous in their support for overseas colonies. The opinions expressed in the pages of the *Hammer* show that some revolutionary antisemites contested the necessity of overseas colonial possessions, contending that Germans should concentrate on the problems at home instead or, if they must, focus on colonizing Eastern Europe. This appears, however, to have been a minority position within the antisemitic movement. The antisemitic political parties all adamantly supported the idea of colonial empire, despite their criticisms of certain policies. Nonpolitical antisemites like Friedrich Lange and his *Deutschbund* devotees championed overseas colonialism, and even the community of *Hammer* readers contained strong supporters of the idea of colonies. The most important divide within the antisemites' ranks over colonialism appears, then, not to have been between its advocates and opponents, but between those who actively participated in the colonial movement through their involvement in the political process or in procolonial pressure groups, and those who did not. Different levels of engagement suggest different levels of commitment to the dream of world empire. The *Hammer* never came out decisively against the colonial project, but the paucity of its discussions of colonial matters relative to other antisemitic and *völkisch* periodicals indicates that colonialism was not a high priority for its editors as it was for Friedrich Lange and the leaders of the German Social Party.

If antisemites were divided among themselves according to their level of engagement with and fervor for the colonies, and if a minority faction rejected the very idea of colonial empire, there were nevertheless certain areas of consensus within the antisemitic community concerning colonialism. The first had to do with the alleged danger that the African colonies posed to the racial purity of the German people. Antisemitic opponents of colonialism identified this danger as yet another reason to abandon the colonies, but even its most vociferous champions emphasized the supposed threat of racial mixing, as did Friedrich Lange, who wrote frequently on this matter in the *Deutsche Welt*. The consternation over interracial sex between Germans and Africans increased after the outbreak of the Herero and Nama uprisings and the accompanying deployment of thousands of young soldiers to German Southwest Africa. Second, antisemites of all stripes also attributed certain problems within the colonial project to Jewish intrigue, although discussions of malicious Jewish interference receded after 1906 once the half-Jewish Bernhard Dernburg assumed control of the Colonial Division of the Foreign Office.

A third area of consensus concerned the policies of colonial development pursued by the government in the 1890s. During this time, the administration attempted to foster colonial development through private capital, in large part because the Reichstag would not approve the necessary public funds. The government made fantastic concessions in order to attract privately owned companies to the colonies, giving away extensive land, mining, and other rights to a handful of corporations. In exchange for these grants, the companies were obligated to construct roads and explore their territories, and by 1903, these "concession companies" controlled vast regions, including almost a third of the land in German Southwest Africa. Contrary to expectations, however, concessionary policy (as it will be referred to hereafter) hindered colonial development. Some companies neglected to construct the necessary infrastructure within their territories, preferring instead to simply wait until the market increased the value of their holdings and then sell them off, and their monopolistic rights prevented local colonial governments from taking action. This created a transportation crisis from 1897 to 1902 in German Southwest Africa, when the German Colonial Corporation failed to act upon its monopolistic right to build railroads within its vast territory along the colony's southern and central coasts.[85] Other companies interpreted the government's concessions as giving them greater control over the exploitation of natural resources than the government intended. This misinterpretation led the South and Northwest Cameroon Companies to exclude rival trading houses from their gigantic zones of influence inside Cameroon, effectively abrogating the government's promise of free trade within these areas.

Given the antisemitic movement's anticapitalist ethos, it is not surprising that antisemites across the board united in condemning the government's concessionary policies. The delivery of huge territories to, and the conferring of special privileges on, privately owned corporations that often failed to live up to their contractual obligations dismayed both the political and revolutionary wings of the antisemitic movement. In addition, several other factors exacerbated the antisemites' anger. In the first place, some of the largest concession companies were partly foreign owned, like the German Colonial Corporation of Southwest Africa. The government also gave extensive aid to the colonial companies above and beyond the original concessions. In Cameroon, local administrators worked closely with the major corporations, building roads in company

---

85. Helmut Bley, *Namibia under German Rule* (Hamburg: LIT Verlag, 1996), 131–32.

land and recruiting indigenous workers for company projects.[86] In German East Africa, the government actually subsidized the DOAG by giving the company 600,000 marks a year from the colony's own customs revenue to help it repay a multimillion-mark loan. The antisemites condemned these policies as the transfer of public wealth into private hands. By the eve of the Herero War, when the failures and abuses of concessionary policy were abundantly clear, articles and editorials attacking the concession companies were standard fare in most antisemitic periodicals.

The Herero War was especially important in galvanizing heated opposition among antisemites to concessionary policy. This arose because the uprising eventually cost the German government 600 million marks to suppress, which amounted to a massive infusion of public funds into a colonial project that so far had only served to enrich a few private corporations. After a period of patriotic silence following the initial outbreak of violence, calls from antisemites and other colonial critics for the renegotiation or outright annulment of the concessions dramatically increased. The parliamentary representatives of the major antisemitic political parties made this a staple of their reform programs for the German colonies, and the vehemence of their attacks on the concession companies even outstripped that of their invective against interracial sex. The same practically held true for the nonpolitical antisemites as well, as strong condemnations of concessionary policy appeared within the pages of the *Deutsche Zeitung* and *Hammer* magazine.[87] This stance reflected the antisemites' realization that these policies thwarted their colonial dreams. The slow pace of development hampered the materialization of the economic and industrial benefits that colonialism was supposed to bring, and the assignment of huge tracts of arable land to the concession companies hindered the growth of colonial settlements. The enrichment of a few privately owned corporations at the expense of national blood and treasure also undermined the antisemites' claim that the German people as a whole would benefit from overseas colonies.

---

86. Harry R. Rudin, *Germans in the Cameroons, 1884–1914: A Case Study in Modern Imperialism* (New Haven: Yale University Press, 1938), 293.

87. For example, the *Hammer* noted in an article during the Nama uprising, "Today, German warriors fight bravely with the black enemy in their adoptive fatherland. But that which they defend has already, for the most part, been given away—by bureaucratic decision makers" ("Boden-Reformer und Kolonial-Politik," *Hammer: Blätter für deutschen Sinn* 4 [1905]: 543).

The most public criticisms of concessionary policy by antisemites were made in the Reichstag, and the most articulate antisemitic spokesman on this matter was the parliamentary deputy Wilhelm Lattmann. Lattmann was a district court judge from the town of Schmalkalden in central Germany who won a seat in the Reichstag as a German Social in 1903, which he held until 1911. The faults of the concessionary system of colonial development were self-evident by the time he entered politics, and he agitated throughout his political career against the concessions granted during the 1890s. In one of his first speeches before the Reichstag on colonial matters, Lattmann classified what he called "the capitalist, in most part English, land companies" as being "among the most evil enemies of Southwest Africa," and he accused them of having incited the Herero rebellion. He also accused them of being "hostilely opposed through their land speculation to the entire settlement question, which is so extraordinarily important for Southwest Africa," and he asked that the treaties between the colonial companies and the government be "rescinded or at least changed to the benefit of our protectorates . . . in the interest of a necessary, thorough, colonization." In his speech, Lattmann proclaimed that the German Social delegates were ready to vote in favor of a resolution to compensate for economic losses in Southwest Africa incurred due to the uprisings, but requested that the resolution exclude the land companies. In his estimation, they had benefited enough "through the enhancement of the value of their lands" due to the infusion of public funds into the colony.[88]

Lattmann sounded the alarm against "the brutal predominance of monopolistic capitalism," "the growing influence of foreign capital," "land speculation," and the "failures of concessionary policy" in almost a dozen deliveries on colonial matters before the Reichstag, in addition to numerous published articles.[89] Although other antisemitic deputies echoed his sentiments with little or no variation, Lattmann's persistence and his knowledge of colonial matters made him stand out from the crowd. Unlike with most of the other outspoken, procolonial antisemites whose contributions to parliamentary debates on colonial matters often elicited little or no response, Lattmann's comments about the evils of concessionary policy and other colonial topics were taken seriously by Reichstag members and

---

88. *Sten. Ber.* XI/I/87, May 9, 1904, 2808.

89. Wilhelm Lattmann, "Küstenklatsch und Kolonialpolitik," *Deutsch-Soziale Blätter,* August 18, 1906; *Sten. Ber.* XI/II/130, November 30, 1906, 4019; *Sten. Ber.* XI/II/24, January 19, 1906, 677.

often generated lengthy discussions. When a bill was introduced in the Reichstag in May 1905 to guarantee the Cameroon Railroad Company against possible financial losses while building a rail line inland from Cameroon's coast, Lattmann's lengthy and detailed objections to the terms of the agreement between the corporation and the government sparked considerable debate during several plenary meetings. Lattmann argued that the government's offer of blocks of land along the rail line to the railroad company, in addition to other important rights, threatened to repeat the errors of concessionary policy.[90] His criticisms were taken seriously enough by his opponents for them to refute or downplay point by point, and his stand probably contributed to the shelving of the bill in committee, where it lingered a year before passing. Lattmann sparked considerable debate among Reichstag deputies again five years later when he advanced a proposal to levy a property tax on landed wealth in Southwest Africa in order to make wealthy investors shoulder a greater part of the financial burden of maintaining the colony. Lattmann intended his tax to raise 36 million marks, and he limited it to a one-time, one-percent levy on landed wealth of 300,000 marks or higher, payable over six years. His proposal won support outside the circle of parliamentary antisemites, but it was eventually rejected along with similar motions from leading members of the Catholic Center and Social Democratic parties.[91]

It must be pointed out that the political antisemites were far from alone in attacking the government's concessionary policies. By the time of the Herero War, anger over the slow pace of colonial development was widespread, and calls for the annulment of the concessions and thoroughgoing reform in colonial matters came not only from the antisemites but also from the more mainstream procolonial political organizations, including the Conservative, National-Liberal, and Catholic Center parties. The call for reform that increased dramatically after the outbreak of violence was spearheaded by Matthias Erzberger, a member of the Catholic Center Party. Soon after his election to the Reichstag in 1903, Erzberger took it upon himself to document and publicize the problems plaguing the colonial project with the intent of forcing the government to remedy them. In addition to exposing the greed of the colonial companies and the inefficiency of concessionary policy, Erzberger chronicled a list of atrocities committed by sadistic colonial administrators against indigenous peoples. But it was the former rather than the latter that most inflamed the an-

90. *Sten. Ber.* II/I/183, May 11, 1905, 5950–51; *Sten. Ber.* II/I/192, May 25, 1905, 6161–66.
91. *Sten. Ber.* XII/II/76, April 30, 1910.

tisemites. When Erzberger revealed in 1906 that the Adolf Woermann shipping company, which held a landing monopoly in all ports in Southwest Africa, and the Tippelskirch company, the sole supplier of equipment for Germany's colonial troops, vastly overcharged for their services, the antisemites joined him in demanding the revocation of their government contracts. This did not stop them, however, from voting to approve the supplementary budget requested by the government to continue the ongoing war with the Nama.[92]

Far from isolating them politically, then, criticisms directed at the administration by Lattmann, Werner, and the other procolonial antisemites in parliament actually grouped them together with more mainstream colonial reformers who also disapproved of contemporary colonial policies but supported the idea of empire. This led to unusual political alliances, as in 1910 when Erzberger supported Lattmann's proposed levy on landed property in Southwest Africa despite the overt anti-Catholicism of the antisemitic political parties. This cooperation suffered, however, when it came to reforming Germany's so-called native policies. In certain matters concerning the treatment of indigenous groups, the antisemites sided not with the more mainstream advocates of reform, like Erzberger, but with the extremists of the colonial movement, overtly demanding, for example, the use of "force" to "educate" blacks to work.[93]

The support given to the colonial cause during the *Kaiserreich* era by political antisemites was evident for all to see. Although procolonial antisemitic newspapers like the *Staatsbürger-Zeitung,* the *Deutsch-Soziale Blätter,* and the *Deutsche Zeitung* had very limited readerships, the procolonial orations of antisemitic Reichstag deputies and their frequent participation in parliamentary debates on colonial matters reached a wide audience. It was therefore common knowledge that the antisemitic political parties identified with the colonial movement and deemed colonial possessions to be of vital importance to the future of the German people. The minority position within the antisemitic movement—skeptical of colonial empire—was probably less well known, given that the revolutionary wing was exclusive by nature and avoided active political involvement. This helps to explain why some contemporaries like the anonymous author of the *Vorwärts* article of 1896, highlighted in the Introduction, perceived an antisemitic element to the colonial movement. The most visible

---

92. Epstein, "Erzberger," 636–63.
93. *Sten. Ber.* XII/I/125, March 18, 1908, 4087. For more on this, refer to chap. 4.

antisemitic politicians trumpeted their procolonial credentials. They took advantage of the opportunities that colonialism offered to articulate crucial elements of their antisemitic agenda, like the campaign against monopoly capitalism.

In addition, an intense antisemitism figured into the *Weltanschauung* of some of the individuals most responsible for the very genesis of colonial empire: men and women who, unlike most procolonial antisemitic politicians and ideologues, had an actual hand in the founding of the colonies. These antisemitic colonialists coalesced in particular around the explorer Carl Peters, and outside observers were aware of, and commented on, the antisemitic ethos of this unusually influential group of colonial actors. This is confirmed in a letter to Peters of 1891 by his friend W. Götz, a copy of which exists in the German Federal Archives. The letter begins with an explanation as to why Götz failed to convince the editor of the *Allgemeine Zeitung* to publish a submission to his newspaper. Götz complained that the editor was most likely a Jew and was therefore disturbed by the antisemitic ethos of Peters's inner circle. "He," Götz wrote, "is likewise at the very least a principled, sworn member of the 'Jewish protective forces,' and he expressed to me that, in this sense, he is a decided enemy of Zelewski's, Bley's, and your antisemitic tendencies. We suppose," Götz continued, "that he himself originates from this race. He even declared that it would be a danger if the Arabs in East Africa learned that these men are antisemites, since this could incite their kin in Tabooa [*sic*] to conspiracies."[94]

Each of the three men mentioned were important participants in the early effort to dominate East Africa. As seen above, Peters had embarked on an initial treaty-signing expedition to the region in 1884, and at the time of the letter's composition, he had recently completed a voyage to the interior. Peters would soon return to East Africa, this time as an imperial commissioner stationed on the slopes of Kilimanjaro. For his part, Fritz Bley had been an agent of the DOAG created—and for a time, headed—by Peters to administer the nascent colony, which it did until the government took control in 1888 during an indigenous uprising. Bley went to East Africa in 1887 to help expand the company's control over trade routes and port towns, and he founded the company station Usungala. In a further connection to Peters, he had also served as the general secretary of the So-

---

94. Walter Götz to Carl Peters, May 1, 1891, no. 7, Walter Frank Papers, Bundesarchiv Koblenz (henceforth BAK). The word *Tabooa* is likely a misspelling of Tabora, a town in the East African interior that was an important way station for trade caravans making their way to the coast. Tabora was dominated by Arabs.

ciety for German Colonization in 1885, and he was the leading editor of its weekly newspaper, the *Kolonial-Politische Correspondenz*. The third individual mentioned, Emil von Zelewski, was a DOAG agent as well, likewise entrusted with the task of expanding the company's grip on the East African coastal economy. Zelewski's outrageous behavior toward local elites in 1888 helped spark the rebellion that ended the DOAG's administrative responsibilities.[95] Zelewski then played an important role in fighting the rebels until his death in June 1891 at the hands of Hehe.

Of the three men, only Zelewski appears to have left no public record of his antisemitism. Bley, on the other hand, had a long career in the antisemitic *völkisch* movement once he returned from Africa, and he professed his antisemitism openly. He collaborated with other antisemitic procolonialists, like the Pan-Germanist Heinrich Class and the novelist Felix Dahn, to found the *völkisch* organizations the National Festival Association and the German League for the Prevention of Female Emancipation in 1899 and 1912, respectively.[96] In addition, Bley took control of the periodical *Zeitfragen* in 1905, which was a weekly edition of the Berlin newspaper, the *Deutsche Tageszeitung,* the official organ of the extremely antisemitic Agrarian League.[97] He wrote an article for the *Zeitfragen* in 1908 where he sharply criticized the leadership of the Society for German Colonization's successor organization, the German Colonial Society, for "hav-

---

95. Several months after the DOAG concluded a treaty with Sultan Kahalifa bin Said giving the company administrative duties in several mainland towns, Zelewski publicly humiliated the Arab governor of the port town of Pangani. As Jonathan Glassman recounts in *Feasts and Riots: Revelry, Rebellion, and Popular Consciousness on the Swahili Coast, 1856–1888* (Portsmouth: Heinemann, 1995), his actions upset a complex web of tensions and resentments among and between local patricians and plebeians, resulting in a prolonged rebellion against the signs of German authority, which came to include the Arabs who ruled in the sultan's name.

96. In her book on imperial Germany's antisemitic *völkish* movement, Uwe Puschner lists Bley alongside Friedrich Lange, Theodor Fritsch, Paul Förster, and Otto Böckel as one of 116 important *völkish* "fore-thinkers, leaders, and agitators" (Puschner, "Die völkische Bewegung," 382).

97. Formed in 1892 as a pressure group representing the interests of German farmers hurt by Chancellor Caprivi's trade treaties, the league became a powerful lobbying agent for the large landholders of East Elbia, and it worked closely with the Conservative Party. According to Richard Levy, the league "displayed an informal antisemitism" from the outset. Ardent antisemites held leadership positions within it—especially on the staff of its newspaper, the *Deutsche Tageszeitung*—and the organization prohibited Jewish members. Yet antisemitism remained subordinate within the league to matters of agricultural policy (Levy, *Downfall,* 3–4, 87–89, 128–29).

ing constantly sunk deeper into Jewification" and having bowed to "the economics of Jewish land speculation."[98] Bley defended the antisemitic movement of the *Kaiserreich* era in two books written during and immediately after the First World War, and he accused German Jews of colluding with Germany's foreign enemies.[99] During these decades, Bley also continued to be a procolonial activist, authoring several books about the colonies.[100]

Peters had a reputation as an antisemite, too, although the depth and intensity of his antisemitism was more difficult to gauge. For one thing, Peters rarely voiced his antisemitic opinions publicly. In addition, he had close dealings with a number of well-known apostate Jews, like his close friend and supporter, the economist and radical nationalist Otto Arendt, as well as the Prussian-born administrator of Equatoria, Emin Pasha, who was the subject of a Peters-led rescue expedition in 1889. What is more, Peters seemed disinterested in antisemitic politics.[101] When he ran unsuccessfully for the Reichstag as a National Liberal in 1895, rumors circulated in the antisemitic press that he had rejected offers to stand as a candidate from both the German Social Reform Party and the Agrarian League.[102]

Yet like Bley, Peters moved in antisemitic circles, both comfortably and intentionally. His letters show that he enjoyed warm relations with well-known members of the antisemitic movement even before he joined Friedrich Lange to form the Society for German Colonization.[103] A casual

---

98. "Die verjudete Kolonialgesellschaft," *Mittheilungen aus dem Verein zur Abwehr des Antisemitismus* 18 (1908): 286 (henceforth *Mittheilungen*). This article reproduces an excerpt from Bley's September 6 piece in the *Zeitfragen*. In it, Bley intimated that Jews are members of a foreign race.

99. Fritz Bley, *Wie kam es doch?* (Leipzig: Erich Matthes, 1918), 69–79, 136–37; ibid., *Am Grabe des deutschen Volkes: Zur Vorgeschichte der Revolution* (Berlin: August Scherl G.m.b.h., 1919), 195–98.

100. Bley's procolonial works include *Deutsche Pionierarbeit in Ostafrika* (Berlin: P. Parey, 1891), *Südafrika niederdeutsch!* (Munich: J. F. Lehmann, 1898), and *Die Buren im Dienste der Menschheit* (Vienna: F. Schalk, 1900). See M. R. Gerstenhauer, "Ein Vorkämpfer nationaler Kolonialpolitik. (Zu Fritz Bleys 60 Geburtstage)," *Deutsche Welt: Wochenschrift der Deutschen Zeitung,* July 20, 1913.

101. Frieda v. Bülow to Hermann Peters, March 24, 1893, no. 99, Carl Peters Papers, Bundesarchiv Berlin (hereafter BAB); Carl Peters to Hermann Peters, May 7, 1893, no. 93, Carl Peters Papers, BAB.

102. "Vereins-u. Parteinachr," *Antisemitisches Volksblatt,* February 15, 1896.

103. In a letter to his brother written in 1883, the future explorer remarked upon his familiarity with Berlin's antisemitic scene. "Am on intimate terms with Pastor Hapke, the Jew-

affiliation continued during his colonial career: in 1896, he spoke at a gathering of the intensely antisemitic Union of German Students, appearing alongside antisemitic politicians—like Liebermann von Sonnenberg—who denounced Jews in their speeches.[104] Perhaps as a result, the *Deutsch-Soziale Blätter* identified Peters later that year as "an outspoken antisemite."[105]

In addition, a tempered antisemitism surfaces in Peters's writings, both public and private. In a short essay on Zionism published in 1903, Peters argued for the resettlement of the Eastern European Jewish proletariat outside Europe "where they could live according to their own customs and tendencies."[106] According to Peters, this was the segment of the Jewish population that retained its original characteristics to the highest degree. Several years earlier, Peters wrote to his brother from Cairo, announcing the arrival of a long-expected sum of money from "Kempebrie Lloyd." Peters complained of the latter's services and denounced his "vile stock rigging." He informed his brother, "I have secured in Luxor a new truly distinguished financial connection in London. I do not need Kempe and other half-Jews any longer."[107] Together, these writings suggest a belief in the incompatibility of Jews and Gentiles and, perhaps, a desire by Peters to be rid of Jews, personally and universally.

Other influential antisemitic colonial actors connected to Peters's Society for German Colonization included Otto Arendt, Joachim von Pfeil, Alexander Merensky, and Frieda von Bülow. All were important members of the early colonial movement, and all were initially close to Peters. Arendt sat on the society's executive committee in the mid-1880s and was a shareholder of the DOAG. He was the editor in chief of the procolonial weekly, the *Deutsches Wochenblatt,* and he championed the colonial cause as a Reichstag deputy for the Reichspartei from 1898 to 1918. Von Pfeil was

---

guzzler," Peters wrote. "Likewise with an antisemitic Jewish junior barrister. . . . Already delivered a lead article on Stoecker for the conservative *Deutsche Tageblatt,* was then at dinner with Diestelkemp." At the time of Peters's letter, Hapke had recently gained fame for refusing to take an oath in a Berlin court before a Jewish judge (Carl Peters to Hermann Peters, November 24, 1883, no. 5, Walter Franks Papers, BAK).

104. *Mittheilungen* 6 (1896): 20. The *Mittheilungen* did not note the content of Peters's speech.

105. "Innerpolitisches," *Deutsch-Soziale Blätter,* March 19, 1896.

106. Carl Peters, *Gesammelte Schriften,* vol. 3, ed. Walter Frank (Munich: C.H. Beck'sche Verlagsbuchhandlung, 1944), 325.

107. Carl Peters to Hermann Peters, February 8, 1900, no. 93, Carl Peters Papers, BAB.

an aristocrat who accompanied Peters on his initial treaty-signing expedition to East Africa. Like Arendt, von Pfeil served as a member of the Society for German Colonization's executive committee, as well as on the DOAG's board of directors. Years later, he emerged as an influential advocate of Boer settlement in German Southwest Africa, and he became the head administrator of the Bismarck Islands in the late 1880s.[108]

For his part, Alexander Merensky was a missionary in the Transvaal from 1859 to 1882, and he was one of the most sought-after spokesmen on Africa in Germany. Merensky also belonged to the society, and in 1884, the organization united behind his suggestion of Angola as the initial target of their first treaty-signing expedition.[109] Finally, Frieda von Bülow—described as "probably the best known woman in the German colonial movement before the First World War"[110]—propagated the colonial cause by writing semiautobiographical accounts of her travels to East Africa, producing a number of popular colonial-themed novels by the turn of the century.[111] Bülow traveled to Zanzibar in 1887 as a nursing representative of the German National Women's League, which she helped found, and she apparently became romantically involved with Peters.

The antisemitic ethos of these members of the Peters circle emerges in their writings more so than from their activities. A Christian convert from Judaism, Arendt's militant nationalism won him entrance into antisemitic circles. The adamantly procolonial *Deutsches Wochenblatt* espoused a consistent religious antisemitism under his leadership in the 1890s. Similarly, von Bülow used her writings as public platforms for both her procolonial and antisemitic beliefs. A frequent underlying theme in her novels on German Africa is the need to relegate Jews and other religious and ethnic minorities to their supposedly proper places in the racial-social hierarchy. Her

---

108. Matthew S. Seligmann, "The Pfeil Family and the Development of German Colonial Ambitions in Southern Africa: A Study of Diplomacy and Colonial Trends," *German History* 12, no. 1 (1994): 27–38; Müller, *Deutschland-Zanzibar-Ostafrika*, 104, 113–16, 157, 183; "Pfeil und Klein-Ellguth, Joachim Graf von.," in *Deutsche Biographische Enzyklopädie*, vol. 7, ed. Walther Killy and Rudolf Vierhaus (Munich: K. G. Saur, 1998), 643.

109. This plan was thwarted when the German government announced in the summer of 1884 that it recognized Portugal's claim to the Angola region. Society members then substituted the area opposite Zanzibar in eastern Africa.

110. Lora Wildenthal, "'When Men are Weak': The Imperial Feminism of Frieda von Bülow," *Gender & History* 10 (1998): 53.

111. Bülow's many colonial-themed novels include *Der Konsul: Vaterländischer Roman aus unseren Tagen* (1891), *Tropenkoller: Episode aus dem deutschen Kolonialleben* (1896), and *Im Lande der Verheissung: Ein Kolonialroman um Carl Peters* (1899).

antisemitism surfaces in her letters as well; in one to Peters, she classified Jews as "this ghostly vampire-people" whose ability to "refresh again and again its senile and rotten blood by unions with strong Teutons capable of outstanding achievement" was "dreadful indeed."[112] Merensky, too, professed his antisemitism publicly: a letter by the missionary appeared in the *Deutsch-Südwestafrikanische Zeitung* in 1906 complaining of the "serious danger" poised to the territory by "the immigration of Russian-Polish Jews and other extremely disagreeable elements over our eastern boundary."[113]

Of the four, only von Pfeil apparently refrained from publicizing his antisemitism, although it, too, surfaces in his private correspondence. In 1887, Joachim informed his brother that he had recently read a book about the mistreatment of Jews in Persia, and he noted, "One must certainly bring these methods to the attention of an antisemitic society."[114] Markus confirmed his older brother's antisemitic hatred in another letter several years later where he attempted to justify his own engagement to a woman with a Jewish heritage. "I know your antipathy against the Jews," Markus wrote, "but unfortunately I must tell you that this is the snag in my engagement. Gertrude originates from a half-Jewish family."[115]

The antisemitism that pervaded the society's leadership also emerges

---

112. Frieda von Bülow to Carl Peters, March 10, 1902, no. 5, Walter Frank's Papers, BAK.

113. Dr. A. Merensky, "Stimmen aus dem Leserkreise," *Deutsch-Südwestafrikanische Zeitung,* August 18, 1906. Merensky recommended against selling Jews land or granting them business licenses as a way to discourage further immigration.

114. Joachim Graf von Pfeil to Markus Graf von Pfeil, January 6, 1887, no. 17, Walter Frank Papers, BAK. Markus, who briefly served as Togo's chief administrator in 1891, is often confused in the secondary literature on German colonialism with his brother, Joachim. This is probably because both men tended to sign their letters as "Graf Pfeil." For an example of this confusion, see Arthur J. Knoll's *Togo under Imperial Germany, 1884–1914: A Case Study in Colonial Rule* (Stanford: Hoover Institution Press, 1978), which names Joachim as Togo's acting commissioner in 1891. Yet the *Deutsches Kolonial-Lexikon,* which does not have an entry for Markus, notes that Joachim was in the British and Dutch Indies in 1889 and 1890 and then German East Africa in 1891. In addition, Alcione M. Amos's essay, "Afro-Brazilians in Togo: The Case of the Olympio Family, 1882–1945," states that the acting commissioner in Togo was Markus (Amos, "Afro-Brazilians in Togo," *Cahier D'Études Africaines* 162 [2001]: 293–314; Seligmann, "The Pfeil Family," 27–34; Knoll, *Togo under Imperial Germany,* 70).

115. Joachim Graf von Pfeil [?] to Markus Graf von Pfeil [?], July 20, 1890, no. 17, Walter Frank Papers, BAK. This letter exists in Koblenz as a typed copy in the collection of the papers of the Nazi-era historian Walter Frank, and it appears that Frank mistakenly attributed it to Joachim. This must be wrong, because in the body of the letter, the author repeatedly addressed the receiver as "mein Alter," meaning my elder or my elder brother. According to Matthew S. Seligmann in his article "The Pfeil Family," Joachim was the older brother, and even contemporaries confused the two. Therefore, this letter must have been authored by Markus, not Joachim.

in the correspondence of its rank and file, which reveals a certain paranoia about anticolonial Jewish intrigue. One petty financier of the DOAG sent a letter to the emperor in early 1889, fulminating against "years of continuous public agitation by the Jewish dictator and its minions in every German party against every German colonial effort."[116] Years later, the public investigation into Carl Peters's behavior in East Africa led a Peters admirer to write to the Reichspartei Reichstag deputy Hermann Graf von Arnim-Muskau, accusing colonial director Paul Kayser—a Christian convert from Judaism—of conspiring with "democratic journalists" against Peters. Referring to recent revelations about the violent abuse of African indigenes by German officials in Cameroon, the author proclaimed that he "and a large number" of his "conservative friends assert freely and frankly that it is not Leist and Wehlau [*sic*] who have done our colonies the most serious injuries, but rather it is Jewry, which also has the direction of our colonies within its hands and which is having an immoral effect upon our German conditions."[117]

Antisemitism, however, was not confined in the colonial movement to individuals directly involved with the Society for German Colonization. Other leading figures in colonialism were avid antisemites as well, and rank-and-file participants beyond the Peters circle openly supported the

---

116. Hornhauer to Wilhelm II, January 12, 1889, Reichskolonialamt (hereafter RKA) 733, BAB. Quoted in Müller, *Deutschland-Zanziber-Ostafrika,* 175. The author was likely incited by a series of recent disappointments. These included a recent transfer of power in the DOAG away from Peters and the investment into the company by the Jewish financial house Mendelssohn-Bartholdy (Fritz Stern, *Gold and Iron: Bismarck, Bleichröder, and the Building of the German Empire* [New York: Vintage Books, 1979], 414; Arne Perras, *Carl Peters and German Imperialism, 1856–1918* [Oxford: Oxford University Press, 2004], 78–79).

117. Anonymous to Graf Hermann von Arnim-Muskau, n.d., no. 7, Walter Frank Papers, BAK. Governor Leist of Cameroon became infamous in the early 1890s for sparking a rebellion among the Dahomey people with his cruelties. Among other things, he prostituted Dahoman women out to colonial whites and beat them in the presence of their husbands. Wehlan was a minor German official working under Leist who also became known for his brutality.

Colonial director Paul Kayser did, in fact, play a role in Peters's downfall. After working for years to bring Peters and his influential supporters to the government's side through appeasement—seen in Peters's appointment to the position of imperial commissioner of German East Africa—Kayser changed course in March 1896 following August Bebel's revelations in the Reichstag concerning Peters's behavior while on Mt. Kilimanjaro. Kayser tried to distance himself and the government from Peters and, in so doing, revealed to parliament certain details meant to discredit him. For example, Kayser informed the Reichstag that Peters had admitted to having sexual relations with black women at his station (Perras, *Carl Peters,* 217).

cause of antisemitism. The onetime colonial governor Eduard von Liebert belonged to the first category. Governor of German East Africa from 1896 to 1900, Liebert later joined the Reichstag as a member of the Reichspartei, where he advocated for colonial railroad construction and championed settler issues, loudly.[118] Although never an outspoken antisemitic ideologue, Liebert was ideologically very close to the leaders of the antisemitic scene, sharing their hatred of socialism, industrialization, and urbanization.[119] He contributed numerous pieces to Friedrich Lange's *Deutsche Zeitung*—articles on military affairs and reviews of books about the colonies—and at least one essay on the threat of Social Democracy to Theodor Fritsch's *Hammer* magazine.[120] In addition, Liebert served on the executive committee of the procolonial Pan-German League at a time when antisemitism was becoming a central part of the league's overall ideology. From 1912 to 1914, the executive committee debated ways to combat Jewish influences on German society. During one such session, Liebert announced his readiness "to undertake even the most 'radical' measures" to reach "a happy solution" to the "Jewish problem."[121] Liebert joined the National Socialist Party in 1929, at the approximate age of eighty.[122]

The list of influential antisemitic colonialists outside the Peters circle also includes the geologist, geographer, and university professor Siegfried Passarge, who participated in a two-man treaty-signing expedition to Cameroon in the early 1890s. In 1908, Passarge became the chair of geographical studies at the Hamburg Colonial Institute (later the University of Hamburg). He wrote extensively on the colonies and their inhabitants throughout his life, authoring geographic, ethnographic, and economic studies of Egypt and South Africa and participating regularly in public debates about colonial policy.[123] Passarge emerged as an antisemitic ideo-

---

118. *Sten. Ber.* XII/I/214, February 26, 1909, 7171–72.

119. Eduard von Liebert, *Aus einem bewegten Leben: Erinnerungen* (Munich: J. F. Lehmann, 1925), 11.

120. E. v. Liebert, "Praktische Erziehung zum National-Bewußtsein," *Hammer: Blätter für deutschen Sinn* 5 (1906): 229–31.

121. Sitzung des Geschäftsführenden Ausschusess des Alldeutschen Verbandes, July 4, 1914, no. 86, Alldeutscher Verband (hereafter ADV), BAB. Quoted in Chickering, *We Men Who,* 244.

122. For useful information on Liebert, see Coetzee, *The German Army League;* Koponen, *Development for Exploitation* (Helsinki: Lit Verlag, 1995); Chickering, *We Men Who.*

123. Siegfried Passarge, *Adamaua: Bericht über die Expedition des Deutschen-Kamerun Komitees in den Jahren 1893/94* (Berlin: Dietrich Reimer, 1895); *Die Buschmänner der Kalahari* (Berlin: Dieter Reimer, 1907); *Die Erde und ihr Wirtschaftsleben, eine Allgemein verständliche Darstellung für Kaufleute, Volkswirte, Lehrer, Studierende der Handelshochschulen und Univer-

logue of some significance in the late 1920s. In 1927, he edited a German-language edition of the infamous *Book of the Kahal,* a fanciful exposé of the Jewish shadow government in nineteenth-century Russia. He delivered antisemitic lectures at the University of Hamburg over the next few years,[124] and in 1929 he wrote his own antisemitic opus: a 450-page self-declared "scientific" study of the origin and nature of Jewry that identifies the existence of a worldwide anti-Gentile Jewish conspiracy.[125] In 1933, Passarge became National Chairman of Geography in the National Socialist Teachers League, and a copy of his book on Jews eventually made its way into Heinrich Himmler's library.[126]

A brief examination of the letters sections of antisemitic newspapers reveals a commitment to the antisemitic cause among an even wider range of colonialists outside the Society for German Colonization and the DOAG. An unnamed army officer stationed in German Southwest Africa wrote to the *Hammer* magazine in 1905, thanking the magazine's editors for sending him copies of the *Hammer* regularly.[127] In 1906, a letter from the colonial trader and missionary society director J. K. Vietor also appeared, complaining about the monopolistic tendencies of the South Cameroon Company.[128] In 1905, a front-page issue of the *Deutsche-Soziale Blätter* featured a letter from Southwest Africa lamenting the "damnable

---

sitäten (Hamburg: Hanseatische Verlagsanstalt, 1926); E. Blanck and S. Passarge, *Die chemische Verwitterung in der ägyptischen Wüste* (Hamburg: Kommissionsverlag L. Friederichsen, 1925). In his informative chapter on Passarge in *Hamiten: Völkerkunde und Antisemitismus* (Frankfurt am Main: Peter Lang, 1996), Michael Spöttel notes that no less than twenty articles by the geographer appeared in the *Deutsche Kolonialzeitung* between 1895 and 1901 (Spöttel, *Hamiten,* 93).

124. Passarge delivered the following antisemitic lectures in 1927 and 1928: "Ethnology of the German People and the Jews," "Oriental Secret Societies in Their Dependency on the Nature of the Land," "The Orient and Occident as a Cultural-Geographical Problem," "The Jewish Racial Problem in Light of Scientific Inquiry," and "Culture Pictures from Palestine" (Spöttel, *Hamiten,* 94).

125. Siegfried Passarge, *Das Judentum als landschaftskundlich-ethnologisches Problem* (Munich: J. F. Lehmann, 1929), 378.

126. The copy of *Das Judentum* held at the research branch of the New York Public Library is stamped with the SS insignia and the words *Bücherei: Reichsführer SS.* Ironically, Passarge's zealous antisemitism proved too much for even Hitler's nascent regime. Fearing for the reputation of German science, the German Foreign Office quickly removed Passarge from his position after he attempted to suspend cooperation between German and French geographers; in Passarge's estimation, the French were still poisoned by Jewish influences, having failed to undergo a National Socialist revolution (Spöttel, *Hamiten,* 94, 111).

127. "Aus Deutsch-Südwestafrika," *Hammer: Blätter für deutschen Sinn* 4 (1905): 334–35.

128. "Kolonial-Gesellschaft Süd-Kamerun," *Hammer: Blätter für deutschen Sinn* 5 (1906): 77–78.

jumble of races" in the colony. The author, only identified as Chr. H., thanked the German Social Party for defending settler interests in parliament.[129] A letter from German East Africa appeared the same year in the *Deutsche Welt,* denouncing missionaries for supposedly sanctioning interracial marriages.[130]

Of these contributors, only Chr. H. evinced antisemitism in his letter, complaining briefly of Jewish immigration into the colony.[131] The other writers focused on other issues. Nevertheless, those they raised, like the dangers of capitalist monopolies and the threat of race mixing, were ones that also preoccupied racial antisemites, and the authors clearly expected a sympathetic reading. Like the careers of Fritz Bley, Eduard von Liebert, Siegfried Passarge, and Carl Peters, the letters show that on-the-ground colonial actors felt quite comfortable moving into the antisemitic fold. There was a common audience for the causes of colonialism and antisemitism.

The *Vörwarts* article of 1896, which claims that Peters shot "Negroes" in Africa as substitutes for Jews, identifies an antisemitic element in German colonialism. More specifically, it recognizes an antisemitic ethos to the unique brutality of colonial violence. Undoubtedly, this is because the colonial actors who became known for their antisemitic passions—the antisemitic colonialists discussed here—figured among the most enthusiastic advocates and active practitioners of a colonizing *Weltanschauung* that was radical in both its racism and its brutality.[132] This outlook identified the alleged savagery, lawlessness, and racial Otherness of black Africans as freeing Germans from any obligation to comply with standard European and Judeo-Christian modes of behavior when on the African continent. In practice, this meant endorsing forced over free labor and an unfettered use of capital and corporal punishment. It also meant supporting the colonizers' right to encourage the disappearance of indigenous peoples deemed

---

129. Chr. H., "Zur Bastardfrage in Südwestafrika," *Deutsch-Soziale Blätter,* April 19, 1905.

130. F. L., "Die Rassenfrage in Deutsch-Ostafrika," *Deutsche Welt: Wochenschrift der Deutschen Zeitung,* June 4, 1905. Lange printed the colonialist's letter within his own article on the dangers of race mixing.

131. Chr.H., "Zur Bastardfrage."

132. The one exception is Alexander Merensky, whose racism was tempered by a paternalism that the other colonial antisemites lacked.

undesirable. This perspective was popular in a radical wing of the colonial movement that was larger than the antisemitic faction and that increased in both its size and influence following the outbreak of the Herero and Nama uprisings. Yet the antisemitic colonialists stood out even within this radical crowd, and their significant participation in the genesis of empire gave them an early leading role in the effort to normalize excessive colonial violence.

Of the antisemitic colonialists mentioned above, Carl Peters exemplified this brutal *Weltanschauung* in his actions most completely. The inquiries into Peters's behavior in East Africa spotlighted his excessive brutality, shocking the public and providing fodder for the political opponents of colonial empire. In 1896, a bitter three-day-long debate erupted in the Reichstag over his conduct while imperial commissioner, sparked by the accusations from Bebel that Peters had ordered the executions of his African concubine and her black lover upon discovering the former's infidelity. Revelations about Peters's cruelty that emerged during the Reichstag debate and an ensuing investigation and disciplinary trial alienated even some inveterate supporters of colonialism on the political right.[133] But in truth, Peters's savagery came as no surprise to many, as the explorer had detailed his sadistic behavior while in Africa in a frank travel account in 1891. Here, he recounted how he had routinely placed men in chains and ordered public whippings in order to terrorize his black porters and soldiers. He described how he induced local peoples to provision his forces by taking hostage village "chiefs" and how he punished those who defied him by burning down their dwellings. In one particularly brutal scene, Peters even described how, after discovering that one of his porters had eaten his guinea fowl, he had forced the offender to vomit up the meal before having him beaten with "twenty-five lashes."[134]

Peters justified his brutality, first and foremost, by attributing responsibility to the black Africans themselves for the violence he inflicted on them. Unlike many of his contemporaries in the colonial movement, Peters rejected the stereotype of the simple, naive, and essentially goodhearted African, deriding as "fanatics" those who believed in a " 'childlike'

---

133. By his own admission, Peters had ordered one execution for stealing cigarettes. Ludwig Werner of the German Social Party condemned Peters's behavior as "obscenities" (*Sten. Ber.* IX/IV/61, March 16, 1896, 1478).

134. Carl Peters, *New Light on Dark Africa: Being the Narrative of the German Emin Pasha Expedition,* trans. H. W. Dulcken (London: Ward, Lock, 1891), 171.

and 'harmless' Negro," and insisting instead that the black African lacked
all virtuous qualities. "He is untruthful, thieving, false, and underhanded,"
Peters wrote in 1892, "and if a superficial observer believes that he sees
within him a certain bonhomie, this is grounded completely in the low irri-
tability of his nervous system and the resulting dull sensitivity of his volition." Peters also accused Africans of craftiness, moral cowardice, and
egoism, plus "an unbelievable measure of brutality, blood-thirstiness, and
bestiality."[135] He argued that these characteristics justified preemptive warfare and forced him to adopt the harshest of measures, even when dealing
with an already defeated African people.[136]

After an official investigation in 1897 concluded that Peters had
hanged one of the Africans without justification, Peters admitted in a public essay that his behavior had exceeded what was acceptable according to
European morality. But he argued that it accorded with the "natural circumstances of the right of the stronger" that existed outside of civilized society.[137] In the same piece, Peters also defended the forced disappearance of
colonized peoples, writing that "the higher culture must eliminate the
lower if it can't incorporate it, in order to allow for the improvement of
earthly humanity." Peters insisted that the perpetrators of such actions
were not accountable to human law. "God, who is revealed in both history
and nature," Peters wrote, "has also a different standard for judging such
personalities."[138]

Peters's brutal colonial *Weltanschauung* was out of step both with the
German public and with majority sentiment within the colonial movement
and government circles. In an explicit rejection of his reasoning, an appeals
court concluded at the end of 1897, "One can't concede that ideas about
justice and decency that are substantially different than in Europe are allowed in Africa."[139] But this was exactly what the antisemites in the colonial movement advocated—alongside other radicals—with Peters being
only the most visible proponent of this philosophy of colonial violence.

Joachim von Pfeil, for example, applied a similar logic in a pamphlet
titled *German Southwest Africa, Now and Later*—written for the Pan-German League in 1905—where he recommended eradicating the Nama and

---

135. Carl Peters, *Gesammelte Schriften*, vol. 2, ed. Walter Frank (Munich: C. H. Beck'sche
Verlagsbuchhandlung, 1943), 520.
136. Peters, *New Light on Dark Africa*, 140.
137. Peters, "Helden und Märtyrer," *Die Zukunft* 6 (1897): 548.
138. Ibid., 545.
139. "Der Peters-Prozeß," *Deutsche Kolonialzeitung,* November 27, 1897.

subjecting the Herero to a strict system of racial domination. Like Peters, von Pfeil acknowledged a fundamental discord between his proposals and European ideas of moral behavior. "It may be that our present opinions do not accord in many ways with justice and law," he admitted. "But in the final analysis, justice is always only that which has been formed into habit through usage and has in this way become accepted as normal according to the peoples' sensibilities." Given this premise, von Pfeil argued specifically against transplanting "opinions of justice that have grown up on German soil to African soil and African people." Instead, he advocated creating "a new perspective" that would lead to a "sense of justice" defined by what was in the interests of white colonizers.[140] Such thinking echoed the logic of Peters's public defenders in 1897, chief among them Frieda von Bülow. Like Peters, she identified the African continent as a place where ordinary rules of behavior did not apply. "Work among savages has as its only great attraction the terrific latitude that it allows for individuality," von Bülow wrote in an essay in 1897. "Freedom of resolution is therefore the most important thing for the colonialist, as it is for him the substitute for the security of orderly relations and for everything that supports the individual in the civilized world."[141]

The idea that colonialism required "a new perspective" that viewed violent coercion, murder, and even genocide as necessary and appropriate everyday tools of colonial rule was also reflected in the conduct and colonizing philosophies of most of the other well-known colonial antisemites. Zelewski, Bley, Liebert, and Passarge all shared Peters's violent proclivities (the missionary Merensky was an exception) and, like Peters, their brutality drew harsh criticism even from other supporters of colonial empire. Zelewski and Bley became infamous during their service in East Africa as DOAG representatives in the 1880s. Zelewski's outrageous behavior helped spark the coastal rebellion of 1888 when he and his marines ran amok in the town of Pangani, seizing men off the streets for manual labor, threatening dissenters with executions, and raping women.[142] Dur-

---

140. *Flugschriften des Alldeutschen Verbandes,* no. 509, ADV, BAB.

141. Frieda Freiin von Bülow, "Ein Mann über Bord," *Die Zukunft* 6 (1897): 554. Otto Arendt defended Peters in a similar fashion, arguing that the dangers Peters faced in East Africa permitted actions that would have been impermissible otherwise (Editorship, "Die Peters-Debatte im Reichstag," *Deutsches Wochenblatt* 9 [1896]: 134).

142. Glassman, *Feasts and Riots,* 217, 257; Edward D. Ropes, Jr., *The Zanzibar Letters of Edward D. Ropes, Jr. 1882–1892,* ed. Norman Robert Bennett (Boston: African Studies Center, Boston University, 1973), 60.

ing the ensuing war, troops under Zelewski's command burned crops, torched villages, and used mosques as barracks.[143] Bley became known for his own excessive cruelty at about the same time. A coworker wrote in 1888 that "many have designated myself and Dr. Bley as brutal." He insisted that "fear," "terror," and "peace" were the results of the "strict discipline" that he and Bley applied.[144]

For his part, Liebert endorsed violent coercion in mobilizing indigenous workers while he was governor of East Africa. He did so with an openness that distinguished him from both his predecessors and successors, all of whom officially shunned the use of force in procuring African labor.[145] Later, Liebert emerged as one of the Reichstag's harshest critics of rules introduced by the central government regulating floggings.[146] Passarge became known for excessive brutality, too. In his travel memoir of 1895, the explorer described in surprisingly frank terms the atrocities that he and his companion had committed in Africa, including extraordinary floggings, chaining men to trees, and taking hostages.[147] A disapproving article appeared in the *Deutsche Kolonialzeitung* following the memoir's publication. Citing Passarge's book, the author accused "many researchers" in the field of "a great deal of whipping" and "the least humanitarianism possible."[148]

The prevailing sentiment among these men was that the nature of black Africans necessitated coercion in the form of forced labor and the

---

143. Even before the Pangani episode, one German observer remarked that Zelewski appeared to be "not entirely in his right mind" (Consul Arendt to Otto von Bismarck, April 3, 1886, RKA 396, BAB. Quoted in Müller, *Deutschland-Zanzibar-Ostafrika,* 223).

144. Leue to Generalvertretung, October 12, 1888, RKA 407, BAB. Quoted in Müller, *Deutschland-Zanzibar-Ostafrika,* 390.

145. This did not mean, however, that other governors opposed coercion, only that they avoided using the word *Zwang* (force) in relation to the mobilization of labor because of their greater sensitivity to public relations issues back home (Koponen, *Development for Exploitation,* 340).

146. The rules prohibited the flogging of women and children, limited the number of floggings for one crime to two, and limited the total number of blows allowable on one occasion to twenty-five. Additional rules were introduced concerning how whips were to be composed and used (Koponen, *Development for Exploitation,* 364).

147. In one particularly brutal scene, *Adamaua* describes how Passarge's companion, von Uechtritz, sentenced two Haussa porters to fifty blows each after they presented him with the choice of either paying them up-front or seeing them leave. The floggings were carried out with the notorious hippopotamus-hide whip that white officials and employers in German East Africa used extensively (Passarge, *Adamaua,* 95, 97).

148. Dr. Siegfried Passarge, "Mission oder Islam?" *Deutsche Kolonialzeitung,* December 14, 1895. Passarge's article is a response to his critic, whom he quoted.

unregulated use of corporal and capital punishment. They spoke in particular of an imagined moral chasm separating blacks from whites and used this to justify real and proposed violence. Peters claimed that blacks lacked an inner impulse to good, which in itself justified the violent requisitioning of their labor by the white colonizer. "The categorical imperative of Kant still has no power with this naive son of the world of the palm and banana," Peters wrote in 1895.[149] "He is a born slave," he insisted elsewhere, "who lacks every noble impulse and who needs his despot like an opium smoker needs his pipe."[150] Similarly, von Pfeil claimed that blacks lacked moral restraint, without which "the right to control one's own destiny degenerates into licentiousness." Von Pfeil became something of a spokesman for a forced labor system, and he argued that a mandatory two-year period of servitude should rotate through East Africa. He also derided what he called the "wretched humanitarian dreams" of more moderate colonialists who denied the unbridgeable racial Otherness of blacks.[151]

Passarge, too, declared that moral absences among blacks justified the regular use of violence. In particular, he insisted that blacks lacked the power to exert will over instinct, but he believed that blacks were extremely intelligent, which made for a dangerous combination: "the result of this absence of every moral strength coinciding with a higher intelligence," Passarge wrote, "is that the Negro stands very low in respect to morals."[152] In Passarge's perspective, this meant that black Africans needed to be treated as adolescents—"with severity but also with the most precise justice"—but he discounted any civilizing mission based on kindness or conversion. "Twenty fife [*sic*] on backside at the right time and place," Passarge wrote, "is an infinitely more effective, culture-promoting measure than all the missionaries with the misconstrued teachings about equality and brotherhood in Christ that, for the poor blacks, only twists their heads and changes them into impudent and useless individuals."[153] Passarge's opposition to Christian proselytization stemmed in part from his idea of an eternal antagonism between blacks and whites. According to Passarge, blacks would

---

149. Peters, *Das Deutsch-Ostafrikanische Schutzgebiet: Im amtlichen Auftrage* (Munich: R. Oldenbourg, 1895), 40–41.

150. Peters, *Gesammelte Schriften,* vol. 2, 520.

151. Quoted in Müller, *Deutschland-Zanzibar-Ostafrika,* 517.

152. Passarge, *Adamaua,* 506.

153. Ibid., 528.

"strive to throw the whites out as quickly as possible" if they had the
means, because "the black race hates the white after a fashion, as far as
their lack of character on the whole allows for hatred."[154] Rather than reconciling blacks to the white colonial order, conversion only made "the
Christianized Negro" into a "hidden opponent," one that was "even more
dangerous for any government."[155]

The antisemitic colonialists who participated directly in the building of
Germany's African empire did not have a monopoly on excessive violence.
The liberation that they felt from the constraints of traditional western European and Judeo-Christian-based morality was a sensation shared by
other colonialists—officials and settlers—who likewise took advantage of
the "freedom of resolution" that the colonial setting offered. But some contemporaries believed that the example set by Peters and his associates was
what inspired brutality in these others: one critic of empire argued during
the Reichstag debate on Peters in 1896 that the sudden descent of "men like
Leist and Wehlan" into "such licentiousness, such brutalities and cruelties"
had much to do with the "psychological" and "demoralizing" effect of Peters's actions in East Africa and his open celebration of his own violence.[156]
From this standpoint, the antisemites among on-the-ground colonialists
not only numbered among the most articulate early proponents and active
practitioners of a "new perspective" that presented Africa as a place beyond
traditional notions of right and wrong. They were also among the most
influential, setting a tone that resonated outward.[157] Significantly, this "new
perspective" gained greater acceptance over time, entering mainstream
colonial discourse and witnessing a partial normalization in the years following the Herero, Nama, and Maji-Maji uprisings. The ascendancy of the
radical outlook led state secretary Bernhard Dernburg to openly complain
in 1909 of a growing inclination among colonialists "to treat the Negro like

---

154. Ibid., 532.

155. Passarge, "Mission oder Islam?" following Passarge's article, the editors of *Deutsche
Kolonialzeitung* printed a rejoinder rejecting several of his points. They contested in particular the geographer's recommendation against Christian proselytization, implicitly refuting his
claim of black immutability (*Deutsche Kolonialzeitung,* December 14, 1895).

156. *Sten. Ber.* IX/IV/60, March 14, 1896, 1465. The speaker was Eugen Richter, a leader
of the Progressive Party.

157. In his biography, Perras notes that Peters's "pseudo-Darwinist ideas" influenced a
number of other important pan-German writers. Perras does not speculate, however, on how
Peters and the men and women around him influenced the actual behavior of other German
officials in the colonies (Perras, *Carl Peters,* 177).

an object to be exploited instead of something to be cultivated" and to speak against what he saw as a rising tide of Social Darwinism.[158]

The evidence presented here suggests a natural relationship between a hardened antisemitism and support for the colonial project, as well as between antisemitism and radical colonial violence. As shown above, not everyone involved in the antisemitic movement championed Germany's colonial project, and not all antisemitic colonial actors preached or practiced extreme brutality in colonial contexts. But these were exceptions to a general pattern, one that suggests an easy infusion of an antisemitic ethos into colonialism.

Undoubtedly, this had much to do with the ideological similarities between the new racial antisemitism and visions of a race-based colonial empire. To take one example, contemporary advocates of extreme anti-Jewish action in Germany marshaled a logic quite similar to that of colonial radicals when it came to justifying extralegal violence. In the 1901 reprint of his 1881 antisemitic opus, *The Jewish Question as a Racial, Moral, and Cultural Question,* the influential ideologue Eugen Dühring argued for the suspension of normal modes of conduct in the "war" against the Jews. Much like colonial extremists, he demanded the adoption of brutal methods of combat in response to the supposedly inhuman qualities of the enemy Other. In confronting what he called "the anti-Aryan, indeed anti-human tactics of foreign parasites," Germans, Dühring insisted, should not shy away from "means of fear and violence."[159] Dühring even hinted at the need for genocide. The ideological proximity of such violent musings on the Jewish Question to radical colonial discourses on race and violence helps explain the easy movement into colonial circles of hardened antisemites—men and women whose antisemitic resentments inclined them toward a type of racially justified radical violence that could actually be realized in the colonies. These same individuals helped radicalize the colonial project.

But racially justified radical violence was only one thread connecting the colonial and antisemitic discourses of the imperial era. There were

---

158. *Sten. Ber.* XII/I/214, February 26, 1909, 7193.

159. Dühring, Eugen, *Die Judenfrage als Frage des Racencharakters und seiner Schädlichkeiten für Völkerexistenz, Sitte und Cultur: Mit einer denkerisch freiheitlichen und praktisch abschliessenden Antwort* (Nowawes-Neuendorf bei Berlin: Ulrich Dühring, 1901), 136, 135.

many others, and the following chapter examines them in detail. Particular attention is paid, however, to the partial normalization within the colonial movement in the later years of empire of the radical perspective on race and violence. This accompanied an extreme Othering of black Africans in the imaginations of an increasing number of procolonial Germans following the 1904 outbreak of the Herero and Nama uprisings. This Othering helped fuse stereotypes of blacks and Jews. It facilitated a remarkable convergence in their representations both within and across the colonial and antisemitic movements in the final decade and a half of the *Kaiserreich*.

Chapter 2

The Meeting of Jews and Africans in the German Imagination

In May 1912, the Christian-conservative newspaper the *Reichsbote* published two front-page articles dealing with the issue of miscegenation. The first, which appeared on May 5, addresses the debate taking place in the Reichstag at the time over the desirability of antimiscegenation laws in place in German Africa since 1905 and their recent extension to the island colony of Samoa. Appearing five days later, the second article focuses on the alleged insincerity of Jewish converts to Christianity and also discusses the phenomenon of interfaith marriage. The newspaper announced its opposition to "miscegenation" in both pieces. Although it did not support the colonial laws banning mixed-race marriages, preferring to rely instead on "moral and national self-discipline," it declared that its "healthy white racial instincts" led it to resist "every easing of racial mixing in our colonies." In the editors' opinion, "the prevention of a further mixing of whites and natives must be and remain the goal of a healthy and competent racial policy."[1] Concerning marriages between Christians and Jews, in the second piece published on May 10 the newspaper reiterated the common stereotype that such interfaith unions were often unfruitful, warning that the few children produced always took after the Jewish parent. The newspaper insisted that "interbreeding therefore goes against the will of nature," and it suggested the necessity of social segregation.[2] As for a more permanent solution to what it saw as the problem of the Jews, the *Reichsbote* admitted that it had none to give.

The chronological and ideological proximity of the discussions in the *Reichsbote* on mixed-race unions in the colonies and on interfaith marriages between Gentiles and Jews suggests a striking compatibility in im-

---

1. "Zur inneren Lage," *Der Reichsbote,* May 5, 1912.
2. "Die Zukunft der Juden," *Der Reichsbote,* May 10, 1912.

perial Germany between colonial issues concerning race and the so-called Jewish Question. As the *Reichsbote* articles show, discourses during the colonial era about Jews and black Africans came to share important features—like the rhetoric of miscegenation—and colonial advocates and antisemites, who were sometimes one and the same, often expressed similar fears using a similar vocabulary. This chapter investigates this phenomenon, studying a merging of representations of blacks and Jews that became more purposeful and apparent over time. It argues that the conflation of representations of blacks and Jews accelerated dramatically in Germany in the final decade before the First World War, and that a radicalization of images of the former facilitated this process.

Discourses on black Africans became increasingly extreme after 1904, resembling more and more the most hate-filled racist rhetoric directed against Jews by racial antisemites. By the last decade and a half of empire, colonial advocates and antisemites not only often expressed similar agendas on matters of race, like protecting German racial purity from blood-incursions and denying citizenship rights to the non-German Other, as demonstrated in the *Reichsbote*. When discussing blacks and Jews, they also often justified their intentions in remarkably similar ways: by attributing both groups with most of the same negative characteristics, attributes that they used to excuse their recommendations for the harshest type of racial domination. The 1904 rebellions in Southwest Africa facilitated this process by making it more acceptable for procolonial advocates to present blacks as a kind of antirace: to demonize them and to present them as the legitimate targets of preventative violence. Before 1904, this type of thinking was highly controversial. It was generally only found within the extreme right wing of the colonial movement, represented by colonialists like Carl Peters.

The merging of representations was largely an undirected and unconscious process. But not always. Sometimes colonial advocates and antisemites explicitly linked blacks and Jews together, often with the purpose of legitimating their claims about one or the other. In addition, colonial issues dealing with matters of race sometimes served as a welcomed impetus in antisemitic circles for transferring notions about blacks onto Jews. Conversely, some colonialists and procolonial advocates consciously drew on ideas about Jews when thinking about black Africans. The merging of representations of blacks and Jews was another way in which the colonial and antisemitic movements and imaginations of the *Kaiserreich* became intertwined.

Images of blacks and Jews in Wilhelminian Germany differed in important ways. The dissimilar positions of both groups within the German empire necessarily resulted in significant differences in their invented representations. Jews lived in the heart of Germany. By the turn of the century, many were highly assimilated, and the Jewish presence in the German middle class had become quite strong in the relatively short time since emancipation. The situation could not have been more different with colonized blacks. Although Germany experienced a trickle of black African immigration following the acquisition of the African territories, the African population within Germany remained minuscule throughout the colonial era.[3] Assimilation for blacks, moreover, was virtually impossible. In addition, the fact that thousands of literate Africans were employed in the colonies in lower middle-class positions—as clerks, interpreters, and telegraphists by the colonial governments and as teachers and evangelists by German missions—made little impression on a German public that was so far away. While Jews were commonly stereotyped as highly intelligent and economically successful, blacks were often depicted as poor savages, inhumanly stupid.

Some of the perceived threats posed by blacks and Jews diverged accordingly. Given the high concentration of Jews in cities and the visibility of Jewish commercial success, Jews came to represent the forces of materialism and modernity for German antisemites. The idea that Jews created and perpetuated the modern capitalist system was common to both the racist and religious wings of the antisemitic movement, as was the notion that Jews were largely responsible for urban living and its vices. Antisemites of all types also accused Jews of exerting strong and deliberately insidious influences on German culture and, to make their case, pointed to the prominent role Jews played in Germany's liberal press and to Jewish support for modernist trends in literature and art. Jews, therefore, represented an internal threat, a danger from within. Blacks, on the other hand, were typically seen to menace Germans only on the outskirts of empire. Their late incorporation into the empire and their location on its periphery

---

3. For information on colonial Africans in the German metropole, see Katharina Oguntoye, *Eine afro-deutsche Geschichte: Zur Lebenssituation von Afrikanern und Afro-Deutschen in Deutschland von 1884 bis 1950* (Berlin: Hoho Verlag Christine Hoffmann, 1997); Leonhard Harding, ed., *Mpundu Akwa: Der Fall des Prinzen von Kamerun. Das neuentdeckte Plädoyer von Dr. M. Levi* (Munster: LIT, 2000); Fatima El-Tayeb, *Schwarze Deutsche: der Diskurs um "Rasse" und nationale Identität 1890–1933* (Frankfurt am Main: Campus, 2001); Andrew Zimmerman, *Anthropology and Antihumanism in Imperial Germany* (Chicago: University of Chicago Press, 2001).

exempted them from blame for Germany's internal problems. Images of Jews as the agents of a corrupting modernity, as a type of willful cancer rotting away the nation from the inside, had virtually no counterpart in images of blacks.

Despite these important differences in the invented representations of blacks and Jews, perceptions of the two during the colonial era merged in a significant fashion. In the imaginations of German racists, Jews and blacks came to occupy unique but comparable positions on the racial scale, not only sharing many of the same negative characteristics but also appearing more foreign and repellent than any of the other human races. This was undoubtedly influenced by an older tendency in Western thought to associate Jews with black Africans.[4] Although Jews were typically seen as "Oriental" in the European imagination—as related to the people of the Middle East—the idea that the Jewish people had interbred with both Arabs and Africans before migrating to Europe spurred discussions among European scientists as far back as the late 1700s about the supposed "blackness" of Jews.[5] Pioneering racial theorists like the Scottish anatomist Robert Knox expounded upon the supposed anatomical similarities between Jews and blacks during the mid-nineteenth century; and the belief that Jewish physiognomy had an African character was consequently widespread well before Germany emerged as a colonial power.[6] Yet the actual acquisition of colonies in Africa gave the merging of representations added impetus. With the incorporation of several million Africans into the German empire in the 1880s, discussions about blacks moved from the confines of the halls of academia into the popular realm. The similarities between antisemitic and colonial discourses intensified, as racists increasingly identified both blacks and Jews as separate and distinct from all other groups of people in crucial ways.

Like the belief that Jews had at one time interbred with Africans, the perception of a significant divide between blacks and Jews and other human groups predated German colonialism as well. European racial taxonomists had placed African blacks on the lower or lowest ends of the racial scale ever since the Enlightenment, commonly ranking them as the least beautiful, intelligent, and cultured race. Although early racial classifiers

---

4. Sander L. Gilman, *The Jew's Body* (New York: Routledge, 1991), 99–172.

5. Jonathan M. Hess, *Germans, Jews, and the Claims of Modernity* (New Haven: Yale University Press, 2002).

6. Robert Knox, *The Races of Men: A Fragment* (Philadelphia: Lea and Blanchard, 1850), 134. Knox wrote about "the African character of the Jew" whose "whole physiognomy, when swarthy, as it often is, has an African look."

saw this more as a difference of degree than a difference of kind and believed in the possibility of improvement and change, their nearly persistent placement of blacks at the bottom of the racial hierarchy influenced the polygenists of the mid-nineteenth century who pictured the distance between blacks and whites as a more permanent and unbridgeable gap. Likewise, the notion that Jews were scarcely human, different from Gentiles in kind, predated the German colonies: the Orientalist German scholar Johann David Michaleis, author of the six-volume *Mosaic Law,* argued in the eighteenth century that Jews were naturally a subject people, suitable for mass enslavement on sugar islands in the West Indies, just like black Africans. It was during the colonial era itself, however, which roughly coincided with the rise and fall of the modern antisemitic movement, that the radical Othering of blacks and Jews reached its furthest development.

Jews experienced several forms of dehumanizing rhetoric at this time. One strategy used by antisemites throughout the colonial period was to compare Jews to parasitical organisms, likening the effect of the Jewish presence upon the German *Volk* to that of a deadly bacteria on a human body. In so doing, antisemites borrowed from what was then cutting-edge science. When the first colonies were acquired in 1884, modern medical bacteriology was less than ten years old, as it was in 1876 that the German scientist Robert Koch demonstrated the role that microorganisms played in causing diseases. Comparing Jews to bacteria or fungi allowed antisemites to appear scientific in their analysis of the Jewish Question and, through the use of metaphor, to rhetorically disassociate Jews from the rest of humankind. The influential antisemitic ideologue Paul de Lagarde used this tactic when he likened Jews to "trichinae and bacilli" that should be eradicated "as quickly and as thoroughly as possible."[7] Similar language appeared in the antisemitic opus of Carl Paasch, a businessman with interests in East Asia who became something of a celebrity in antisemitic circles in the 1890s. In *A Jewish-German Embassy and Its Helper,* Paasch wrote of the supposed infiltration of Jews into Germany's foreign service, and he documented centuries of alleged Jewish crimes. Working from the premise that Jews were a race and, therefore, incapable of change, Paasch compared the Jewish attack on Gentile society to a ringworm infection.[8]

---

7. Paul de Lagarde, *Ausgewählte Schriften,* ed. Paul Fischer, 2nd ed. (Munich: J. F. Lehmann, 1934), 239.

8. Carl Paasch, *Der jüdische Dämon I,* section 3 of *Eine jüdisch-deutsche Gesandtschaft und ihre Helfer. Geheimes Judenthum, Nebenregierungen und jüdische Weltherrschaft* (Leipzig: Carl Paasch, 1891), 67–68. For more on Paasch, see chap. 3.

Such comparisons dehumanized the Jews while making the antisemites' diagnoses seem progressive and modern.[9]

Antisemitic ideologues of the colonial era also contrasted Jewish and German-Gentile characteristics in order to create the impression of a diametrical opposition between two types. Since German racial theorists both within and without the antisemitic movement typically identified their own people as the highest representatives of the Aryan race and pictured Aryans as the apex of human development, such negative comparisons effectively relegated Jews to the opposite end of the racial scale, putting their very humanity in doubt. This perspective remained highly controversial, never gaining wide acceptance during the *Kaiserreich* era outside the ranks of convinced racial antisemites. This did not stop them, however, from boldly depicting Jews and Germans as inversely related, presenting the former as unique human beings, alien to a degree that distinguished them qualitatively from the German type. The antisemitic publisher Theodor Fritsch encapsulated this radical view in an article in the *Hammer* in 1910, when he identified Jews as being even lower than Slavs, "different and more foreign than all other European peoples." In Fritsch's opinion, Jews were "the deepest antithesis" to Germans, "our spiritual antipode in the strictest sense of the word."[10] The pan-Germanist Heinrich Class echoed these sentiments in a political tract three years later when he likened Jews and Germans to "fire and water" in their "innermost essences."[11]

The extreme positioning of Jews within the racial hierarchy during the colonial era and their dehumanization by racial antisemites paralleled contemporaneous developments in popular perceptions of black Africans. As noted above, blacks had occupied a special place in the European imagination for centuries. In Germany, racial taxonomists and philosophers of the human condition first positioned blacks at the bottom of the racial scale during the Enlightenment, identifying the black African type as represen-

---

9. Other examples abound. In Friedrich Lange's *Reines Deutschtum,* Lange described "civilization" as the "gelatine" that feeds the "Bazillus judaicus" (*Reines Deutschtum: Gründzuge einer nationalen Weltanschauung* [Berlin: Verlag von Alexander Duncker, 1904], 105).

10. Th. Fritsch, "Die geistige Unterjochung Deutschlands," *Hammer: Blätter für deutschen Sinn* 9 (1910): 150.

11. Heinrich Class [Daniel Frymann, pseud.], *Wenn ich der Kaiser wär-Politische Wahrheiten und Notwendigkeiten,* 4th ed. (Leipzig: Dieterich'schen Verlagsbuchhandlung, 1913), 30.

tative of the lowest stage of human development.[12] By the late nineteenth century, this positioning gained added significance, as the older belief in human mutability among European scientists—based on the idea that mental and physical differences were environmentally determined and could therefore change—had generally receded, and theories about the essential permanence of racial characteristics became widely accepted.[13] With the acquisition of gigantic African territories in the 1880s, the alleged peculiarities of black African nature suddenly assumed a new relevance in Germany, and discussions about blacks proliferated. Many advocates of empire seized on preexisting theories about their radical Otherness and propagated them in simplified but exaggerated forms in order to win support for the aggressive subjugation, or even eradication, of black Africans. The essentializing discourse, prone to generalizations about a specific "black" nature, coexisted with more complicated perspectives—among colonial administrators, missionaries, and other "experts"—that differentiated between different types of black Africans.[14]

The political debate in Germany over the humanity of blacks peaked in the decade following the outbreak of the Herero and Nama Wars. The uprising forced a reevaluation of previous official policies toward colonial blacks, which were condemned on virtually all sides after January 1904 for allegedly encouraging the rebellion. The parliamentary critics of empire on the Left and Center who blamed the uprising on the forced impoverishment of the Herero and Nama peoples through the appropriation of their land and cattle gained a crucial ally in 1906 when the reformer Bernhard Dern-

---

12. Susanne Zantop, *Colonial Fantasies: Conquest, Family, and Nation in Precolonial Germany, 1770–1870* (Durham: Duke University Press, 1997).

13. With some notable exceptions, like the Darwinist Hermann Schaaffhausen, German anthropologists generally stood out from their British and French counterparts in the late nineteenth century by continuing to believe in the responsibility of climatic conditions for racial characteristics. Yet most German anthropologists of this period also believed in the permanence of human variation, arguing that once characteristics are acquired, they become inherited traits (see Zimmerman's *Anthropology and Antihumanism in Imperial Germany*). Anthropologists did not, however, monopolize the debate in Germany about the meaning and origin of human difference. They had to contend for the public's attention with racial theorists and *völkisch* mystics who had little or no scientific training, and also with the organizers of sensationalistic *Völkerschauen* and freak shows who often presented their supposedly primitive or atavistic subjects as proof of Darwin's theory of evolution based on the principle of natural selection.

14. For a discussion of the latter, see George Steinmetz, *The Devil's Handwriting: Precoloniality and the German Colonial State in Qingdao, Samoa, and Southwest Africa* (Chicago: University of Chicago Press, 2007).

burg assumed the directorship of the Colonial Division of the Foreign Office. Although Dernburg was not uncompromising in his opposition to colonial violence, allowing as he did for a tremendous increase in racial oppression in Southwest Africa, the new director nevertheless pursued a program of reform in the remaining colonies aimed at improving relations between indigenes and whites by lessening the brutality of colonialism. Among other steps, Dernburg instituted government oversight of the hiring of indigenous workers by whites, mandating fair treatment and giving workers certain rights. Dernburg also attempted to limit white employers and officials in their ability to inflict corporal punishment, prescribing a maximum number of blows and other stipulations. Together, the Herero and Nama revolts and the humanitarian aspects of Dernburg's colonial philosophy generated a backlash among hardened racists who argued for a more inflexible system of racial domination, especially in Africa. These pro-colonial extremists dehumanized the subjects of their rhetoric, much like antisemitic ideologues, but seemed to enjoy greater success by the end of the colonial era in propagating their ideas across the political spectrum.

Two books representative of this backlash appeared in 1907 and 1908. The first, *The Negro-Soul and Germans in Africa: A Battle against Missions, Moral-Fanaticism, and Bureaucracy from the Standpoint of Modern Psychology,* gained some fame shortly after publication when it was cited several times by deputies in the Reichstag during plenary debates about colonial matters.[15] Written by a former director of the health service in German East Africa, Dr. Karl Oetker, *The Negro-Soul* articulates the growing dissatisfaction within the radical wing of the colonial movement with what extremists deemed the excessive humanitarianism of administrators who worked to moderate colonial violence. Oetker argued against the promulgation of "native policy" from Berlin on the grounds that officials in the metropole lacked a real understanding of the nature of black Africans. Much like Frieda von Bülow a decade earlier, he insisted that men on the ground in the colonies be given "complete freedom of action."[16] The second book, suggestively titled *Black Against White: The Native Question as the Turning Point of Our Colonial Policy,* written by the colonial enthusiast Woldemar Schütze, reiterates Oetker's complaints

---

15. *Stenographische Berichte über die Verhandlungen des Reichstags* (hereafter *Sten. Ber.*) XII/I/45, May 3, 1907, 1366; *Sten. Ber.* XII/I/124, March 17, 1908, 4048.

16. Karl Oetker, *Die Neger-Seele und die Deutschen in Afrika: Ein Kampf gegen Missionen Sittlichkeits-Fanatismus und Bürokratie vom Standpunkt moderner Psychologie* (Munich: J. F. Lehmanns, 1907), 39.

about contemporary colonial policy. Schütze condemned the limitations placed on colonial whites in their treatment of blacks by the central government. He argued for an "unconditional, unrestricted right"[17] of whites to flog, and he derided as "absurd" regulations concerning corporal punishment.[18] Both Oetker and Schütze accused contemporary colonial policymakers of mollycoddling Africans, and they advocated a state of permanent servitude in the form of an uncompromising and openly exploitative system of racial domination. Accordingly, they opposed any attempt to educate Africans that did not directly serve the selfish needs of the colonizing nation.

Oetker and Schütze justified their proposals by explicitly contesting the very humanity of African blacks. Both authors likened blacks to animals. Oetker compared Africans to dogs and wild horses in need of expert training, and Schütze attributed them with an apelike physique and a simian's ability to imitate. At one point in *Black Against White,* Schütze even went so far as to insist that "if one designates as 'human' only that type that has taken the spiritually highest-standing direction of development, and which we ourselves belong to, then the Negro, strictly taken, is no human in this sense of the word!"[19] Oetker dehumanized black Africans further by claiming that they were less sensitive to pain than whites, an idea borrowed from Robert Knox from the mid-nineteenth century. Both Oetker and Schütze ascribed the radical Otherness of blacks in part to an unusual inability to progress and change. Oetker argued that blacks had accomplished nothing "despite centuries of contact with Europeans" in Africa and decades of political freedom in the Americas. By way of contrast, he noted that the Chinese had produced "a Confucius and a Li Hung Tschang" and that the Japanese had adopted many of the achievements of "the culturally superior races."[20] Likewise, Schütze insisted that "all influences of culture passed over the Negroes,"[21] and he, too, remarked upon the cultural accomplishments of Asians.

Oetker and Schütze were extremists, and their ideas were controversial. But they represented a segment within the colonial movement that gained strength in the aftermath of the Herero and Nama uprisings. In June 1908, Schütze presented his views on blacks to a meeting of the gen-

---

17. Woldemar Schütze, *Schwarz gegen Weiss: Die Eingeborenenfrage als Kernpunkt unsere Kolonialpolitik in Afrika* (Berlin: C. A. Schwetschke und Sohn, 1908), 82.

18. Ibid., 85.

19. Ibid., 12.

20. Oetker, *Die Neger-Seele,* 22.

21. Schütze, *Schwarz gegen Weiss,* 104.

eral assembly of the German Colonial Society. In a sign of the ascendancy
of like-minded men, a majority of speakers at the event openly criticized
Dernburg's advocacy of a more humane treatment of blacks,[22] and the society later adopted a resolution stating the need for white colonizers to
maintain "unconditional mastery over the colored populations."[23] The
more mainstream proponents of colonialism recognized the growing popularity of the radical viewpoint and so challenged it directly. A member of
the conservative Reichspartei registered his disapproval of Oetker's book
in the Reichstag soon after it appeared in print. In an acknowledgment of
its importance, however, the deputy also labeled *The Negro-Soul* as "a
work that will play a large role" in the controversy over missionary education.[24] Another parliamentary deputy attacked Oetker's viewpoint ten
months later. Speaking at the end of a parliamentary debate on the
colonies, Dr. Peter Spahn of the Catholic Center Party contested Oetker's
view that, as Spahn put it, German colonizers faced in the African black
"an organism that is dissimilar in nature." Contra Oetker, Spahn argued
that "blacks do not differ in their spiritual development from us qualitatively, rather, it is only a matter of quantity."[25] Likewise, state secretary
Bernhard Dernburg criticized colonial radicals for dehumanizing Africans.
Speaking in parliament in February 1909, Dernburg insisted on treating
black laborers "like men." He condemned what he saw as a growing inclination among colonialists "to treat the Negro like an object to be exploited
instead of something to be cultivated."[26]

Despite the opposition of procolonial moderates, the antiblack
rhetoric of the extremists had an important effect: by the end of the
Kaiserreich era, both proponents and critics of the colonial project shared
a hierarchical view of humankind that placed blacks on the lowest level.
The near universality of this outlook was made evident in the last years of
empire by the debate in the Reichstag in May 1912 over the legality of antimiscegenation laws in the colonies. These laws had existed in German
Africa since 1905, and Dernburg's successor, Wilhelm Solf, extended them
to Samoa seven years later. Resentful of their own lack of influence over
colonial policy, opposition parties introduced a resolution in favor of a

---

22. "Hauptversammlung im Saale des Künstlervereins am 12 Juni 1908," *Deutsche Kolonialzeitung,* June 20, 1908.
23. "Wintertagung der Deutschen Kolonialgeschaft zu Berlin am 4 Dezember 1908,"
Deutsche Kolonialzeitung, December 12, 1908.
24. *Sten. Ber.* XII/I/45, May 3, 1907, 1366.
25. *Sten. Ber.* XII/I/124, March 17, 1908, 4048.
26. *Sten. Ber.* XII/I/214, February 26, 1909, 7193.

law declaring mixed-race marriages valid, sparking a debate that lasted three days. Although a majority in the Reichstag voted in the resolution's favor, the deliberation revealed the extent to which ideas about the radical Otherness of blacks—like those propagated by Oetker and Schütze—came to affect even the most progressive and liberal-minded parliamentary deputies.

Proponents of the laws evinced their special bias toward blacks quite clearly. Although it was the extension of the ban to the island colony of Samoa that motivated the resolution, its opponents both within and without the Reichstag focused on mixed-race marriages between whites and blacks, indicating that they considered this the very worst offense. When Wilhelm Solf opened the discussion of the decrees on May 2 with an impassioned defense, he evoked the specter of German sons returning home from the colonies with African, rather than Samoan, wives.[27] His supporters focused on blacks as well. Freiherr von Richthofen of the National Liberal Party denounced racial mixing with blacks in a lengthy speech on May 7. He differentiated between blacks and Pacific Islanders in the course of his delivery by identifying Samoan women as "substantially prettier" than their African counterparts and categorizing Samoans on the whole as "better educated" and at "a much higher cultural level."[28] This special, antiblack prejudice was also echoed in the procolonial press. A contributor to the *Deutsche Zeitung* proclaimed in mid-May that racial mixing with Samoans was "not so morally depressing and perhaps also not so culturally contaminating" as marriages with black women or, "horrible even to think of it," between white women and black men. The author insisted that Samoans, Indians, and Japanese were all higher types, possessing positive qualities that blacks lacked.[29] Several weeks later, a contributor to the official organ of the Women's League of the German Colonial Society, *Kolonie und Heimat,* identified unions between whites and blacks as "naturally 1,000 times worse" than unions between whites and Pacific Islanders.[30]

The most adamant opponents of the ban also privileged Samoans

---

27. Solf asked the assembled Reichstag deputies if they wished to see white colonial women marrying "Hereros, Hottentots, and Bastards." To the laughter of his audience, he spoke of the possibility of having to receive "black daughter-in-laws" or "woolly haired grandchildren" (*Sten. Ber.* XIII/I/53, May 2, 1912, 1648).

28. *Sten. Ber.* XIII/I/55, May 7, 1912, 1730.

29. O. E., "Wochenschau," *Deutsche Zeitung,* May 12, 1912.

30. Leonore Niessen-Deiters, "Rassenreinheit! Eine deutsche Frau über die Mischehen in den Kolonien," *Kolonie und Heimat,* May 26, 1912. Niessen-Deiters equated the legalization of interracial marriages with "racial suicide."

during the debate and expressed special discomfort with the idea of sexual unions involving blacks. This was even the case for men who had previously defended Africans against dehumanizing policies and language. The Social Democratic deputy Georg Ledebour is a case in point. An opponent of colonialism on principle, Ledebour was well known as a champion of the rights and humanity of blacks. He denounced Southwest African officials in 1905 for treating blacks "like cattle."[31] He censored army officials in 1906 for using the term *hunting down* when describing their pursuit of indigenous rebels.[32] That same year, he also astutely ascribed blame for atrocities against the colonized to the exercise of "an almost unlimited authority" by colonial officials "over men whom they view as inferior."[33] And yet, Ledebour identified blacks in May 1912 as lower than other races. He warned against the rhetorical conflation of blacks and Samoans—admonishing other deputies not to "degrade" the latter to the former's status—and he classified Pacific Islanders as "closely related physically and spiritually to Europeans."[34] What is more, he admitted to "sharing completely" in the indignation occasionally voiced in the socialist press over the alleged propensity of German women to "make advances to Negroes."[35]

Other opponents of the ban from the Left and Center expressed similar sentiments, likewise appearing to reject the idea of a shared humanity with blacks on an almost intuitive level. Dr. David of the Social Democratic Party reiterated Ledebour's complaint that supporters of the antimiscegenation ban were confusing Samoans with Africans. David stated on the final day of the debate that "from a racial standpoint, Samoan women are not to be lumped together with Negresses, which has happened here." He complained that this was "an entirely inadmissible comparison," because Samoans were "probably more closely related to the Javanese and Japanese" than to blacks.[36] Even the Catholic Center Party deputy Matthias Erzberger expressed a general aversion toward black Africans. Years before, Erzberger had offended his colleagues in the Reichstag by stating that

---

31. *Sten. Ber.* XI/I/180, April 6, 1905, 5890.

32. *Sten. Ber.* XI/II/128, November 28, 1906, 3979.

33. *Sten. Ber.* XI/II/66, March 15, 1906, 2042.

34. Specifically, Ledebour accused deputies like Richthofen of misrepresenting the situation by speaking almost exclusively of blacks when, to his knowledge, the majority of mixed-race unions actually occurred between whites and Samoans or with the mixed-race Rehoboth Bastards (*Sten. Ber.* XIII/I/55, May 7, 1912, 1735).

35. Ibid., 1737.

36. *Sten. Ber.* XIII/I/56, May 8, 1912, 1745.

the black man was "a human being possessing an immortal soul and a divinely appointed destiny identical to our own."[37] Yet in May 1912, he admitted that he, too, did not wish to acquire "a black daughter-in-law" or a "black uncle." He also suggested punishing colonial officials who had sexual relations with blacks.[38] Together, these comments betray the power of the rhetoric of radical difference, showing that it eventually influenced the thinking of even colonialism's harshest critics.[39]

The rhetoric of radical difference aimed against Jews during the colonial era had much in common with that directed against black Africans. Both relegated their subjects to extreme positions on the racial scale, contrasting them negatively to other human groups while comparing them to animals, rhetorically disassociating them from all other human races. The extreme positioning of blacks and Jews by colonial radicals and racial antisemites also coincided with an undeniable conflation of their invented representations. As expressed in the major antisemitic and colonial newspapers of the day, as well as in other publications meant for popular consumption—like books, novels, and pamphlets—racist discourses about blacks and Jews attributed both with many of the same negative characteristics, setting them apart from the rest of humanity in remarkably similar ways.

On the most basic level, it was the rhetoric of radical difference itself that brought colonial and antisemitic discourses together. During the colonial era, racists commonly used the German racial type to negatively contrast the accomplishments, characteristics, and mentalities of non-German groups with German achievements and ways. While Germans were spiritually profound and honorable, productive, creative people, tied to the land and capable of building their own independent states, non-Germans lacked these virtues and abilities to varying degrees, according to the racist literature of the day. The rhetoric of radical difference aimed at blacks and Jews was unique, however, in that it often denied them *any* of the qualities that supposedly characterized German nature, while racialists usually ascribed at least some positive attributes to most other non-German groups, be they Slavs, Arabs, American Indians, or East Asians. Blacks and Jews

---

37. Ibid., XII/I/126, March 19, 1908, 4098.

38. Ibid., XIII/I/56, May 8, 1912, 1741, 1742.

39. Ledebour and other deputies on the Left and Center nevertheless opposed the bans on mixed-race marriages. Ledebour interpreted the issue in moral terms, insisting that by withdrawing the right of marriage, the government was, in effect, condemning indigenous women involved with white men to lives of prostitution or concubinage. Ledebour and others also argued that the bans did nothing to stop the rise in the colonies of mixed-race populations.

competed in the imaginations of radicals within the colonial and antisemitic movements as the most un-German of the non-German races.

The character trait most commonly attributed to both blacks and
Jews was a disinclination to labor. For most racial theorists, the defining
German characteristic was a proclivity for hard work, and in establishing a
diametrical opposition between blacks and Germans, or Germans and
Jews, colonialists and antisemites often juxtaposed German industry with
African sloth or Jewish indolence.[40] The accusation made in the antisemitic
newspaper the *Deutsche Wacht* in 1892 that "the Jew . . . understands not a
single handicraft or profession and on the whole knows nothing of 'work'
itself" was repeated ad nauseam throughout the colonial era in the antisemitic press.[41] This was matched by frequent complaints in colonial publications about a negative attitude toward labor among black Africans.
When Woldemar Schütze wrote in *Black Against White* that the black man
"hates work deep down in his heart" and perceives it as "shameful," he articulated what for many had already become a cliché.[42] Such complaints
about black and Jewish laziness contrasted with the common contemporary stereotype that certain Asian groups, like the Chinese, were hard-
working, although they, too, were deemed racially inferior.[43]

Racists who spoke of a German penchant for hard work also described Germans as being inherently creative. In response, colonialists and
antisemites frequently depicted blacks and Jews as lacking creative talent.
The *völkisch* ideologue and literary historian Adolf Bartels encapsulated
this perspective on Jews in an article in the *Deutsche Welt* in 1909 when he
insisted that "Jewry has in general no, or only very little, creative ability
and simply acquires foreign things, albeit in a masterly way."[44] The former
governor of German East Africa, Captain Adolf von Götzen, lent author-

40. Friedrich Lange encapsulated this view in 1893 when he wrote, "Every German has a
natural desire to work, to organize, to accomplish something, and to have the uplifting realization at the end of his life that his efforts have brought his children forward" (*Reines
Deutschtum,* 122).

41. Gr, "Arbeit und Judenthum," *Deutsche Wacht: Wochenschrift für nationales Deutschtum und soziale Reform,* June 19, 1892.

42. Schütze, *Schwarz gegen Weiss,* 77.

43. Ferdinand Freiherr von Richthofen, *Schantung und seine Eingangspforte Kiautschou*
(Berlin: Dietrich Reimer, [Ernst Vohsen], 1898), 114–15. Von Richthofen wrote of the "dili-
gence and frugality" of the Chinese popular classes, that "the common man amazes us with
the amount of work he accomplishes and the length of time he labors" (quoted in Steinmetz,
Devil's Handwriting, 410).

44. Adolf Bartels, "Judentum und Literatur," *Deutsche Welt: Wochenschrift der
Deutschen Zeitung,* May 2, 1909. Bartels (1862–1945) led a campaign to "dejudaize" German
literature. He became an enthusiast of National Socialism in the 1920s.

ity to a similar myth about blacks in his 1906 memoir of the Maji-Maji uprising when he proclaimed, "I personally belong to those who cannot believe that blacks are capable of the same developmental possibilities as we,
since the Negro appears to lack every faculty for creative thought and action."[45] Such sentiments contrasted, again, with conventional perceptions
of Asians, who were recognized as having created past great civilizations.

Some authors compounded the allegation of a fundamental absence
of creativity among blacks and Jews by attributing the one or the other
with an inherently destructive nature. Contributors to Theodor Fritsch's
Hammer magazine concerned with preserving Europe's natural spaces
identified Jews as "nature-destroyers" who, in their thoughtless pursuit of
profit and pleasure, wreaked havoc on the environment.[46] "He who is familiar with how the Russian Jews over the last fifty years have attacked the
forests in Wolhynien, Podolien and from the Ural to the Krim," one author
wrote in 1910, "doesn't wonder why it is that the entirety of western Russia
is constantly barren and suffers periodically from famine."[47] Blacks stood
accused in the colonial press of a similarly destructive and uncreative exploitation of their natural resources. "They are much too indolent and ir-
responsible and have too few wants to approach a sensible vocation in a serious manner," insisted a contributor familiar with German East Africa in
the *Koloniale Monatsblätter* in 1913. "They know very well how to ruth-
lessly exploit their surroundings. They will slaughter a goat in order to get
its hide. Once the material runs out, their exports fall off, as seen with the
trade in wax, caout-chouc, ivory, and copal."[48]

The racist literature of the day frequently interprets a nomadic
lifestyle as the natural consequence of these negative qualities. As a result,
while racist ideologues attributed Germans with a rootedness to the soil
and a long-standing and productive relationship with their land, they often
depicted both Jews and blacks as lacking a similar connectedness to their
own natural surroundings. The ancient myth of the wandering Jew, Aha-

---

45. Adolf von Götzen, *Deutsch-Ostafrika im Aufstand 1905/06* (Berlin: D. Reimer, 1909),
10. Quoted in Carl v. Stengel, "Die Eingeborenenfrage und die Regelung der Rechtsverhält-
nisse der Eingeborenen in den deutschen Schutzgebieten," *Zeitschrift für Kolonialpolitik,
Kolonialrecht und Kolonialwirtschaft* 12 (1910): 191.

46. Ewald Haufe, "Die Jüdin auf dem Berge," *Hammer: Blätter für deutschen Sinn* 4
(1905): 356.

47. Hans der Bauer, "Der moderne 'Kulturmensch' als Schöpfer der Wüste," *Hammer:
Blätter für deutschen Sinn* 9 (1910): 79.

48. Hauptmann a. D. A. Leue, "Unsere Eingeborenen," *Koloniale Monatsblätter:
Zeitschrift für Kolonialpolitik, Kolonialrecht und Kolonialwirtschaft* 15 (1913): 368. The German Colonial Society published the *KM* monthly from Berlin.

suerus, condemned by Christ to walk the earth until Judgment Day, was among the most enduring of antisemitic legends. Modern antisemites compounded it by attributing the very existence of the Jewish diaspora to a Jewish "nomadic spirit" conditioned by historical, cultural, or racial factors.[49] Antisemitic ideologues like Theodor Fritsch insisted that the Jewish incapability for productive labor helped motivate their wanderings, making it necessary for Jews to seek out and live off of productive settled people. Colonialists who attributed blacks with nomadism made a similar connection. Woldemar Schütze insisted in *Black Against White* that "the political unit for the Negro is the village, and this is because he is not stationary and never will be, since he never works for more than what is sufficient to make a bare living. For this reason," Schütze continued, "farming is only a stopgap for him, and cattle breeding has by no means become common to all Negro tribes. When the soil becomes exhausted or the grazing land depleted, he leaves his village to erect his home elsewhere."[50]

Allegations of a vagabond lifestyle correlated well with another popular stereotype: the supposed fixation of blacks and Jews on their immediate existence, their alleged inability to project themselves beyond the here and now. Some in the German military blamed the government's total unpreparedness for the Herero uprising in Southwest Africa on this alleged African trait, claiming that the present-mindedness of blacks had precluded any advance warning of the outbreak of hostilities. "The Negroes are true children of the moment," wrote one army officer who marshaled this argument. "Once they have set off on an action, they do not ask after the consequences, and they concern themselves little with 'tomorrow' when 'today' pleases them."[51] For blacks, this trait was often portrayed as the result of an immature temperament or limited intellect, but for Jews, it was seen as a product of a lack of spiritual profundity. Discussing Jewish religiosity, one contributor to the antisemitic *Deutsch-Soziale Blätter* proclaimed in 1908 that "the Jew does not know, and has never known, of a hereafter. He concerns himself as little with the question of the mystery of

---

49. Werner Sombart, *The Jews and Modern Capitalism,* trans. M. Epstein (New York: B. Franklin, 1969), 323–54.

50. Schütze, *Schwarz gegen Weiss,* 33.

51. "Afrikanische Ueberraschungen," *National-Zeitung,* January 30, 1904. This piece consists almost entirely of a letter from a Major Richelmann that was originally printed in the army newspaper, *Militärwochenblatt.* Karl Oetker repeated this allegation about blacks in *Die Neger-Seele und die Deutschen in Afrika.* He insisted that "the Negro . . . seldom, or never, gives thought to the future and thinks even less over the past" (Oetker, *Neger-Seele,* 19).

his existence as with the matter of what follows death. Although apparently only lasting a short minute long, the momentary existence appears to him as an end in itself, and the earth as an *Etablissement,* where everyone must strive to amuse themselves as far as possible."[52] "The nomad lives completely and utterly in the present, and concerns himself not at all with either the this-worldly or the otherworldly future," insisted another contributor to the *Blätter* almost two decades earlier. "Thus the Arab, the old Hebrew, and the present-day Jew. 'Every Jew,' says Göthe, 'is interested in the immediate.'"[53]

According to racists in the antisemitic and colonial movements, all these qualities, combined, prevented blacks and Jews alike from either forming their own self-sustaining independent states or maintaining those that they managed to take over. This alleged incapacity for state formation was a frequent topic of discussion in the antisemitic press. "A talent for political organization and a wise and just rule is denied to the Hebrews," wrote Fritsch in the *Hammer* in 1906. "In their boundless mania for exploiting all resources, they have repeatedly quickly exhausted the productive power of the people and have brought the lands to the abyss of economic and social ruin."[54] Fritsch asked derisively a year later, "Why, then, hasn't the Jewish nation been able to form its own self-supporting state? Because they lack all serious ability to do it," he answered, "lacking all creating and shaping talents, all true power and wisdom, all qualifications for a self-established and fixed culture."[55]

Lengthy deliberations over the failure of blacks to create or sustain successful states appeared in colonial newspapers at about the same time. The main organ of the German Colonial Society, the *Deutsche Kolonialzeitung,* ran an article on this subject in November 1904. "Both of the great Negro races, the Sudan- and Bantu-Negroes, resemble each other in their dispositions and their cultural conditions," the author proclaimed. "Neither of the two races has achieved the formation of true states, since transitory despots that disappear without a trace after several generations or that fall to pieces upon the ruler's death cannot be perceived as such." The author referred to independent Haiti and Liberia as cases in point.

---

52. "Ecce homines. Ein Wort über Juden- und Christentum," *Deutsch-Soziale Blätter,* December 30, 1908.

53. "Das Gesetz des Nomadentums," *Deutsch-Soziale Blätter,* June 14, 1891.

54. Theod. Fritsch, "'Israel Triumphator,'" *Hammer: Blätter für deutschen Sinn* 5 (1906): 166.

55. "Gibt es eine Judenfrage?," *Hammer: Blätter für deutschen Sinn* 6 (1907): 198. Fritsch is almost certainly the author of this unsigned lead article.

Speaking of the former, he insisted that blacks had transformed "what was once an excellently cultivated island" into "almost a wilderness" plagued by "perpetual revolutions, universal depravity, and a relapse into barbarism." Concerning Liberia, the author noted sardonically that, despite a "chronic lack of funds," the state maintained "an army with the most unbelievable uniforms of any nation and an order with the most diverse ranks." He attributed the fiscal crisis in part to a lack of industrial production, itself a result of the "work-shy, indolent, and conceited" nature of the "civilized" black.[56] Another article on Liberia in the *Deutsche Kolonialzeitung* reached similar conclusions several years later. Its author insisted that the Liberian experiment "clearly proved" the inability of blacks to build states or maintain them.[57]

The rhetoric of radical difference common to the colonial era did much more than ascribe an absence of German characteristics and capabilities to Jews and blacks. Extremists in both the colonial and antisemitic movements attributed to both groups a fundamentally malicious nature: a hateful and pernicious, insidious, brutal essence that neither education nor conversion could change. From this perspective, Jews and blacks did not simply lack positive and productive traits, like a capacity for creative thought or an appreciation for fruitful labor. They also possessed evil dispositions enhanced by specific malignant qualities that together threatened Germans in many different ways. Jews had long suffered such extremely negative representations. During the Middle Ages, allegations of ritual murder, host desecration, and well-poisoning dramatically compounded the image of the evil Jew that originated with the biblical story of deicide by attributing to Jews murderous intentions toward their Gentile neighbors. Modern antisemites secularized many of their prejudices, but the accusation of malevolent intent remained much the same. For blacks, however, the dark and threatening image painted by colonial extremists had much shallower historical roots. While Europeans demonized Jews as Satan's helpers during the Middle Ages, medieval European art and literature often depicted blacks positively, a development encouraged by the popularity of stories about black Christian converts like the legendary Prester

---

56. P. Walther, "Einiges über unsere schwarzen Mitbürger in Afrika," *Deutsche Kolonialzeitung,* November 24, 1904.

57. "Was geht in Liberia vor?" *Deutsche Kolonialzeitung,* November 7, 1908.

John, whose African Christian kingdom was said to be in Ethiopia.[58] But the attacks on German soldiers and settlers at the outset of the Herero uprising helped discredit older stereotypes of black amiability and childlike naïveté, encouraging representations that mimicked the image of the hate-filled, conspiratorial, and inherently evil Jew on many levels.

Not all antisemites believed that Jews consciously intended to injure their Gentile neighbors. Some within the racist wing of the antisemitic movement denied the existence of a Jewish conspiracy, arguing instead that Jews were simply compelled by their nature, independent of their own volition, to engage in activities harmful to the Christian German nation.[59] Yet this was a minority position, even among racial antisemites. Much more common was the allegation of a deep-seated hatred among Jews for Gentiles and a burning desire by Jews to dominate them, feelings that supposedly motivated Jews to deliberately encourage, and even plan, the moral, political, and cultural ruin of Christian states. Although these sentiments were often identified as a product of Jewish religious teachings, racial antisemites frequently blurred the line between religion and ethnicity, or race. "While Christianity is the doctrine of universal love, Judaism is the doctrine of universal hatred for everyone who doesn't belong to the Jewish tribe," wrote one contributor to the *Hammer* magazine in November 1912.[60] "Rabbinical law expressly says that Jews must not bend down before other laws, or if they do, only for appearance's sake," wrote Theodor Fritsch several years earlier in an article where he used the terms *Jew, Hebrew,* and *Semite* interchangeably. "It demands for all Jews an unlimited right of dominion and allocates non-Jews to them as slaves," he continued.[61] In this piece, Fritsch also wrote of a "Semitic instinct of destruction" arrayed "with hatred and scorn" against everything good and noble in the German nation.[62] Siegfried Passarge adopted the theme of Jewish animosity as well in his antisemitic opus, *Das Judentum als landschafts-*

---

58. Positive medieval representations of blacks included the black Magi, Caspar (also known as Gaspar), Saint Gregory the Moor, and Saint Maurice (George M. Fredrickson, *Racism: A Short History* [Princeton: Princeton University Press, 2002], 26–28).

59. Heinrich Class took this position in his 1912 book *If I were the Kaiser,* which he wrote using the pseudonym Daniel Frymann.

60. "Bekenntnisse einer jüdischen Seele," *Hammer: Blätter für deutschen Sinn* 11 (1912): 609. The theme of Jewish hatred reoccurs throughout the antisemitic literature of the day.

61. Th. Fritsch, "Die geistige Unterjochung Deutschlands," *Hammer: Blätter für deutschen Sinn* 9 (1910): 150.

62. Ibid., 152.

kundlich-ethnologisches Problem, twenty-five years later. Unlike Fritsch, however, Passarge insisted that "the hatred that Jews have against all non-Jews" had little to do with Talmudic teachings but stemmed instead from what he called a "daily making of scorn" of Gentiles that infected Jewish ghetto children at an early age.[63]

Following the outbreak of fighting in German Southwest Africa, some colonialists voiced allegations of a similarly intense and general hatred among blacks toward whites that, like anti-Gentile Jewish enmity, rendered impossible peaceful relations. Barely a month after the hostilities began, an editorial speaking of black hatred appeared on the front page of the *National-Zeitung,* the main organ of the National Liberal Party. The anonymous author, identified only as "someone who knows the conditions in South Africa," argued for an application to the situation in the German colonies of the lessons learned by the Boers and the British in their dealings with black Africans. Insisting that "all coloreds" were alike "to a certain degree" in their "ways of thinking and feeling," the author suggested that experiences in British Africa showed that Germans should not try to win over the Hereros "with love" but rather with respect through the application of a "strict justice," because, in his estimation, South African blacks "hated the English as they hated the Boers, despite the fact that the English frequently did nothing short of coddle them."[64]

Irreconcilable black antipathy for whites was a topic of discussion the following year at the annual meeting of the Colonial Congress. In a speech titled "The Meaning of the Study of Native Languages for the Colonial Administration," the famous professor of linguistics Carl Meinhof argued that the failure of English-speaking American blacks to assimilate into the majority population boded poorly for the future of race relations in German Africa. In language reminiscent of antisemitic rhetoric about Jewish anti-Gentile hatred, Meinhof insisted that "racial strife between whites and blacks is an impregnable partition, and because of it, one has with the English speaking colored people a state within a state, an element full of murderous hatred toward the whites, whose danger only increases with the terrific growth in the size of the black population.[65]

Woldemar Schütze elaborated several years later on the reasons for the alleged hatred for whites among colonized Africans. In *Black Against*

---

63. Siegfried Passarge, *Das Judentum als landschaftskundlich-ethnologisches Problem* (Munich: J. F. Lehmann, 1929), 382, 383.

64. "Südafrikanische Eingeborenenpolitik," *National-Zeitung,* February 3, 1904.

65. Quoted in Stengel, "Die Eingeborenenfrage," 200.

White, Schütze argued that whites were "the most evil sworn enemy from the Negro's perspective," because white rule had ended the black man's lifestyle of continuous warfare and nomadic wanderings.[66] "What, then, is the Negro left to do?" Schütze asked. "If he can no longer effortlessly give up his former residence as before, then the Negro must work, and he hates work no less than the white man. Therefore, he has in this way a double reason to hate whites."[67] Schütze insisted that the purpose of the uprising in Southwest Africa was to regain this former freedom: "The Negro still has not forgotten the blessed times of earlier centuries when he was the free master of his own shores until he was suppressed by someone stronger, when he could make war, rob, murder, burn, and ravage to his heart's content."[68]

According to many antisemites and colonial extremists, Jews and blacks also lacked a sense of morality. They shared an indifference to matters of right and wrong that allowed them to employ the most immoral brutal tactics against those they hated, and, in the minds of German racists, this trait set them apart in the depth of their wickedness and perfidy from other races. The assertion made by the *Deutsch-Soziale Blätter* in June 1891 that Jews "know of no categorical imperative" typifies opinions about Jewish immorality expressed in the antisemitic press.[69] The Jew "threw ethics overboard," wrote a contributor to the *Hammer* in 1905, because "they stood in the way of his march of conquest through the world." In their quest to "materially exploit and rule other people," he continued, "they set all ethics behind them and bump up against no moral considerations of any sort. Juda's advantage is their only moral philosophy."[70] Years later, Heinrich Class wrote of the Jews' "indifference toward right and wrong" and their "moral heartlessness" in their economic dealings.[71] The image of the Jew as eternally malevolent and incurably immoral evoked older religious stereotypes demonizing Jews as Satan's helpers. In his article of March 1910, where he spoke of a "Semitic instinct of destruction," Theodor Fritsch labeled the Jews a "demon-people."[72]

Comparable allegations of black African immorality appeared in the

---

66. Schütze, *Schwarz gegen Weiss,* 32.
67. Ibid., 34.
68. Ibid., 38.
69. "Das Gesetz des Nomadentums," *Deutsch-Soziale Blätter,* June 14, 1891.
70. Dr. Franz Lüdtke, "Schlaglichter," *Hammer: Blätter für deutschen Sinn* 4 (1905): 474.
71. Class [pseudonym Frymann], *Wenn ich der Kaiser wär—Politische Wahrheiten und Notwendigkeiten,* 4th ed. (Leipzig: Dieterich'schen Verlagsbuchhandlung, 1913), 32.
72. Th. Fritsch, "Die geistige Unterjochung Deutschlands," 151.

colonial press during the Herero and Nama uprisings. Although some colonial pioneers like the explorer Carl Peters had insisted for decades that blacks lacked virtue and a moral sense, the outbreak of war in 1904 and rumors about atrocities against German settlers and soldiers encouraged others to write of blacks in this vein. In his November article in the *Deutsche Kolonialzeitung* on the inability of black Africans to form their own viable states, P. Walther identified blacks as lacking "courage, loyalty, chastity, and a respect for the female sex." He argued that these deficiencies made blacks inferior in "character and disposition" to even the most ancient of German people.[73] An article specifically devoted to the topic of black immorality, titled "Reflections upon the Negro Character," appeared in the *Deutsche Kolonialzeitung* several years later. The author, identified only as Z, argued that ethics, and not intelligence, separated blacks from whites. He insisted that "the Negro" was "in no way mentally inferior" and offered as proof his own encounters in Cameroon with intelligent blacks, some with facilities for "elementary science," others for European languages. For Z, the difference lay in the black man's "moral inferiority." "I believe," Z wrote, "that we can never, not in the course of many centuries, lift Negro tribes to the level of western European culture; for this, they are simply not morally fit. In this fact lies the primary decisive partition between ourselves and the Negro, and, in my opinion," he continued, "a comparison between us and him can never be made."[74]

Woldemar Schütze painted an even darker image of black Africans. Like the contributors to the *Deutsche Kolonialzeitung,* Schütze insisted that blacks lacked moral qualities. But he went much further, presenting blacks as cruel—even ghoulish—and he explicitly refuted the stereotype equating them with innocent children. "The Negro has nothing, absolutely nothing of the childish pure innocence and impartiality of a child," Schütze wrote. "One says, it is true, that every child, even the best, is unconsciously cruel, and people attempt to prove this by showing that even normally good natured ones like to torture animals. But to a child, it is not at all clear that his actions cause the animal pain and torment. The Negro, to the contrary, delights with diabolical pleasure in the agony of men and beasts, knowing full well that he is giving the object of his enjoyment the most dreadful agonies." Taking stories about Herero wartime atrocities against whites at face value, Schütze insisted that events during the uprising revealed the de-

---

73. P. Walther, "Einiges über unsere schwarzen Mitbürger in Afrika."
74. Z., "Betrachtungen über den Neger-charakter," *Deutsche Kolonialzeitung,* August 17, 1907.

monic nature of black Africans. "We certainly, and repeatedly, sufficiently experienced at the beginning of the Herero rebellion in German Southwest Africa just how frightfully cruel and inhuman the Negro can be, and is," Schütze wrote, "when he finds himself in the ecstasy of martial blood-lust."[75]

For racists in the colonial and antisemitic movements, Jews and blacks were particularly threatening because their negative, dangerous qualities were indelible. Antisemitic and procolonial authors who insisted that these characteristics were racially determined argued that neither education nor conversion could erase or change them. "Even with the most 'civilized' Negro," Schütze wrote in *Black Against White,* "the bestial, brutal Negro-nature will always burst forth in unguarded moments (like the bloodthirsty predatory nature of a cat), and, therefore, the culture of the whites that was grafted on him is only a veneer."[76] Concerning the uselessness of Christian conversion, Schütze believed that the participation of Christian converts in the Herero uprising and in wartime atrocities of "murder, beatings, and burnings" showed just how little Christianity affected "the heart" of "the Negro."[77] In *The Negro-Soul,* the medical doctor Karl Oetker painted a more genial, although no less racist, picture. He did not, for example, attribute a malicious essence to blacks, but he, too, insisted that Christianity could not improve them. Oetker maintained that Christian blacks were even "lazier, more unreliable, more dishonest, and more insubordinate" than the unconverted.[78] Such statements mirror assertions in the antisemitic press and elsewhere that even converted Jews exhibited stereotypically Jewish traits and passed them on to their offspring, unchanged. For racial antisemites, conversion only exacerbated the Jewish threat by making Jews more hidden and covert enemies.[79]

Racists within the colonial and antisemitic movements who wished to construct negative, threatening representations of the Jewish or black African Other invented additional characteristics that made them appear even more similar and dangerous. For example, racists presented Jews and black Africans as each having an inherited sense of racial solidarity that strengthened their power vis-à-vis outsiders and facilitated crimes against

---

75. Schütze, *Schwarz gegen Weiss,* 79.
76. Ibid., 13.
77. Ibid., 57, 56.
78. Oetker, *Neger-Seele,* 24.
79. In *The Jews and Modern Capitalism,* Werner Sombart discussed at great length the failure of Jewish converts to shed their specifically Jewish characteristics.

members of other races. For Jews, this allegation had a long history and figured into antisemitic accusations of malicious Jewish intent. Carl Paasch wrote at length in his 1891 book of a "secret Jewry which, in alliance with overt Jewry, seeks to secure for their own kind all important offices and positions for the end goal of world domination."[80] Theodor Fritsch elaborated on Jewish racial exclusivity in the *Hammer* several decades later. He argued in an article in March 1910 that "even if the Aryan people could adopt all characteristics of the Semites, they would surely still be worsted by them in free enterprise, so long as they do not at the same time belong to the inner society of interests which hides under the guise of the Jewish religion." Fritsch insisted that "Talmudic law" likened non-Jews to animals and promised Jews "'dominion over all other people.'" He argued that this law was founded on "a society of blood, on race."[81]

Comparable discussions of a dangerous racial unity among blacks appeared in 1904 in the procolonial press. Soon after the outbreak of violence in German Southwest Africa, the *National-Zeitung* printed an article by a Major Richelmann who wrote of a "positive feeling of solidarity" among blacks that, in his words, "allows very seldom for one black to betray another."[82] Several months later, a rumor supposedly testifying to the strength of black racial consciousness circulated in colonial newspapers. According to the story, printed first in the *Deutsch-Südwestafrikanische Zeitung,* the Herero had executed a "fully *verkaffert*" white man, cutting his throat "like a sheep," despite the fact that he lived among them and considered himself one with the Herero people.[83] The issue of black group solidarity and its nefarious consequences emerged again in 1909 during a debate played out in the Reichstag and in the pages of the colonial press over the value of sworn testimonies from black witnesses. In March of that year, state secretary Bernhard Dernburg made clear his desire to end the custom of refusing blacks the right to testify under oath in colonial courts. Proponents of this tradition challenged Dernburg's position during the German Colonial Society's annual meeting, arguing that a black man, in addition to being predisposed to dishonesty, would never testify truthfully "were his testimony directed against kin."[84]

Another common allegation made against blacks and Jews was that of

80. Carl Paasch, *Eine jüdisch-deutsche Gesandtschaft,* viii.
81. Th. Fritsch, "Die geistige Unterjochung Deutschlands," 149.
82. "Afrikanische Ueberraschungen," *National-Zeitung,* January 30, 1904.
83. "Wieß und Schwarz," *Deutsche Kolonialzeitung,* July 28, 1904.
84. "Hauptversammlung der Deutschen Kolonial-Gesellschaft. III." *Deutsch-Ostafrikanische Zeitung,* July 31, 1909.

insincere conversion to Christianity. Racial antisemites and procolonial advocates frequently insisted that conversions by blacks and Jews were rarely, if ever, authentic. "Most baptized Jews observe baptism only as a *Passepartout,* as something with which to achieve a higher standing, 'as an entrance ticket for European culture,' as Heine says," claimed a contributor to the *Deutsch-Soziale Blätter* in February 1910. "Cases where genuine conviction is said to have occasioned conversion would seem to be extremely rare."[85] Months later, the *Deutsch-Soziale Blätter* quoted, approving, from an article in the *Deutsche Tageszeitung* that proclaimed the irreconcilable nature of Christianity and "the Jewish spirit."[86]

Colonial extremists made similar allegations about the incompatibility of Christianity with the sensibilities of black Africans. Schütze argued in *Black Against White* that the Christian values of love, kindness, and forgiveness were foreign to black nature. While Europeans showed "leniency" to "defeated and defenseless" opponents as a result of their "ethical development," blacks were incapable of understanding such behavior, meaning that they failed to grasp "the first principle of Christianity."[87] Schütze also insisted that when blacks did convert, they did so superficially and often perverted the Christian faith. "Christianity is no religion for the Negro," Schütze wrote. "Either he understands it not at all and adopts it only externally, or he understands it falsely, arranges it as it should be after his own methods, and makes from it a Negro-Christianity which is no longer Christianity."[88] Allegations of black opportunism concerning conversion were voiced in the Reichstag several years later. During a discussion of the budget for Cameroon in March 1909, parliamentary deputy Goller of the left-liberal German Progressive Party warned his audience of the probability that conversions among blacks were motivated less by faith than by the knowledge that Christian converts were more employable. Goller spoke of a similar problem in China. But he intimated that the African situation was more difficult when he insisted that black Africans had a "partiality toward lies and hypocrisy."[89]

Perhaps the most emotionally charged accusation leveled at both blacks and Jews was that of racial pollution. As seen above, concerns over race mixing led to the promulgation of a series of antimiscegenation laws

85. "Ueber das Taufjudentum," *Deutsch-Soziale Blätter,* February 19, 1910.
86. "Rundschau. Christentum und Antisemitismus," *Deutsch-Soziale Blätter,* May 18, 1910.
87. Schütze, *Schwarz gegen Weiss,* 31.
88. Ibid., 56.
89. *Sten. Ber.* XII/I/217, March 2, 1909, 7258.

in the German colonies. During the debate in the Reichstag over their legality in May 1912, even opponents of the laws expressed special discomfort with the idea of sexual relations between blacks and whites, as compared to relations between whites and Samoans. Allegations of sexual
intentions by black men toward white women circulated in the colonial
press soon after. In August 1912, the magazine *Kolonie und Heimat*
reprinted a letter originally published in the *Deutsch-Südwestafrikanische
Zeitung* purportedly by a Southwest African black man living in Germany
writing home to his parents. The alleged author remarked on the abun-
dance in Germany of "pretty girls." He stated that white girls "pleased"
him the best and told of a white woman who had agreed to marry him. According to the *Kolonie und Heimat,* the letter indicated "the difficult danger that our women and girls in the colonies are exposed to if blacks are
not restrained by the most stringent regulations."[90]

The Reichstag debate of May 1912 also exposed fears in certain circles
about the allure of black male sexuality; in addition to prompting discussions in the procolonial press about the sexual intentions of black men toward white women, the debate incited deliberations about the supposed
problem of German women seeking out black men. An early article on this
topic appeared in the pages of the *Deutsche Kolonialzeitung* in September
1909. Titled "Racial Questions," the piece reports on young German
women corresponding with black men in Togo—men educated in German
schools—supposedly on the pretext of adding to their stamp collections.
According to the report, one woman included a photograph of herself to
her correspondent, while another offered herself in marriage.[91] Similar stories surfaced during the 1912 Reichstag debate. On May 7, an article appeared in the *Deutsche Tageszeitung* condemning mixed-race marriages as
endangering colonial rule by lessening the esteem for whites among black
Africans. Its author also remarked upon reported instances of correspondence between white German women and black men in the colonies. He labeled this a "race scandal" and suggested that the government publish the
letters and name their authors, presumably to expose them to public
ridicule.[92] Another article briefly mentioning this correspondence appeared in the *National-Zeitung* the following day. Its author condemned
"the perversity of certain German women who run after Negroes." He

---

90. "Ein widerlicher Beitrag zur Rassenfrage," *Kolonie und Heimat,* August 4, 1912.
91. "Rassenfragen," *Deutsche Kolonialzeitung,* September 4, 1909.
92. "Ein beherzigenswertes Wort zur Mischlingsfrage," *Deutsche Tageszeitung,* May 7,
1912. Published in Berlin, the *DT* was the official organ of the Agrarian League.

lamented the lack of German racial consciousness, claiming that English and American women would never dream of sending "a love letter to a Cameroon Negro or a Samoan."[93]

Similar concerns about sexual relations between Gentile women and Jewish men surfaced in the antisemitic press. During the colonial era, newspapers and periodicals that embraced racial antisemitism depicted adult Jewish males as sexual predators, frequently reporting on alleged instances of sexual molestation by the Jewish employers of young Gentile women. The *Staatsbürger-Zeitung* raised the alarm about the plight of "Christian girls" working in Jewish households in a front-page article in December 1903.[94] The *Hammer* printed a letter from a self-described former female employee in March 1906 who wrote of "hundreds" of teenage girls suffering regular sexual abuse in Jewish-owned shops and businesses.[95] Several weeks later, another contributor to the magazine lamented what he saw as "the transformation of the German nation through Jewish blood" as a result of illegitimate sex between Jewish men and Gentile women. Contrasting the situation in Germany with that in Romania—where most Jews still lacked civic equality—the author insisted that Germany "sacrificed everything" to the Jews: "its citizenship, its money, its professorships, its theater—and its women."[96] Much like the colonialists who feared that German women were sexually attracted to blacks, racial antisemites also depicted Jewish men as possessing an incomprehensible sexual allure. In *The Riddle of Jewish Success,* published in 1919, Theodor Fritsch wrote of a Jewish ability to "dominate female psychology" and entice Gentile women.[97]

Discussions in colonial and antisemitic circles about the undesirability of sexual relations between blacks and whites, and Jews and Gentiles, encouraged deliberations about the outcome of these unions, namely, children. As is to be expected, colonialists and racial antisemites sharply condemned the creation of what both called a *Mischlingsrasse.* Each identified the mixed-race individual as particularly dangerous, representing, at least for some, an even greater threat than his or her full-blooded non-German

---

93. Otto Jöhlinger, "Mischenen und Rassenfragen," *National-Zeitung,* May 8, 1912.

94. "Haltung für falsche Anschuldigung," *Staatsbürger-Zeitung,* December 11, 1903, evening edition.

95. Frau B, "Gefahren für junge Mädchen," *Hammer: Blätter für deutschen Sinn* 5 (1906): 176.

96. G. B., "Zur Frage der Ein-Ehe," *Hammer: Blätter für deutschen Sinn* 5 (1906): 245.

97. F. Roderich-Stotheim [Theodor Fritsch], *Das Rätsel des jüdischen Erfolges* (Leipzig: Hammer-Verlag, 1919), 247.

parent. In 1905, a contributor to the *Hammer* denounced mixed-race marriages in general but singled out unions between Jews and Gentiles as especially problematic, stating that Jewish blood possessed "an extraordinary penetrating power" that ensured the inheritance of Jewish characteristics.[98] In *If I Were the Kaiser,* Heinrich Class wrote of the "disastrous role" played by "half-blood" individuals who, in his account, were largely responsible for the penetration of the Jewish spirit into the German people.[99]

Deliberations about the danger posed to German rule in the colonies by mixed-race offspring preoccupied some colonialists at about the same time. The German Colonial Society passed a resolution in December 1908 stating its opposition to the creation of a *"Mischlingsrasse"* in German Africa. In the deliberation before its passage, one of the resolution's most avid advocates, Dr. Friedrich Hupfeld, compared blacks unfavorably to East Asians and identified sexual unions between blacks and whites as race mixing in its worst form. Hupfeld insisted that the offspring of such unions were politically dangerous, because, in his opinion, "Mulattos" saw themselves as "leaders" who would lead the black race against whites.[100] The conservative newspaper the *Neue Preußische Zeitung* reiterated this concern in a front-page article four years later. Its author claimed that a *"Mischlingsrasse"* possessing both "Negro vices and European intelligence" would endanger the "healthy development" of German Africa. He insisted most colonial uprisings were led by individuals of mixed race.[101]

The most negative and violent discussions of blacks and Jews resembled each other in at least one other important way. Given what they saw as the irreconcilable natures of Gentiles and Jews, or Germans and black Africans, the most extreme members of both the antisemitic and colonial movements predicted an eventual race war that would determine, once and for all, the mastery or defeat of the ethnic German nation. Woldemar Schütze insisted in *Black Against White* that the hatred for whites common

---

98. Hans Heinrich von Schwießel, "Zum Kapitel 'Schamlose Ehen,'" *Hammer: Blätter für deutschen Sinn* 4 (1905): 525.

99. Class, [pseudonym Frymann], *Wenn ich der Kaiser wär,* 76.

100. *Bericht über die Sitzung des Vorstandes der Deutschen Kolonialgesellschaft im Sitzungssaale der Stadtverordneten im Rathause zu Berlin am Freitag den 4. Dezember 1908* (Berlin: Deutsche Kolonialgesellschaft, 1908), 44–45. Hupfeld worked in Togo as a planter and representative of the *Deutsche Togo Gesellschaft* during the 1890s.

101. Privatdozent Dr. F. Zadow, "Mischehen und Rassenmischung," *Neue Preußische Zeitung,* May 7, 1912, evening edition.

to black Africans would lead to "a terrible *Entscheidungskampf* [decisive battle] of the races," beginning in South Africa.[102] Two articles appeared a few years later in the Society for German Colonization's most prestigious periodical, the *Zeitschrift für Kolonialpolitik, Kolonialrecht und Kolonial-wirtschaft,* that also warn of a future race war predicated on black resentment or seething black hatred.

The first article, published in March 1910, prophesies an eventual attempt by colonized blacks to throw off the yoke of white rule. However, its author, Carl v. Stengel, played down the actual danger posed by a black uprising, insisting that a rebellion in Asia would be more threatening because, in his opinion, "Mongols" possessed a higher culture.[103] The second article is much more alarmist. Written by H. Berthold and running over forty pages, this piece has the idea of a future *"Endkampf,"* or final battle, between blacks and whites as its central theme. Unlike Stengel, its author also claimed that a coordinated black uprising could put German "domination" on the African continent "in question."[104] He clamored for immediate preparation: "In the *Endkampf* which must come, there will not be Suahelis, or Zulus, or Basutos, or Hereros, or Aschantis, et cetera, nor English, Germans, French, Dutch, or Italians, but only blacks and whites. And all whites must prepare and organize for this struggle in good time, since it will break out when we least of all expect it." Like Schütze, Berthold attributed the coming war to black animosity, insisting that a "collective enmity for all whites" would form "a bridge" among Africa's different populations.[105] To convince his readers of the seriousness of the threat, Berthold informed them that whites had "no rights of any sort" in black-ruled Haiti.[106]

The idea of a future *Endkampf* between blacks and whites parallels the apocalyptic visions of the most extreme racial antisemites of a final violent showdown between Jews and Gentile Germans. One of the earliest expressions of this vision came from the antisemitic journalist and ideologue Wilhelm Marr, famous for having popularized the word *anti-Semitism.* In his book, *The Victory of the Jews over the Germans,* first published in 1879, Marr wrote of a state of mortal combat between the two, and he

---

102. Schütze, *Schwarz gegen Weiss,* 38.

103. Stengel, "Die Eingeborenenfrage," 188, 191.

104. H. Berthold, "Ziele und Wege der kolonialen Besiedlung," *Zeitschrift für Kolonialpolitik, Kolonialrecht und Kolonialwirtschaft* 12 (1910): 468.

105. Ibid., 471.

106. Ibid., 469. Berthold quoted here from Hesketh Pritchard in *Where Black Rules White.*

pressed the German people to make a concerted counterattack against the Jewish enemy, for their own preservation.[107] Hints of a final violent reckoning inform the works of other influential contemporary antisemites as well, such as Eugen Dühring and Carl Paasch, both of whom intimated in their public writings their hopes for a bloody future confrontation.[108] Metaphorical references to an ongoing war between Jews and Gentiles are also scattered through the antisemitic literature of the day, as in the *Hammer* and the *Deutsch-Soziale Blätter*. For the antisemites and colonialists who envisioned a coming battle, the burning hatred that they attributed to their opponents, whether Jews or blacks, had the effect of enhancing their imagined potency and, therefore, threat. It also rhetorically transformed into perpetrators the actual victims of racial discrimination and violence, while nullifying any hope for a peaceful compromise with the enemy.[109]

The ascription of similar characteristics to blacks and Jews and the relegation of both to unique, but comparable, positions on the racial scale is one example of how antisemites and colonialists came to think about African and Jewish Others in similar ways. The similarity between the prescriptions given by racial antisemites for dealing with the Jewish Question and the actual, ongoing, colonial practices of racial discrimination is another. Just as antisemitic and colonial discourses converged during the colonial era—with or without the awareness of participants—certain colonial policies closely approximated elements of antisemitic fantasies of racial domination.

Broadly speaking, the primary goals of political antisemitism were realized in the colonies, albeit not for Jews but for indigenous populations. Beginning with the Antisemites' Petition of 1880, racial antisemites made

---

107. Klaus P. Fischer, *The History of an Obsession: German Judeophobia and the Holocaust* (New York: Continuum, 2001), 110.

108. Dühring, for example, wrote that "only the complete disappearance of the Hebrews could be a solution to the Jewish Question worth the name." To this end, he suggested the necessity of "extremely energetic means" and "means of fear and violence" (Eugen Dühring, *Die Judenfrage als frage des Racencharakters und seiner schädlichkeiten für Völkerexistenz, Sitte und Cultur: mit einer denkerisch freiheitlichen und praktisch abschliessenden Antwort* [Nowawes-Neuendorf bei Berlin: Ulrich Dühring, 1901], 139, 135–36).

109. Even the idea of the exceptional "good Jew" had its parallel in contemporary images of blacks. It was not uncommon for colonial officials who had worked with black troops to speak well of certain groups or individuals, but poorly of blacks or "coloreds" in general. Similarly, some antisemites spoke of the occasional "good Jew" who was the rare exception to the rule. For examples of both, see von Hauptmann a. D. A. Leue, "Unsere Eingeborenen," *Koloniale Monatsblätter* 15 (1913): 363, 364, 368, and Class, [pseudonym Frymann], *Wenn ich der Kaiser wär,* 77.

the annulment of Jewish civic equality the focus of their campaigns. They demanded the revocation of Jewish equal rights and the placing of Jews under a "special alien law," under which Jews would suffer special taxes and regulations and would lose the right to vote and hold elective office, plus the ability to serve in the military.[110] These demands, stated in the petition and reiterated in the programs of the major antisemitic political parties, would create, in effect, a racial state that would deny Jews both the rights and duties of citizenship. This imagined system anticipated, then paralleled, actual policies in the colonies, where the constitutional rules of the German Reich extended only to "non-natives" following the proclamation of the Law Concerning the Legal Position of the German Protectorates (known as the *Schutzgebietsgesetz*) in 1886. Individuals classified as "native" were subject not to German civil or criminal law, but to a special "native law" determined by the different colonial governments, allegedly in accordance with various "native" customs. They enjoyed none of the rights or duties of German citizenship and, therefore, had no recourse to the legal protections afforded under German law to German citizens—or even to non-German Europeans—in their dealings with colonial administrators. By creating a category of people subject to German rule but excluded from the German body politic and forced to live under special separate jurisdictions, the *Schutzgebietsgesetz* realized for "natives" much of what contemporary racial antisemites envisioned for Jews back in Germany.[111]

The treatment of blacks in colonial courts is a case in point. A comparison with the aims of political antisemites regarding the legal standing of Jews vis-à-vis Gentiles in German courts of law shows just how closely some colonial practices concerning black Africans approximated the antisemites' own intentions. Although no law in the German colonies expressly prohibited the administration of oaths to blacks, white German judges

---

110. "Program of the Antisemitic German Social Party (1890)," quoted in George Bernstein, "Anti-Semitism in Imperial Germany, 1871–1914: Selected Documents" (EdD diss., Columbia University, 1973), 376.

111. Jürgen Haunss, "Weiß und Schwarz, und Mann und Frau: Die Diskussion um die sog. Mischehen in den deutschen Kolonien unter besonderer Berücksichtigung des 'Schutzgebietes' Deutsch-Südwestafrika. Ein Beispiel für die Konstruktion von Geschlechterdifferenz als Mittel zur Legitimation von Herrschaft im wilhelminischen Deutschland" (Wissenschaftliche Hausarbeit zur Erlangung des akademischen Grades eines Magister Artium der Universität Hamburg, 1997), 18; Ralph Erbar, "Kolonialismus, Rassismus und Recht. Die Versuchte Kodifizierung Afrikanischer Gewohnheitsrechte und deren Konsequenzen für das Kolonialrecht in der Deutschen Kolonie Togo," in *Rassendiskriminierung, Kolonialpolitik und ethnisch-nationale Identität*, ed. Wilfried Wagner (Munster: LIT, 1992), 134–38.

commonly refused blacks the right to testify under oath on the pretense of a black penchant for mendacity, a practice that devalued the statements of black witnesses.[112] Antisemites intent on revoking Jewish emancipation demanded a similar treatment of Jews for a similar reason. They alleged that Jewish tradition allowed Jews to perjure themselves in court, and, to protect the integrity of the legal system, they advocated banning Jews from the judiciary and making Jewish witnesses take a special oath, different from that given to Gentiles. The antisemitic press occasionally hinted at the need for an even more drastic measure: the prohibition of sworn testimonies from Jewish witnesses altogether when such testimonies might help other Jews or harm Gentiles. By using the issue of perjury to justify similar discriminatory judicial practices, colonialists and antisemites adopted a common strategy to ensure the supremacy of whites and Gentiles, respectively, by disempowering blacks and Jews in legal matters. An examination of the similarities between the rhetoric of the antisemitic advocates and colonial defenders of such practices also demonstrates, once again, a merging across the antisemitic and colonial movements of representations of Jews and black Africans.

Articles attacking the trustworthiness of Jews appeared frequently during the 1890s in the antisemitic newspapers the *Deutsch-Soziale Blätter,* the *Staatsbürger-Zeitung,* the *Deutsche Wacht,* and the *Reichsgeldmonopol* (also known as the *Antisemitisches Volksblatt*).[113] Many of these articles support their allegations of a Jewish culture of deceit by pointing to the *kol nidrei,* an ancient saying found in the Talmud and recited in synagogue on the eve of Yom Kippur.[114] Dating back at least as far as the ninth century, the *kol nidrei*—whose author and original purpose are unclear—consisted in its original form of a statement declaring null and void vows made by its reciters during the preceding year. According to one historian, the *kol nidrei* became a "hallowed folk custom" throughout most of the Jewish world by the Middle Ages, during which time it also was amended to refer to vows made in the future, although this change was not universally ac-

---

112. Christian von Bornhaupt, "Die Vereidigung von Eingebornen in den deutschen Schutzgebieten," *Koloniale Rundschau,* July 1909: 427–32.

113. The *Reichsgeldmonopol* was published in Cassel. Ludwig Werner served as lead editor from 1890 to 1893.

114. In his informative history of the *kol nidrei,* Stuart Weinberg Gerhson argued that the saying cannot be classified as a prayer, because God is never mentioned (Gerhson, *Kol Nidrei: Its Origins, Developments, and Significance* [Northvale, NJ: Jason Aronson Inc., 1994]).

cepted.[115] Despite the insistence of religious leaders that only vows made to oneself were annulled, and not vows made to God or other people, the medieval Jewish laity commonly assumed the saying's power to nullify interpersonal vows, including those made in legal situations. Aware of this belief, medieval Gentiles forced Jews to swear a special oath in courts of law—sometimes accompanied by a humiliating rite—renouncing the *kol nidrei*'s power. Despite the fact that the *kol nidrei* was rewritten by reform Jews in Hanover in 1870 in a way that transformed its declaration nullifying oaths into a statement confirming them—a rendition that became the standard version in all European Liberal and Reform prayer books until 1929—the saying provided fodder for antisemites throughout the colonial era in their campaign to revoke Jewish emancipation.

For example, when Dresden's *Deutsche Wacht* reported on an instance of perjury involving a Romanian Jew in a German criminal court in May 1892, the newspaper insisted that Jewish religious law endorsed such behavior. According to the report, the individual on trial convinced a family member to provide a false alibi, and the *Deutsche Wacht* insisted that the Talmud actually allowed one Jew to commit perjury in another's favor. "This involuntarily evokes the question," the *Deutsche Wacht* stated, "can, under such circumstances, one Jew testify in court for another? Can people with the morality of thieves be permitted to hold titular offices or administer justice?"[116] That same year, the German Antisemites' League—an organization formed by Liebermann von Sonnenberg at an antisemites' congress in Kassel in 1886—published a translation of the *kol nidrei* titled "The Value of Jewish Oaths" and distributed it on Yom Kippur in Cologne and Friedeberg R. M.[117] Almost two decades later, the *Staatsbürger-Zeitung* printed a front-page article insisting that the Jew's "religious persuasion" sanctioned perjury and that, as a result, "the Aryan is delivered to him hand over foot" in legal matters. The *Staatsbürger-Zeitung* denounced what it called the "immoral

---

115. "All vows, prohibitive vows, oaths, vows of dedication, *konam*-vows, *konas*-vows, and equivalent terms that we have vowed, sworn, declared, and imposed upon ourselves from this day of atonement until the next day of atonement, may it come upon us for good. Regarding them all, we regret them. Let them all be released, forgiven, erased, null and void. They are not valid nor are they in force. Our vows are not vows. Our prohibitive vows are not prohibitive vows. Our oaths are not oaths" (Gershon, *Kol Nidrei*, ix).

116. "Schlagender Beweis von jüdischer Unmoral," *Deutsche Wacht: Wochenschrift für nationales Deutschtum und sociale Reform,* May 15, 1892.

117. "Der Werth des jüdischen Eides," *Mittheilungen aus dem Verein zur Abwehr des Antisemitismus* 2 (1892): 309–10; "In Köln," *Mittheilungen* 2 (1892): 339.

conceptions of Judaism," labeling them "a serious danger for the people and state that must be fought with the most radical measures because, together, they undermine the most primitive rules in the people's existence."[118]

Near-contemporaneous discussions in colonial newspapers about the value of the sworn testimonies of indigenous Africans parallel the deliberations over the *kol nidrei* in the antisemitic press. Unlike antisemites, however, colonialists defended discriminatory practices already in place from moderates who demanded a more equitable treatment of blacks and whites in legal matters. The most serious challenge to the practice of denying indigenous witnesses the right to testify under oath came in March 1909 in the form of state secretary Bernhard Dernburg's stated opposition to the practice.[119] Dernburg's belief that a prosperous colonial economy lay in the encouragement and facilitation of indigenous agricultural production led him to champion a more equitable treatment of the colonized, and, in this vein, he opposed the current judicial custom. Speaking before the Reichstag, Dernburg insisted that he was "especially of the opinion that the present judicial practice where a native cannot be administered an oath is actually not very practical. . . . I cannot understand why a Christian native should not be allowed to take an oath," Dernburg proclaimed, "and it is also not understood why one cannot give a heathen native a formula by which he says: I swear to have told the pure truth and to have withheld nothing, and I am further aware that such and such punishments may befall me. This is indeed necessary to sharpen the people's conscience and elevate esteem for the court of law."[120]

Responses to Dernburg were quick in coming. Like antisemites in their depictions of Jews, procolonial activists described blacks as inveterate liars who manipulated the judicial system to the detriment of Germans. Deputies from the National Liberal Party warned Dernburg of the black African's penchant for lying; one deputy proclaimed that "the Negro takes the circumnavigation of the truth to be a sign of cleverness,"[121] while another spoke of the easy suggestibility and childlike nature of blacks.[122] Re-

---

118. "Jüdische Eide. Eine sensationalle Feststellung," *Staatsbürger-Zeitung,* September 3, 1909.

119. However, deliberations in the colonial press over the value of the sworn testimonies of "native witnesses" predated 1909. See "Zur Eingeborenenfrage. II.," *Deutsch-Südwesafrikanische Zeitung,* November 3, 1903, and Altera Pars., "Nochmals zur Eingeborenenfrage," *Deutsch-Südwestafrikanische Zeitung,* December 8, 1903.

120. *Sten. Ber.* XII/I/217, March 2, 1909, 7271.

121. *Sten. Ber.* XII/I/218, March 3, 1909, 7289.

122. Ibid., 7298. The speaker here was Dr. Semler.

sponses from the colonial press are much more strident. The *Windhuker Nachrichten* printed a letter from "an Afrikaner" classifying Dernburg's recent statements as "frightful." The author insisted that "every Negro would lie about the color of the sky if he deems it to his advantage, or if he believes that, by so doing, he could cast aspersions on an unpleasant white."[123] The *Deutsch-Ostafrikanische Zeitung* echoed these sentiments, insisting that colonial judges "know precisely from their own rich experience that a member of the colored races does not have the smallest moral misgiving to lie if he can win his trial."[124]

Other procolonial advocates who sharply opposed Dernburg included the conservative *Neue Preußische Zeitung* and the influential German Colonial Society. Claiming that "the Negro lacks all prerequisites for appreciating the sanctity of oaths, because his propensity for untruthfulness, for lies, appears indestructible," the *Neue Preußische Zeitung* argued that the idea of allowing blacks to testify under oath courted disaster: "The white man would be at the black's mercy, since he is not restrained by honor or a feeling of duty, and the black would know how to make the most of this situation." The *Neue Preußische Zeitung* also warned that "the policy of establishing an equality of rights between blacks and whites must lead to the destruction of whites or their expulsion from the colonies."[125] Equally dire predictions came from the Colonial Society. "With the permitting of oaths, the white man would be placed completely in the black man's hand," stated one society member at the organization's annual meeting, "since he would pay no heed to the punishments for perjury."[126]

By painting blacks and Jews as unscrupulous liars whose only loyalties lay with their own kind, colonialists and antisemites argued in nearly identical terms for a similar goal: the preservation, or establishment, of a system of discrimination in German courts of law that would enforce, or create, a racial hierarchy. Like the advocates of race war, both the supporters of a revocation of Jewish legal equality and the defenders of current colonial practices justified the subjugation of Jews and blacks, respectively, as a defensive measure against the machinations of an unscrupulous and

---

123. "Deutsch-Südwestafrika. Der Negereid nach Dernburgs Anschauung," *Windhuker Nachrichten: Unabhängige Zeitung für Deutsch-Südwestafrika*, April 17, 1909.

124. "Der Eid des Farbigen," *Deutsch-Ostafrikanische Zeitung*, April 21, 1909.

125. "Nochmals der Eid des Farbigen," *Deutsch-Ostafrikanische Zeitung*, May 1, 1909. Here, the *DOZ* reprinted excerpts from the *Neue Preußische Zeitung.*

126. "Hauptversammlung der Deutschen Kolonial-Gesellschaft. III.," *Deutsch-Ostafrikanische Zeitung*, July 31, 1909. The speaker was Dr. Hindorf, and the *DOZ* paraphrased his statement.

threatening racial Other. They appealed to a similar fear, namely, the possibility that Aryans might be delivered to Jews "hand over foot," or that white men might be at "the black's mercy" in legal affairs. In short, they spoke the same language. The important difference was that colonialists defended a system of subjugation already in place, while antisemites argued with not a little desperation for its creation.

In *A Jewish-German Embassy,* Carl Paasch wrote that genocide was "out of the question, at least for us Germans" as a practical solution to the so-called Jewish problem. But he added—half jokingly—that such an action might be entrusted to the black population of the United States: "A joker opines that one would have liked to export them to America with the upmost speed before the MacKinley Bill was expanded to the Jews. There, one would have been inclined to, perhaps, call the Negro to the cultural task of taking care of slaying the Jews, which we resist."

Paasch did not continue the jest. After making this statement, he then discussed in earnest what he saw as a more realistic course of action: sending the Jews to New Guinea, which he deemed "large enough and suited to receive and nourish the world's entire Jewish people."[127] Despite its brevity, however, Paasch's joke about allocating the monstrous task of annihilating the Jews to American blacks is indicative of a trend in antisemitic writing contemporary to the colonial era: namely, attributing to blacks and Jews a similar inhumanity based on common characteristics and thinking of both groups together. The following sections show that images of blacks and Jews merged not just across, but also within, the antisemitic and colonial movements, and that this was strongest in the writings of procolonial antisemites.

For example, Siegfried Passarge's depictions of black Africans smack, undeniably, of antisemitism. To a remarkable degree, the negative characteristics commonly ascribed by antisemites to Jews are transferred in Passarge's works to the generic "Negro" or "black." Blacks appear in Passarge's books as highly intelligent but uncreative and immoral beings, possessed of a hatred for whites. Much like converted Jews, black Christians are depicted as insincere converts, moved to conversion "from mo-

---

127. Carl Paasch, *Der jüdische Dämon I,* section 3 of *Eine jüdisch-deutsch Gesandtschaft,* 252. The "MacKinley Bill" is undoubtedly a reference to the McKinley Act that became law in the United States in October 1890. The act imposed extremely high tariffs on goods imported into the United States.

tives of self-interest."[128] Blacks are also presented as incapable of self-rule, lacking the "character," if not the intelligence, of maintaining their own successful, independent states.[129] Passarge's memoir, *Adamaua,* even evokes antisemitic rhetoric about Jewish parasitism by comparing blacks to "ivy" on a tree, forever in need of the superstructure of white culture and governance.[130] As seen in chapter 1, Passarge identified black Christians as especially dangerous—"a hidden opponent" as opposed to "an open enemy"—a sentiment that mimics antisemitic thinking about Jewish converts; in *The Jews and Modern Capitalism,* for example, the antisemitic economist Werner Sombart warned at length of the historical threat posed to Gentiles by what he called "crypto-Jews" who "passed as Christians and Mohammedans."[131]

Passarge's attitude toward acculturated blacks evokes antisemitism as well. He expressed contempt in *Adamaua* for blacks who adopted Western ways, deriding them as caricatures while attributing a "moral superiority" to those who retained their traditional clothes and customs.[132] Years later, Werner Sombart wrote similarly of "assimilation Jews." He denounced them as "yes-men and sneaks" while identifying "the honorable National Jew" as "an entirely different fellow, one that a person may hate, but nevertheless must have respect for."[133] Like antisemites, Passarge also fixated on mannerisms, insinuating that the behavioral traits of Western-educated blacks betrayed the resilience of their African characters. He made this point in *Adamaua* while recounting a visit to a court session in Lagos during his trip to western Africa: "The white chief judge at the podium, at his feet the black lawyers, everything as by us. The lawyers are all very educated gentlemen who have studied in England. . . . But their behavior! These giggles and whispers, this foolishness and self-entertainment, like schoolboys behind the back of the teacher!"[134] Fifteen years later, the antisemitic *Deutsch-Soziale Blätter*—quoting from the *Kölner Lokal-Anzeiger*—gave a remarkably similar description of state secretary Bernhard Dernburg's conduct in the Reichstag: "His thumbs in the sleeve holes

---

128. Siegfried Passarge, *Adamaua: Bericht über die Expedition des Deutschen-Kamerun Komitees in den Jahren 1893/94* (Berlin: Dietrich Reimer, 1895), 529.
129. Ibid., 532.
130. Ibid.
131. Sombart, *The Jews,* 8.
132. Passarge, *Adamaua,* 530.
133. Werner Sombart et al., *Judentaufen* (Munich: Georg Müller, 1912), 16–17.
134. Passarge, *Adamaua,* 530–31.

of his vest—that is his favorite position—he took care to move back and forth near the speaker and to, no doubt, immediately work on his critic with laughter, shakes of the head, shrugs of the shoulders, long looks at the assembly, and interruptions." The *Deutsch-Soziale Blätter* concluded, "Baptism has, therefore, not been able to expel racial characteristics with Dernburg as well."[135] As with the black lawyers, an undignified lack of composure was seen to signify the persistence of racial Otherness.

Numerous examples exist of a similar coming-together of perceptions of and attitudes toward blacks and Jews in the antisemitic press. Here, the enthusiastic support for colonialism among the leaders of the antisemitic movement translated into a close following of colonial developments. Like Siegfried Passarge, the staff and contributing readerships transferred many of the negative characteristics commonly ascribed to Jews onto black Africans. In an article on Jewish criminality in 1902, the antisemitic *Neue Preußische Zeitung* declared that Jews "can only live as either oppressed or oppressors" and that "for the Jew it is not possible to respect the rights of another person equal to his own rights."[136] This parallels quite closely the picture of black Africans painted in Friedrich Lange's *Deutsche Welt* during the Herero War. While arguing for an uncompromising domination of the African colonized, one contributor insisted in an eighteen-page article in 1904 that "the Kaffer understands his relationship to ourselves as the relationship of master to servant, or the reverse. As long as he had the means, he exploited to his ability the white trader and abused him in certain cases."[137] This accords with the opinions of colonial radicals like Woldemar Schütze and antisemitic colonialists like Carl Peters. Both men accused blacks of subscribing to a might-makes-right philosophy and being incapable of assuming any other role than that of the oppressor or the oppressed.[138]

---

135. "Rassen-Eigentümlichkeiten," *Deutsch-Soziale Blätter,* May 21, 1910.

136. "Das Judenthum in Amerika," *Neue Preußische Zeitung,* November 29, 1902, morning edition. Quoted in Eric A. Johnson, *Urbanization and Crime: Germany 1871–1914* (Cambridge: Cambridge University Press, 1995), 82.

137. Fr. Henkel, "Der Hereroaufstand. Entweder—oder!" *Deutsche Welt: Wochenschrift der Deutschen Zeitung,* July 31, 1904.

138. Schütze wrote in *Schwarz gegen Weiss:* "The Negro makes unlimited and ruthless use of the right of the stronger in the struggle for existence. The victor in this battle becomes the master, the vanquished, the slave. The Negro only esteems those who are stronger who seize him with clenched fist at the nape of the neck and, as the vanquished, would see it as nothing less than a matter of course if he were made into a slave; since as victor, he would do nothing else. The Negro despises the weak and handles him with callous hardness as his unlimited property, as something that has in reality lost its right of existence" (Schütze, *Schwarz gegen*

The antisemitic press ascribed many other qualities in common to blacks and Jews. These included an inability to speak proper German, an obscene and ridiculous love of finery, and an inherent laziness, among others. Concerning the first, antisemites had long accused Jews of failing to master the German language.[139] Like the *völkisch* ideologue Adolf Bartels, who insisted that "a Jew will never learn proper German"—and who wrote of the persistence of a "Jewish style" of speech even among the offspring of interfaith marriages—German antisemites identified the alleged tenacity of Jewish accents and intonations as a signifier of permanent racial Otherness.[140] Similarly, some colonialists attributed blacks with an inability to speak good German or to learn the language altogether, and these myths made their way into the antisemitic press. An article in the *Hammer* in 1912 supportive of colonial bans on interracial marriages stresses the reality and significance of the racial differences between blacks and whites. In this vein, its author declared that "a black will never learn German" given the difficulty of the language.[141]

Likewise, allegations made in antisemitic publications of an excessive love of finery and an inherent laziness among blacks echo familiar antisemitic refrains. For example, in October 1909, an article on Liberia appeared in the *Deutsche Welt,* painting a ridiculous picture of its inhabitants. The author attributed Liberians with a dislike for hard work and a penchant for fantastic adornment—in particular, a love of shiny medals and colorful uniforms by the Liberian army.[142] The following month, another contributor wrote of a Jewish predilection for "haggling, trading, and usury" and a penchant for "tasteless ostentation."[143] Discussions among antisemites about the alleged immutability of African nature mirror anti-Jewish rhetoric as well. Friedrich Lange insinuated in the *Deutsche Welt* in 1905 that Jews retain their "outer and inner" racial characteristics

---

Weiss, 29–30). Carl Peters articulated similar sentiments in his 1911 essay, "Die Rassenfrage in Südafrika" (Carl Peters, *Gesammelte Schrifte,* vol. 3, ed. Walter Frank [Munich: C. H. Beck'sche Verlagsbuchhandlung, 1944], 422–26).

139. Sander L. Gilman, *The Case of Sigmund Freud: Medicine and Identity at the Fin de Siècle* (Baltimore: Johns Hopkins University Press, 1993), 26–37.

140. Adolf Bartels, "Zur Rassenforschung," *Deutsche Welt: Wochenschrift der Deutschen Zeitung,* April 10, 1904.

141. "Reine Rasse," *Hammer: Blätter für deutschen Sinn* 11 (1912): 438.

142. Hans Fischer, "Liberia," *Deutsche Welt: Wochenschrift der Deutschen Zeitung,* October 3, 1909.

143. Dr. Otto Schmidt-Gibichenfels, "Das religiöse Problem unserer Zeit," *Deutsche Welt: Wochenschrift der Deutschen Zeitung,* November 28, 1909.

despite "environmental and educational influences."[144] Three years later, the *Deutsch-Soziale Blätter* proclaimed in a lead article about black Africans that "even a centuries-long education is not capable of making a European out of them, although they, like ourselves, bear a human face."[145]

Images of blacks and Jews also merged in the antisemitic press in a much more direct fashion; articles and editorials explicitly linking the two appeared throughout the colonial era in all the major antisemitic newspapers and magazines. By comparing blacks to Jews directly, and the racial situation in colonial Africa or the American South to that in Germany, newspapers like the *Deutsch-Soziale Blätter,* the *Deutsche Welt,* and the *Staatsbürger-Zeitung* suggested the applicability at home of lessons about race learned abroad, especially in the colonies. These lessons dealt with the reality and significance of racial difference, the dangers of race mixing, and both the need for and possibility of a thorough domestic *Rassenpolitik* like that implemented in German Africa.

From the standpoint of those who called for a revocation of Jewish civic equality on the basis of Jewish racial Otherness, the examples of German Africa and the American South were useful in supporting the veracity of their claims about the importance of racial difference. This was because the reality of race and its implications seemed more apparent in these contexts; even the uninitiated could perceive the physical and cultural differences that separated blacks from whites, whereas the divide between Jews and Gentiles was less manifest. Accordingly, one tactic used during the colonial era by the staff and contributing readership of the antisemitic press was to make passing references to blacks in antisemitic articles. This had the effect of hammering home the point that Jews were racially alien, unassimilable to the German ethnic nation, no different in this respect from black Africans.

The *Deutsche Welt* used this tactic repeatedly in the months and years following the outbreak of the Herero War, when, after prolonged disinterest, public attention returned to colonial matters. In April 1904, the newspaper printed a long front-page article by Adolf Bartels defending the im-

---

144. F. L., "Unbehagen über das Rasseproblem," *Deutsche Welt: Wochenschrift der Deutschen Zeitung,* January 22, 1905.

145. Adolf Stein, "Die Bastardgefahr," *Deutsch-Soziale Blätter,* July 8, 1908.

portance and validity of racial research and, in this context, discussing at length the persistence of Jewish racial characteristics. Bartels argued that the physical markers of race were, in fact, less permanent and important than mental and spiritual features. With this in mind, he ended the first section of his article by explicitly likening blacks and Jews: "Indeed, they are also men, but that a Jew will become a true German poet and one of the Hereros a professor of Ethnology in the not-too-distant future is, in the end, surely to be rejected, despite the declared 'insignificant difference in the mental developmental capabilities of the human races.'"[146] The following year, another contributor to the *Deutsche Welt* also mobilized the image of blacks to strengthen his case for Jewish difference. Responding to an article in a literary magazine written by a self-proclaimed German of Jewish descent, the author contested the nomenclature "Jewish-German." He argued that this was an oxymoron, tantamount to the term "Mongolian-German" or "Negro-Teuton."[147]

Another tactic used by the antisemitic press was to discuss Jews within reports on race relations between blacks and whites, effectively the reverse of the above strategy. Frequently, these remarks took the form of short antisemitic asides but were occasionally more substantial. For example, in June 1891, the *Deutsch-Soziale Blätter* printed a brief report on the travel essays of the German playwright and publisher Paul Lindau, who had recently visited the American South. The *Blätter* noted that Lindau's descriptions of "the Negro question" in Louisiana closely resembled what it deemed "our Jewish Question." To make the point, it printed an excerpt from one of Lindau's reports but replaced the words "Negro" with "Jew" and "whites" with "Germans."

> In general, the Jews do not appear able to surpass a certain level of development and haven't achieved anything distinguished in scholarship or industry. It is now a fact that the Jews increase more numerously than the Germans. Under these conditions, it can become truly quite precarious if they achieve political dominance, constitutionally, with their numerical superiority. All Germans regardless of party differences share in the opinion (would they do this, indeed!) that to allow the Jews the fair exercise of their constitutional rights is completely

146. Bartels, "Zur Rassenforschung."
147. K. M., "Unbequemes Rassenbewußtsein," *Deutsche Welt: Wochenschrift der Deutschen Zeitung,* April 30, 1905.

impossible, since that would mean in truth making laziness and a lack of education the mistress of intelligence and industry. With knowledge of this undeniable truth, it would now be the easiest and most natural thing to do to put an end to this unhealthy state of affairs and replace the questionable paragraph concerning equal rights with one that agrees with, and is more truthful to, the situation.

The *Blätter* insisted that altering the text in this way transformed it into "an accurate picture of how it appears in our Germany and also the means for how it can become better."[148]

References to Jews in articles on the colonies increased in frequency with the initiation of hostilities in German Southwest Africa. The commencement of fighting in early 1904 galvanized the editors of the *Deutsch-Soziale Blätter* to impress upon their audience the relevance of colonial experiences for antisemitism. In September 1904, the *Blätter* printed a front-page article titled "A Word over our Colonial Policy" that intimates the need to treat Jews like the rebelling Hereros. Written by the newspaper's editors, the piece presents, and then responds to, a lengthy letter from a reader who argued for the application of "Christian neighborly love" toward the indigenous rebels. The editors rejected this position as excessively "humane," and they faulted what they deemed as the government's "all-too-great compliance" not only toward blacks in Africa but also toward Poles and Jews at home. They classified the application of Christian love toward non-Germans as a type of "religious fanaticism" and declared the "call to Christianity" by colonial critics to be a way to weaken the German people "be it vis-à-vis oriental or African blacks." By using the term *oriental blacks,* the editors deliberately conflated Jews and Africans, intimating the need in Germany for the same type of "thorough" retaliation, one unrestrained by Christian values, that they recommended for Southwest Africa.[149]

Many other examples exist of antisemitic asides inserted into reports on race relations between blacks and whites. The *Deutsch-Soziale Blätter* used this ploy again in August 1905 when it reported on the public whipping of a white laborer by a black man in German Southwest Africa. The punishment was ordered by a German officer on account of lèse-majesté, and it caused an uproar in the colonial press. After voicing its own indig-

---

148. "Paul Lindau und die Louisiana-Neger," *Deutsch-Soziale Blätter,* June 21, 1891.
149. "Ein Wort über unsere Kolonialpolitik," *Deutsch-Soziale Blätter,* September 14, 1904.

nation over the event, the *Deutsch-Soziale Blätter* stated its refusal to accept "not only the black man, but also Jews as judges of our people."[150] The *Hammer* magazine followed suit the following year when it suggested adopting for domestic purposes the outlook of colonial radicals concerning race and education. The newspaper printed the opinion of an official from East Africa that Africans must "learn to do bodily work" before learning to read and write in order to combat their "inborn laziness." The *Hammer* concluded that this advice was valid "not only for the savages in Africa, but also for the savages at home with us" in Germany.[151] In these different ways, the antisemitic press linked blacks and Jews together, implying the applicability at home of lessons learned abroad about racial domination.

Antisemites did this most aggressively with the issue of race mixing toward the very end of empire. For those who subscribed to Arthur de Gobineau's theory of racial degeneration, protecting the purity of the German racial stock from infusions of Jewish blood was at the very heart of antisemitism. Accordingly, denunciations of interfaith marriage filled the antisemitic press, and revolutionary antisemites like Friedrich Lange advocated specific strategies to elevate public awareness about the importance of racial purity.[152] With the outbreak of war in German Southwest Africa in 1904 and the shipment of thousands of young German soldiers to the territory, racial antisemites also became highly concerned with race mixing between blacks and whites. From April 1904 through the summer of 1912, no fewer than thirty articles and reports discussing interracial mixing in the colonies appeared in the *Deutsche Welt,* the *Deutsch-Soziale Blätter,* and the *Hammer* magazine. When the Reichstag passed the resolution of May 1912 contesting the prohibitions in the colonies of interracial marriages, the antisemitic press responded with outrage, printing a series of articles tying the campaign against race mixing in colonial Africa to that against interfaith marriages at home between Jews and Gentile Germans.

Before May 1912, however, only a few articles in the antisemitic press made this connection explicitly. One early example appeared in the *Deutsche Welt* in a 1904 piece titled "Racial Shame," authored by "F. L.," who was most likely Friedrich Lange, the newspaper's editor. Referring,

---

150. "Rassenehre," *Deutsch-Soziale Blätter,* August 9, 1905.

151. "Die Schul-Bildung und die Wilden," *Hammer: Blätter für deutschen Sinn* 5 (1906): 600.

152. Lange suggested mandating that every German district display records of family lineages and alert the public when community members married non-Aryans (Friedrich Lange, *Reines Deutschtum,* 246).

perhaps, to a recent essay in the newspaper concerning mixed marriages in German Southwest Africa, Lange opened his article by noting that "we have recently illuminated this theme [of racial shame] for our fellow countrymen in the colonies as seriously and clearly as it must be illuminated." Following this, Lange complained about German "indifference" toward "racial shame" at home and cited instances of Germans marrying Asians. He then quoted at length from an article in the weekly newspaper *Der Deutsche* whose author approvingly discussed the prohibition of black and white intermarriage among the Boers in southern Africa. In his ensuing commentary, Lange asked of the author, "what does he think about the marriages between Germans and Jews?" "For ourselves," Lange continued a little further down, "it is not doubtful for a moment that the idea of 'racial shame,' if it were to be legally determined, could not ignore the issue of Jewish mixed marriages." Lange admitted, however, that any domestic law against intermarriages with Jews would be a long time in coming. As a more realistic solution, he proposed passing laws requiring each community to keep close records of everyone's ancestry. This would, he reasoned, help raise German racial consciousness while permitting racially conscious individuals to avoid those with "non-Aryan blood."[153]

Likely as a result of these and other public statements by antisemites, it was quite evident to the political opponents of antisemitism well before 1912 that antisemitic opposition to race mixing in the colonies also extended to interfaith marriages, and that when antisemites raised the former issue, the latter was never far from their minds. This was made clear during a Reichstag debate on foreign policy matters in March 1905, when Count Ludwig zu Reventlow of the German Social Party raised the issue of race mixing in the colonies before the legislature for the very first time. The deputy voiced his hope that the German chancellor would give "wholly extra-special attention to the handling of the racial question for the coming year." He spoke of the necessity of preventing "with fire and sword" the creation of a "black-white *Mischungsrasse*" and insisted on punishing "every sexual relationship" between blacks and whites.[154] Although Reventlow made no mention of unions between Jews and Gentiles, the Social Democratic leader August Bebel accused him the following day of also

---

153. F. L. "Rassenschande," *Deutsche Welt: Wochenschrift der Deutschen Zeitung,* November 17, 1904.

154. *Sten. Ber.* XI/I/164, March 15, 1905, 5275. Reventlow entered antisemitic politics when he became the vice-chairman of the Agrarian League for Schleswig-Holstein in 1901. He served as a Reichstag deputy for the German Socials for several years before his death in May 1906.

having designs on interfaith marriages: "if the Herr Count has such a feeling for the purity of German nationality . . . I assume that, according to the antisemitic disposition that the Herr Count possesses, he is also ready to raise an emphatic objection against the mixing of Jews and Germans." The antisemitic deputies nodded in agreement, and Bebel noted their silent affirmation for the record.[155] The antisemites then confirmed this sentiment more directly. That same day, Otto Böckler of the German Reform Party noted while defending Reventlow's statements that "mixes of Jews and Germans are very often childless" and that "a smaller or less valuable generation arises from them." Böckler also cited racial strife in Asia and Africa as proof that the twentieth century was to be "the century of *Rassenkampfe*," or racial struggles, while the 1800s had been "the century of the contest of nationalities."[156]

Antisemites continued to warn against the dangers of race mixing in the intervening years before 1912. But until the passing of the Reichstag resolution condemning colonial bans on interracial marriages, discussions about race mixing in the colonies remained largely separate from discussions of the Jewish Question. Reflections on the one in the antisemitic press and elsewhere, however, often followed reflections on the other, indicating a relationship between the two from the antisemitic perspective and, perhaps, a subtle attempt to link them. For example, in June 1905 a lengthy article by Friedrich Lange titled "The Race Question in German East Africa" appeared in the *Deutsche Welt* that speaks approvingly of the increased attention paid in the colony to the dangers of race mixing.[157] In another piece on racialism printed several months later, Lange predicted that the current strengthening of "racial-thinking" among "civilized humanity" in general would eventually prove "fatal" to the Jews.[158] In January 1906, a short report appeared in the *Deutsch-Soziale Blätter* warning of the "*Verjudung* [Judaizing] of the Christian German population through mixed marriages" in Berlin.[159] Then in March, Wilhelm Lattmann of the German Social Party raised in the Reichstag the issue of race mixing in the

---

155. "The gentlemen antisemites corroborate this understanding with nods of the head," Bebel stated (*Sten. Ber.* XI/I/165, March 16, 1905, 5292).

156. Ibid., 5311.

157. F. L., "Die Rassenfrage in Deutsch-Ostafrika," *Deutsche Welt: Wochenschrift der Deutschen Zeitung,* June 4, 1905.

158. F. L., "Der Rassegedanke am Toilettentisch," *Deutsche Welt: Wochenschrift der Deutschen Zeitung,* October 15, 1905.

159. "Die Verjudung der christlichen deutschen Einwohnerschaft durch Mischehen," *Deutsch-Soziale Blätter,* January 24, 1906.

colonies, something that parliamentary deputies had ignored since Reventlow's speech. Lattmann spoke of a pressing need to take the *"Mischlings
frage"* in German Southwest Africa seriously now that the colony contained "a white army of over 10,000 men." He also noted with approval
that the evangelical kindergarten in Windhuk had recently closed its doors
to half-white children.[160]

The staff and readership of the *Hammer* magazine also dealt separately during these years with the issues of race mixing at home and
abroad, for the most part. One exception is a letter printed in November
1905. Reacting to Reventlow's speech, its author acknowledged the alleged
problem of race mixing between blacks and whites, but insisted that unions
with Jews were more dangerous, because mulattos knew their place.[161]
Most other deliberations in the *Hammer* about race mixing treat the situations in Germany and colonial Africa separately, but express similar concerns and use similar language. In April 1906, the *Hammer* reported with
approval on the intensification of social discrimination against the German husbands of indigenous women in settler society in Southwest
Africa.[162] The same issue printed a letter warning of an ongoing "transformation" of Germany through "Jewish blood" due to a high rate of illegitimate sex between Jews and Gentiles.[163] Two years later, another reader
warned of Germany's inevitable Negroification. This contributor wrote of
the appearance on German streets of "black nannies, servants, waiters,
porters and workers," even "mulatto-children" attending school, and also
of black officers in the military.[164] He concluded that the *"Vernegerung* of
our people and army" would be colonialism's probable outcome.[165]

In the aftermath of the Reichstag debate of May 1912, antisemites
linked the case against mixed-race unions in the colonies with that against
marriages between Jews and Gentiles much more openly. Although the
passing of the resolution did not actually change the situation on the
ground in German Africa due to the Reichstag's lack of control over colo-

---

160. *Sten. Ber.* XI/II/73, March 23, 1906, 2228.

161. Hans Heinrich von Schweißel, "Zum Kapitel 'Schamlose Ehen,'" *Hammer: Blätter
für deutschen Sinn* 4 (1905): 525.

162. "Die Menschen sind doch nicht alle gleich!" *Hammer: Blätter für deutschen Sinn* 5
(1906): 247.

163. G. B., "Zur Frage der Ein-Ehe," *Hammer: Blätter für deutschen Sinn* 5 (1906): 245.

164. Alb. Grimpen, "Die Negerfrage in Deutschland," *Hammer: Blätter für deutschen
Sinn* 7 (1908): 147.

165. Ibid., 149.

nial policy, antisemites were dismayed, interpreting the event as a defeat for the principle of *Rassenpolitik*.[166] The episode was especially galling for political antisemites, because several members of the small parliamentary group known as the Economic Union, which contained most of the deputies from the antisemitic political parties, had voted with the majority.[167] One Christian Social deputy, the Protestant pastor Reinhard Mumm, had even argued in the resolution's favor, insisting that banning interracial marriages in German Africa was impractical so long as neighboring colonial powers did not do the same.[168] In their response to the resolution's passage, contributors to the antisemitic press were particularly concerned with rejecting the argument advanced by some that the Christian status of the black spouses of white settlers trumped racial differences and legitimated interracial marriage. In the months following the May debate, some contributors also went further than before in linking blacks and Jews by attributing the latter with an African heritage.

Two articles printed in late May express the first concern most strongly. The earlier piece appeared in the *Staatsburger-Zeitung* and was composed by the *völkisch* ideologue Heinrich Pudor, who looked with disfavor on the very idea of colonial empire.[169] In his editorial, Pudor attacked colonialism for facilitating what he called "race-mixing between a master race and a slave race," more specifically, "between Germans and Africans." He also accused the members of the Economic Union who voted for the resolution of betraying the essence of antisemitism, namely,

---

166. The Reichstag's power over colonial affairs was limited to rejecting or approving colonial budgets.

167. The Economic Union (*Wirtschaftliche Vereinigung*) came into being after the parliamentary elections of 1903, when the antisemites managed to win only eleven seats. The reconstituted German Social Party (previously the German Social Reform Party) formed the Union as a small multiparty bloc in order to gain *Fraktion* status, but to do so, it had to accept a number of deputies from outside the three main antisemitic political parties (the German Social, Christian Social, and German Reform Parties).

168. "Rundschau," *Mittheilungen* 22 (1912): 82.

169. Heinrich Pudor (1865–1943) was a prolific essayist and publisher from Dresden who espoused nudism, *völkisch* nationalism, and racial antisemitism. Most of his writings were self-published, such as his 1912 book, *Deutschland für die Deutschen. Vorarbeiten zu Gesetzen gegen die jüdische Ansiedlung in Deutschland.* According to Thomas Adam, Pudor was an occasional speaker at German Social Party meetings, but his effect on the antisemitic and *völkisch* movements "can only be estimated with difficulty." Adam concluded that Pudor was less influential than his rival, Theodor Fritsch, who made a better living from his antisemitic writings (Adam, "Heinrich Pudor—Lebensreformer, Antisemit und Verleger," in *Das bewegte Buch. Buchwesen und soziale, nationale und kulturelle Bewegungen um 1900,* ed. Mark Lehmstedt and Andreas Herzog [Wiesbaden: Harrassowitz Verlag, 1999], 183–96).

"keeping the race pure," and he lamented that unions between "Germans and Negroes" were now "fundamentally supported." Pudor noted that marriages between Jews and Gentiles had been "punished with death" during the Middle Ages, a period that he classified as "not so dark as is always imagined." He concluded by insisting that the issue before the Reichstag was "not a question of belief, but rather a purely racial question," as with marriages between Jews and Gentile Germans. "If we reject the latter," Pudor wrote, "we must also reject the former."[170]

An article in the *Deutsch-Soziale Blätter* the following day makes a similar argument. Its author, identified as B. W., also attacked the idea that conversion legitimated interracial marriage. After insisting that the Reichstag resolution revealed "the enormous devastation caused by the miserable idea of equality for all 'wingless bipeds,'" B. W. asked his audience to imagine what would happen if a German farmer circumcised his child. "Is he for this reason, perchance, a Jew? Will the Jewish community taken him seriously? Will his blood have changed? Not true, gentlemen," B. W. replied, but then noted, sarcastically, that baptizing "Negroes" transformed them into "valid members" of the German community. In his concluding paragraph, B. W. intimated that fear of an increase in German racial consciousness had motivated the parliamentary supporters of the Reichstag resolution. "Once the German becomes aware of his rank, of his racial responsibility," B. W. wrote, "then the domination of the Jews will be over."[171]

Antisemites continued in the coming months to link racial policies in German Africa with their own domestic antisemitic agendas. The *Deutsch-Soziale Blätter* printed another such article in June. Its author, Wardein, noted with approval that the German Colonial Society had disavowed the Reichstag resolution, and he quoted at length from the organization's public statements. Wardein then compared the dangers of race mixing at home and in the colonies. Referring to the common belief in colonial circles that the offspring of mixed-race unions took leadership positions during indigenous uprisings, Warden asked: "Is it different with us? Isn't it the sad *Mischlinge*-products of Jewish and Aryan blood who form the cruelest haters of German culture?" Wardein proclaimed that the Jews were themselves a "*Mischlingsrasse*" and, what was more, that they were part black, the result of a centuries-long process of race mixing where "Semitic-

---

170. Dr. Heinrich Pudor, "Mischehen," *Staatsbürger-Zeitung,* May 24, 1912.
171. B. W., "Rassenbewußtsein," *Deutsch-Soziale Blätter,* May 25, 1912.

Negroid components" had crossed with "Turanian-Mongolian blood." Drawing on the colonial example yet again, Wardein warned that Germany would decline like Spain and Portugal—themselves old colonial powers—if it did not resume the practice of forbidding marriages between "Germans and Jews."[172] Four months later, the issues of race mixing at home and abroad became topics of discussion at the German Social Party's annual meeting in Erfurt. As reported by the *Staatsbürger-Zeitung*, a German Social parliamentary deputy delivered a lengthy lecture at the meeting on race, in the course of which he declared that antisemites would, "before everything else," fight race mixing "not only in the colonies, but also in our own land." Afterward, the party produced a statement declaring its expectation that the government "remain firm in the face of the regrettably miscegenation-friendly Reichstag majority."[173]

Another article by Heinrich Pudor appeared in November, this time on the front page of the *Deutsch-Soziale Blätter*. More so than the articles that preceded it, this piece demonstrates the merging of blacks and Jews in the antisemitic imagination at this time and the increased tendency among antisemites to borrow from colonial language. In part a celebration of the racial purity of certain northern European groups, the article begins with a description of the physical attributes of pure-blooded Germanic people: Pudor described them as having "blue eyes," "whitish, sparkling hair," and, "above everything else . . . clear, light skin." After giving this description, Pudor complained of the general lack of racial consciousness in Europe, for which he faulted race mixing both with Jews at home and with blacks in the colonies. If, according to Pudor, Europeans were more aware of their racial duty, then "miscegenation with Negroes in Africa [would] never have been allowed to come into question, but also in Germany we would have had so much racial pride and tribal consciousness that any marriages between Germans and Jews would have been precluded." Pudor ended his piece by recounting his encounter with "two Jews" and "a Germanic family" while traveling from Prussia to Finland. "Semites with Negroid infusions and pure-blooded representatives of the white race!" Pudor wrote. "There is no reconciliation between the two, just as little as among white and black and yellow."[174] Theodor Fritsch's *Hammer* magazine also explicitly connected blacks to Jews two years later. In a lengthy article printed

172. Wardein, "Deutsche Kolonialgesellschaft," *Deutsch-Soziale Blätter*, June 12, 1912.

173. "Deutschsozialer Parteitag," *Staatsbürger-Zeitung*, October 9, 1912.

174. Dr. Heinrich Pudor, "Rassenpflichten," *Deutsch-Soziale Blätter*, November 13, 1912.

on the eve of the First World War, an anonymous author discussed the supposed attraction of German women to "dark-haired, dark-eyed men," specifically, Jews and "Negroes."[175]

Antisemites were not alone in thinking of blacks and Jews together. Following the outbreak of violence in Southwest Africa in 1904, some colonialists openly attributed a Jewish identity or Jewish characteristics to indigenous rebels. For example, rumors circulated in colonial circles that some Nama leaders had Jewish roots. The influential Berliner weekly the *Allgemeine Zeitung des Judenthums* brought this story to the attention of its readers in December 1906 when it reported on recent references in the Reichstag to what it deemed "the old fairy-tale" that a leader of one of the Nama tribes was "a rabbi's son from Posen."[176] The *Zeitung* refuted the story. Quoting at length from a soon-to-be-published book on Southwest Africa by its former governor, Theodor Leutwein, the newspaper insisted that the individual in question, Abraham Morris of the Bondelzwarts, descended from a Nama woman and an Englishman of the Cape Colony.

The idea of a Nama-Jewish connection persisted, nevertheless. The *Allgemeine Zeitung* reported the following year on a disturbing quote attributed in a government publication to another Nama leader that again raised this specter. According to the German General Staff's official written account of the war, Samuel Isaak of the Witbooi tribe described to German interrogators his men's reaction to a German artillery barrage with the following statement: "Before and behind us . . . to the right and to the left, the shells exploded, we had such *Judenangst* that we all turned entirely white and thought, o God, o God, how shall it end?"[177] In this context, the term *Judenangst* denotes a special type of cowardice—namely, the intense cowardice of Jews. The author of the *Allgemeine Zeitung*'s editorial

---

175. "Deutsche Mädchen und fremdrassige Männer," *Hammer: Blätter für deutschen Sinn* 13 (1914): 318.

176. *Allgemeine Zeitung des Judenthums,* December 28, 1906. Matthias Erzberger of the Catholic Center Party referred, in passing, to Abraham Morris's supposed Jewish identity while speaking in the Reichstag in December 1906 (*Sten. Ber.* XI/II/133, December 4, 1906, 4151).

177. Department I of the Military History Section of the General Staff, *Der Hottentottenkrieg: Ausbruch des Aufstandes; die Kämpfe am Auob und in den Karrasbergen,* book 4 of *Die Kämpfe der deutschen Truppen in Südwestafrika. Auf Grund amtlichen Materials bearbeitet von Kriegsgeschichtlichen Abteilung I des Großen Generalstabes* (Berlin: Ernst Siegfried Mittler und Sohn, 1907), 60.

suggested that perhaps this was a "joke of the translator," a play on the word *Heidenangst*.[178] The author denounced the appearance in an official publication of such an antisemitic term. He denied any sense of religious camaraderie with either Samuel Isaak or Moses Meier, another Nama leader with a Jewish-sounding name.

Some procolonial advocates linked blacks and Jews in a different way: by using the example of older German antisemitic policies to guide their thinking about colonial practices. From 1909 to 1912, several contributors to the procolonial press argued for the legality of colonial laws against marriages between blacks and whites in the colonies by pointing to the defunct Prussian policy of hindering marriages between Jews and Gentiles. This was part of a lengthy debate involving multiple participants, sparked in part by the German Colonial Society's public announcement in 1908 of its support for the antimiscegenation policy. In the deliberations that followed, some contributors to the society's own newspapers argued that the existing prohibitions in the colonies against mixed-race unions were not, in fact, sanctioned by German law, and they suggested ways to make them legal. Others argued that they were legal already and needed no changes.

Edler von Hoffmann leaned toward the second position in his essay "The Question of Mixed Marriages," which appeared on the front page of the *Deutsche Kolonialzeitung* in November 1909. Although Hoffmann insisted that there was nothing in the German civil code that allowed the government to deny a person the right to marry on the basis of skin color, he argued that historical precedent showed that governments have the right to hinder marriages that are against state interests. He pointed out that Prussia had effectively impeded unions "between the baptized and the unbaptized" until March 1874 by failing to establish a civil procedure for this particular type of interfaith marriage. Hoffmann insisted that marriages between whites and "coloreds" in the colonies could be prevented in the same way: by providing one procedure for marrying whites, another for marrying indigenes, but none for marrying the two together. According to Hoffmann, this solution, which reflected the current situation on the ground, accorded with public opinion, both at home and abroad. He claimed that just as "the legal exclusion of marriages because of religious difference isn't seen in the motherland as being in conflict with moral feel-

---

178. Dr. M. Spanier, "Judenangst," *Allgemeine Zeitung des Judenthums,* March 8, 1907. *Heidenangst* means "mortal fear." *Heide* means "heathen" or "pagan" and *Angst* means "fear" or "dread."

ing, so it should be in agreement with the viewpoint of the vast majority of whites settled in the protectorates that racial difference rules out sexual unions in general and also in its particular legal form, being marriage." Hoffmann recommended registering all mixed-race individuals as "coloreds" to further ensure the prohibition of mixed-race marriages.[179]

Carl v. Stengel used Hoffmann's argument the following year. In a twenty-two-page article on the so-called native question in the *Zeitschrift für Kolonialpolitik, Kolonialrecht und Kolonialwirtschaft,* Stengel repeated Hoffmann's assertion that colonial authorities could adopt the old Prussian strategy for hindering unions between Jews and Gentiles in order to prevent interracial marriages.[180] Stengel went beyond Hoffmann in combining antisemitism with colonial discourse. Mirroring the logic of procolonial antisemites who referred to blacks in antisemitic articles to support their contentions about the reality and importance of race, Stengel argued for the permanent racial otherness of blacks by pointing to the Jewish example. Insisting that "the most weight" should be given to racial differences when determining how to handle "the native problem," Stengel proclaimed that "not all races . . . are of the same kind and are equal to each other. Already, this has been felt regarding the subdivisions in which the different races are divided after complexion, as the opposition between Aryans and Semites shows, although the difference between Aryans and Semites is small compared with the opposition between Negroes and whites."[181] Stengel made a similar point in another article on race mixing in 1912. Here, he insisted that blacks would still be unequal to whites even if they achieved the same cultural and civilizational levels, because the "difference of the races" would remain. For Stengel, this difference is manifest "above all in the difference

---

179. H. Edler v. Hoffmann, "Die Mischehenfrage," *Deutsche Kolonialzeitung,* November 27, 1909. Hoffmann's piece was in response to four preceding articles in the *Deutsche Kolonialzeitung* concerning the legality of the bans on interracial marriage: v. Bornhaupt, "Zur Frage der Mischehen zwischen Reichsangehörigen und Eingeborenen in Deutsch-Südwestafrika vom Rechtsstandpunkte," *Deutsche Kolonialzeitung,* January 2, 1909; Staatsanwalt Dr. B. Fuchs, "Zur Frage der Mischehen zwischen Reichsangehörigen und Eingeborenen in Deutsch-Südwestafrika," *Deutsche Kolonialzeitung,* January 16, 1909; idem, "Zur Frage der Mischehen zwischen Reichsangehörigen und Eingeborenen in Deutsch-Südwestafrika," *Deutsche Kolonialzeitung,* January 23, 1909; von Bornhaupt, "Zur Frage der Mischehen zwischen Reichsangehörigen und Eingeborenen in Deutsch-Südwestafrika," *Deutsche Kolonialzeitung,* February 13, 1909.

180. Hoffmann's argument also resonated with readers of the Christian-conservative *Neue Preußische Zeitung.* The newspaper printed an article reiterating Hoffmann's views in May 1912 (Privatdozent Dr. F. Zadow, "Mischehen und Rassenmischung," *Neue Preußische Zeitung: Kreuz-Zeitung,* May 7, 1912).

181. Stengel, "Die Eingeborenenfrage," 190.

in mental predispositions and attributes," things that cannot be removed "either through education or conversion to Christianity or an equalization in legal relationships." Stengel added in a footnote, "One needs . . . only to point to how the opposition between Aryans and Semites prevails time and again in all states, despite the so-called emancipation of the Jews."[182]

That even the movers and shakers of colonialism may have thought of blacks in antisemitic terms is suggested by a letter that appeared in Friedrich Lange's avidly antisemitic *Deutsche Zeitung* by the military commander responsible for virtually destroying the Herero people. That year, state secretary Bernhard Dernburg criticized von Trotha's actions during the Herero War for contributing to the contemporary labor shortage in the colony. Trotha defended himself in his letter to the *Deutsche Zeitung*. He designated Africans as a "treacherous rabble whose only law is force," and he hinted at the need for their eventual eradication.[183] He also accused the Herero of adhering to the Old Testament. "The deeply bloody history of the Old Testament with the frightful pictures of the Barmer bibles were found in the Pontocs, obviously used and well-thumbed," Trotha wrote, "and it had filled the instincts of the band, which knew nothing of the reconciling teachings of Christ. The generations that bore arms against us, that murdered our farmers and violated our wounded . . . had to be pursued to the last weapon."[184] Even if he did not consciously mean to, Trotha linked Jews and Hereros together for the *Deutsche Zeitung*'s readers by referring to the Old Testament. His letter revealed, perhaps, an inclination to let antisemitism shape his own perspective on black Africans.

The merging of representations of blacks and Jews both across and within the antisemitic and colonial movements of the *Kaiserreich* era was part of a long-established practice among Western colonizers of assigning Jewish characteristics to foreign peoples and imagining blood ties between Jews and non-European groups. As Tudor Parfitt has pointed out in her essay on this phenomenon, medieval Christians viewed the world as divided into

---

182. Carl v. Stengel, "Zur Frage der Mischehen in den deutschen Schutzgebieten," *Zeitschrift für Kolonialpolitik, Kolonialrecht und Kolonialwirtschaft* 14 (1912): 771.

183. "Especially in the beginning, we cannot do without them, but they must ultimately recede," Trotha wrote.

184. H. Teut., "Deutsche Kolonialpolitik," *Deutsch-Soziale Blätter,* February 6, 1909. The *Deutsch-Soziale Blätter* reprinted excerpts from Trotha's letter.

185. Tudor Parfitt, "The Use of the Jew in Colonial Discourse," in *Orientalism and the Jews,* ed. Ivan Davidson Kalmar and Derek J. Penslar (Waltham, MA: Brandeis University Press, 2005), 51–67.

four religions: Christianity, Islam, paganism, and Judaism.[185] When Christian explorers began spreading across the globe beginning in the late fifteenth century, they tried to make sense of new populations by fitting them into one of these categories. The myth of the Lost Tribes of Israel—the ancient Jews who disappeared from history following the conquest of the Kingdom of Israel by the Assyrians—encouraged many European travelers to speculate that newly discovered peoples were, in fact, the descendants of scattered long-lost Jews. At one point or another, the Japanese, the Chinese, Native Americans, the Maoris of New Zealand, and many others were deemed "Jewish" by early modern Western observers—missionaries or traders who often claimed that specific cultural or religious traits supported the hypothesis that these people were the progeny of the Lost Tribes. But the ascription of Jewishness to foreign peoples in early modern times was usually meant as a compliment; it was done to explain why some non-Western groups seemed more Western than others in their culture, capabilities, or physical appearance, and it helped justify the privileging of certain populations by Western colonizers. The "Jew," therefore, had a place in European colonial discourse that stretched back many centuries. The merging of representations of blacks and Jews in German colonial discourse during the age of high imperialism departed from this tradition by associating "Jewishness" only with that which was negative and threatening.

For this reason, the merging of representations of blacks and Jews both across and within the antisemitic and colonial movements of the *Kaiserreich* era had obvious potential negative ramifications for Germany's Jewish community. As discussions about black Africans increasingly resembled antisemitism—focusing on the same issues, like mixed-race marriages, and attributing blacks with characteristics common to antisemitic stereotypes—ordinary Germans unconnected to the antisemitic movement became familiar with a logic and rhetoric that, though colonial, paralleled the antisemites' own. The propagation of racist discourses of exclusion akin to antisemitism came at a time when the antisemitic movement was itself in decline. After 1900, political antisemitism receded, but, as seen here, a type of racial thinking easily redirected toward Jews was alive and well, advanced from within colonial circles and spurred by dramatic events in the colonies. Admittedly, ardent opposition to the most radical of colonial discourses continued within the colonial movement until the very end of empire. But as the Reichstag debate of May 1912 shows, the rhetoric of radical difference aimed at blacks—which shared with racial antisemitism common goals and vocabulary—affected even colonialism's harshest critics, who came to express a hierarchical view of humankind, rejecting, almost intuitively, the idea of a shared humanity with black Africans. It is easy to see how the easy identification of one human group as lower than all the rest could serve antisemitic interests later on.

Some antisemites understood the advantages that colonialism offered them. Although there was no coordinated effort to harness it to the antisemitic cause, some used colonialism to strengthen their case against the Jews, arguing for Jewish racial Otherness by linking blacks and Jews together, stressing their similarities and attributing Jews with African ancestry. In addition, some used the example of racial domination in the colonies to hint at the possibility of implementing *Rassenpolitik,* or racial policies, at home, suggesting the potential applicability to the Jewish Question of lessons about race and racial domination learned abroad. These discussions were largely internal to the antisemitic movement, played out in the pages of the antisemitic press, but, as shown above, colonialism also offered opportunities to engage the wider public in discussions about race in a way that could benefit antisemitism. Count Ludwig zu Reventlow seized this opportunity in 1905 when he introduced the Reichstag to the issue of race mixing in the colonies for the very first time. Reventlow's comments were greeted with laughter, but seven years later, race mixing was a weighty topic, taken seriously by deputies from across the political spectrum.

Colonialism undoubtedly influenced antisemitic thinking. Although the modern antisemitic movement predated the acquisition of the colonies—as did fantasies of racial domination through the revocation of Jewish civil rights—the creation of colonial racial states showed antisemites what was possible, if not for Germany in the near future, then perhaps in the very long run. While none of the official platforms of the antisemitic political parties written in the 1880s and 1890s demanded the prohibition of interfaith marriages, this desire became more prominent in antisemitic thought by the last decade and a half of colonial empire. As in the Reichstag debate of March 1905 and again during the annual meeting of the German Social Party of 1912, it was sometimes expressed in the context of discussions of colonial matters. For antisemites who paid close attention to colonial developments, colonialism also strengthened their conviction in the overriding importance of race, proving, in

Otto Böckler's words, that the twentieth century was to be "the century of *Rassenkampfe.*"[186] For some like Friedrich Lange, colonial events suggested an encouraging increase in German racial consciousness. The Reichstag resolution of May 1912 may have crushed this optimism, but it renewed dedication in certain circles to the antisemitic cause.[187]

What is more, the relationship between colonialism and antisemitism was not one-directional. The evidence presented here shows that some colonialists and procolonial advocates thought about blacks in antisemitic terms, while others looked to older Prussian antisemitic policies to guide decision making in the colonies. The remarkable similarity between antisemitic representations of Jews and radical notions about blacks speaks, in itself, of a similar mind-set among colonial radicals and racial antisemites: in particular, a shared need to invent an antirace and to project their worst fears and hatreds upon it. The tendency of both to attribute an eternal hostility toward Germans to their un-German Other, to suggest a coming *Endkampf,* and to justify preemptive violence in its anticipation is especially striking, indicative of a shared millenarianism that anticipated aspects of National Socialism. The eventual mainstreaming of the radical perspective within the colonial movement is exemplified by its repeated expression toward the end of empire in the *Zeitschrift für Kolonialpolitik, Kolonialrecht und Kolonialwirtschaft,* a magazine that, unlike the *Deutsche Kolonialzeitung,* was not prone to sensationalism or written in a popular style. The articulation of aspects of the radical colonial viewpoint by voices on even the political Left and Center is further evidence of this troubling normalization.

From the standpoint of German Jews, the partial normalization of the radical colonial viewpoint should have been particularly worrisome. Although focused on blacks, its ideological proximity to racial antisemitism promised an easy refocusing upon the Jewish Question once the colonies were gone. At the time, it surely made the violent racist visions of antisemitic ideologues like Eugen Dühring seem less outlandish by comparison. Acutely aware of their own delicate position as insider-outsiders in German society, some Jewish contemporaries recognized a danger to themselves in discourses on blacks. As we shall see in the following chapters, this may have encouraged a liberal mind-set on racial matters among some individuals of Jewish descent involved in creating and maintaining German Africa.

---

186. *Sten. Ber.* XI/I/165, March 16, 1905, 5311.
187. "Deutschsozialer Parteitag," *Staatsbürger-Zeitung,* October 9, 1912.

CHAPTER 3

Jews, Germans of Jewish Descent, and German Colonialism

When colonial director Paul Kayser resigned in October 1896 from his position as the chief administrator of the Colonial Division of the German Foreign Office, he did so under a cloud of scandal. In late July and early August, the German press had been abuzz with news of the recent sentencing to fifteen years imprisonment of an official of the German East Africa Plantation Company for raping young girls and mistreating his workers "with fatal results."[1] The individual in question, Friedrich Schröder, had run the company's plantation at Lewa from 1887 until 1895, during which time he gained a reputation for truly pathological brutality.[2] Reports in the press about Schröder's sentencing were coupled with allegations that the Colonial Division of the Foreign Office in Berlin had known about Schröder's savagery for years but had done nothing about it. These allegations and the revelations about Schröder's conduct emerged only a few months after the Carl Peters affair broke in the Reichstag. Together, they cemented the impression first given by the Leist and Wehlan affairs of 1894 that the colonial administration did little to vet its officials and, perhaps, was unconcerned with moderating colonial violence.[3] Kayser was criticized from across the political spectrum following Schröder's sentenc-

---

1. *Voss. Zeitung,* July 27, 1896, Reichskolonialamt (hereafter RKA) 4812/1, Bundesarchiv Berlin (hereafter BAB). The German East Africa Plantation Company shared important leading members with Carl Peters's German East Africa Company (or DOAG).

2. Schröder's brutality toward his workers was such that the plantation constantly suffered from the problem of runaways (Jonathon Glassman, *Feasts and Riot: Revelry, Rebellion, and Popular Consciousness on the Swahili Coast, 1856–1888* [Portsmouth: Heinemann, 1995], 188–90, 260–61; Fritz Ferdinand Müller, *Deutschland-Zanzibar-Ostafrika: Geschichte einer deutschen Kolonialeroberung, 1884–1890* [Berlin: Rütten und Loening, 1959], 242–44). The Schröder case is also detailed in RKA 4812/1 and 4812/2.

3. See chap. 1 for information on Leist and Wehlan.

ing. It was widely reported that he had actually visited the Lewa plantation during his 1892 trip to German East Africa and, therefore, had firsthand knowledge of its horrors.

Kayser received especially sharp criticism from the antisemitic press upon his resignation. Before 1896, the press had not made his Jewish ancestry a focus of attention in its coverage of colonialism, but this changed in the final months of Kayser's directorship. On the heels of the Schröder scandal, the short-lived Berlin-based antisemitic newspaper *Der Moderne Völkergeist* printed a scathing indictment of German colonial policy, alleging a change in recent years from relatively peaceful and productive trade to "zealous commerce, eager for plunder" and "a practice of violence." The author faulted Kayser in particular for this "unfortunate change." "Herr Kayser is also a Jew, and this says much already," he wrote. Referring to Kayser's apparent reluctance to deal in a timely fashion with the problem of excessive violence by colonial officials, he added that the director possessed "the businesslike spirit of his race: with diplomatic flexibility, he understood not to cause offense, at all events not where it could develop into inconveniences for himself." The author also faulted Kayser, "a Jew," for lacking "an understanding of true justice" and sending "scandalous people" to the colonies.[4] Other, more procolonial antisemitic periodicals attacked Kayser in a similar fashion. In an article in October, the *Staatsbürger-Zeitung* implicitly criticized Kayser's concessionary policies (see chapter 1) and blamed him for the outbreak of the Peters and Schröder scandals. It then declared its expectation that "henceforth, men who are not even connected through their lineage with the interests and ideas of the German people will not be permitted in our imperial offices."[5] The newspaper also noted, however, that Kayser was not to blame for all recent setbacks and disappointments with German colonialism.

Paul Kayser's exit from the colonial administration in the aftermath of a scandal that revolved around excessive violence, and the antisemitic attacks upon him before and after his departure, point to a hitherto ignored aspect of German colonialism: the influential participation in the creation and administration of colonial racial states of individuals who were themselves subjected to racist dehumanizing discourses because of

---

4. P. Kufhal, "Christische Gewaltpolitik und jüdischdeutsche Kolonialpolitik," *Moderne Völkergeist: Organ des Socialitären Bundes* 3 (1896): 139–40. The Socialitärer Bund followed the teachings of the racial antisemite Eugen Dühring.

5. "Der Wechsel in der Leitung der Colonial-Abteilung," *Staatsbürger-Zeitung,* October 16, 1896, morning edition.

their Jewish backgrounds. As seen in chapter 2, these antisemitic discourses sometimes closely paralleled contemporary colonizing language, even going so far as to explicitly link Jews to colonized groups like black Africans. Paul Kayser, who headed the Colonial Division of the German Foreign Office from 1890 to 1896, was but one of a number of Germans of Jewish descent who lived this paradox by figuring prominently in the *Kaiserreich*'s colonial projects. Bernhard Dernburg, who assumed the post of colonial director in 1906 and then headed the newly formed Colonial Office from 1907 to 1910, was another. Other famous and influential German-Jewish colonial actors included Emin Pasha, Ernst Vohsen, Otto Arendt, and Julius Scharlach—explorers, publicists, administrators, and financiers—men whose names appear in the historiography of imperial Germany's colonies. These men were important figures who affected the course and character of German colonialism and public attitudes toward overseas empire. Their Jewish ancestry was public knowledge, and they all suffered from racial and religious antisemitism to varying degrees as a result.

This chapter is the first of two investigating the involvement of Jews and Germans of Jewish descent in colonialism, and it focuses on the first two decades of empire. It examines the important and varied roles that individuals identified—and denigrated—as "Jewish" by their peers played in the German colonial project: for example, through exploration, by providing financial backing for colonialism as investors, or in setting important colonial policies as administrators. Of particular interest is their attitude toward the African colonized. One scholar of German-Jewish history has argued that minority groups subject to discrimination tend to recognize which elements of public discourse impinge negatively upon their own existence. If true, then the parallels between antisemitic and antiblack language, and the tendency of antisemites to conflate Jews with black Africans, might well have encouraged a more liberal attitude toward race among procolonial Germans of Jewish descent.[6] Although heavily implicated in the violence of colonialism, Paul Kayser repeatedly clashed with more racist and conservative colonial officials over the meaning of racial difference and, in particular, the treatment of individual blacks. We will see in these last two chapters whether this was characteristic of colonialists like him or was anomalous.

---

6. Yfaat Weiss, "Identity and Essentialism: Race, Racism, and the Jews at the Fin de Siècle," in *German History from the Margins,* ed. Neil Gregor, Nils Roemer, and Mark Roseman (Bloomington: Indiana University Press, 2006), 49–68.

In addition, this and the following chapter use the stories of these German-Jewish colonial actors to investigate further the complexities of the relationship between colonialism and antisemitism during the *Kaiserreich* period, as well as the meaning that colonialism had for the lives of the Germans of Jewish descent involved. As seen in chapters 1 and 2, colonialism aided the antisemitic movement in various ways, by providing antisemites, for example, with new opportunities to make the case for the reality and importance of race and by popularizing colonizing discourses that approximated racial antisemitism. But these chapters also show that colonialism introduced new divisions into an already deeply divided movement, such as over the purpose, nature, and benefits of overseas empire. We will see in the remainder of this book that the prominent participation of Germans of Jewish descent in German colonialism furthered this fragmentation, as the antisemitic movement, which contained a strong procolonial majority, split over the merits of the colonizing activities of men with Jewish heritage. This was especially true when it came to Emin Pasha and Bernhard Dernburg; both became extremely popular with the procolonial Right and with a large segment of the observing public as a result of their colonizing efforts. This popularity existed despite public knowledge of their Jewish heritage, and the idea that these men were German heroes even extended into the ranks of some procolonial antisemites.

By providing the public with such prominent examples of "Jewish" German patriots, colonialism seemed to undermine—in a most public way—racial antisemitism's basic principle of a diametrical opposition between "Jews" and "Germans." Colonialism gave these individuals unique opportunities to earn patriotic credentials. Even so, antisemitism against these figures persisted. Some antisemites saw in the colonizing activities of Paul Kayser, Emin Pasha, Bernhard Dernburg, and others a confirmation, rather than a refutation, of their antisemitic preconceptions, like their perceived connection between Jews and violence.

Jews and Germans of Jewish descent participated in German colonialism in relatively large numbers compared to the total number of individuals who had a hand in founding, running, and settling the colonies. By the eve of the First World War, Germany's largest settler colony, German Southwest Africa, contained 300 to 400 Jews out of a total white population of 15,000, making the territory's Jewish population proportionally larger than that in Germany. A majority of these were Russian Jews who had come from the Cape Colony, but a significant percentage were German. The

Jews were merchants, traders, craftsmen, farmers, prostitutes, and gamblers, and their numbers increased following the end of the Herero and Nama revolts in 1907. The town of Swakopmund even witnessed the formation of a Jewish *Gemeinde,* or congregation, in 1905.[7] Jews were also in the army sent to the colony to quell the uprisings. The German-Jewish press noted the death of one such individual—a lieutenant in the reserves—and the decoration of two others for bravery.[8]

In addition to contributing to the ranks of relatively anonymous settlers and soldiers, Jews and Germans of Jewish descent also numbered among the most prominent personalities of the early colonial movement. One of the best known and most colorful colonialists of Jewish descent was the explorer Eduard Schnitzer, who became world-famous in the late 1880s as Emin Pasha, the besieged European governor of the Egyptian province of Equatoria in the southern Sudan. Born Isaak (soon changed to Eduard) Karl Oscar Theodor Schnitzer in Silesia (Prussia) in 1840, Schnitzer converted to Lutheranism along with his widowed mother upon her remarriage to a Christian when Schnitzer was a small child. As a young man, he attended medical school in Germany and afterward left for the Ottoman Empire where he served as a quarantine medical officer in Albania before becoming the personal physician to Ismail Hakki Pasha, the Albanian governor.[9] By 1876, Schnitzer had changed locations completely and was living in Lado on the upper Nile, serving as a medical officer for the British general Charles George Gordon, who administered the region of Equatoria for the Egyptians. By now, Schnitzer was calling himself Emin, meaning "the loyal one," and he had long since adopted the dress and customs of a Turk.

---

7. G. A., "Die Juden und die deutschen Kolonien," *Im deutschen Reich: Zeitschrift des Centralvereins deutscher Staatsbürger jüdischen Glaubens* 16 (1910): 723–25. The author, identified only by initials, based his or her figure on the official 1907 census of the colony's white population. G. A. noted that the Jewish presence in the remaining German colonies was negligible.

8. Josef Bendix died in 1904 while in German Southwest Africa. Abraham Gutmann, a noncommissioned officer, won the Bavarian military-service cross in recognition of his bravery against the Herero. Dr. Alexander Lion of the 8th Bavarian Infantry Regiment was awarded the Knight's Cross of the order of the Bavarian military-service, the Prussian *rote Adlerorden 4. Klasse,* and the Southwest Africa medal (*Mittheilungen aus dem Verein zur Abwehr des Antisemitismus* 18 [1908]: 200; "Korrespondenzen," *Im deutschen Reich: Zeitschrift des Centralvereins deutscher Staatsbürger jüdischen Glaubens* 19 [1913]: 364).

9. Emin Pasha, *Emin Pasha, His Life and Work Compiled from His Journals, Letters, Scientific Notes and Official Documents by Georg Schweitzer with an Introduction by R. W. Felkin,* vol. 1 (New York: Negro Universities Press, 1969), 17.

Emin became not just a medical officer but also a political envoy for Gordon's government, and he traveled on diplomatic missions to the kingdom of Uganda and elsewhere. Then, in 1878, Gordon appointed him as his replacement as the governor of Equatoria, after Gordon accepted for himself the governorship of the entire Egyptian Sudan, relocating to Khartoum further north. Within several years, the Sudan was ablaze with the Mahdist rebellion against Egypt, led by the onetime Islamic ascetic Muhammad Ahmad, who preached that the Egyptians were not true Muslims.[10] The Mahdists captured Khartoum in 1884, killing Gordon in the process, and they established a Mahdist state south of Egypt. Emin and his government became trapped in Equatoria as a result.

Emin—known as Emin Bey until 1886 and then as Emin Pasha—became an obsession of the European press by the late 1880s.[11] This was due in large part to his acquired reputation in Europe as the embodiment of the civilizing mission in central Africa. Supporters painted him as the paternalistic colonizer extraordinaire, as a gentle governor who loved his subjects and elevated them to a more civilized way of life through good administration. The publication of his letters to European contacts solidified this image; they outlined his efforts to foster Equatoria's economic development through the introduction of cotton cloth production and the cultivation of tropical crops like rice and indigo. They also revealed a certain esteem for the capabilities of blacks, whom Emin praised for their relative "unselfishness" and likened to children.[12] Emin's fame provoked multiple rescue expeditions from Europe designed to bring him supplies or otherwise relieve him. The two best-organized and best-financed were an English expedition begun in 1888, led by the British-American journalist-turned-adventurer Henry Morton Stanley, and a German one begun in 1889, organized and led by Carl Peters.

Stanley reached Emin first. He convinced the governor to accompany him to Zanzibar via German East Africa. To the tremendous enthusiasm of the procolonial public in Germany—and to British consternation— Emin entered German service soon after arriving on the coast with Stanley. The German government assigned him the task of expanding German

---

10. Muhammad Ahmad claimed to be the Mahdi, a messianic figure prophesied to appear during the thirteenth Islamic century (1785–1882 C.E.) who would unite the world in an Islamic state. The Mahdist state he helped establish ended in 1898 at the battle of Omdurman.

11. Emin received the title of "Bey" from Gordon when he became the governor of the Equatorial Provinces. The Egyptian government awarded him the title "Pasha" in 1886 ("Emin Pasha," *Times,* December 10, 1886).

12. "Emin Bey," *Times,* December 2, 1886.

control in eastern Africa northward, from Lake Victoria up to Lake Albert. With the signing of the Helgoland-Zanzibar Treaty with Britain in the summer of 1890, however, Germany renounced its claims to the Uganda region, thwarting this plan. Emin busied himself for a time establishing a German presence in the northwestern regions of the colony. He raised the flag in Tabora—an important Arab trading town—and founded the station Bukoba near the shores of Lake Victoria.

Contrary to his reputation back in Europe as an inveterate man of peace, Emin began furnishing his men at this time by attacking Arab caravans. While in the colony's interior, he wrote a letter fulminating against European missionaries who gave Africans "checkered trousers" and taught them "mechanical bible reading" instead of turning them into soldiers or craftsmen.[13] This did not, however, affect Emin's by now well-established image back in Europe as a paternalist and model colonizer. In fact, his stature with German colonial enthusiasts only increased as time went on. In 1891, news reached Europe that Emin had left East Africa to try to reach Cameroon, purportedly to create a gigantic German-controlled land bridge connecting the two colonies. The governor of East Africa, Julius von Soden, encouraged Emin in this project but insisted that he undertake his trek as a private citizen.[14] Emin failed to reach Cameroon, and Islamic slave hunters killed him in the Congo in 1892. Reported sightings of the explorer continued for several years, however, fueling rumors that he had survived.[15]

At about the same time that Emin Pasha was busy establishing a German presence in the hinterland of German East Africa, another individual of Jewish descent, Ernst Vohsen, worked to solidify German control in its coastal regions. Although never as famous as Emin Pasha, Vohsen was much more important to German colonialism. Dubbed by historian Richard Pierard as "one of the most industrious supporters of colonial ventures of all kinds," Vohsen was a leading member of numerous colonial organizations, including, among others, the German East Africa Company (DOAG), the German Colonial Society, and the advisory board of private

---

13. "Korrespondenzen," *Deutsche Kolonialzeitung,* November 29, 1890.

14. Julius von Soden to Emin Pasha, May 12, 1891, R1001/274, BAB.

15. L. H. Gann and Peter Duignan, *The Rulers of German Africa, 1884–1914* (Stanford: Stanford University Press, 1977), 59–63; Müller, *Deutschland-Zanzibar-Ostafrika,* 458–87; Richard Victor Pierard, "The German Colonial Society, 1882–1914" (PhD diss., Graduate College of the State University of Iowa, 1964), 117–28; Martin Reuss, "The Disgrace and Fall of Carl Peters: Morality, Politics, and *Staatsräson* in the Time of Wilhelm II," *Central European History* 15 (1981): 114.

citizens known as the Colonial Council established in 1891 by colonial director Paul Kayser.[16] Born to Jewish parents in Mainz in 1853, Vohsen never converted from Judaism. He did not, however, embrace the Jewish faith; upon his death in 1919, one contemporary described him as a "free thinker" who lacked any specific religious affiliation.[17]

Vohsen became involved with colonialism at an early age, and he furthered Germany's colonial cause in both a public and private capacity. In 1876, he traveled to Sierra Leone as an employee of the Compagnie Française du Sénégal de la Côte Occidentale de l'Afrique, where he quickly assumed direction of a company factory. In 1881, the German government named him Sierra Leone's first German consul, a post he held until leaving for Germany in 1887. Back home, he became acquainted with the DOAG and, in 1888, he left for German East Africa as the company's chief representative—a position previously held by Carl Peters. The company charged him with the task of establishing an effective administration of a coastal region across from Zanzibar, but Vohsen was hampered in his efforts, in part, by the violence of DOAG agents like the antisemite Emil von Zelewski.[18] Following the suppression of the uprising of 1888, which Zelewski helped spark, Vohsen oversaw the transference of administrative duties from the company to the German government in 1891. He left the employ of the DOAG soon after.

Vohsen remained active in colonial affairs for the next three decades. The same year that he resigned from the DOAG, he assumed control of the geographical publishing firm Dietrich Reimer, which he turned into one of Germany's most prolific publishers of colonial-related material. He also joined the German Colonial Society, chairing a committee organized in 1891 to oversee and fund an expedition to the interior of Cameroon. The expedition took place in 1893 under the leadership of Edgar von Uechtritz and the antisemite Siegfried Passarge, and it had the effect of strengthening the German claim to the interior of the colony. Vohsen chaired a similar committee in 1895 that funded an expedition into Togo's hinterland, and, two years later, the German Foreign Office sent him to Paris to negotiate a treaty with France settling border disputes in Togo's interior.

---

16. Pierard, "The German Colonial Society," 137.

17. Missionsdirektor D. A. W. Schreiber, Prof. D. Meinhof, and Prof. D. Julius Richter, "Eingeborenenschutz, Kongo-Liga und Missionswesen," *Koloniale Rundschau: Zeitschrift für Weltwirtschaft und Kolonialpolitik* (January–March 1919): 114.

18. Following the outbreak of violence, Vohsen sojourned in Germany, where he helped direct the DOAG's business. He returned to Zanzibar in 1890.

Vohsen was also a member of the Colonial Council from its inception in 1890 until its disbandment in 1908 and, as such, participated in the regular advising of the Colonial Division of the Foreign Office on colonial policy. During this period, he served for a time as the director of the Settlement Society for Southwest Africa, which held large tracts of land in the colony, ceded by the government. In addition, Vohsen played a leading role in the German Navy League Abroad. Formed in 1898, largely on the initiative of Colonial Society members, the league raised money from German émigrés for the purpose of funding a larger German navy.

None of these activities distinguished Vohsen as much from his contemporaries as his outlook on "native policy." Vohsen was extremely progressive when it came to matters of race. In the German Colonial Society, he represented the view that rejected the stereotype of the lazy black who needed to be forced to labor. He insisted instead that blacks, like whites, were rational economic beings who would produce for the colonial economy under their own volition, given the right circumstances. Like many of his contemporaries, Vohsen was a paternalist, but he stood out in the depth of his egalitarianism. He believed that whites had a moral duty to uplift the colonized, and that colonialism was necessary to bring peace and prosperity to indigenous people. Yet he insisted that blacks be treated by whites as colleagues, not subjects, and he claimed that "economic and constitution conditions" in Africa, as opposed to racial factors, accounted for the continent's limited development.[19] Vohsen openly opposed society members who argued for the permanent subjugation and unapologetic exploitation of colonized people, and he stood out as a lonely progressive voice in the organization's governing body during the last decade of empire. In 1908, he opposed a society resolution demanding the "unconditional mastery" of "colored populations," and, the following year, he objected to the society's stated support for the custom of denying indigenes the right to testify under oath in colonial courts of law. He also voiced opposition in 1912 to the prohibitions against interracial marriage in the colonies, and he founded

---

19. Missionsdirektor D. A. W. Schreiber, Prof. D. Meinhof, and Prof. D. Julius Richter, "Eingeborenenschutz," 106. Vohsen made this statement in a foreword to a German translation of Booker T. Washington's autobiography. Vohsen also wrote (as reproduced in the Schreiber essay) that Washington's book "confirmed" his own view "that the Negro differs from the European essentially only in color and that he possesses all the necessary qualities to bring about with and alongside him the economic development and utilization of the tropical territories of Africa, indeed, that he is, moreover, indispensable if the European nations want to accomplish this task in their colonies."

his own magazine, the *Koloniale Rundschau,* in 1909 to air his progressive views. Four years later, he joined the newly formed German Society for the Protection of Aborigines.[20]

Jews and Germans of Jewish descent also participated in colonialism as political advocates and financiers. The Reichstag deputy and pan-Germanist Otto Arendt was a Christian convert, born into a family of Jewish entrepreneurs in Berlin in 1854. He became a leading conservative politician, joining the Prussian House of Deputies as a member of the Free Conservative Party, or Reichspartei, in 1885, and then served in the Reichstag from 1898 to 1918, where he became one of the most outspoken advocates of colonial empire. Arendt lobbied the government to increase its colonial expenditures, agitating, for example, for public funding for railroad construction and for government subsidies for colonial businesses. Arendt viewed Africa as a potential market for German industrial goods. He championed colonialism through his weekly newspaper, the *Deutsches Wochenblatt,* published in Berlin during the 1890s.

As seen in chapter 1, Arendt was also an influential member of the Society for German Colonization, and he was a close associate of Carl Peters. He joined the society's executive committee a year after the organization was founded, and he became a shareholder of the DOAG. He cooperated with Peters on a number of other projects over the next half-decade. He was a founding member of the short-lived General German League to Represent German National Interests, which had Peters as its chair. Formed in 1886 with the purpose of uniting foreign and domestic German associations to better coordinate German nationalist efforts, the General German League anticipated the pan-Germanism of its better-known successor, the Pan-German League. Arendt cooperated with Peters as well in the "rescuing" of Emin Pasha. He joined the Emin Pasha Committee, organized under Peters's leadership in 1888 to raise funds for the expedition. Arendt also distinguished himself as one of Peters's most loyal and vocal supporters. He publicly defended the explorer during and after the scandal of 1896, and he led an effort to rehabilitate him ten years later, agitating for

---

20. S. Passarge, "Ernst Vohsen," *Deutsche Kolonialzeitung,* July 20, 1919; Pierard, "The German Colonial Society," 137, 148, 151, 156, 180, 196, 258, 331–39; *Deutsches Kolonial-Lexikon,* s.v. "Vohsen, Ernst"; Glassman, 200, 202–4, 207, 215, 221–23; Arthur Knoll, *Togo under Imperial Germany, 1884–1914: A Case Study in Imperial Rule* (Stanford: Hoover Institution Press, 1978), 29–31, 85; Müller, *Deutschland-Zanzibar-Ostafrika,* 318, 384, 388–90. The entire 1919 April–June issue of the *Koloniale Rundschau* is devoted to documenting Vohsen's colonial activities.

a government pardon. Accordingly, Arendt was an outspoken apologist for colonial violence. He saw colonialism first and foremost as a "policy of conquest" that required violent action.[21]

As an apologist for brutality, Arendt was outstripped by Julius Scharlach, another German of Jewish descent with strong business interests in the colonies. A lawyer from Hamburg born in 1842, Scharlach was also an entrepreneur who helped found and direct a number of the most important colonial concession companies. He participated in the formation in 1898 of the South Cameroon Company, an organization that enjoyed special privileges from the government over the exploitation of Cameroon's natural resources. He was also a controlling member of the Southwest Africa Company, which owned a gigantic swath of land along Southwest Africa's coast, possessed most of the mining rights in the colony, and received huge government subsidies. In addition, Scharlach served on the board of directors of the German Colonial Society's Economic Committee, formed for the purpose of encouraging public interest in colonial products. He was also a member of the Colonial Council and, like Vohsen, advised the Colonial Division of the Foreign Office. In this capacity, Scharlach helped conceive, and was the primary advocate of, concessionary policy, meaning the pursuit of colonial development through government-subsidized private companies endowed with fantastic privileges and monopoly rights. The government pursued concessionary policy throughout the 1890s.[22]

Much like Arendt, Scharlach viewed the colonies in utilitarian terms, as objects of exploitation. Unlike Vohsen, he had no interest in a civilizing mission, and during his tenure in the Colonial Council, he advocated violent coercion in the frankest terms possible as a means to mobilize African labor for white purposes. Accordingly, he argued against placing any

---

21. *Stenographische Berichte über die Verhandlungen des Reichstags* (hereafter *Sten. Ber.*) XI/II/66, March 15, 1906, 2024. Information on Arendt can be found in Pierard, "The German Colonial Society," 52, 81–82, 88, 92, 175, 239, 322; Müller, *Deutschland-Zanzibar-Ostafrika*, 180, 182, 187, 402, 463, 474; Hans Ulrich Wehler, *Bismarck und der Imperialismus* (Cologne: Kiepenheuer und Witsch, 1969), 141, 447, 485; Woodruff D. Smith, *The Ideological Origins of Nazi Imperialism* (Oxford: Oxford University Press, 1986), 121, 96; M. B., "Arendt, Otto," in *The Jewish Encyclopedia*, vol. 2, ed. Isidore Singer (New York: Funk and Wagnalls, 1901–6), 88. Members of Arendt's family were also involved in colonialism. His brother-in-law worked as a railroad director in German Southwest Africa, and his mother-in-law was a member of the Patriotic Women's Leagues (Lora Wildenthal, *German Women for Empire, 1884–1945* [Durham: Duke University Press, 2001], 39).

22. One contemporary later labeled Scharlach as "the most influential man in the Colonial Department," despite the fact that he never served in the colonial bureaucracy (J. K. Vietor, *Geschichtliche und Kulturelle Entwickelung unserer Schutzgebiete* [Berlin: D. Reimer, 1913], 62).

meaningful limitations by the central government on the power of officials to coerce and punish indigenes. He insisted before the Colonial Council in October 1894 that restricting the discretion of men on the ground was "far worse" than occasional "excesses."[23] As a Colonial Council member, Scharlach also advocated capital punishment for the slightest challenge to white rule: in his words, for "all actions directed against German domination."[24] Concerning the African colonized, he insisted that blacks were an inferior race, and he rejected the stereotype of the naive childlike black; like other colonial radicals, Scharlach claimed that blacks were "predisposed to cruelty" and, as a result, needed a harsh and uncompromising domination. Other members of the Colonial Council criticized his extremism and likened Scharlach to a Spanish conquistador.[25] In the main, however, his ideas were no different from those expressed by Carl Peters.[26]

Other Jewish and Jewish-descended colonialists of note included the scholar Moritz J. Bonn, the administrator Richard Kandt, and the military doctor Alexander Lion. Although much more peripheral to the colonial movement than Emin Pasha, Vohsen, Arendt, or Scharlach, each gained a certain amount of fame during his lifetime. Moritz J. Bonn was a Jewish professor of economics from Frankfurt who taught in Munich. He visited British South Africa in 1906 and German Southwest Africa in 1907 in order to study the "interpenetration of native life by Western capitalism."[27] Bonn became convinced during his trip of the follies of settler colonialism, and he published a series of articles in the *Frankfurter Zeitung* where he argued that Africa needed to remain a "black man's country," although developed under white guidance.[28] He also argued against forced labor. His writings caught the eye of state secretary Bernhard Dernburg, who met with Bonn upon the professor's return and asked him to compile a study of legislation concerning "native affairs" in British Africa.[29] Bonn joined the German Colonial Society and the International Colonial Institute, becoming an important vocal advocate of Dernburg's efforts to moderate colonial violence (outside of German Southwest Africa) and improve relations between blacks and whites in the colonies.

---

23. Kolonialrat, 3rd session, October 18, 1894, 13, RKA 6960, BAB.
24. Kolonialrat, 4th session, December 1, 1897, 205, RKA 6971, BAB.
25. Kolonialrat, 4th session, December 2, 1897, 214, RKA 6971, BAB.
26. Like Frieda von Bülow and Otto Arendt, Scharlach defended Peters following his public disgrace in March 1896.
27. M. J. Bonn, *Wandering Scholar* (London: Cohen and West, 1949), 115.
28. Ibid., 118.
29. Ibid., 147.

Richard Kandt and Alexander Lion participated in empire building in official capacities. Kandt, a Jewish physician from Posen, explored the far eastern territories of German East Africa as a private citizen from 1897 to 1901. He published a book on his experiences several years later with Ernst Vohsen's publishing house, after which the colonial administration appointed him as Rwanda's chief resident administrator in 1907. Alexander Lion was a medical doctor from Berlin. He served as a medical officer with German troops in Southwest Africa during the Herero and Nama uprisings, and he wrote a book in 1908 concerning the cultural capacities of black Africans.

Like Vohsen, both Kandt and Lion rejected the radical perspective of colonial extremists concerning racial matters. Kandt perceived black Africans in a sympathetic light. In his written work, he rejected the myth of black African immorality, arguing that African customs could not be judged by European standards. Kandt also insisted that blacks were not nearly as violent and brutal as often depicted in popular writings, noting, for example, that African warfare usually produced few casualties. In addition, he challenged the idea that blacks were relatively insensitive to pain, a myth used by radicals to justify extreme corporal punishment.[30] Lion, too, was something of a moderate. He rejected what he called "the standpoint of the conquistadors" who "do not shrink from racial extermination." He attributed blacks with what he deemed to be childlike qualities, like a "fine sense for justice and injustice," and he argued that whites should give blacks positive reasons to accept white dominance, like better economic opportunities and the rule of law. He argued that so-called native policy should be paternalistic, that whites should rule "less with a domineering than with a fatherly severity."[31]

Antisemites were well aware of the Jewish heritage of these and other prominent participants in colonialism. In the political arena, however, there appeared to be a convention against attacking them openly and from an antisemitic standpoint. Deputies in the Reichstag from the antisemitic political parties rarely singled out specific Jewish colonialists or procolonial activists for public ridicule or denunciation.

---

30. Richard Kandt, *Caput Nili: Eine empfindsame Reise zu den Quellen des Nils* (Berlin: Dietrich Reimer, 1904), 152, 168–69, 175.

31. Arthur Dix, "Koloniale Rundschau," *Deutsche Welt: Wochenschrift der Deutschen Zeitung,* September 19, 1909. Dix quoted at length from Lion in his review of Lion's book *Die Kulturfähigkeit des Negers und die Erziehungsaufgaben der Kulturnationen* (Berlin: Wilhelm Süsserott, 1908).

More common were allegations of a Jewish anticolonial bias, directed toward individual political actors or German Jews in general. In the Reichstag in May 1890, for example, Reichspartei deputy Wilhelm von Kardoff attributed the critical stance toward German colonialism of Ludwig Bamberger of the Progressive Party to the fact that he was an "Israelite." Specifically, von Kardoff stated that the "Israelite" Bamberger could be forgiven for forgetting the important role that colonialism played in "the spreading of Christianity."[32] The following month, Reichstag deputy von Frege accused the Rothschilds of failing to invest in the German colonies. Antisemitic Reichstag deputies occasionally alleged Jewish profiteering from German colonial efforts as well. Liebermann von Sonnenberg attacked the colonial administration's concessionary policies in 1899 for effortlessly enriching "Jews and Jewish companions," and, in this context, briefly mentioned Julius Scharlach.[33] Five years later, he joined deputy Bieberstein of the Conservative Party in accusing Jewish merchants of selling horses for the war effort in Southwest Africa to the government at inflated prices.[34]

In addition, the antisemites in parliament occasionally complained of a Jewish presence in the colonies. An antisemitic deputy raised the issue of Jewish colonial settlers in 1896 during a plenary session debate over colonial director Paul Kayser's request for funding to increase troop strength in Southwest Africa in light of recent fighting. Eugen Richter of the Progressive Party joked, in Kayser's presence, that antisemitic deputies who supported the director's demand should send themselves to Africa, seeing that it was "*judenrein*," or "Jew free." Deputy Paul Förster of the German Social Reformers, who supported Kayser's request, replied that "Abraham's seed" was already widely dispersed in the region, attracted by South Africa's diamond fields. Without offering any details, Förster remarked that the Jews in southern Africa were engaged in what he called their "characteristic activity," bribery.[35] Antisemites in the Reichstag brought the body's attention to Jewish settlement in Southwest Africa again eleven years later. During a plenary session in March 1907, deputies Wilhelm Lattmann and Friedrich Bindewald lamented in state secretary Bernhard Dernburg's presence the existence of a "racially alien Jewish element" in the colony.[36]

---

32. *Sten. Ber.* 4, May 12, 1890, 47.
33. *Sten. Ber.* X/I/122, December 14, 1899, 3399.
34. *Sten. Ber.* XI/I/73, April 22, 1904, 2337.
35. *Sten. Ber.* IX/IV/93–94, May 19, 1896, 2357.
36. *Sten. Ber.* XII/I/11, March 6, 1907, 295.

Allegations of the undue infiltration of Jews, or Jewishness, into German colonialism were made more vociferously in the antisemitic press. After Carl Peters set out to rescue Emin Pasha, the *Deutsche Wacht* erroneously reported the former's death and characterized him a victim of "Jewish money-interests." It also alleged "an increasing Jewification" of German "colonial efforts," perhaps a subtle reference to Ernst Vohsen's appointment as the DOAG's chief representative in German East Africa or to the recent investment by Jewish financial houses—like Mendelssohn-Bartholdy—in the company.[37] In 1894, Friedrich Lange's *Tägliche Rundschau* alleged an incursion of a "semitic business acumen" into the DOAG leadership and warned that German East Africa was turning into a "*Daitsch-Neujudäa.*"[38] The *Antisemitisches Volksblatt* lamented in 1895 the presence of "Jewish military doctors" and a Jewish colonial judge in German East Africa.[39]

The participation of high-profile Germans of Jewish descent in colonialism had the potential to compromise, however, allegations of Jewish anticolonial bias. When von Frege made his accusation in the Reichstag against the Rothschilds in June 1890, another deputy quickly pointed out that both Emin Pasha and Ernst Vohsen were related to "Semitic elements" and had done much for the "economic development" of German East Africa.[40] The examples of Emin Pasha and Ernst Vohsen went against the grain of other emerging antisemitic axioms as well, in particular, the idea that Jews were not Germans by virtue of their race and that German citizens of Jewish descent could never be loyal German patriots. Much to the contrary, the dominant narrative that emerged over Emin Pasha in Germany, beginning in the late 1880s, painted him as a German colonial hero. In the context of international colonial rivalry between Germany and England, it even positioned him, at times, as the epitome of Germanness and a stand-in in Africa for Germany itself. The men behind the German Emin Pasha relief expedition drove this narrative, which they began before Emin's Jewish heritage became public knowledge. But it continued and intensified even after the mainstream press reported on his Jewish family background.

37. "Dr. Peters todt!" *Deutsche Wacht,* November 10, 1889; Stern, *Gold and Iron: Bismarck, Bleichröder, and the Building of the German Empire* (New York: Vintage Books, 1979), 414.

38. The *Tägliche Rundschau* is quoted in "'Echt semitischer Geschäftsgeist," *Mittheilungen* 4 (1894): 303.

39. "Umschau in Israel," *Antisemitisches Volksblatt,* March 2, 1895.

40. *Sten. Ber.* 15, June 12, 1890, 288. The speakers were Dr. von Frege and Dr. Dohrn.

Establishing Emin Pasha as not just a German citizen in technical terms, but as German in outlook and sentiment was so important for his supporters in Germany because of initial doubts about his origins and loyalties. Early reports about Emin in the European press elided his national origins or labeled him an Austrian, a mistake that persisted even after his German supporters had set the record straight.[41] The fact that Emin had adopted a Turkish alias made him seem even more exotic. In addition, as the Egyptian governor of Equatoria, Emin was a de facto agent of the British Empire, and by late 1886, the idea that Emin was a standard-bearer of not just European but British colonial efforts became an underlying assumption of British reporting on him. This was encouraged by the publication in Britain of several of Emin's letters, wherein he wrote—in general terms—of his loyalty to the colonial vision of the deceased Charles Gordon. In the British press, Emin became Gordon's "ablest and most loyal lieutenant," the last remaining pillar of Gordon's—and therefore Britain's—civilizing mission in the Sudan.[42]

The founders of the German Emin Pasha relief expedition believed that they could use a trek to Emin in Equatoria to expand German influence in central Africa. They organized the German Emin Pasha Committee in the summer of 1888 with Carl Peters at its head, and the group set about the task of raising funds to cover the expedition's projected expenses. This entailed a propaganda campaign to convince public opinion of the worthiness of the cause. Committee members emphasized the potential gains for German business that would come from opening up an overland trade route to Equatoria from German territory. They also stressed that Emin was a loyal German, that he was worthy of relief by dint of his accomplishments and characteristics as a model colonizer, and that helping him was a matter of German-national pride. In labeling Emin Pasha as a loyal German, committee members worked to create an alternative narrative from what was found in the European press at large. In describing him as a model colonizer, they expanded upon precedents in both British and German sources that predated the German relief effort.

One of the first articles emphasizing Emin's Germanness appeared in the *Deutsche Kolonialzeitung* in early 1887. Titled "Our Compatriot Emin Bei" by A. Woldt, it contains no specifics, however, about Emin's background.[43] This was rectified in the pamphlet "A German Task," published

---

41. *Times,* September 28, 1887. Here, the *Times* calls Emin an "Austrian naturalist."
42. "Emin Bey," *Times,* December 2, 1886.
43. A. Woldt, "Unser Landsmann Emin Bei," *Deutsche Kolonialzeitung,* no. 1 (1887): 7–10.

in April 1888 by the executive committee of the Nuremberg division of the German Colonial Society, some of whose members went on to participate in the Emin Pasha relief effort. The pamphlet identifies Emin as "this brave German man, Dr. Eduard Schnitzer, born on March 28, 1840 in Oppeln in the Prussian province of Schlesien." It assures its readers that "despite his Egyptian title, Emin Pasha (Emin means the 'Loyal One') has remained a good Christian." In bold type, it labels Emin a "German master" who had effectively ruled a large territory in eastern Africa for an entire decade.[44]

The first of several German-published collections of Emin's letters and journals appeared in 1888 as well, compiled and introduced by a member of the German Emin Pasha Committee, Dr. Georg Schweinfurth, who had corresponded with Emin. Schweinfurth wrote in his introduction that it was "the tremendous loyal adherence to the old homeland expressed by Emin in many places" that had convinced him to make his letters available to a German audience. "Emin belongs to us entirely, a German, a Prussian!" he proclaimed before recounting details of Emin's early life, like the history of his education.[45] Schweinfurth explained that Emin had adopted his Turkish alias while working for the Ottomans because he feared that his German identity would distance him from his Islamic patients. As proof, he quoted from a letter Emin wrote to his sister in 1871 where he assured her that he had "not become a Turk" and that it was "only the name" that had changed.[46] Advocates of the German relief expedition trumpeted Emin's German-national loyalties in public speeches as well. At a September event in Wiesbaden, a speaker quoted from two of Emin's letters where he expressed his preference for "German research" and his hopes for an expedition from Germany. The speaker concluded that "this is truly, indeed, not the speech of a man who has disregarded or disowned his fatherland."[47]

According to the British narrative, Emin was not just any colonial

---

44. Eine deutsche Aufgabe, by Der Vorstand der Abtheilung Nürnberg der Deutschen Kolonial-Gesellschaft, April 11, 1888, R8023-852, BAB.

45. Georg Schweinfurth and Friedrich Ratzel, introduction to *Emin-Pascha: Eine Sammlung von Reisebriefen und Berichten Dr. Emin-Pascha's aus den ehemals ägyptischen Aequatorialprovinzen und deren Grenzländern,* compiled by Dr. Georg Schweinfurth and Dr. Friedrich Ratzel (Leipzig: F. A. Brockhaus, 1888), vi.

46. Ibid., xii.

47. Vortrage des Herrn Direktors im Reichs-Postamt Sachse über die Emin Pascha-Expedition gehalten in der Vorstandssitzung der Deutschen Kolonialgesellschaft am 11 September 1888 zu Wiesbaden, R1001/249/3, BAB.

governor. As stated above, the British identified his rule in Equatoria as a model of white paternalism and good governance. According to the British press, Emin was a foe of the slave trade who protected Equatoria from its blight. He was a gentle scientist who esteemed, rather than despised, the local black population and who uplifted it through economic development. Emin was also a selfless colonizer who refused to desert his post out of a noble concern for his charges.[48] Emin's British supporters used his own letters to Europe to craft this image; in his missives, Emin wrote of his commitment to remaining in Equatoria in order to continue Gordon's project of "civilization and progress."[49]

Emin's supporters in Germany seized upon this narrative and expanded it, magnifying what was already in British newspapers. A. Woldt claimed that Emin had forged a "flowering empire almost the circumference of the Prussian kingdom" and that he had done so "entirely independently" and with "mildness and kindness"; employing a "fatherly manner" toward his subjects, he had created "a selfless, loyal, devoted and capable race" out of "the indolent, dark-colored, lazy native inhabitants."[50] Schweinfurth called Emin an "apostle of culture" who applied himself to his administrative tasks with "loyalty and commitment." Concerning the letters in his compilation, he insisted, "No one can read them without being filled with respect and affection for the person of our resolved, noble-minded, and brilliant compatriot."[51] The speaker at Wiesbaden insisted that Emin combined "in rare fashion the attributes of a distinguished scholar and natural scientist with those of an energetic and agile administrator." He quoted at length from a Scottish missionary, Robert Felkin. According to Felkin, Emin's "entire activity arose from a pure love of one's fellow man. . . . he esteems the ways of the natives and is convinced that it is possible to raise them to a high level of civilization and to build in central Africa a lasting empire where right and justice dominates, where oppression and the slave trade could be unknown and where trade and industry could thrive." The

---

48. See, for example, "The Rescue of Emin Pasha," *Times,* December 15, 1886. The correspondent wrote of Emin: "With absolute disinterestedness he has cast his lot in with his men, whom he refuses to desert, and at the same time he is governing his province with much success that even after all the Mahdi troubles, that province is a going concern which, with a little outside help, might be made to yield a large annual surplus."

49. "Emin Pasha," *Times,* September 27, 1887. Also see "Emin Bey," *Times,* December 2, 1886.

50. Woldt, "Unser Landsmann."

51. Schweinfurth and Ratzel, introduction to *Emin-Pascha: Eine Sammlung von Reisebriefen und Berichten,* viii.

speaker insisted that one could come to know Emin "in his entire touching simplicity and selflessness" by reading his letters.[52]

In the committee's rhetoric, helping such a man was "a duty of humanity."[53] Emin was "the last bulwark" in the southern Sudan "of European culture," the one remaining hindrance to Arabic slavers and Islamic fanatics, and so relieving him would serve the general good of humankind.[54] At the same time, the committee couched it as a specifically German responsibility, arguing that Germans were duty-bound to help their own "heroically noble compatriot."[55] Supporting the expedition was also equal to supporting the greater German-national cause in the competition of nations, as an expedition would strengthen German business—the committee claimed—by opening up trading routes to the interior of east Africa.[56] A successful expedition meant advancing the greater cause of German civilization as well; the Equatorial Province had been cultivated through "German activity," making it only natural that Germans—and not the English—should continue Emin's civilizing work in, or around, the Sudan.[57] Committee members insisted that it was the "love of our German breed and nation" and a "rock-steady trust in the world-historical future of our people" that inspired them.[58] In this way, they positioned helping Emin Pasha as an act not just of solidarity with a fellow German but of the highest importance to the future of the nation and a matter of national pride.

These arguments resonated with colonial enthusiasts, and the pro-colonial press repeated them. The *National-Zeitung* connected the relief effort to the competition of nations and German national pride. "England sent out expedition after expedition when its Franklin went missing in the northern seas," the newspaper declared in August 1888, "and the entire civilized world admiringly recognized these efforts. Should it be necessary in Germany to point to sober motives of political interest to suggest to our people the rescue of a deserving compatriot in Africa?"[59] "If the German

---

52. Vortrage des Herrn Direktors im Reichs-Postamt Sachse.
53. Eine deutsche Aufgabe.
54. Der Deutsche Emin Pasha-Comité, "Aufruf!," *National-Zeitung,* September 23, 1888.
55. Ibid.
56. "Die Emin Pascha-Versammlung in Hannover," *National-Zeitung,* September 22, 1888.
57. Der Deutsche Emin Pasha-Comité, "Aufruf!"; Streng vertraulich, by Die geschäfts-führende Commission des Emin-Pascha-Comité, July 1888, R1001/249/3, BAB.
58. "Die Emin Pascha-Versammlung in Hannover."
59. "Die Rettung Emin Paschas," *National-Zeitung,* August 31, 1888. English rear admiral Sir John Franklin was the subject of multiple rescue expeditions after disappearing in the Arctic in 1845 while searching for the Northwest Passage.

people should stop short, if the Reich should not powerfully and irre-sistibly intervene for its members," the newspaper proclaimed in Septem-ber, "then the dreamed-of world-position of the Germans will probably, indeed, be long gone."[60] That same month, the *Kölnische Zeitung* argued that relieving "our compatriot" would be "an act of human kindness." It also insisted that it would strengthen the German presence in the region of the great lakes, thereby consolidating "the German occupancy of east Africa."[61] The liberal *Berliner Tageblatt* came out for the expedition as well and affirmed Emin's Germanness. The newspaper declared in October that Emin had become a Muslim only for professional reasons and that "inside he has remained a Christian and a German."[62]

The first German reports detailing Emin's background did not mention his Jewish heritage. A. Woldt said nothing about it, while Schweinfurth identified both his parents as being of the "evangelical confession."[63] The Emin Pasha Committee placed special emphasis in its propaganda on the fact that Emin was a Christian in order to dispel suspicions that he was Muslim. In addition, part of the committee's argument for aiding Emin was that he represented "the last bulwark of Christian rule on the upper Nile."[64]

Yet news of Emin's Jewish heritage quickly emerged following the start of the committee's campaign to win over the German public. The Christian conservative *Neue Preußische Zeitung* printed a piece in Septem-ber 1888 stating that Emin was, reportedly, "a Jew who had subsequently turned to Mohammedanism."[65] The *Kölnische Zeitung* printed an inves-tigative report about the same time detailing Emin's Jewish background, replete with evidence from the synagogue's registry of births at Oppeln and from the registry of Oppeln's Jewish congregation. This information showed that Emin had been born as "Isaak"—soon changed to "Ed-uard"—to two Jewish parents, and the report traced his paternal grand-father's roots to Poland. Antisemitic newspapers such as the *Deutsche*

60. "Die deutsche Kolonial-Bewegung," *National-Zeitung,* October 7, 1888.

61. "Eine deutsche Emin Pascha-Expedition," *Kölnische Zeitung,* September 30, 1888.

62. *Berliner Tageblatt,* October 1, 1888.

63. Schweinfurth and Ratzel, introduction to *Emin-Pascha,* vii. This was misleading, be-cause Emin's biological father had never converted to Christianity.

64. Streng vertraulich, by Die geschäftsführende Commission des Emin-Pascha-Comité, July 1888, R1001/249/3, BAB.

65. "Deutschland," *Neue Preußische Zeitung,* September 18, 1888, morning edition.

Wacht and the *Antisemitische Correspondenz* reprinted parts of this report in October and November.[66] The *Berliner Tageblatt* printed its own piece in January 1890 titled "The Origins of Emin Pasha." It informed its readers that Emin was born in 1840 but was baptized in 1846, an abnormality because "the law back then prescribed that the baptism of a child must take place within six weeks of the birth."[67] The article revealed by way of explanation that the Schnitzer family was registered with Oppeln's synagogue.

The revelation that Emin had been born a Jew did not, however, dampen enthusiasm for his cause. Procolonial newspapers like the *National-Zeitung* continued to champion the German relief expedition. Eulogies to Emin only increased in grandiosity once he entered German service in late 1889, and again in early 1890 when news emerged that he was to head an expedition into the interior of German East Africa. Even newspapers that had reported on his Jewish background reflected the heightened excitement that these events caused. The *Kölnische Zeitung* effused in April 1890 that the application of Emin's "rich knowledge" to German colonialism was "cheerful tidings and of great meaning for the development of our African colonies."[68] The *Neue Preußische Zeitung* printed a report from Zanzibar the following month, praising Emin as "an admirable picture of a scholar informed by ideals . . . a . . . pioneer fired up with German-national enthusiasm." The author gushed that Emin's "full vigor and vivacity . . . his love of work, the sweeping knowledge of scholarly and political domains, his talent for languages simply amazes," and he wrote that Emin entered German service "from conviction and with his entire essence."[69] One of the most laudatory books on Emin Pasha appeared the following year, and it, too, acknowledged his Jewish background. In *Dr. Emin Pasha, A Champion of Culture in Inner Africa*, author Paul Reichard praised Emin as "this important, ingenious, man of ideals" and "a man of whom the German nation can be proud as one of their own." He noted on the same page that Emin was "born of Israelite parents."[70]

By now, Emin had become a reference point not only in procolonial

---

66. "Zur Judenfrage," *Deutsche Wacht,* October 7, 1888; "Emin Pascha—Jude," *Antisemitische Correspondenz,* November 1, 1888.

67. "Die Herkunft Emin Paschas," *Berliner Tageblatt,* January 7, 1890.

68. "Deutschland. Emin Pascha im deutschen Dienst," *Kölnische Zeitung,* April 4, 1890.

69. "Emin Pascha und die deutsche Seen-Expedition," *Neue Preußische Zeitung,* May 12, 1890.

70. Paul Reichard, *Dr. Emin Pascha. Ein Vorkämpfer der Kultur im Innern Afrikas* (Leipzig: Verlag Otto Spamer, 1891), 41.

circles but also in German popular culture. In 1890, his picture graced the front page of the middle-class magazine *Die Gartenlaube,* and children as young as six could be heard in the streets discussing "Emil Pascha."[71] Light satire on him appeared in the humor magazine *Kladderadatsch,* and the novelist Karl May used Emin as an example of a model colonizer in his book *The Slave Caravan.*[72] Serialized in the magazine *Der Gute Kamerad* between 1889 and 1890, the story repeats the narrative that Emin was a peaceful benevolent colonialist, someone "who does everything in order to establish and raise the prosperity of his subjects."[73] Characters in May's story contrast him with "those Christians who go into other lands in order to subjugate and exploit the people."[74] By the end of the decade, it was even possible to smoke "Emin Pascha" cigarettes manufactured in Dresden by the company Brussig & Wollmann.[75]

Several factors explain the uptick in Emin's popularity beginning in late 1889. As stated above, his rapid entrance into German service endeared him to the procolonial Right. But this gained added significance with the revelation that Emin had turned down repeated overtures from the British, including promises of a lucrative position in a private colonial company.[76] In addition, when Emin departed on his expedition to the interior of German East Africa in 1890, he did so without first sojourning in Europe. This appeared even more remarkable given the fact that Emin had severely injured himself upon reaching the coast with Stanley; he fell out of a second-story window during a banquet in Bagamoyo hosted in his honor.[77] His rapid return to the interior despite his injuries was seen as proof of his tremendous dedication to the German colonial cause.[78] In addition, Emin's reputation as a peaceful colonizer—one who expanded his territory in Equatoria through negotiation instead of war—made him the antithesis of violent adventurers like Carl Peters in the minds of his supporters. Segments of the German press hypothesized that Emin's employment in Ger-

---

71. *Die Gartenlaube: Illustriertes Familienblatt,* 1890, no. 27; Karl von den (illegible) to Emin Pascha, April 25, 1890, N2063-08, BAB. The author of the letter wrote to Emin, "You are truly popular. Yesterday I heard two small girls of approximately 6 and 8 years old talking in the street about 'Emil Pascha.'"

72. None of *Kladderadatsch*'s short pieces on Emin and illustrations of him referred to his Jewish heritage.

73. Karl May, *Die Sklavenkarawane* (Bamberg: Karl-May-Verlag, 1949), 224.

74. Ibid., 225.

75. "Mosaik," *Deutsch-Soziale Blätter,* January 19, 1899.

76. "Emin Pascha," *Berliner Börsen-Zeitung,* April 4, 1890.

77. Emin almost died from the fall, and it took him two months to recover.

78. "Ostafrika," *Magdeburgische Zeitung,* April 4, 1890.

man service would initiate a "sharp turn" in policy: the replacement of warlike undertakings with a more peaceful type of colonialism in East Africa.[79]

Finally, animosity toward Emin in Britain increased his appeal with the procolonial crowd. Emin's quick entrance into German service generated tremendous vitriol, especially when news broke of his imminent expedition into the interior of German East Africa.[80] Segments of the British press interpreted the expedition in the worst possible light, as "an enterprise intended to work as much mischief as possible" for the British nation, and lambasted Emin for his apparent ingratitude.[81] Prominent members of the Stanley rescue expedition who had soured on Emin fed the animosity by painting unflattering pictures of him in their memoirs. Stanley's *In Darkest Africa* faulted Emin for an "excess of sentiment" and "childish pettishness" and for being strangely ungrateful to his British rescuers.[82] Stanley's companion, A. J. Mounteney-Jephson, gave a more critical account, describing Emin as "eminently a man of compromises" and "morally a coward."[83] Both men faulted him for many of the difficulties they encountered on the long march with him to the coast of East Africa. A *Times* editorial printed in September 1893 encapsulates the dramatic transformation of Emin's reputation in Britain by this time. Emin was "a weak man, of no particular principles," the newspaper declared. "That he was worthy of all the sacrifices that were made for him, and of the heroic position allotted him by the enthusiasm of six years ago, few will now be inclined to admit."[84]

The sense in Germany that the "noble compatriot" was under attack by the British began even earlier, however: reports in the German press in late 1889 suggest that Stanley's appearance in Equatoria had actually led to

---

79. "Frankfurt, 5 April," *Frankfürter Zeitung,* April 6, 1890. Also see "Emin Pascha in deutschen Diensten," *Weser-Zeitung,* April 5, 1890.

80. "The Gratitude of Emin Pasha," *St. James's Gazette,* April 2, 1890.

81. *Times,* April 3, 1890. The *Times* argued that Emin's government-funded expedition was intended to extend German control deep into Central Africa at the expense of British interests. It condemned Emin for repaying in this way "the heavy expenditure of British lives and British money on extracting him from a position of a decidedly precarious kind."

82. Henry M. Stanley, *In Darkest Africa or the Quest, Rescue, and Retreat of Emin, Governor of Equatoria* (London: Sampson Low, Marston, Searle, and Rivington, 1890), 1:8; ibid., 2:469.

83. A. J. Mounteney-Jephson, *Emin Pasha and the Rebellion at the Equator: A Story of Nine Months' Experience in the Last of the Soudan Princes* (New York: Charles Schribner's Sons, 1891), 409, 479.

84. "Emin Pasha," *Times,* September 23, 1893.

the collapse of Emin's government.[85] Later accounts indicate that Stanley had harshly bullied Emin into accompanying him to the coast. It was also reported that Stanley had spoken against German colonialism while trying to convince Emin to rejoin the British colonial cause. For all these reasons, defending Emin—and celebrating him—became a matter of German national pride. This was the position taken by *Die Gartenlaube* in 1890 when it reviewed Stanley's memoir. The reviewer concluded that Stanley had intended "to darken Emin's stature in the eyes of Europe. This attitude is only another reason for us Germans to stand firm in our admiration of our grand compatriot until he has appeared to defend his name himself against the attacks of his liberator, just as he once defended his province against his enemies."[86] The fact that Emin did not do so—that he returned to the African interior without mounting his own defense—was interpreted as proof of his nobility of spirit, of his desire to rise above the fray and concentrate his energies on helping German colonial efforts.[87]

Surprisingly, these attitudes made their way into segments of the antisemitic press. The *Neue Preußische Zeitung* reported the German Emin Pasha Committee's laudatory propaganda on Emin and, as seen above, printed its own panegyric in 1890. This occurred despite the newspaper's initial hostility. When it reported in September 1888 that Emin was a Jewish convert to Islam, the newspaper wrote that "the Semitic background of Dr. Schnitzer and his religious defection makes supporting him not easy." Nevertheless, it attributed the German Emin Pasha relief expedition with the potential to strengthen German "national consciousness" and declared that this was reason enough to support it.[88]

Conversely, the antisemitic *Staatsbürger-Zeitung* backed the relief expedition without any apparent reserve. It detailed the progress of the Stanley and Peters rescue attempts and reported on Emin's activities once he entered German service. Ironically, the editors accused Jewish interests of opposing Carl Peters's expedition, and the Jewish press in general of dissuading private investments by painting the colonies in a negative light.[89] The Protestant newspaper *Der Reichsbote* went even further, actually defending the onetime Egyptian governor from antisemitic attacks after he

---

85. *Tägliche Rundschau,* November 26, 1889.

86. "Stanley im dunkelsten Afrika," *Die Gartenlaube: Illustriertes Familienblatt,* no. 27 (1890), 456.

87. Emin's side of the story did come out, however, in the form of interviews conducted after his arrival in Bagamoyo and in the posthumous publication of his journals and letters.

88. "Deutschland," *Neue Preußische Zeitung,* September 18, 1888.

89. "Die Freigabe der 'Nerra,'" *Staatsbürger-Zeitung,* August 8, 1889.

died. Responding to an article in the *Deutsche Ostwacht* that called Emin "the colonial and ivory-Jew Schnitzer," *Der Reichsbote* insisted that Emin had rendered greater service "than all Ahlwardts, Pikenbachs, Schwenn-bagens, and Böckels combined."[90]

The *Neue Preußische Zeitung* and *Der Reichsbote* belonged to the wing of the antisemitic movement that—for the most part—viewed the "Jewish problem" as a religious rather than a racial one. But praise for Emin Pasha from the *Staatsbürger-Zeitung* showed that support for the explorer also extended into circles that included racial antisemites. The antisemitic and adamantly procolonial *Tägliche Rundschau*—which complained in 1894 that the DOAG was becoming "Semitic"—even emerged as one of Emin's strongest advocates, despite having Friedrich Lange as an editor until 1895. The *Rundschau* praised Emin in 1890 for "immediately offering his services to his old fatherland . . . even though it had previously done almost nothing to care for him." It romanticized his decision to return to the interior, stating that he had "become unaccustomed to the hustle and bustle of Europe during his long, peaceful, contemplative life in inner Africa" and therefore "has no desire to return to the so-called civilized world."[91] In addition, the *Rundschau* went further than practically any other newspaper in making Emin into the epitome of "Germanness" and in insisting that an attack on him was an attack on Germans in general.

The *Rundschau* made these points in its harsh review of *In Darkest Africa* in 1890. The reviewer complained that Stanley "attempts to diminish Emin Pasha in the eyes of the world and makes every effort to damage the Germans." He insisted that "every patriotic-feeling German" now felt "open hatred or silent judicious disdain" for Stanley.[92] The reviewer also equated Stanley's mode of colonialism with the English mode in general, and he contrasted it with Emin's: whereas Stanley colonized "after the English style, with the bible and the sword to first subjugate and plunder the natives," Emin Pasha "attempted to improve and better his subjects from within and without." Surprisingly, the reviewer implied that Emin's talents were due, at least in part, to his Jewish heritage: "Stanley is, with his violent, brutal energy and his mercantile streak (exemplified by the fact that no officer of his expedition was allowed to publish anything before the ap-

90. "Der conservativ-antisemitische 'Reichsbote,'" *Mittheilungen* 3 (1893): 236. Ahlwardt, Pikenbach, and Böckel were well-known antisemitic politicians of the early *Kaiserreich*.

91. Br., "Vom ostafrikanischen Kriegsschauplatze. XI.," *Tägliche Rundschau*, April 26, 1890.

92. Dr. H. Pastenaci, "Stanley und Emin," *Tägliche Rundschau*, July 6, 1890.

Emin Pasha.
Nach der neuesten Aufnahme in Sansibar.

Fig. 1. An idealized drawing of
Emin Pasha on the front page of
the middle-class magazine *Die
Gartenlaube,* in 1890

Fig. 2. Emin Pasha
(in the dark suit)
and Carl Peters
during a brief
meeting in Mpuapua
in German East
Africa in the
summer of 1890

pearance of this book) the true Englishman, half businessman, half explorer; Emin to the contrary is a true German *Gelehrtennatur* with the administrative talents and the diplomatic inclination of the Jews."[93] None of this, however, blunted the newspaper's antisemitism: during the 1890s, it continued to lament the "frivolous" nature of contemporary Jewish baptisms and accuse the "Jewish press" of a lack of patriotism.[94]

Not all antisemites jumped on the Emin Pasha bandwagon. The organs of the two major racially antisemitic political organizations, the German Reform Party and the German Social Party, remained constant in their opposition, and they based it on the fact of Emin's Jewish heritage.

The *Deutsche Wacht* (of the Reform Party) argued against a German relief expedition from the very beginning. It attributed the pro–Emin Pasha craze to the "Jewish press" that, it insisted, normally opposed colonialism but championed Emin because he was a "tribal companion."[95] The newspaper also refuted the common arguments made in favor of a German rescue effort. "Let us look for once at the facts calmly and soberly," wrote the author of a front-page editorial in September 1889. "Emin Pasha is no German, but rather a Jew and a truly international Jew at that. . . . What is the fate of an Egyptian Pasha to us Germans," he asked, "especially one who, as a Jew and Mohammedan, has nothing to fear from the fanaticism of the Mahdists, unlike Gordon?"[96] The author insisted that aiding Emin would only damage German foreign policy, because it would increase tensions with England, to Germany's detriment. Similarly, the *Antisemitische Correspondenz*—which became the *Deutsch-Soziale Blätter* of the German Social Party in 1890—condemned Emin as a Jew early on. Both newspapers maintained their hostility even after Emin reached German East Africa.

As time passed, Emin's antisemitic critics insisted that he confirmed, rather than confounded, their antisemitism. To make their argument, they pointed to certain specific developments. In late 1890, the governor of German East Africa, Hermann von Wissmann, complained to the Foreign Office that Emin had disobeyed orders by raising the German flag at Tab-

---

93. Ibid.

94. "Aus Kunst, Wissenschaft und Leben," *Tägliche Rundschau,* December 13, 1893; ibid., December 16, 1893.

95. "Tagesfragen. Der Lärm um Emin Pascha," *Deutsche Wacht,* October 21, 1888.

96. "Hat Deutschland Verpflichtungen gegen Emin Pascha?", *Deutsche Wacht,* September 15, 1889.

ora and that his actions disrupted important plans for the region. Then, in the summer and fall of 1891, reports emerged that Emin had left German service, commanding his German troops to march back to the coast while he himself embarked further into the interior, purportedly to connect Cameroon to East Africa. Although Governor von Soden tacitly endorsed this plan, the government in Berlin publicly announced that Emin had left German territory against official orders.[97] Emin's detractors accused him of attempting to return to Equatoria to recover the gigantic hordes of ivory that he had reportedly left behind, accumulated during his long stay in the region.

Consequently, Emin became "the ivory-Jew" and the "Jewish-African idler" in newspapers like the *Leipziger Tagesanzeiger* and the *Antisemitische Correspondenz,* which painted him as a paradigm of "Jewishness."[98] His antisemitic critics argued that Emin proved the merits of an uncompromising antisemitism. The *Deutsch-Soziale Blätter* declared in late 1891 that "our colonial-Jew Emin Pascha (more correctly Dr. Eduard Schnitzer) increasingly shows himself in his inherent light. We constantly advised mistrust toward this Hebrew colonial genie," it wrote, "and indeed there were even usually-reasonable people under the antisemites and conservatives who, since a few months ago, believed it necessary to doff their caps to Emin's 'accomplishments.' We always supposed that this adventurer was led in his enterprises merely by a Hebrew business-spirit and a little ambition." The newspaper echoed the accusation that Emin left German territory against orders in order to make "an ivory haul" in Equatoria, and it insisted that his raising the flag in Tabora had destabilized the region. It asserted that Emin's example proved the unsuitability of "Jews" for government service.[99] Reichstag deputy and German Social Party founder Liebermann von Sonnenberg repeated this claim several weeks later before an assembly of party members in Leipzig.[100]

Emin's antisemitic critics used information about his private life against him as well. When the news broke in 1888 that Emin had been named "Isaak" before becoming Eduard, the *Antisemitische Correspon-*

---

97. *Deutscher Reichsanzeiger,* October 28, 1891.

98. "Der Antisemitismus und die Wissenschaft," *Mittheilungen* no. 4 (1891): 6; "Der pövelhaften Angriff," *Mittheilungen* 3 (1893): 333.

99. "Emin Schnitzer has now, again, clearly established just how unreliable Jewish elements in official positions are" ("Unser Kolonial-Jude Emin Pascha," *Deutsch-Soziale Blätter,* November 15, 1891).

100. Verträgt sich die Talmud-Moral mit dem deutschen Staatsbürger-Recht?, by Liebermann von Sonnenberg, N2177-6, BAB.

denz declared this an example of "the unscrupulous substitution of names and taking of double names by Jews" in general.[101] Several years later, reports emerged that Emin had abandoned his mistress—the widow of the Albanian governor, Ismail Hakki Pasha—during a brief visit to Germany in the mid-1870s, and that he had misrepresented her as his wife. The *Deutsch-Soziale Blätter* argued that Emin had deceived her "in a truly Jewish, underhanded way," proof again of his true nature.[102]

None of this, however, did much to dim Emin's light. The controversies concerning the raising of the flag in Tabora and Emin's departure from government service split the procolonial press, but majority opinion sided heavily with Emin against critics like Wissmann. Liberal newspapers like the *National-Zeitung* and the *Vossische Zeitung* countered attacks on Emin by recounting his accomplishments and defending his patriotism.[103] Procolonial enthusiasts also thrilled at the prospect of a land bridge connecting Cameroon to German East Africa.

What is more, Emin's stature only grew after his death, despite the attempts by his antisemitic opponents to tear him down. The publication in 1894 of a memoir by Franz Stuhlmann, *With Emin Pasha in the Heart of Africa,* helped this along. Stuhlmann, who had accompanied Emin into the interior in 1890, presented the former governor in almost superhuman terms: as a "man of peace" who nevertheless "shrank back from no dangers," as someone with "heroic willpower" who "overcame us all in stamina by a wide margin," as a selfless patriot whom "applause . . . left cold," and as someone who was animated by "a warm love of the fatherland . . . despite his long stay in foreign lands."[104] Far from rendering Emin ridiculous, this became the dominant popular image, spurred in part by anger against Britain. Emin "governed as a ruler, doctor and sage. . . . Never has a white man exerted a nobler domination over his colored Brothers," declared a contributor to the *Berliner Morgen-Zeitung* following his death.[105] Emin Pasha was "a true German man" wrote *Das Kleine Journal* in 1897, "one of

---

101. "Emin Pascha—Jude," *Antisemitische Correspondenz.*

102. "Enthüllungen über Emin Pascha's Privatleben," *Deutsch-Soziale Blätter,* March 26, 1896.

103. "Nachrichten von Emin Pascha," *National-Zeitung,* November 2, 1891, evening edition; "Der Herrscher von Wadelai," *Vossische Zeitung,* May 2, 1892.

104. Franz Stuhlmann, *Mit Emin Pascha ins Herz von Afrika* (Berlin: Geographische Verlagsbuchhandlung von Dietrich Reimer, 1894), 610–11, 614.

105. Friedrich Dernburg, "Emins Tod," *Familienblatt: Tägliche Unterhaltungsbeilage zur "Berliner Morgenzeitung,"* September 12, 1893.

the best and most steadfast champions of Germanness for the people at large."[106]

Praise continued to come from within antisemitic circles as well. Reichstag deputy Wilhelm Lattmann of the German Social Party lauded Emin in 1910 for having combined a "healthy humanitarianism" with a "healthy attitude of domination" in his outlook on the African colonized.[107] During the First World War, the *Tägliche Rundschau* held up Emin Pasha's life history as exemplifying "German industry and ability." The newspaper declared that Emin was an exemplar of Germanness at a time when "the German breed and German ways" were "so thoroughly misunderstood."[108]

As Emin Pasha, Eduard Schnitzer achieved greater public acclaim in imperial Germany than perhaps any individual of Jewish descent up until that time. His genuine popularity testified to the special opportunities for assimilation afforded to Germans of Jewish descent through participation in the new project of overseas empire: despite the fact that he was born a Jew, Emin became a German patriot in the imagination of his German supporters, and this, during the age of racial antisemitism. Emin had the fortune, however, of being far removed from the antisemitic cauldron back in Germany, having left before the rise of the modern antisemitic movement. With the exception of a very brief meeting with Carl Peters in the interior of East Africa in 1890, Emin had no interaction with anyone of significance from antisemitic circles. In addition, Emin's early death—combined with his long absence from Europe—meant that his saintly image suffered little damage from the reality of the flesh-and-blood man.

None of this was the case for other colonial actors of Jewish descent. For men like Paul Kayser and Bernhard Dernburg, colonialism was much more a double-edged sword. They, too, benefited from participation in the patriotic project of empire building, earning respect for their activities on behalf of colonialism. As we shall see in chapter 4, Dernburg's reputation with the public as a German patriot even rivaled Emin's. But both Kayser and Dernburg came under attack by antisemites who could not believe that

---

106. Wilh. Tappert, "Emin Pasha," *Das Kleine Journal: Zeitung für alle Gesellschaftsklassen,* December 6, 1897.

107. *Sten. Ber.* XII/II/29, February 3, 1910, 1001.

108. Hans Ellenberg, "Die Tagebücher von Emin Pascha," *Unterhaltungsbeilage der Täglichen Rundschau,* April 3, 1917.

a "Jew" could act for Germany's greater good. As seen above, this had also been the case with Emin Pasha. Unlike him, however, Kayser and Dernburg had to closely interact with antisemitic forces in Germany. In their capacity of representing and defending official colonial policy in parliament, they often found themselves arrayed with procolonial antisemites against the political Left, which produced the most outspoken critics of both colonialism and the antisemitic movement. For these two Germans of Jewish descent, participation in colonialism was therefore a precarious undertaking. Kayser and Dernburg never knew what sort of public embarrassment they might suffer from their dubious political allies, individuals who could speak vociferously on the Jewish Question and then, almost in the same breath, defend colonialism against its political opponents.

This uncertainty seriously affected Paul Kayser. His private correspondence shows that antisemitism was a constant worry, that he felt under continuous attack by antisemitic forces in the military, the nobility, and the press throughout the 1890s.[109] The decade was an inauspicious time for a converted Jew to head the colonial bureaucracy, as it witnessed the high point in the fortunes of the new antisemitic political parties. During Kayser's tenure, the powerful Conservative Party publicly endorsed the antisemitic cause. In 1893, the antisemites increased their seats in the Reichstag from six to sixteen. In 1894, representatives from the antisemitic German Social and German Reform Parties gained *Fraktion* status in the Reichstag by uniting into one group with fifteen members. Antisemitic deputies introduced legislation that same year to restrict Jewish immigration into Germany from Eastern Europe, and the radical independent antisemite Hermann Ahlwardt called for Germans to "exterminate" Jewry during a plenary session in 1895. This was the legislative body to which Kayser had to defend the colonial budget and official colonial policies while serving as *Dirigent* of the Colonial Division of the Foreign Office

---

109. Parts of Paul Kayser's private correspondence survive in the form of excerpts typed by the Nazi-era (and antisemitic) historian Walter Frank, found today in the Walter Frank Papers (hereafter WFP) at the Bundesarchiv in Koblenz. A small number of letters from Kayser to his political confidants also exist in the Paul Kayser Papers, the Count Philipp zu Eulenburg Papers, and the Prince Chlodwig Hohenlohe-Schillingsfürst Papers, all in the Koblenz archive (Kayser's collection is in two parts, however, one of which is in Berlin). Walter Frank wrote an article on Kayser in 1943 using some of this material (Walter Frank, "Der Geheime Rat Paul Kayser. Neues Material aus seinem Nachlass," *Historische Zeitschrift* 168 [1943]: 302–35, 541–63).

from 1890 to 1894, then *Direktor* until late 1896.[110] For Kayser, the situation was unnerving. In August 1892—even before the Conservatives inserted an antisemitic statement into their official party platform—Kayser wrote to his uncle that he "could not bear" a "clerical-conservative, that is to say, antisemitic government."[111]

Kayser's rise to the top of the colonial bureaucracy was a result of his own ambition and his fortuitous connections with leading members of the ruling aristocracy. Much like Eduard Schnitzer, Kayser was born to two Jewish parents in Silesia, although slightly later, in 1845. Instead of medicine, he chose a career in law, becoming a judge and university lecturer in Strasbourg in the 1870s, where he also tutored members of the ruling noble class in their university studies on the side. In this way, he became acquainted with Herbert and Bill Bismarck, the sons of the German chancellor, as well as Alfred von Bülow, the brother of Bernhard von Bülow, one of Bismarck's future successors. Kayser also met in this fashion the young Count Philipp Eulenburg, who became a trusted friend of and favorite adviser to Emperor Wilhelm II.[112] Kayser left Strasbourg for Berlin in 1875, becoming first a city judge, then a privy councillor for the Imperial Justice Office. After converting to evangelical Christianity in 1882, he joined the Reich Chancellory. With the help of Herbert Bismarck, then secretary of state for foreign affairs, Kayser became a jurist in the Foreign Office in 1885, gaining the titles *Wirklicher Geheimer Legationsrat* and *Vortragender Rat* that same year.[113] In this capacity, he became strongly involved in drafting legislation for the new colonies, and in 1886, he was appointed the government's representative overseeing the reorganization of the German East Africa Company.[114] Between 1886 and 1889, he received

110. The Colonial Division of the Foreign Office gained the right to represent colonial affairs for the chancellor only in 1894. Kayser helped to defend colonial policies in the Reichstag before this, however (Harry R. Rudin, *Germans in the Cameroons, 1884–1914: A Case Study in Modern Imperialism* [New Haven: Yale University Press, 1938], 134).

111. Paul Kayser to Professor Baron, August 5, 1892, no. 14, WFP, BAK.

112. Isabel V. Hull, *The Entourage of Kaiser Wilhelm II, 1888–1918* (Cambridge: Cambridge University Press, 1982), 45.

113. Akta personalia des Kgl. Stadtgerichts zu Berlin betr. die Anstellung des früheren Gerichtsassessors Dr. jur. Paul Kayser, no. 21, WFP, BAK.

114. "Kolonialabtheilung und Kolonialrath," *Koloniales Jahrbuch* 3 (1890): 107–8; Arne Perras, *Carl Peters and German Imperialism, 1856–1918: A Political Biography* (Oxford: Oxford University Press, 2004), 79. Carl Peters approached the government for help with the company in 1886 following his failure to raise sufficient capital for it from the private sector. The state became involved in helping secure the necessary funds, but it demanded a reorganization of the company that shifted power from Peters to a new board of directors. Kayser had

two decorations for his service: the Roten Adler medals of the fourth and third orders.[115]

Kayser maintained his connections with Bismarck's sons during this time. Both the sons and their father drew on his legal expertise in several private matters, for example, asking Kayser to prepare some of the legal work for proceedings against the publicist Heinrich Geffcken, one of the chancellor's political enemies.[116] Kayser also became close to Count Friedrich August von Holstein, a Bismarck opponent who worked to sabotage the chancellor's foreign policies. Kayser maintained his relationship with Philipp Eulenburg as well, and it was through Eulenburg that he met the emperor in early 1890. This was the period of Wilhelm's interest in the so-called social question. Against Bismarck's recommendations, the emperor was intent on introducing legislation to improve the plight of German workers in order to win their loyalty and lessen the attractions of Social Democracy. Eulenburg recommended Kayser to Wilhelm in early 1890 as a man of considerable knowledge about the "socialist and worker questions," and also as someone with an "eminent capacity and natural talent."[117] Kayser met with both the emperor and empress in March, presumably to discuss social legislation.[118] He was appointed chief administrator of the Colonial Division of the Foreign Office approximately five months later.

Kayser's appointment was greeted with general approval. The *Koloniales Jahrbuch,* published by Gustav Meinecke, the lead editor of the *Deutsche Kolonialzeitung,* remarked in 1890 that Kayser enjoyed "unusual confidence in all colonial circles" and that he raised "happy expectations" for the future of the Colonial Division of the Foreign Office.[119] Despite this positive reception, however, Kayser's tenure in office was difficult, to say the least. As *Dirigent* and then *Direktor* of the Colonial Division, Kayser was charged with creating a development policy for the colonies.

---

the power to oversee the board and review its accounts and correspondence. Peters stayed on as the director of the corporation (Perras, *Carl Peters,* 78–79).

115. Abschriften aus dem Bestand Reichskolonialamt, no. 21, WFP, BAK.

116. According to Carl Peters, Chancellor Bismarck referred to Kayser as a "wandering legal reference book" (Frank, "Der Geheime Rat Paul Kayser," 307).

117. Philipp zu Eulenburg to Wilhelm II, January 20, 1890, no. 8, Fürst Philipp zu Eulenburg und Hertefeld Papers, BAK.

118. Holstein to Philipp zu Eulenburg, March 2, 1890, no. 9, Fürst Philipp zu Eulenburg und Hertefeld Papers, BAK. Holstein wrote that the emperor "conferred a great honor on Kayser" during their meeting by letting him kiss the empress's hand.

119. "Kolonialabtheilung und Kolonialrath."

But he only had a small budget with which to operate, because neither the Caprivi government nor a majority in the Reichstag gave the colonies a high funding priority. Another problem that Kayser faced was the confused nature of the decision-making process for colonial affairs, a result of the competition between the civilian bureaucracy and military forces. The *Schutztruppe,* or colonial troops, were not under civilian control, and, as a result, the Colonial Division had to contend with a military presence on the ground that acted independently of its authority.

Kayser attempted to solve the first problem through concessionary policy, granting private companies fantastic land rights and privileges in the expectation that they assume the costs of developing the colonies. To attract private capital, he created the advisory board know as the Colonial Council, whose membership, appointed by the chancellor, contained representatives of colonial companies plus other interested parties, like missionaries. Kayser also fought a long-running battle with the military to assert the Colonial Division's control, and he had more success on this front than with his development policies. Backed by Chancellor Hohenlohe, the Colonial Division of the Foreign Office eventually won out over the recalcitrant military governor of German East Africa, Friedrich von Schele, making headway in its efforts to concentrate the decision-making process for colonial affairs in the hands of the civilian authorities.[120] But concessionary policy was a failure, because concession companies proved reluctant to assume the costs of developing the territories they controlled. Other difficulties that Kayser faced included a staunch opposition to colonialism and a deep suspicion of concessionary policy from the political Left and, of course, the Peters, Schröder, and Leist and Wehlan scandals.[121]

Antisemitism was also a problem. Despite his conversion, Kayser was widely perceived as a Jew, even by friends and supporters. For example, Philipp Eulenburg held Kayser in the highest esteem for his drive and intellect, but never forgot his Jewish roots. Upon Kayser's resignation in 1896, Eulenburg authored a short essay on him where he highlighted both Kayser's intellectual gifts and his outsider status. "He is the *only state official* that I have come to know . . . whom I *deeply revere* and *admire* and

---

120. Arthur J. Knoll, "Decision-Making for the German Colonies," in *Germans in the Tropics: Essays in German Colonial History,* ed. Knoll and Lewis H. Gann (New York: Greenwood Press, 1987), 133–37.

121. Beginning in 1892, the Reichstag assumed greater control of colonial finances, demanding for its approval a detailed budget for each colony. The Reichstag also assumed the power to approve or reject colonial loans and their guarantees.

whose miserable, poor, small, broken, Jewish form will always remain luminous before my soul and heart," Eulenburg wrote.[122] Compared to the vitriol leveled at Emin Pasha from newspapers like the *Deutsche Wacht,* however, the treatment Kayser received from the antisemitic press was extremely mild; the harshest criticisms with an antisemitic tone came only toward the end of his six-year stay in office, shortly before and then immediately after the announcement of his resignation, and then after his death in 1898, when segments of the press and individual antisemites blamed Kayser for the follies of concessionary policy.[123] Before this time, the most embarrassing antisemitic attacks came from other sources.

Perhaps the greatest embarrassment came in 1891, when the emotionally and mentally unbalanced businessman Carl Paasch used Kayser as an example in *A Jewish-German Embassy* of the penetration of Jews into the highest levels of government.[124] Although Paasch only mentioned Kayser in passing—albeit repeatedly—he included a chapter titled "Jews and Colonial Policy" where he attributed a "semitic tinge" to all contemporary colonial efforts.[125] Paasch distributed his book to practically the entire political establishment with Theodor Fritsch's help, reportedly mailing one thousand copies to German princes and members of the Bundesrat, the Reichstag, and the various Landtags, plus other important political personalities. In addition, Paasch wrote an "Open Letter" to the German chancellor, Caprivi, where he again accused the Foreign Office of being dominated by Jews subservient to Jewish interests. The Foreign Office accused Paasch of libel, and, after several court cases, he was sentenced in May 1893 to fifteen months imprisonment.[126] Kayser's name came up repeatedly during the proceedings. Some of Paasch's libelous statements against him were read out loud in court, like the accusation that Kayser

---

122. "Der kleine Kayser," no. 43, Fürst Philipp zu Eulenburg und Hertefeld Papers, BAK. The emphases are Eulenburg's own.

123. Fr. Henkel, "Der Hereroaufstand. Entweder—oder!" *Deutsche Welt: Wochenschrift der Deutschen Zeitung,* July 31, 1904; Friedrich Lange, *Reines Deutschtum: Gründzuge einer nationalen Weltanschauung* (Berlin: Alexander Duncker, 1904), 283.

124. A German court confined Paasch to a mental institution for seven weeks of observation in June 1893. The medical official who made the recommendation testified that Paasch appeared to suffer from a persecution complex, fearing that he was caught up in a "net of intrigue" ("Prozeß Paasch und Genossen," *Mittheilungen* 3 [1893]: 261).

125. Carl Paasch, *Der jüdische Damon I,* section 3 of *Eine jüdisch-deutsch Gesandtschaft und ihre Helfer. Geheimes Judentum, Nebenreigerungen und jüdische Weltherrschaft* (Leipzig: Carl Paasch, 1891), 204. Like the antisemitic press, Paasch fixated on Emin Pasha rather than Kayser.

126. "Der 'Fall Paasch,'" *Mittheilungen* 3 (1893): 219.

had delivered in the Reichstag a "truly Jewish" speech that showed Talmudic influences.[127]

Another embarrassing incident for Kayser occurred in late 1892 or early 1893, this time in the form of an antisemitic slight from one of his own subordinates. The civilian governor of German East Africa, Baron Julius von Soden, insinuated in a report to the chancellor that Kayser had privileged a Jewish firm while commissioning construction work for the colony. Given Kayser's background, the implication was clear: that Kayser was still a Jew and, as such, had Jewish interests at heart.[128]

Both incidents came at a time when the growing boldness of the antisemitic political parties would have been increasingly obvious to Kayser. On March 13, 1891, Kayser spoke in the Reichstag about the budget for Cameroon shortly after deputy Liebermann von Sonnenberg complained that "always more people of Jewish ancestry are penetrating into our overseas foreign service."[129] On November 17, Kayser spoke in the Reichstag about the slave trade in German Togo and East Africa.[130] After a long interval, his speech was followed by a lengthy exchange between von Sonnenberg and Progressive Peoples Party deputy Heinrich Rickert about Jewish morals and usury, preceded by a delivery on usury by Otto Böckel.[131] Four months later, a long discussion took place involving Adolf Stöcker, von Sonnenberg, and members of the Social Democratic and Progressive Peoples parties concerning a recent antisemitic riot. Von Sonnenberg referred in his delivery to killing Jews and stealing their property. He prophesied that the Jewish Question would be solved in this way should the Social Democrats become infused with antisemitism.[132]

Made in this context, the attacks by Paasch and von Soden troubled Kayser greatly and exacerbated his awareness of his own outsider status. He wrote about each incident to his uncle, a professor in Bonn, voicing fear and anger. Concerning Paasch's slander, Kayser was as much disturbed by the lukewarm response of important members of the Colonial Division of the Foreign Office as he was by Paasch's accusation that the colonial ad-

---

127. "Gerichts-Zeitung. Verhandlungen. Prozeß Paasch. II.," *Staatsbürger-Zeitung,* August 7, 1892, evening edition.
128. Paul Kayser to Professor Baron, January 22, 1893, no. 14, WFP, BAK.
129. *Sten. Ber.* 88, March 13, 1891, 2027.
130. *Sten. Ber.* 120, November 17, 1891, 2891–95.
131. Ibid., 2901–6, 2907–12.
132. *Sten. Ber.* 204, March 26, 1892, 5028.

ministration was essentially a Jewish cabal.[133] "All in all, the book and its treatment is indeed a bad sign of a wretched time and thoroughly spoils for me what is a difficult and troubled vocation anyway," Kayser wrote in April 1891. "Suddenly, one sees oneself surrounded by enraged fanatics, by political slanderers, by shoulder-shrugging colleagues and superiors who inwardly rejoice." Kayser wrote of his desire to "throw the whole show away" and "become a lawyer and perhaps a Social Democrat." He complained that his efforts in office simply prepared "a more comfortable place for the future Aryan successor."[134]

The antisemitic slight from Soden angered Kayser even more. Initially, Chancellor Caprivi refused to publicly discipline the governor, fearing a scandal, and preferred instead to quietly remove him from his post by barring his return from a current vacation. Faced with the prospect of no immediate public official response to Soden's insubordination, Kayser threatened to resign.[135] In a letter to his uncle, where he protested that he "did not know" if the director of the building firm in question was Jewish, Kayser professed a need for "atonement."[136] In the end, Caprivi publicly dismissed Soden from his post, although the official announcement cited Soden's poor health as the reason, and Kayser remained.[137]

Antisemitism was a concern for Kayser even before these incidents, and it remained so afterward. His private correspondence shows that he was quite sensitive to antisemitism well before ascending to the very public position as head of the Colonial Division of the Foreign Office. In 1886, he wrote to Chancellor Bismarck's younger son, Wilhelm, complaining of a public antisemitic slight, most likely from the press.[138] Two years later, he warned his uncle against relocating to Breslau where, in his estimation,

---

133. One important official, Anton Hellwig, favored ignoring Paasch's attacks rather than responding to them through the courts, a suggestion that appalled Kayser.

134. Paul Kayser to Professor Baron, April 28, 1891, no. 14, WFP, BAK.

135. Paul Kayser to Leo von Caprivi, January 21, 1892, no. 14, WFP, BAK. The date of the transcribed letter should actually be 1893.

136. Paul Kayser to Professor Baron, January 22, 1893, no. 14, WFP, BAK.

137. Frank, "Der Geheime Rat Paul Kayser," 331.

138. The Bundesarchiv in Koblenz contains a letter from Wilhelm Bismarck to Kayser, responding to an "excerpt" sent to him by Kayser that troubled Kayser greatly. Bismarck's letter gives no clear indication of what the excerpt said. However, he insisted that Kayser's outrage was unjustified because the piece in question—likely a newspaper article—contained "only facts" (Graf Wilhelm von Bismarck to Paul Kayser, October 14, 1886, no. 10, Kleine Erwerbungen, BAK).

"antisemitism stands in full bloom."[139] He then expressed repeated concern about the antisemitic press and political parties after assuming the
leadership of the colonial bureaucracy. He voiced suspicion to his uncle in
a letter of 1891 that "antisemitic parties" had been behind an article appearing in a French newspaper accusing him of involvement in the anti-
Bismarck machinations that contributed to the chancellor's recent resignation.[140] Seven months later, in the same letter where he wrote that he "could
not bear" a "clerical-conservative, that is to say, antisemitic government,"
Kayser also remarked that both the Catholic Center and Conservative Parties would rather "sacrifice" the colonies than see them "surrendered to the
Jews."[141] Kayser complained later that month about comments in the antisemitic press over his recent three-month-long trip to German East Africa.
Kayser's wife, Alwine, had accompanied him, and the *Hamburger Nachrichten* reported that the sultan of Zanzibar gave her "sumptuous gifts"
during their visit to the island.[142] Kayser wrote that this report occasioned
"attacks" from the antisemitic *Staatsbürger-Zeitung,* which had made several snide remarks about Kayser's "'traveling' wife" and her "expensive
presents."[143]

Kayser might have taken some comfort in the fact that, unlike Chancellor Bismarck, Chancellors Caprivi and Hohenlohe had no patience for
political antisemitism. Bismarck had himself been the target of antisemitic
attacks during the 1870s by opponents in the Conservative Party who used
the chancellor's close relationship with his Jewish banker, Gerson Bleichröder, to accuse him of being under Jewish influences.[144] But Bismarck
never spoke out officially against the political antisemites, and he was not
averse to making common cause with Adolf Stöcker against the Progres-

---

139. Paul Kayser to Professor Baron, May 6, 1888, no. 14, WFP, BAK. For a discussion of
political antisemitism in Breslau during the 1880s, see Till van Rahden, *Jews and Other Germans: Civil Society, Religious Diversity, and Urban Politics in Breslau, 1860–1925,* trans. Marcus Brainard (Madison: University of Wisconsin Press, 2008).
    140. Paul Kayser to Professor Baron, December 27, 1891, no. 14, WFP, BAK.
    141. Paul Kayser to Professor Baron, August 5, 1892, no. 14, WFP, BAK. Kayser likely
made the first remark in light of the increased cooperation between political antisemites and
the Conservative Party.
    142. Frank, "Der Geheime Rat Paul Kayser," 329.
    143. Paul Kayser to Professor Baron, August 25, 1892, no. 14, WFP, BAK; "Zeitung der
Thatsachen. Deutschland," *Staatsbürger-Zeitung,* August 16, 1892, evening edition; "Local-
Zeitung. Die Frau Geheimrat Kayser," *Staatsbürger-Zeitung,* August 17, 1892.
    144. Stern, *Gold and Iron,* 187.

sive Party.[145] In contrast, his successor, Leo von Caprivi, took a strong public stance against political antisemitism. Shortly after the Conservative Party made waves by adopting an antisemitic statement into its official party platform in 1892, Caprivi announced his intention while speaking before the Reichstag to "actively" oppose any "legislative step" to revoke Jewish emancipation.[146] Caprivi reiterated his position toward the end of 1893 during a parliamentary plenary debate over the next year's colonial budget. Representative Oswald Zimmermann of the antisemitic German Reform Party denounced Jewish overrepresentation in the judiciary and warned that Germany was "setting a course to become a pure Jewish state."[147] Caprivi responded by attacking Zimmermann as a demagogue, and antisemitism as a prelude to Social Democracy. He accused the antisemites of targeting not just Jews but also their relatives: "anyone who has a Jewish father or a Jewish wife."[148]

Before this, however, Kayser had little faith that Caprivi would be of much help against antisemitic opposition. During the summer of 1893, he wrote to his uncle that Caprivi "would be the first to let me fall should I no longer be suitable to the current antisemitic majority in the Reichstag."[149] Kayser had greater faith in Caprivi's successor, Prince Chlodwig zu Hohenlohe-Schillingsfürst, who backed him in 1894 against a reluctant Wilhelm II in his effort to assert civilian control over the military governor of German East Africa. Early the next year, Kayser complained to his uncle that "antisemitic, military, noble, and Bismarckian agitators" were working against him, but he insisted that he still enjoyed Hohenlohe's support. "Were Caprivi still at the helm," Kayser wrote, "I would not doubt for a moment under the prevailing circumstances that my days are numbered."[150]

Antisemitism played a role in Kayser's decision to resign. The letters from his last eight months in office refer repeatedly to antisemitic opposition both within and without the Reichstag. This period was particularly

145. Weiss, *Ideology of Death: Why the Holocaust Happened in Germany* (Chicago: Elephant Paperbacks, 1996), 93; Richard S. Levy, *The Downfall of the Anti-Semitic Political Parties in Imperial Germany* (New Haven: Yale University Press, 1975), 132.

146. *Sten. Ber.* 13, December 12, 1892, 273.

147. *Sten. Ber.* IX/II/9, November 30, 1893, 179. Kayser did not speak during this plenary meeting.

148. Ibid., 192.

149. Paul Kayser to Professor Baron, June 25, 1893, no. 14, WFP, BAK.

150. Paul Kayser to Professor Baron, February 15, 1895, no. 14, WFP, BAK.

stressful for Kayser. In addition to experiencing continued opposition from military circles, he suffered harsh castigation from a wide spectrum of the press over his handling of the Peters and Schröder scandals. To make matters worse, his decision to abandon Carl Peters to his Reichstag critics in March 1896, when the scandal over his actions in German East Africa was in full bloom, created an upsurge of animosity from the explorer's powerful supporters in the Pan-German League and Reichspartei. His handling of the affair also drew the attention of the antisemitic *Deutsch-Soziale Blätter*. The *Blätter* labeled Kayser a "Jew" and accused him of undermining Peters, whom the newspaper identified as "an outspoken antisemite."[151] Kayser then experienced another disappointment in the Reichstag during the summer of 1896, when the body rejected a proposed treaty that would have transferred administrative authority of the German New Guinea Company's island possessions to the government in exchange for far-reaching monopolistic powers granted to the company.[152] Kayser seemed to perceive an antisemitic undercurrent to the attacks upon him, as antisemites and fellow travelers like Otto Arendt were among Peters's and Schröder's most vocal supporters. In addition, segments of the antisemitic press joined the opposition in denouncing the proposed treaty with the New Guinea Company.[153]

Kayser complained in his correspondence of "agitation" both from "vulgar antisemites" and "Peters's people" at this time.[154] He also accused his superiors of giving him insufficient public support and, in June, indicated to Chancellor Hohenlohe that he was at the end of his endurance. It all came to a head when Ludwig Werner of the German Social Reform Party joined the Social Democratic leader August Bebel and the Reichspartei deputy Count von Arnim in attacking Kayser in a Reichstag debate over the new treaty.[155] "To fight alone against antisemites, Social Demo-

---

151. "Innerpolitisches," *Deutsch-Soziale Blätter,* March 19, 1896.

152. S. G. Frith, "The New Guinea Company, 1885–1899: A Case of Unprofitable Imperialism," *Historical Studies* 15 (1972): 376.

153. The *Staatsbürger-Zeitung* accused Kayser in June of not being "sufficiently true" to the interests of the German Reich (*Sten. Ber.* IX/IV/105, June 15, 1896, 2623).

154. Paul Kayser to Professor Baron, June 11, 1896, no. 14, WFP, BAK.

155. The attacks on Kayser during this Reichstag debate took an unusually personal tone. While discussing the proposed deal with the German New Guinea Company, the Reichspartei deputy Count von Arnim accused Kayser of lacking the "moral power of resistance" that one would expect from "a man in such a responsible position" (*Sten. Ber.* IX/IV/105, June 15, 1896, 2626). Arnim was a close friend of Carl Peters. His hostility to Kayser was undoubtedly fueled by the perception that the colonial director had abandoned the explorer to his critics during the Reichstag debate of March.

crats, and Count von Arnim," Kayser wrote the following day, "becomes in reality too much for me," adding that "it would be best to resign from this position with the end of summer."[156] Kayser resigned in the early fall and, afterward, cited in a letter to his uncle antisemitic opposition as one of the reasons for his departure: "I had precisely to deal with opponents who do not shrink from any measures and who had immense power, since as a bimetallist, Dr. Arendt had all agrarian organs, and as an antisemite, Peters had all newspapers of this gang on his side."[157]

The reaction of the antisemitic press to Kayser's resignation confirmed their hostility, which had in fact been muted until 1896. Once the news of Kayser's imminent departure broke, the Berlin-based *Tägliche Rundschau* and *Deutsche Tageszeitung* joined *Der Moderne Völkergeist* in attacking Kayser in an antisemitic fashion. Formerly edited by Friedrich Lange, the *Rundschau* accused Kayser of allowing the representatives of big capital into the Colonial Council. It insisted that the future colonial leadership be "sustained by the national spirit."[158] The official organ of the Agrarian League, the *Deutsche Tageszeitung,* was more direct. It printed a short biography of Kayser, mentioning his Jewish parents, and declared that "it would be better if in the future we dispense with men of his type and descent filling such singular and responsible positions."[159] The newspaper went even further several days later following Kayser's official resignation speech, delivered before the Colonial Council. In it, Kayser defended his record, reminding his audience of his achievements and of the praise he had received from the government. He also attacked his opponents. He criticized the Reichstag for its lack of support in colonial matters, and he censured Otto Arendt for improperly pressuring him in previous years to make Carl Peters the governor of German East Africa.[160] The speech provided more ammunition for antisemites. The *Staatsbürger-Zeitung* criticized it for lacking "Christian humility."[161] The *Deutsche Tageszeitung* proclaimed that Kayser "remained in his heart a Jewish par-

---

156. Paul Kayser to Chlodwig zu Hohenlohe-Schillingsfürst, June 16, 1896, no. 1603, Chlodwig Fürst zu Hohenlohe-Schillingsfürst Papers, BAK.

157. Paul Kayser to Professor Baron, October 25, 1896, no. 14, WFP, BAK. Otto Arendt was one of Germany's leading proponents of a bimetallic monetary system, where both gold and silver are used as legal tender.

158. "Politische Rundschau," *Tägliche Rundschau,* October 16, 1896.

159. "Der Rücktritt des Kolonialdirektors Dr. Kayser," *Deutsche Tageszeitung,* October 15, 1896.

160. Kolonialrat, 4th session, October 19, 1896, 5, RKA 6969, BAB.

161. "Dr. Kayser's Abschied," *Staatsbürger-Zeitung,* October 20, 1896, morning edition.

Fig. 3. Paul Kayser, circa 1890. (Bundesarchiv, Bild 137-029852.)

venue" and insisted that greater attention be paid in the future to "the *völ-kiche* [*sic*] lineage" of candidates for high office.[162]

Paul Kayser was one of the original articulators of the imperialist ideology of *Weltpolitik,* which, according to historian Woodruff D. Smith, competed with the *Lebensraum* approach to colonial development.[163] He wrote several position papers early in his career at the Colonial Division of the Foreign Office that Smith characterized as "the first comprehensive treatments of foreign and colonial policy couched in terms of *Weltpolitik* . . . taken seriously at the highest levels of government."[164] Accordingly,

162. "Herr Dr. Kayser," *Deutsche Tageszeitung,* October 20, 1896.
163. See chap. 1.
164. Woodruff D. Smith, *The Ideological Origins of Nazi Imperialism* (New York: Oxford University Press, 1986), 56.

Kayser was concerned with colonialism's potential economic and industrial benefits. He desired to transform the colonies into dependable markets for German goods and producers of raw materials, and he pursued concessionary policy to this end because of the meagerness of the public funds allotted for colonial development. For concessionary policy to work, Kayser needed to attract capital investment, and, in his mind, this required creating an impression of stability and order in colonial affairs in Berlin and the colonies.

A concern with creating such an impression helped determine Kayser's response to colonial issues dealing with race and violence. From Kayser's perspective, anything that might scare away potential private investors in the colonies was to be avoided. This included public scandals concerning the mistreatment of colonized people, and this attitude contributed in large part to his own mixed record in confronting abuses by officials and free agents in the colonies. By Kayser's own admission, it played a leading role in his muted reaction during the summer of 1892 to news of Friedrich Schröder's pathological brutality. Kayser explained in his resignation speech in 1896 that Governor von Soden himself informed him during his trip to the colony of Schröder's violent conduct, which was so bad that his plantation suffered a chronic labor shortage because of continuous desertion.[165] Soden planned to force Schröder from the colony, but Kayser objected, because Soden had previously expelled a troublesome German journalist. As Kayser put it, he feared that the expulsion of another European might frighten away "faint-hearted capital."[166] Kayser chose to deal with the problem indirectly. After returning home to Germany, he quietly pressured Schröder's brother—a leading member of the German East Africa Plantation Company—to recall the troublesome plantation director.[167]

A fear of scandal, likely motivated by similar concerns over capital investment, also contributed to Kayser's muted response to Carl Peters's brutalities. As was widely pointed out in the press in March 1896, Kayser had heard as early as 1892 of reports that Peters had hanged two Africans

---

165. Schröder's brutality was such that it earned him the nickname *Bana Magongo,* meaning "Bludgeons" (*Essener Volkszeitung,* August 3, 1896, RKA 4812/1, BAB).

166. Kolonialrat, 4th session, October 19, 1896, 5, RKA 6969, BAB.

167. This is the account that Kayser gave to the Colonial Council during his resignation speech, delivered on October 19, 1896. It accords with what Kayser told Governor Hermann von Wissmann in a letter in late September (Paul Kayser to Das Ks. Gouvernement Dar-es-Salam, September 26, 1896, RKA 4812/1, BAB). Schröder was recalled from German East Africa but later returned.

out of sexual jealousy while in the Kilimanjaro region.[168] Yet upon Kayser's recommendation, Peters was appointed a permanent imperial commissioner in 1894. In addition, the Colonial Division of the Foreign Office took no steps to investigate the allegations until they were repeated in public by a Social Democratic Reichstag deputy in 1895. Even worse, Kayser initially sided with Peters during the Reichstag debate in March. He reminded Reichstag deputies that Christopher Columbus and Amerigo Vespucci also committed condemnable acts but, likewise, achieved greatness. He spoke as well of the difficulty of judging from Berlin actions taken in dangerous colonial contexts.[169] When Kayser defended his own actions during the Peters affair in his resignation speech before the Colonial Council, he admitted that a fear of scandal had played a part. He claimed that he had not considered the information against Peters provided in 1892 as enough to prove a punishable impropriety. "A further continuation of the matter would, in my belief, according to the contemporary known evidence, have only given rise to a scandal detrimental to colonial affairs," Kayser stated, "without achieving a conviction."[170]

Kayser's dedication to the *Weltpolitik* model of colonization and his interest in attracting private capital investment did not, however, make him a radical—like Scharlach or Peters—when it came to matters of race and violence. Far from it. As a *Weltpolitiker*, Kayser was not driven by *völkisch* nationalism, and settlement colonialism played no great part in his vision for the colonies. Accordingly, he did not subscribe to the hard-edged racism and violent ethos that often typified *völkisch* nationalists and *Lebensraum* advocates. Instead, Kayser possessed a strikingly liberal outlook on the meaning and importance of race, especially concerning the nature, characteristics, and capabilities of individual black Africans. This put him more in line with colonialists like Ernst Vohsen.

In addition, he was not unconcerned with moderating colonial violence. Although revealing in terms of Kayser's priorities, his behavior during the Peters affair and his apparent inaction against Schröder actually belied his liberal side. His attempt to rationalize Peters's brutalities in

---

168. Governor von Soden initiated his own investigation into the hangings that spring and came to the conclusion that Peters had executed the two Africans out of sexual jealousy. He informed Berlin of this during the summer and pressed the government, unsuccessfully, to take action against Peters (Julius von Soden to Leo von Caprivi, September 16, 1906, no. 21, WFP, BAK; Julius von Soden to Leo von Caprivi, July 4, 1892, no. 21, WFP, BAK; Julius von Soden to Colonial Division, July 31, 1892, no. 21, WFP, BAK).

169. *Sten. Ber.* IX/IV/59, March 13, 1896, 1440.

170. Kolonialrat, 4th session, October 19, 1896, 5, RKA 6969, BAB.

March 1896 was not ideologically driven; rather, it was an opportunistic effort to head off the coming debate in order to spare the colonial administration damaging embarrassment.[171] Kayser admitted as much in private. Shortly after the debate, he labeled what he had said in Peters's defense as "nonsense."[172] He also expressed his opposition to Peters's actions in a letter to the emperor, where he attributed colonial excesses to "the inclination of a section of the younger generation" to see "an ideal worth emulating in the Nietzschean superman."[173]

The greatest difference between Kayser and colonial radicals like Peters lay in the colonial director's outlook on black Africans. For Kayser, blacks were not wild, treacherous, demonic creatures who needed to be ruled with an iron hand. Rather, they were economically rational and potentially peaceable beings who were not incapable of progress and change, an optimistic outlook more in line with the aims of *Weltpolitik* than with *Lebensraum* colonialism. This viewpoint may have stemmed from—or, possibly, was reaffirmed by—Kayser's own experiences in German East Africa in 1892, when he traveled to the colony to investigate the strained relationships between Governor von Soden and two of his strong-willed imperial commissioners, Carl Peters and Hermann von Wissmann.[174] Kayser emerged from the trip with favorable impressions of Arab and African urban settings. He wrote positive descriptions of the multiethnic inhabitants of the port cities of Arden and Tanga in his unpublished travel diary.[175] He described as "thoroughly . . . civilized" the "behavior" of what he called

---

171. Perras points out that, in dealing with Peters in the past, Kayser pursued a policy of appeasement because he did not want to alienate Peters's powerful supporters on the political right from the government. This concern probably motivated Kayser's initial defense of Peters in March 1896 (Perras, *Carl Peters,* 172).

172. Ludwig Raschdau, *In Weimar als preussischer Gesandter* (Berlin: E. S. Mittler, 1939), 66–67.

173. Chlodwig zu Hohenlohe-Schillingsfürst to Wilhelm II, March 22, 1896, no. 21, Walter Frank Papers, BAK. Frank notes that the draft of this letter is in Kayser's hand, and he attributes the above-mentioned quote to him.

174. Peters resented Soden for assigning him to reside in the hostile Kilimanjaro region in 1891 instead of along German East Africa's northern coast. Peters submitted his resignation in protest but eventually relented. Tension increased between the two when Soden announced that he would not pacify the colony's interior after the Hehe decimated forces commanded by Emil von Zelewski. Wissmann resented Soden as well, angered by the governor's refusal to support his plan to explore the Lake Tanganyika region (Reuss, "The Disgrace and Fall," 116–19).

175. Arden lies on the tip of the Arabian Peninsula in present-day Yemen. Tanga is on the northern coast of present-day Tanzania, formerly German East Africa. Kayser noted that both cities contained a mixture of Arabs, Indians, and black Africans.

Arden's "colored nature's children."[176] In Tanga, he was impressed by local market activity and noted the city's atmosphere of "peace" and "contentment."[177]

Kayser's optimistic outlook concerning the ability of blacks to progress and change was reflected above all in his promotion of the education and training in Germany of a handful of black male children almost entirely from Cameroon for the purpose of creating skilled laborers for that colony. He allocated official funds from his department to subsidize this endeavor from 1891 to 1896, funds that he intended to recover by requiring the subsidized blacks to return to Africa to work for limited pay for a prescribed period under their local colonial government. The paucity of the white population in the colonies during the 1890s and its vulnerability to tropical diseases made the supplementation of colonial whites with skilled black workers a reasonable course of action.[178] But from the perspective of local administrators, it was a dangerous policy. According to whites on the ground, European trained or European educated blacks were a disruptive element that threatened white rule by reducing the cultural and educational divide between themselves and the colonized. Governor Eugen von Zimmerer of Cameroon and his acting governor Heinrich Leist both attempted to dissuade Kayser with these concerns, claiming in multiple letters to the Foreign Office that experiences abroad made Africans uncontrollable. When this failed, they marshaled racist arguments, suggesting the immutability of black nature by insisting upon the ultimate futility of cultural enlightenment. Kayser promoted the education and training of blacks in Germany over these objections and, in so doing, demonstrated what his behavior during the Schröder and Peters affairs obscured: the existence of a real difference of opinion between the chief administrator in Berlin and his subordinates in the colonies concerning black potential and the means and meaning of racial domination.

The first expression of dissent came from Zimmerer in July 1892, after Kayser had instructed him to select four Cameroonian boys to apprentice with the building and architectural firm F. H. Schmidt in Altona, Germany. The colonial government had commissioned the firm to build a port on the Cameroonian coast, and the firm, which was already experienced in

---

176. Paul Kayser's Travel Diary, May 23, 1892, no. 63, Paul Kayser Papers, BAK.

177. Ibid., June 1, 1892, no. 63, Paul Kayser Papers, BAK.

178. Cameroon continued a total white population of 105 in 1890. Whites fell victim in tropical colonies to malaria, black-water fever, and sleeping sickness.

training Africans, requested boys to apprentice for this purpose at its own cost, but asked Kayser to help arrange their selection.[179] In his reply to Kayser's request, Zimmerer dissented. He announced his success in securing four boys with the permission of their fathers but declared his strong disapproval, arguing that Africans trained in Europe become "pampered" and "spoiled" and fall under Social Democratic influences. Such "Negroes," Zimmerer wrote, "lose their belief in authority in relation to whites, on which, of course, a predominant part of our influence in Africa is based."[180] Acting governor Leist expressed similar sentiments the following year. Leist reported to the Foreign Office in August that an increasing number of Cameroonians were leaving the colony for Europe to gain an education at a "Congo Institute" established by a "Reverend Hughes" in Wales. He noted that the experience in Cameroon with "Negroes 'educated' in Germany" was "not very pleasant."[181] He proposed stopping the continued departure of Africans from the colony for educational purposes by making emigration dependent upon the governor's approval.

Kayser's response established his clear opposition to this way of thinking and his loyalty to the idea of black progress. In January 1893, he forwarded to Zimmerer a report from F. H. Schmidt concerning the four boys, and he made it clear in a brief preface that he had read the governor's letter. The report describes the boys as "domestic, clean, and industrious." It notes that they were "serious" about learning their respective handicrafts and that they attended church "regularly." Along with their professional training, the boys also received a basic education. The report includes a review by their teacher, who wrote that three of the four were sufficiently "industrious" and that one boy had earned high marks (a "*besonderes gut*") for "language and writing."[182] Kayser responded to Leist's complaints in the fall by investigating Reverend Hughes's activities in Wales. He found that Hughes's institute instructed young Africans "in Christian teaching and living, field- and housework" in order to provide skilled help to white missionaries in Africa.[183] He informed Leist that his discoveries "consider-

---

179. F. H. Schmidt apprenticed four African boys in Alton, Germany, in 1887.

180. Eugen von Zimmerer to Leo von Caprivi, July 24, 1892, RKA 5571, BAB.

181. Heinrich Leist to Colonial Division of the Foreign Office, August 8, 1893, RKA 5572, BAB.

182. Paul Kayser to Eugen von Zimmerer, January 1893, RKA 5572, BAB; F. H. Schmidt to Colonial Division of the Foreign Office, January 11, 1893, RKA 5572, BAB.

183. Dr. C. Büttner to Colonial Division of the Foreign Office, October 7, 1893, RKA 5572, BAB.

ably diminished existing misgivings" about the situation, and he opined that the colonies might benefit from "the education of such natives."[184]

In the face of Zimmerer's and Leist's opposition, Kayser also increased the very small number of African boys living and learning in Germany subsidized by the Colonial Division of the Foreign Office. He began his experimental subsidies in November 1891, when he agreed to have the Colonial Division assume half the cost (500 marks) for at least one year of the upkeep and formal education of a young Cameroonian boy named Tube Metom. Tube's father worked as a translator for Cameroon's colonial government, and he sent his young son to Germany to attend an evangelical primary school in Aalen with the ultimate goal of becoming a physician. The father requested a government subsidy, and Kayser agreed after reading extremely positive reports on Tube's intelligence from his German host, a schoolteacher.[185] Kayser renewed the subsidy several times, helping Tube attend a Latin school. When tragedy overtook Tube's father in 1894, and, as a result, Tube was no longer able to continue his formal education, Kayser paid for Tube's apprenticeship in the "culinary arts" with a German field artillery regiment in Ulm.[186] In return, Tube promised to work for four years for the Cameroon government upon the completion of his training.

Kayser aided a number of other boys in a similar fashion. In the summer of 1892, he and his wife returned from German East Africa with a young black servant named Ali ben Said. They furnished Ali with a basic education for three years then returned him to the colony, where he became an aid in a German school for Africans.[187] In the fall of 1893, Kayser allocated official funds to subsidize the upkeep and vocational training in

---

184. Paul Kayser to Heinrich Leist, October 14, 1893, RKA 5572, BAB.

185. Oesterle to Colonial Division of the Foreign Office, November 1, 1891, RKA 5571, BAB. Oesterle claimed that Tube not only exhibited good moral behavior but also was "a bright, intelligent youth, who has already surpassed his classmates and justified the best hopes. As far as it is possible to judge at this point," Oesterle wrote, "he possesses all capabilities in order to later study medicine, which is the actual goal of his presence."

186. Oesterle to Colonial Division of the Foreign Office, July 4, 1894, RKA 5572, BAB. Tube's father was arrested in 1894 for misusing his position as the government's official translator for the purpose of blackmail. As a consequence, he could no longer contribute to Tube's education. The situation became permanent when the father was executed eleven months later.

187. Alwine Kayser, *Aus den Anfängen unserer Kolonien. Meine Erlebnisse als Begleiterin meines Gatten, des ersten Kolonialdirektors, Wirkl. Geh. Legationsrats Dr. Kayser auf seiner Inspektionsreise nach Deutsch-Ostafrika 1892* (Berlin: Dietrich Reimer [Ernst Vohsen], 1912), 31–32, 68.

Germany of two additional Cameroonians on the condition that, afterward, they work for four years in the colony for the colonial government.[188] Three years later, Kayser had the Colonial Division of the Foreign Office assume the costs of the culinary training in Berlin of an African servant boy from Togo brought to Germany by a colonial official for this purpose.[189]

Kayser received additional protests from Zimmerer during this period. In August 1894, Zimmerer complained in a letter to Chancellor Caprivi that the past success rate with European-educated Africans was only 10 percent. "Most Negroes," Zimmerer insisted, "learnt in Germany only things that they should not have and, as a rule, became incredibly spoiled and conceited, but nevertheless brought with them only an entirely insufficient knowledge for their vocation." Zimmerer also claimed that time abroad had no lasting positive effects. He argued that European-educated blacks had a propensity to "*vernegern,*" or "re-negroize," after returning to the colonies.[190] These complaints did not, however, seem to significantly diminish Kayser's optimism about black potential.

This optimism was reflected as well in the extremely active interest that Kayser took in educating Africans inside the colonies. A handful of government-run primary and secondary schools were founded in Togo and Cameroon (along with missionary schools) during the first decade of empire, and, as chief administrator of the Colonial Division of the Foreign Office, Kayser championed these institutions. He not only allocated the necessary funds for the government schools, but he also helped recruit white teachers and acquire scholastic supplies. He wrote to publishing firms in 1893 concerning books, maps, and other materials, and he asked the German Colonial Society in 1895 for donations for the creation in Cameroon of a school library.[191]

Once again, Kayser's optimistic progressive attitude concerning black potential put him at odds with officials on the ground. The governor of

188. Paul Kayser to Frau Dörfling, October 9, 1893, RKA 5572, BAB. For more on these individuals, see Christian Stuart Davis, "'Coddling' Africans Abroad: Colonial Director Paul Kayser and the Education of Africans in Germany, 1891–96," *Journal of Colonialism and Colonial History* 9, no. 1 (Spring 2008).

189. Paul Kayser to Hering, January 31, 1896, RKA 5573, BAB. As in the other cases, the subsidy came with the stipulation of four years of service to the colonial government.

190. Eugen von Zimmerer to Leo von Caprivi, August 30, 1894, RKA 5572, BAB. This, like other letters to the chancellor from the colonies, almost certainly went through the Colonial Division of the Foreign Office.

191. Paul Kayser to [?], February 6, 1893, RKA 4077, BAB; Paul Kayser to Government in Cameroon, November 23, 1895, RKA 4073, BAB.

Cameroon from 1895 to 1906, Jesko von Puttkamer, adamantly opposed the government schools because they benefitted the Duala people, an ethnic group that he despised.[192] Soon after Kayser's resignation, Puttkamer informed Chancellor Hohenlohe of his poor opinion of the Duala and voiced his desire to shut the government schools down. "I see it as no great success," he wrote, "if thieves and burglars . . . can now write and speak a little German . . . the mission-Duala is the same thief and liar as the heathen or as those raised in school, the last of which are certainly in general the worst, as far as their intelligence has sufficiently developed."[193]

Kayser also differed with administrators over the school curricula, to which he paid close attention.[194] When he discovered in the winter of 1892 that religious instruction was excluded, he wrote to Togo's *Kommissariat* expressing his extreme dissatisfaction. He insisted that "the biblical history of the Old and New Testaments" needed to form the "foundation of instruction," particularly for "heathen natives."[195] Kayser was assured later that year that religious instruction would be included. In the interim, however, Chancellor Caprivi received a dissenting letter from colonial administrator Markus Graf von Pfeil, who argued that a successful instruction in the Christian religion in government schools would be too time-consuming.[196]

The emphasis that Kayser put on religious instruction was consistent with his support for mission activity. Unlike colonial radicals who believed that black Africans were set in their ways and, therefore, that proselytization was a waste of time, Kayser took mission work seriously, and he differentiated between unconverted and Christian blacks. He articulated his commitment to the missions publicly while speaking before the Reichstag

---

192. German administrators and businessmen greatly resented the Duala for resisting their efforts to recruit them as laborers.

193. Jesko von Puttkamer to Hohenlohe, November 11, 1896, RKA 4073, BAB. Even before Puttkamer became governor in August 1895, the German director of one of the government schools, J. Christaller, complained to Kayser of a lack of sympathy on the part of local colonial administrators. In the same letter, Christaller—who had recently visited the Kaysers in Berlin—indicated that he was nevertheless buoyed by Kayser's support. "Since I have now seen through my visit with you that my work has also found appreciation with my superiors," he wrote, "I turn there all the more so to work further" (Christaller to Herr Geheimrat, May 11, 1895, RKA 4073, BAB).

194. Kayser requested detailed outlines of the curricula used in Togo and Cameroon.

195. Paul Kayser to [?], March 21, 1892, RKA 4077, BAB. Kayser also suggested changes to the school curriculums in Togo and Cameroon in 1893, recommending that recent history with an emphasis on Germany supplant ancient history in instruction (Paul Kayser to Jesko von Puttkamer, January 5, 1893, RKA 4073, BAB).

196. Jesko von Puttkamer to Leo von Caprivi, October 25, 1892, RKA 4077, BAB; Markus Graf von Pfeil to Leo von Caprivi, June 21, 1892, RKA 4077, BAB.

in February 1891. The occasion was a proposal advanced by Christian Social deputy Adolf Stöcker to divide the colonies into zones exclusive to particular denominations. Kayser rejected the idea. He argued that its implementation could upset the colonial administration's positive working relationship with missions already active in the colonies. During his speech, Kayser proclaimed that, "without the activity of the mission societies," colonization would be "unthinkable."[197] He also spoke of his constant readiness to provide assistance to the missions through his officials on the ground.

Kayser proved his commitment to the missions later that year, when he interceded for the North German Mission Society in Togo against a hostile Markus Graf von Pfeil. As Togo's chief administrator, Pfeil issued an edict prohibiting English instruction in mission schools, a practice that continued in North German missions that had been located in British-controlled territory before the Heligoland Treaty of 1890. Pfeil's order threatened to confound contemporary missionary activity, and mission director Zahn wrote Kayser to complain.[198] Kayser sympathized with Pfeil's reasoning that German colonial subjects needed to know German, and he conceded that a "gradual" replacement of German for English was "urgently desirable." Kayser insisted, however, that he could not approve "an intrusion in the teaching activities" of the missions, nonetheless, and he instructed Pfeil to rescind his order.[199]

Unlike many of his more conservative and racist subordinates, then, Kayser did not believe that race was the absolute, overriding factor in determining the capabilities and individual value of blacks. His support for education and his concern for religious instruction reflected his progressive, albeit paternalistic, belief that Africans could change for the better under white guidance, making progress in their personal development to better serve the needs of the colonial state. His willingness to educate blacks in Germany revealed an optimism for a peaceful coexistence between colonizers and the colonized even when the cultural gap between them narrowed. Governor Zimmerer and acting governor Heinrich Leist did not share this belief and viewed an education abroad as dangerous.

---

197. *Sten. Ber.* 63, February 11, 1891, 1443.

198. F. M. Zahn to Colonial Division of the Foreign Office, September 24, 1891, RKA 4077, BAB.

199. Paul Kayser to Jacobi, October 13, 1891, RKA 4077, BAB; Paul Kayser to Markus Graf von Pfeil, October 13, 1891, RKA 4077, BAB.

They also perceived an essential immutability to the black African character, arguing that blacks educated abroad would eventually "re-negroize."
Some, like Puttkamer, directed the allegation of immutability more toward
particular groups, like the Duala, whom Puttkamer believed were incapable of positive change.

Kayser, on the other hand, was deeply influenced in his perceptions of
blacks by their educational and religious standing. This was especially true
for individuals. In Kayser's opinion, some educated Christian blacks deserved differential treatment and, in appropriate circumstances, special
considerations. This outlook led him to intervene on the behalf of individual Africans on more than one occasion, much to the dismay of some of
his subordinates who viewed educated blacks with suspicion and did not
credit acculturation with engendering a deep or meaningful positive
change. These men disapproved of Kayser's interventions. Their responses
reaffirmed the divide between the colonial director and local officials concerning the moral and mental potential of black Africans.

One important intervention occurred in the summer of 1894. During
this time, Kayser helped a leading member of the Afro-Brazilian elite in
Togo's coastal trading town of Lomé obtain a mortgage from the English
firm Lionel Hart and Company for the purpose of founding a coffee plantation. The individual in question, Octaviano Olympio, was the son of a
man of mixed Portuguese, African, and Amerindian descent who left
Brazil for western Africa as a teenager, where he made a living in the slave
trade before switching to legal commerce. The son, Octaviano, received an
education in accounting and business in London, and he moved to Lomé
in 1882 as the local representative of the British trading company A. & F.
Swanzy. He also went into business for himself while serving in this capacity. He established the town's first coconut plantation in 1889 and, also, its
only brickyard. He quickly became one of Lomé's wealthiest men.[200]

Kayser received a letter from Lionel Hart in the summer of 1894 inquiring if he could affirm that Octaviano had the power under German
law, as "a black man and a British subject," to mortgage his property in
Lomé to an English firm.[201] Kayser contacted Togo's chief administrator,
Jesko von Puttkamer, asking if Octaviano's "educational level and esteem"
qualified him for treatment "as a European."[202] Puttkamer replied that Oc-

---

200. Alcione M. Amos, "Afro-Brazilians in Togo: The Case of the Olympio Family,
1882–1945," *Cahier D'Études Africaines* 41 (2001): 293–314.

201. Lionel Hart and Co. to Paul Kayser, July 19, 1894, RKA 4980, BAB.

202. Paul Kayser to Jesko von Puttkamer, August 5, 1894, RKA 4980, BAB.

taviano was "a native," but that A. & F. Swanzy described him as "a very refined, educated, and unassuming man."[203] Octaviano traveled to Berlin in late August and met with Kayser. Afterward, Kayser instructed Puttkamer to aid Octaviano in the transaction.[204] Puttkamer then informed Berlin that members of the Olympio family had attained the right to be treated like Europeans due to their "educational level and esteem."[205]

This outcome did not sit well with Puttkamer's successor, August Köhler, who attempted to discredit Octaviano after replacing Puttkamer in 1895. Köhler wrote to Berlin that year, insisting that Octaviano was not the "honorable man" previously assumed. Rather, Köhler proclaimed that Octaviano owed money to local creditors and had recently left Togo for the Gold Coast, presumably to avoid paying. Köhler added that Octaviano's good reception in Europe had gone to his head, and he intimated that the experience should guide the government in the future when dealing with educated and acculturated blacks. "The changes in him that have been observed," Köhler wrote, "accordingly constitute, at any rate, an interesting contribution to a judgement concerning the native question."[206]

Köhler's allegations against Octaviano did not dissuade Kayser from attempting to aid another educated Christian black the following year, this time to redress physical harm resulting from prejudicial treatment. As in the case with Octaviano, Kayser's intercession on behalf of J. R. Harley revealed his ideological distance from his subordinates, whose hard-edged racism led them to discount the importance of an individual's education, religion, or wealth in determining their place in the colonial hierarchy. J. R. Harley was a black British subject born in Sierra Leone who worked as a clerk in Cameroon for the English trading firm John Holt. Harley wrote

---

203. "Notiz betr. den Mulatten Olympia," RKA 4980, BAB.

204. Paul Kayser to Jesko von Puttkamer, August 23, 1894, RKA 4980, BAB.

205. Jesko von Puttkamer to Leo von Caprivi, September 11, 1894, RKA 4980, BAB.

206. August Köhler to Chlodwig zu Hohenlohe-Schillingsfürst, September 18, 1895, RKA 4980, BAB. Octaviano had not fled Togo, as Köhler suggested. According to Alcione M. Amos, he continued to operate his coconut plantation in northwest Lomé, and he built new plantations with his brothers near Agoue, in French territory. He had an uneasy relationship with German officials. Acting commissioner Markus Graf von Pfeil had Octaviano flogged in 1891 for "insolent behaviour" when the latter refused to doctor Pfeil's horse. Octaviano was fined in 1898 for offenses against German trade and tax ordinances and in 1899 for a "rude" remark about the colonial government. Octaviano subsequently became involved in an effort by the Afro-Brazilian elite to gain more rights from the Germans. He took part in a petition submitted to the government in 1909 that requested, among other things, equal treatment for indigenes under the law. He signed another petition in 1913 requesting the elimination of chaining and flogging and the inclusion of indigenous representatives in government council meetings (Amos, "Afro-Brazilians"; Knoll, *Togo under Imperial Germany,* 70).

Kayser a lengthy letter in December, complaining of severe mistreatment at the hands of German officials. According to his statement, he had been unjustly imprisoned and beaten by officials who had conspired against him in order to secure his position in the John Holt factory at Dido for a white. Harley wrote that the excuse for his mistreatment was a transaction that he had authorized with local indigenes. He had given stock from the Holt factory in the amount of 3,998 marks "to natives for trade," which, he claimed, was customary. Complaints were brought against him to local officials, who then arrested him and held him responsible for the goods in question. A trial pursued, but Harley was unable to defend himself. Whenever he tried to speak, he was shouted down with insults by the presiding German officer.

Harley was sentenced to nine months imprisonment, and all his property was forfeited to repay the trust. Later, he was also charged with owning a firearm and was sentenced to three more months in prison. Eventually, his sentence was commuted to thirty lashes. After this was carried out, he was put on a ship going back to Sierra Leone. He left Cameroon "naked," "destitute," and "hatless," possessing "nothing else but a pyjama singlet."[207] Harley complained to Kayser that "the tenor of this treatment from what could be gathered is nothing else than prejudice."[208] He insisted that his right of free speech had been "forfeited" in court because he was "a Negro" and "African."[209]

Kayser had dealt with excessive violence in Cameroon once before. In October 1893, he investigated reports of a dramatic increase in the severity of punishments meted out in the colony to black Africans, writing acting governor Heinrich Leist to express his concerns and demanding a report on all sentences handed out over the previous two years. Back then, Kayser counseled greater moderation, but with subtlety. He recommended that "political and cultural points of view" be privileged over "an exclusively judicial perspective" in the "treatment of natives."[210] This time, Kayser was much more direct. Receiving Harley's letter in December, he wrote to the governor of Cameroon in January, requesting a report on the legal documents concerning Harley and his trial. He asked if the trial judge had, in fact, allowed the court recorder, Meyer, to adjudicate the case, something

207. J. R. Harley to the Secretary of States Foreign Affairs, December 4, 1895, RKA 4771, BAB.

208. Ibid.

209. Ibid.

210. Paul Kayser to Heinrich Leist, October 21, 1893, RKA 4770, BAB; Kayser to Eugen von Zimmerer, April 3, 1894, RKA 4770, BAB.

that Harley alleged. Then, in a paragraph running several pages, Kayser registered his strong disapproval over Harley's flogging, which he considered unacceptable, given that Harley was clearly an educated man. Kayser insisted that "the application of flogging toward Harley is not unobjectionable and will need a further explanation."

> As may be known . . . corporal punishment, which is foreign to German criminal law, is permitted in the exercise of criminal law over natives, because the latter, due to the low state of their development, are not capable of perceiving imprisonment as a real evil, and, for this reason, harder types of punishments are necessary. The consideration that was, according to this, decisive in the adoption of flogging in applicable criminal proceedings against natives is not valid for persons who, like the complainant, have enjoyed an orderly, statutory education and acquired sufficient knowledge in order to become drawn to a commercial life through independent and responsible work. An individual of this type differs, undoubtedly, not insignificantly from a Duala Negro or a *Kruneger,* who is customarily suitable only for bodily work. A considerable regard for this difference cannot be denied precisely when it comes to the exercise of criminal justice toward natives if the judicial activity connected to the legal opinions of your subordinate persons is to be appropriately administered.[211]

Despite the obvious importance that Kayser placed on this matter, the authorities in Cameroon were slow to respond. Over six months passed before Kayser received a reply, and, in the interim, he wrote to the local government a second time with a reminder.[212] He finally got a response from colonial administrator Theodor Seitz in the summer of 1896.[213] Seitz informed him that the case could not be investigated further because the judge who originally presided was dead, and Governor Puttkamer and Secretary Meyer were both on vacation. Although Seitz wrote that he did not know the exact reason why Meyer had been given authority in the case by the judge, he insisted that such a delegation of power was not unusual, given that there were only two judicial officials on hand, besides the gover-

---

211. Paul Kayser to the Imperial Government in Cameroon, January 19, 1896, RKA 4771, BAB.

212. Paul Kayser to the Imperial Government in Cameroon, July 1, 1896, RKA 4771, BAB.

213. Seitz served as the governor of Cameroon from 1907 to 1910 and then as the governor of German Southwest Africa.

nor. Seitz insisted that a review of the legal documents concerning the case showed that Meyer was not prejudiced against Harley.

Seitz also argued for the continued use of corporal punishment on educated blacks, insisting that education and acculturation did not moderate the negative essence of black Africans.

> A pecuniary punishment for a Negro who, through his knowledge, towers considerably over the others is, generally speaking, no punishment, since he is constantly in the position to easily obtain money through a deceptive cheating of other Negroes. Likewise, an imprisonment has no profound effect, since an increase in modesty doesn't keep pace with an increase in education and self-reliance. Impudence and refinement, as is often encountered these days with the educated Negro, can only be countered effectively with corporal punishment.

In an even further departure from Kayser's viewpoint, and perhaps in a reference to recent regulations from Berlin prohibiting the whipping of Arabs and Indians, Seitz stated his support for the flogging of other non-whites.[214] He asked that the colonial director understand the need for "the application of corporal punishment in exceptional cases also against educated coloreds."[215]

Kayser differed from his subordinates concerning differential treatment for acculturated blacks in at least one other important area: intermarriage. In accordance with his opposition to the hard-edged racism of many officials on the ground and his own conviction that education, religion, and wealth merited individual blacks special considerations, Kayser had no fundamental disagreement with the idea of intermarriage, so long as the nonwhite person in the relationship was a Christian. Kayser first dealt with this issue while working as a jurist in the Foreign Office in 1887, when he received a request for clarification on mixed-race marriages from mission inspector Carl Gotthilf Büttner of the Bielefeld Mission Society. Büttner had lived in Southwest Africa for several years, and he insisted that accepting as legal the marriages between "whites and coloreds" (by proclaiming, for example, that marriages performed in Africa had the force of

---

214. The regulations on corporal punishment were issued from Berlin in May (*Deutscher Reichsanzeiger,* May 1, 1896, RKA 4771, BAB).

215. Theodor Seitz to Chlodwig zu Hohenlohe-Schillingsfürst, June 26, 1896, RKA 4771, BAB. Seitz's letter was not the end of the matter. Correspondence between Berlin and Cameroon over Harley continued into 1898, well after Kayser resigned.

law) would benefit the colony by promoting an "orderly family life" for people in interracial relationships.[216]

Kayser wrote to the colony's chief administrator, Heinrich Goering, informing him of Büttner's inquiry and also of his own opinion that marriages between "natives" and whites could indeed take place.[217] Kayser stated that an extension to "all members of civilized nations living in the Protectorates" of the consular law of May 4, 1870, which enabled German citizens living abroad to marry in accordance with German law and endow wives and children with German nationality, could also cover Christian, although not "heathen," "natives."[218] Goering confirmed this several months later, stating his recognition of the legality of interracial marriages. Goering made clear, however, that he did not share Büttner's enthusiasm. He insisted that the particular "'moral, political, and national-economic' results" of interracial unions, as mentioned by the missionary, "are not seen much here by me." "The right thing to do," he concluded, "is to neither limit nor promote such marriages."[219]

Kayser dealt with this issue on several other occasions, and his attitude remained much the same. In September 1893, he reviewed and rejected a proposal by Goering's successor, Captain Curt von François, that the designation *native* include all individuals possessing a great-grandfather originating from "a colored race." Kayser rejected this type of formal definition as unnecessary and, in his response, reaffirmed his acceptance of the idea of interracial marriage. This time, however, he went even further, also countenancing the transmission of German citizenship to "*Mischlinge*" children, the products of unions between whites and "natives." For Kayser, the issue was purely a legal one, depending on whether or not the mixed-race offspring were from legitimate marriages. If they were, then the children would have "the nationality of the white father" and also "the same civic rights and duties."[220] Although the *Reichskolonialamt* records do not contain a response from François, Kayser's letter in the archives is marked in a way that suggests how it was received. Dramatic red lines underline Kayser's statements concerning interracial marriage, "*Mischlinge*,"

---

216. Mission Inspector C. G. Büttner to Otto von Bismarck, May 7,1887, RKA 5423, BAB.

217. Goering's son was Hermann Goering, Adolf Hitler's designated successor and the commander in chief of the *Luftwaffe* during the National Socialist era.

218. Paul Kayser to Heinrich Goering, June 23, 1887, RKA 5423, BAB. Kayser specified that the law should not be extended to "heathen natives."

219. Heinrich Goering to Otto von Bismarck, September 17, 1887, RKA 5423, BAB.

220. Paul Kayser to Curt von François, September 24, 1893, R151/5180, BAB.

and citizenship rights. These are accompanied by exclamation marks in the margins.

The issue of mixed-race unions rose at least once more during Kayser's tenure, soon before his resignation. As in 1887, it was a German missionary who broached the subject. Dr. A. Schreiber, a member of the Rhenish Mission, wrote Kayser in March 1896, asking about rumored restrictions on marriages between indigenous women and former German soldiers who decided to settle in the colony. Schreiber claimed that Kayser informed him years ago of a decision to expropriate land given by the government to former soldiers if they entered into mixed marriages.[221] Schreiber asked if this rule was still in effect and, if so, requested its revocation. He insisted that such a policy would result in concubinage. He also pointed out that the indigenous women involved in relationships with former soldiers were Christians "almost without exception."[222] True to form, Kayser wrote to governor Leutwein after receiving Schreiber's letter and asked if "an abolition or relaxation of the existing rules" was "feasible."[223] Leutwein replied that nothing currently impeded mixed-race marriages, but he added that these were "a necessary evil" and were "by no means desirable."[224]

Like his support for educating blacks abroad and his willingness to intercede on behalf of educated Christian blacks, Kayser's countenance of interracial marriages illustrates the distance between himself and some of his subordinates over the importance of race and the means and meaning of racial domination. For Kayser, Christian conversion and a Western-style education should have opened the door to a more equitable treatment for individual blacks—if not systematically, then on a case-by-case basis—while giving them claim to special rights, like the right to marry across the races. Conservative colonial administrators on the ground saw things differently. They denied that blacks had the potential for positive change. More intimately concerned than Kayser with issues of domination and control, they also perceived too much acculturation to be a threat to colonial rule. In time, the colonial administration in Berlin drew closer to the viewpoint of its administrators on the ground. After Kayser's departure, the Colonial Division of the Foreign Office lost inter-

---

221. A question mark, presumably by Kayser, is written in the margin of Schreiber's letter next to his claim that Kayser had informed him years ago of restrictions on interracial marriages. Presumably, Kayser did not remember telling him this.
222. A. Schreiber to Paul Kayser, March 10, 1896, RKA 5423, BAB.
223. Paul Kayser to Theodor Leutwein, March 26, 1896, R151/5180, BAB.
224. Theodor Leutwein to Hohenlohe, June 21, 1896, RKA 5423, BAB.

est in subsidizing Africans in Germany in their education and vocational training. Later, it reemphasized the divide between whites and blacks by banning intermarriage.

The above discussion of Jews and Germans of Jewish descent involved in colonialism shows that there was no monolithic attitude within this group toward the colonized, in particular, no single "Jewish" outlook on the nature and capabilities of black Africans. Some, like Ernst Vohsen, saw no substantial difference between blacks and whites beyond color. Others, like Julius Scharlach, denied blacks their humanity, painting an image of Africans in accordance with the darkest fantasies of the most radical procolonial racists. There was also no monolithic outlook on colonial violence. Some, like Kayser, attempted to moderate the violence endemic to colonization; it was in the final months of Kayser's tenure that the central government issued rules regulating the application in the colonies of corporal punishment.[225] Others, like Scharlach, chafed at any limitations.

These differences impede any facile equation of "Jewishness" with a certain outlook on colonial issues concerning race and violence. Being the target of antisemitism, the most inclusive definition of "Jewishness," was not enough in itself to ensure a liberal or moderate colonizing philosophy.[226] Like Kayser, Scharlach suffered from antisemitic hatred. As seen above, no less a prominent antisemite than Liebermann von Sonnenberg targeted Scharlach publicly. Even colonial radicals like Frieda von Bülow considered him a Jew and discussed him, privately, in an antisemitic fashion.[227] Otto Arendt—a friend of conservative antisemites—was himself not immune to antisemitism: parliamentary opponents on the left drew attention to Arendt's Jewish roots, and antisemites on the right attacked him as a Jew on occasion.[228] Yet as procolonial advocates, both men embraced the radical viewpoint when it came to race and violence.

---

225. In addition to prohibiting the whipping of Indians, Arabs, women, and children, the rules also limited the number of blows permissible on one occasion to twenty-five.

226. "Jewishness" can be defined in the loosest possible terms à la Isaac Deutscher as an awareness of belonging to the persecuted minority of individuals who are perceived as "Jewish" by others. Although Deutscher wrote with the Holocaust fresh in his mind, his idea of a "negative community" can be applied to the *Kaiserreich* era, when even Christian converts like Paul Kayser were aware that others perceived them as belonging to the so-called Semitic race (Deutscher, *The Non-Jewish Jew and Other Essays* [London: Oxford University Press, 1968], 50–51).

227. Wildenthal, *German Women for Empire*, 232.

228. *Sten. Ber.* XI/I/129, January 30, 1905, 4123; "Aus dem antisemitischen Lager. Herr Dr. Arendt," *Mittheilungen* 18 (1908): 396.

This phenomenon was not limited to a handful of extremists; the liberal Jewish-owned *Berliner Tageblatt,* an organ that antisemites reviled, also voiced the radical perspective on occasion. One contributor insisted in 1904 that blacks were vicious creatures for whom "a mere nothing" sufficed to "unleash the wild gang, like when the first drops of an enemy's blood brings beasts to full savagery . . . the educational methods of the different missions," he continued, "cannot make an impression on such natures."[229] A foreign correspondent wrote the following year that blacks were inherently lethargic beings who limited their activities "exclusively to the territory of murder and theft."[230]

The fact that Jews and Germans of Jewish descent ran the spectrum in their perspectives on race and colonial violence does not mean, however, that the experience of antisemitism can be discounted as an explanation for the very liberal outlooks of some. Race liberals Kayser and Vohsen may well have been influenced in their opposition to the hard-edged racism and violent colonizing philosophies of colonial radicals by their own experiences with racial prejudice. That this was, at the very least, possible is shown by the fact that segments of the wider German-Jewish community and its supporters recognized a danger to Jews in the dehumanizing discourses about non-European Others and acknowledged a kinship in suffering between the two based on racial discrimination. These sentiments appeared on occasion in the German-Jewish press (newspapers written specifically for a Jewish audience) and in Jewish-friendly periodicals in the final decade and a half of empire.

For example, the Union for the Defense Against Antisemitism hotly contested in its monthly newsletter in 1904 the idea of racial predestination, in particular, the notion that "primitive races" were incapable of progressive change. The anonymous author of a lengthy article on the topic labeled this "the main argument of racial theory" and denounced it as a justification for "a newly introduced bondage."[231] He rejected the idea of fixed racial characteristics, insisting that negative perceptions of other races were based on hasty observations. He claimed that the so-called low races could change, arguing that "external circumstances" rather than a "fixed racial natural predisposition" determined a people's development.[232]

---

229. E. Tappenbeck, "Heidenmission und Kolonialarbeit," *Der Zeitgeist: Beiblatt zum "Berliner Tageblatt,"* November 7, 1904.

230. "Die Lage in Deutsch-Südwestafrika," *Berliner Tageblatt,* June 10, 1905.

231. "Die Fortschrittsfähigkeit der Menschenrassen," *Mittheilungen* 14 (1904): 190.

232. Ibid., 192.

Along the way, he also refuted the most common antiblack stereotypes. Although he did not mention antisemitism, the connection was clear, given that the union's main purpose was combating anti-Jewish prejudices and discrimination.

The *Allgemeine Zeitung des Judentums,* published from Berlin, expressed more explicitly an awareness of similarities between antisemitism and actions and attitudes toward "primitive races." In an anonymous front-page article in 1904, a contributor to the newspaper compared the hatred of Jews in Russia to that of blacks in America by the majority populations. "In Russia many Jews, and in the United States, many Negroes, wish to be elsewhere," he wrote, "in order to finally escape persecutions and torments." He attributed the animosity toward both groups to "instinctive racial hatred" and noted that the result was the same in both places: "Jewish massacres" in Russia and "lynch justice" in the United States.[233]

Years later, another contributor to the *Allgemeine Zeitung* also acknowledged a kinship in suffering between blacks and Jews, this time, in an article celebrating Harriet Beecher Stowe's one hundredth birthday. The author, Marcus Landau, compared antiblack to anti-Jewish discrimination. Slavery in the Americas and serfdom in Russia had both been lifted, but "in reality," he wrote, "in social life, in influence on the government and the administration, 'blacks' in North America compared with whites are on the same footing as, indeed, even weaker than, Prussian 'citizens of Jewish confession' and peasants in Russia to Christian townsmen." Lindau understood the relevance for European Jews of the situation faced by American blacks. "Which discriminations and infringements of rights the Negro is still now exposed to in North America, even in the Union States where there has been no slavery for a hundred years, I do not want to detail here," he wrote, "in order to offer our European antisemites any attractions for imitation."[234]

Clearly, German antisemites did not have to look as far as America to discover appropriate models of racial discrimination, but only to Germany's own colonies. As far as can be determined, however, race liberals Kayser and Vohsen never expressed a recognition of this in their public or private writings. Nevertheless, it seems unlikely that men so intimately involved with Germany's African colonial projects and, as seen in Kayser's case, deeply affected by antisemitic hatred were not influenced in their own

233. "Der Rassenhaß," *Allgemeine Zeitung des Judentums,* February 5, 1904.

234. Marcus Landau, "Zum 100. Geburtstage der Vorkämpferin der Neger-Emanzipation," *Allgemeine Zeitung des Judentums,* June 21, 1912.

strikingly liberal approaches to racial issues by an understanding of the re
lationship between contemporary actions and attitudes toward non-European Others and the difficulties that they, themselves, faced. In light of the
sympathies with the plight of American blacks expressed in the *Mittheilungen* and the *Allgemeine Zeitung,* such an understanding must be
seen as a possible, if not probable, contributing factor to the rejection by
these men of the idea of black African immutability—of the notion that
education, wealth, and Christian conversion did not change a black's character and that race alone determined a black's capabilities.

If, therefore, the examples of Scharlach and Arendt show that personal experiences with antisemitism did not guarantee a liberal colonizing
philosophy, and although there was no single "Jewish" colonial outlook,
Jews and Germans of Jewish descent in colonialism still often represented
forces of moderation. Undoubtedly, experiencing racism opened the possibility of a greater empathetic viewing of the colonized than colonial actors
who were not targeted by racist discourses that sometimes likened them to
the colonized and advocated a similar subjugation. In this light, it is not
surprising that Kayser judged some blacks according to their religion and
education. As a highly educated converted Jew who knew firsthand the lie
in theories of racial predestination, he was in a special position to assume
a progressive stance on colonial matters dealing with race. The public narrative on Emin Pasha even hints at the possibility of a link in the wider
public imagination between "Jewishness" and a more thoughtful, moderate form of colonization and a more tempered outlook on race. At the
time, Jews were associated with intellectualism. As seen above, Emin's supporters heralded the entrance into German colonial service of the "scholarly" Emin as a turn in colonial policy: as the beginning of a new phase
where the type of harsh racial violence practiced by men like Carl Peters
would now be rejected and a more paternalistic relationship with the
African colonized would take its place.

On a final note, the evidence presented here shows that participating
in the nationalist project of empire building could affect, but not eradicate,
the antisemitism that Jews and Germans of Jewish descent faced. Participation offered these individuals a unique opportunity to symbolically join
the racial mainstream, given that colonialism gave new importance to the
imagined racial divides between "whites" and "natives." Colonialism also
provided them with new ways to demonstrate their patriotism, even to
members of the antisemitic movement, something that was quite remarkable for the time. And yet, an unbridgeable dichotomy between "Jew" and

"German" persisted in the minds of many antisemites, and German-Jewish colonial actors remained vulnerable to the threat of antisemitism. What is more, involvement in colonialism could put Germans of Jewish descent under a public microscope, inviting attacks of an antisemitic nature. Colonialism, therefore, provided German Jews with the ability to earn patriotic credentials that were widely accepted but lacked universal currency, and participation made them targets for antisemitism.

The actions and attitudes of those involved in colonialism had some bearing on the amount of antisemitic hostility against them. Kayser's poor handling of the Schröder and Peters scandals and his advocacy of what came be seen as a flawed policy of colonial development opened him to criticisms that fueled the fires of antisemitic resentment. Had his resignation speech in October 1896 been more modest and measured, the antisemitic vitriol upon his retirement may have been less.[235] The degree to which Jews and Germans of Jewish descent involved in colonialism could, through their actions and attitudes, affect antisemitic anger is explored in greater detail in the next chapter, which focuses on Bernhard Dernburg, one of Kayser's successors and, like Kayser himself, of Jewish descent. It was easier for some procolonial antisemites to downplay or ignore Dernburg's Jewish heritage when he acted in accordance with what they believed was in the colonies' best interests. Once their visions of colonial development diverged, antisemitic hostility intensified, and, as with Kayser, some antisemites used Dernburg's Jewish heritage as a weapon against him. In addition, Dernburg's story further illuminates the degree to which colonialism splintered the antisemitic movement over the question of "Jewish" participation in the construction and maintenance of the colonies.

---

235. See Stern, *Gold and Iron,* 522–23, for a discussion of the "yearning for 'the modest Jew'" among late nineteenth-century antisemites.

CHAPTER 4

Colonial Director Bernhard Dernburg: A "Jew" with "German Spirit"?

German chancellor Bernhard von Bülow introduced Bernhard Dernburg to the Reichstag as the new colonial director on November 28, 1906. Almost immediately, deputies from the political Left and Center attempted to draw the new director into a discussion of colonial atrocities. Following Bülow's introduction and Dernburg's own lengthy inaugural speech, deputy Schaedler of the Catholic Center Party pressed the new director on the need for reform, insisting that "embezzlement, falsifications, lascivious cruelties, the violation of women, [and] horrible ill-treatments" had hitherto characterized "the history of our colonies."[1] The next speaker, Georg Ledebour of the Social Democrats, went further, accusing the government of pursuing "policies of extermination" in German Southwest Africa.[2] Others joined the attack over the next several days. Deputies from the Left and Center denounced colonial practices like whipping, and they detailed reports of the murder and abuse by colonial officials of indigenous Africans. The critics accused the government of failing to investigate, or to investigate thoroughly, credible stories of rapes, beatings, and mutilations and unjustified and unorthodox executions, some dating back a decade.

Dernburg responded cautiously at first. On November 29, he made only a passing reference to the accusations of the previous day, denying in a few sentences that the army intended to "hunt down" the remaining Nama in Southwest Africa, as Ledebour claimed.[3] On November 30, he

---

A shorter version of this chapter first appeared under the title "Colonialism and Anti-semitism during the *Kaiserreich:* Bernhard Dernburg and the Antisemites" in the *Leo Baeck Institute Yearbook* 53 (2008): 31–56.

1. *Stenographische Berichte über die Verhandlungen des Reichstags* (hereafter *Sten. Ber.*) XI/II/128, November 28, 1906, 3973.

2. Ibid., 3981.

3. *Sten. Ber.* XI/II/129, November 29, 1906, 4001.

addressed the criticisms at greater length, promising investigations into all allegations of abuse and thanking Matthias Erzberger of the Catholic Center Party for providing him, privately, with information. Dernburg also defended colonial officialdom in general, noting that only a handful of officials had ever been disciplined for bad behavior.

These assurances did not silence the colonial critics, however, and so on December 3, Dernburg mounted a vigorous counterattack, criticizing the critics themselves and challenging their more sensational accusations. He censured Social Democratic leader August Bebel for publicly naming the subjects of ongoing investigations. He defended several of the officials named, and he also attacked the reliability of black witnesses involved in the cases. Then, Dernburg impugned the motives and methods of the Catholic Center Party colonial critics. He detailed to the Reichstag past communications between the chancellor and party member Hermann Roeren that suggested an attempt by the latter to influence administrative affairs by threatening parliamentary opposition from the Center Party. Dramatically, Dernburg labeled this as "a type of backstairs government." To thunderous applause from the Right, he declared that an "abscess" needed to be lanced and that he had lanced it, implying that the real problem was the behavior of the colonial critics, not the abuses they criticized.[4]

Dernburg's passionate response thrilled supporters of colonialism. The new director's energetic stance contrasted sharply with the helplessness of his predecessor when faced the previous year with similar complaints and opposition. When Matthias Erzberger initiated his campaign

---

4. *Sten. Ber.* XI/II/132, December 3, 1906, 4101, 4118. In 1904, a civil servant of the colonial administration in Togo named Wistuba arrived in Berlin with a dossier of information detailing the abuse of both indigenous Africans and white Catholic missionaries by German officials in the colony. Wistuba met a minor official in the Colonial Division of the Foreign Office, O. Pöplau, who took the dossier to an important Liberal Party deputy, who in turn showed it to Chancellor Bülow. Horrified at the leakage of official documents, Bülow had both Pöplau and Wistuba charged with divulging state secrets. In response, Pöplau and Wistuba gave their collected material to Center Party deputies Erzberger and Roeren. Erzberger based some of his criticisms of colonial policy on this material, using it to support his claim that the Reichstag should have a greater say in colonial matters. Roeren adopted Wistuba's cause. Believing that a public trial of Wistuba could only embarrass the government, as it might lead to the publication of Wistuba's material, Roeren tried to convince Chancellor Bülow to settle the matter secretly, using his administrative powers. In his communications with Bülow, Roeren suggested that revelations about colonial atrocities resulting from a public trial might motivate the Center Party to reject the colonial budget. The government interpreted this as a threat and documented the dialogue between Roeren and Bülow for political advantage (Klaus Epstein, "German Colonial Scandals, 1905–1910," *English Historical Review* 74 [1959]: 654–59; George Dunlap Crothers, A.M., "The German Elections of 1907" [PhD diss., Columbia University, 1941], 78–82).

of exposure in 1905, hoping to force reform by detailing scandals, then–colonial director Prince Ernst zu Hohenlohe-Langenburg responded weakly. Hohenlohe-Langenburg eventually resigned, worn down by Erzberger's persistent attacks.[5] Dernburg's vocal denunciation of the critics stood out in contrast and made him the instant hero of colonial enthusiasts. Shortly after his performance, hundreds of congratulatory postcards, letters, and telegrams flooded to him, thanking him for his actions in the Reichstag. One representative note celebrated his "manly words" and declared him him a true "German man" and even a new "Luther" who "rose from the dead in parliament."[6] Dernburg's popularity increased in the following weeks when he traveled the country during the Reichstag election campaign of December and January, lecturing to crowds as large as 5,000 on the importance and viability of the African colonies.[7] These speeches—printed in pamphlets and widely circulated—cemented the impression that Dernburg was a fighting champion of colonialism and a "manly" advocate of empire.

The widespread popularity that Dernburg won in December 1906 was both broad and deep, moving even many within the antisemitic movement to praise him, his Jewish ancestry notwithstanding. For example, in a front-page article titled "Finally, a man!" the antisemitic *Deutsche Zeitung* described Dernburg on December 5, 1906, as a "man of industry, of ability, with the courage of truthfulness, and of a higher moral sense of accountability, who walked into the hailstorm without an umbrella."[8] The hundreds of congratulatory letters and telegrams sent over the following months included a speaking invitation from Adolf Stöcker's Christian Social Party and an invitation to attend a meeting of the Berlin branch of the Pan-German League,[9] as well as a letter from the *völkisch* antisemite Wil-

---

5. Following Erzberger's lead, the Catholic Center Party helped defeat three colonial budgetary bills in the spring of 1906. The Center Party deputies who voted down the bills wished to rein in government spending on the colonies and force reforms on the colonial administration, making it more effective, efficient, humane, and responsible.

6. Paul du Vignau to Bernhard Dernburg, December 14, 1906, no. 12, Bernhard Dernburg Papers (henceforth BDP), Bundesarchiv Koblenz (henceforth BAK).

7. After the Reichstag rejected the government's colonial budget on December 13, Chancellor Bülow dissolved parliament, forcing new elections. By traveling the country and lecturing on the colonies, Dernburg implicitly campaigned for the government-friendly procolonial parties.

8. O. E., "Endlich ein Mann!" *Deutsche Zeitung,* December 5, 1906.

9. Hernst Bämmer, Vorstand der Christl. soz. Partei des Wahlkreises Elberfeld-Barmen to Bernhard Dernburg, February 13, 1907, nr. 40, BDP, BAK; Erich Stolta to Bernhard Dernburg, May 1, 1907, no. 40, BDP, BAK.

helm Schwaner expressing the "heartfelt" thanks of the "10,000 German teachers" he claimed to represent.[10] Another *völkisch* antisemite, Heinrich Pudor, wrote Dernburg twice in 1907, requesting his collaboration on *Die Berliner Weltausstellung,* one of Pudor's monthly magazines.[11] That same year, the antisemite Siegfried Passarge sent Dernburg a complimentary copy of one of his recent books on South Africa.[12] Later, Dernburg also received a speaking invitation from the very antisemtic Union of German Students.[13] All this occurred despite public knowledge that Dernburg's father had converted to Christianity from Judaism as a child.

This popularity, however, waned over time. Dernburg became one of the most controversial figures in colonial affairs well before his retirement in the summer of 1910. The outspokenness and lack of tact that worked in his favor when confronting colonial critics eventually hurt his standing with many in the colonial movement who had different ideas about the proper direction of colonial development. Supporters on the right were surprised when, in 1907, Dernburg began privileging indigenous agriculture in German East Africa over white-owned plantation production, something that eroded his support among advocates of settlement colonialism. And yet, Dernburg's strong showing against colonialism's critics in 1906 and the fact that the colonial empire was on a much stronger footing upon his retirement ensured him a certain degree of continued respect even from many who adamantly opposed some of his policies.

The following pages examine the problem that Dernburg posed for antisemites. Like Paul Kayser, Dernburg was widely perceived to be a Jew. Even so, he gained a reputation as a patriot and a man above politics, a crusader against colonial critics and the special interests of Catholicism and Social Democracy. For a time, he enjoyed unprecedented public popularity for a colonial director. Moreover, he helped alleviate many problems plaguing German colonialism, instituting reforms that fulfilled some of the long-standing wishes of colonial enthusiasts, antisemites among them. These facts were hard to deny. Although some antisemites distrusted Dern-

---

10. Wilhelm Schwaner to Bernhard Dernburg, December 6, 1906, no. 12, BDP, BAK. For information on Schwaner, see Uwe Puschner, *Die völkische Bewegung im wilhelminischen Kaiserreich: Sprache, Rasse, Religion* (Darmstadt, 2001), 11, 53f, 69, 73, 91, 164, 170, 203, 215, 234, 239, 240–50, 253f, 258, 268, 275, 284, 392.

11. Heinrich Pudor to Bernhard Dernburg, April 15, 1907, no. 24, BDP, BAK; Heinrich Pudor to Bernhard Dernburg, March 25, 1907, no. 40, BDP, BAK.

12. Siegfried Passarge to Bernhard Dernburg, November 24, 1907, no. 28, BDP, BAK.

13. Verein Deutscher Studenten zu Leipzig to Bernhard Dernburg, February 27, 1909, no. 42, BDP, BAK.

burg all along, others credited him with "German spirit" and defended him from antisemitic attacks.[14] Still others remained suspicious and denounced him as a Jew shortly before, and then after, his retirement. By examining these reactions to Dernburg by antisemites in parliament and the press, this chapter studies the confusion and divisions that Dernburg's appointment and performance generated in the antisemitic movement. More than any other German of Jewish descent since Emin Pasha, Dernburg forced even racial antisemites to ponder the degree to which a person could overcome his "Jewishness" by having the right ideological orientation.

This chapter also delves deeper into the peculiar nature of the participation in colonialism of individuals of Jewish descent. Like Paul Kayser, Dernburg was aware of antisemitism. During his tenure, he wrote at least once in a personal letter of the deep impression that antisemitism had made on him as a child. As Germany's chief colonial administrator, however, Dernburg helped create and enforce colonial racial states that—despite his own rejection of the *Herrenvolk* mentality of colonial radicals—perpetuated, validated, and reified the same type of racial thinking that infused the worldview of many dedicated antisemites. What is more, pro-colonial antisemites in the Reichstag supported Dernburg, despite disagreements over certain colonial policies, and even defended him for years from critics on both the political Left and Right. Dernburg's tenure in office demonstrates that colonialism offered the possibility of cooperation between representatives of the antisemitic movement and those they persecuted, even when the two were in close proximity on a regular basis. Colonialism provided a common enemy in the opponents of empire and furnished common identities as colonizers.

Dernburg's appointment as the new director of the Colonial Division of the Foreign Office in September 1906 caused a stir in both the German press and government. In the first place, Dernburg was not a politician, noble, or bureaucrat, but a businessman from Berlin who had spent time working as a young man in America.[15] He had strong connections in the world of high finance, and he had recently served as a director of the

---

14. Dr. Fritz Krone, "Zur Dernburg-Frage," *Hammer: Blätter für deutschen Sinn* 6 (1907): 153.

15. The young Bernhard secured a position in New York during the late 1880s first with the American Metal Company and then the bank firm Ladenburg, Thalmann and Co. (Werner Schiefel, *Bernhard Dernburg. 1865–1937. Kolonialpolitiker und Bankier im wilhelminischen Deutschland* [Zurich: Atlantis, 1974]).

Darmstädter Bank. His appointment, therefore, marked a break from official tradition, because most of his predecessors were nobles and came from within the ranks of the imperial bureaucracy.

In the second place, Dernburg was widely perceived as a liberal Jew. His father, Friedrich, had been born a Jew but had been baptized as a child along with his siblings when his own father converted to Christianity. Friedrich was also a well-known writer and editor for the Jewish-owned liberal newspaper the *Berliner Tageblatt,* and he had served in the 1870s as a Reichstag deputy for the National Liberal Party before joining the progressive successionists. At a time when the question of the existence of a Jewish race was hotly debated, and at least a mild antisemitism pervaded much of the political spectrum, Dernburg's Jewish ancestry exacerbated his outsider status. It made him an even more unorthodox choice for the new colonial director, despite the fact that his mother came from a family of distinguished Protestant pastors. The surprise within the political establishment was heightened by the widespread expectation that the Colonial Division of the Foreign Office would soon become an independent ministry with cabinet status for its leader. This occurred in May 1907, making Dernburg the first person of Jewish descent since 1879 to enjoy the title of state secretary. As state secretary, he was a more powerful and prominent political figure than his predecessors, including Paul Kayser.

Recognition of the need for change motivated Chancellor Bernhard von Bülow's selection. By 1906, German colonialism was in crisis. Reichstag proceedings on colonial budgets were bogged down by discussions of administrative mismanagement, corruption, and atrocious colonial violence. Colonial development was stymied. A handful of large British- and German-owned companies controlled gigantic tracts of colonial land and enjoyed monopolistic privileges over settlement, mining, and road and railroad building in the colonies. This hindered the expansion of white settlements and the development of a colonial infrastructure, which deterred new investors. German Southwest Africa was also still at war, as Nama guerrillas continued to fight. Since several decades of administration by bureaucratic (and court) insiders had not put the colonies on a path to secure development, Bülow turned to new blood. Dernburg had a reputation in the business world for energetic decisive management and positive results, having helped triple the market value of the Darmstädter Bank while serving as director since 1901. Bülow hoped that someone like him from the world of business or high finance would attract more private investors to the colonies. By appointing an outsider, he also wished to prove to colonial critics the government's desire for reform in colonial matters. Bülow turned first to the current director of the Dresdner Bank, who declined. Then, after considering the industrialist Walther Rathenau, Bülow chose Dernburg upon the recommendation of the leader of the Press Division of the Foreign Office.[16]

For many, Dernburg did not disappoint. He had no experience in colonial affairs or in politics, but he pursued a policy of reform with energy and determination hitherto unseen in the Colonial Division of the Foreign Office. He announced the cancellation of the much-criticized government contracts with the Tippelskirch and Woermann companies during his very first speech in the Reichstag. Here, he also set forth a positive new vision of colonial development, declaring his intention to create "administratively independent, economically healthy colonies" run by an "efficient and reliable civil service, loyal to the homeland, developed in good traditions," and composed of "the best men and characters."[17] Dernburg followed his words with action. Over the next three and a half years, he successfully negotiated with the concession companies of German Southwest Africa to reduce the territories under their control, freeing land for white settlement.[18] He won government control over the administration of mining in areas held by the German Colonial Corporation of Southwest Africa. In addition, Dernburg reorganized colonial finances; during his tenure, the civil administrations of the various colonies began paying for their own operating costs with revenue raised internally or through loans guaranteed by the government.[19] Dernburg also oversaw a dramatic expansion of railroad lines in German Africa, setting the stage for an economic upswing.[20] Finally, to create a better educated and trained colonial officialdom, Dernburg collaborated with academics in Hamburg to create a Colonial Insti-

---

16. Schiefel, *Berhard Dernburg*, 38. In his memoirs, Bernhard von Bülow wrote (perhaps flippantly) that he appointed "a Jew" as colonial director to placate Catholics and Protestants, who would not accept Christians of the opposite denomination (Bernhard Fürst von Bülow, *From the Morocco Crisis to Resignation, 1903–1909*, vol. 2 of *Memoirs of Prince von Bülow*, trans. Geoffrey Dunlop [Boston: Little, Brown, and Company, 1931–32], 293).

17. *Sten. Ber.* XI/II/128, November 28, 1906, 3961–62.

18. In 1903, nine companies owned one-third of the land in German Southwest Africa, but by 1908, their holdings had been reduced to one-seventh (Schiefel, *Bernhard Dernburg*, 99–100).

19. Ibid., 89–90. The discovery of diamonds in Southwest Africa in 1908 helped its administration pay for its own operating costs, outside of military expenses.

20. Ibid., 92–96. From 1908 to 1911, approximately 125 million marks were spent on railroad construction. The money was raised through loans so as not to burden the imperial budget.

tute, which opened in October 1908. Under Dernburg, the Colonial Office sent at least twenty officials a year to study at the institute for terms of two semesters.[21]

Just as important to nationalists, Dernburg also helped elevate colonial enthusiasm among the public. For years, supporters of colonialism lamented the lack of a German colonial consciousness.[22] The events of late 1906 and early 1907, however, helped rekindle public interest in the colonies. Dernburg's energetic performance in the Reichstag attracted widespread attention, and colonial issues were put front and center in the election campaign of December and January. The government attempted to "educate" the public on the importance of colonialism during the campaign in order to drum up support for progovernment parties to create a working parliamentary bloc. Dernburg led this effort, lecturing on the colonies before packed audiences in Berlin, Munich, Stuttgart, and Frankfurt from December through early February. In these speeches, he called upon Germans to unite behind the national project of empire building, and he repeatedly presented colonialism as something that could subsume political, religious, and social differences and unify the nation. Dernburg's insistence that "all members of the German race" and "all confessions" and "all occupations" could partake in colonialism reinforced the impression that he was a man above politics.[23] The election campaign returned a government majority—decreasing Social Democratic seats by almost half—and raised public awareness of colonial matters.

Despite these successes, however, it was not all smooth sailing for Dernburg. To the contrary, Dernburg managed to alienate important segments of the colonial movement when barely into his second year in office. The primary reason was his reevaluation, made during a trip to German East Africa in the summer and fall of 1907, of the value of settler colonialism, white-owned plantations, and the productive capabilities of blacks. In short, Dernburg returned from Africa with negative opinions of

---

21. Ibid., 83. Another of Dernburg's accomplishments was the dissolution of the Colonial Council, which had been criticized from its inception for representing special interests—as opposed to the German people—in its dealings with the government.

22. In his unpublished and unfinished memoir, Dernburg wrote that "the popularity of the German colonies" was at a "low point" when he assumed office (see page 9 of his memoirs, found in no. 11, BDP, BAK).

23. D. über Koloniale Erziehung, January 21, 1907, no. 39, BDP, BAK. Dernburg cultivated the image of himself as a man above politics. "I have nothing to do with politics," he declared in the Reichstag on December 4, 1906. "I have thrown the politicians out of the Colonial Division, and they should stay out" (*Sten. Ber.* XI/II/133, December 4, 1906, 4154).

the former two and a positive outlook on the latter. Much like Paul Kayser, he became convinced that blacks were rational economically motivated beings with productive abilities and a sense for commerce, capable of being drawn into a German-structured agricultural economy without the use of force through the creation of markets and a supporting infrastructure. At the same time, he found East Africa unsuitable for large settlements and the existing settlers disappointingly ignorant, greedy, and violent. When Dernburg returned, he articulated a policy of colonial development that would discourage white settlement in East Africa and strengthen, through strategically placed railroad lines, existing networks of native production.[24] This brought Dernburg into direct conflict with the advocates of settler colonialism, and also with racists, who saw blacks as lazy children, incapable of productive labor without white oversight. In addition, his rejection of settler colonialism appeared to conflict with his insistence during the election of 1907 that the German people as a whole needed to become involved with the colonies.

Dernburg antagonized white settlers and their supporters even more with decrees that protected the rights of black workers and restricted corporal punishment. In July 1907, the Colonial Office issued new regulations concerning whipping, limiting the number of blows in most cases to fifteen and mandating the presence of a doctor during floggings.[25] In February 1909, the governor of German East Africa, supported by, and in collaboration with, the Colonial Office, issued detailed rules concerning the recruitment and treatment of black workers, giving the state control over recruitment and limiting the length of work contracts.[26] These orders also regulated wages, working hours, and the condition of worker lodgings, and they created a system to monitor compliance. German settlers and planters were infuriated, and they accused Dernburg of being a "fanatical Negrophil."[27] To many, his concern over the treatment of blacks jarred with the impression given in late 1906 in the Reichstag, when Dernburg adopted a somewhat cavalier attitude toward reports of excessive violence. Here, he had insisted that the vast majority of colonial officials needed protection

24. Bradley D. Naranch, "'Colonized Body,' 'Oriental Machine': Debating Race, Railroads, and the Politics of Reconstruction in Germany and East Africa, 1906–1910," *Central European History* 33, no. 3 (2000): 299–338.

25. Schiefel, *Bernhard Dernburg*, 219.

26. Juhani Koponen, *Development for Exploitation: German Colonial Policies in Mainland Tanzania, 1884–1914* (Helsinki: Finnish Historical Society, 1995), 372.

27. Schröder-Poggelow to Reichskanzler Bülow, March 21, 1909, Reichskolonialamt (henceforth RKA) 121, Bundesarchiv Berlin (henceforth BAB).

Fig. 4. A cartoon titled "Dernburg everywhere!!" satirizing Dernburg's apparent ubiquity during the so-called Hottentot election of 1907, when he traveled the country giving frequent public speeches promoting the colonies. (Bildarchiv Preussischer Kulturbesitz, Image nr. 00079641.)

from "unjustified and malicious attacks."[28] He had also explained away certain atrocities.[29]

Finally, critics both within and without the colonial movement sharply attacked Dernburg in early 1910 for his handling of the diamond fields of German Southwest Africa. Following the discovery of the fields in April 1908, Dernburg gave monopolistic control over the mining and sale of diamonds to the German Colonial Corporation of Southwest Africa and a consortium of banks, respectively. He acted to prevent land speculation—which he believed would hurt the colony's economy—and a flooding of the world diamond market. He also wished to secure a reliable source of revenue for the government, and he negotiated with the companies involved for a share of the diamond profits.[30] The shutting-out of local firms from the diamond business enraged the Southwest African settler community, sparking protest meetings. Critics at home accused Dernburg of undermining his earlier efforts to limit the power of concession companies. Yet, Dernburg's policies received broad support in the Reichstag from both progovernment parties like the National Liberals and colonial critics within the Catholic Center and Social Democratic parties.[31] This accord disintegrated, however, in late January 1910, when the details of a new proposed treaty with the German Colonial Corporation came to light. Many who supported the previous arrangements argued that the new proposal gave too much to the company. Dernburg rejected these concerns and asserted his right to decide the diamond matter on his own authority. He concluded the controversial treaty shortly before resigning in May, sparking outrage in the Reichstag.

Dernburg's three-and-a-half-year stint as colonial director and then

---

28. *Sten. Ber.* XI/II/128, November 28, 1906, 3962.

29. On December 1, parliamentary deputy Dr. Ablass accused a German official in Togo of shooting an indigenous "chief," decapitating the body, and keeping the head as a trophy on his dinner table. In his rebuttal, Dernburg admitted the truth of the execution and decapitation, but defended the official involved. He argued that a "medicine man" had been shot after disobeying an order and that the head had been removed for scientific purposes and sent to the Natural History Museum in Berlin (*Sten. Ber.* XI/II/131, December 1, 1906, 4077; ibid., XI/II/132, December 3, 1906, 4100).

30. Schiefel, *Bernhard Dernburg,* 102; Arthur J. Knoll and Lewis H. Gann, eds., *Germans in the Tropics: Essays in German Colonial History* (New York: Greenwood Press, 1987), 140.

31. Dernburg argued successfully that company control over the mining and sale of the diamonds was the safest and most efficient way to develop the fields and secure some of the profits for the government. For speeches by colonial critics Matthias Erzberger and Georg Ledebour in favor of Dernburg's diamond policies, see *Sten. Ber.* XII/II/23, January 25, 1910, 767–74, 789–94.

state secretary of the Colonial Office was, therefore, tumultuous. After becoming the darling of the colonial movement and the German Right, he alienated many supporters with his policies on native production, settler colonialism, labor relations, and corporal punishment, and by appearing to reverse his stance on concession companies. Dernburg's difficult personality also cost him; often visibly impatient with those who disagreed with him, Dernburg could exude an arrogant and irritating overconfidence. Yet, by objective standards, Dernburg's leadership was a success. He left office with an extensive transportation system in place, which, combined with the discovery of diamonds, contributed to an economic upswing in the African colonies. Trade and private capital investment increased during and after his tenure, as did the public's colonial consciousness.[32] For all these reasons, Dernburg retained considerable support from within the procolonial parties, and from the Catholic Center Party as well, which saw its concerns over the treatment of indigenes addressed by his so-called native policies.[33] As late as April 1910, even a radical like Eduard von Liebert—who adamantly protested limitations on corporal punishment—felt moved to publicly thank Dernburg for "the industrious, careful, and farsighted work" that he did for the colonies.[34]

Throughout his leadership of the colonial bureaucracy, Dernburg also enjoyed considerable support from the antisemites in parliament. Like Paul Kayser, he faced a legislature containing representatives of the Christian Social, German Social, and German Reform Parties, whose combined representation actually grew during his tenure in office. Riding the wave of nationalism that followed Bülow's dissolution of the Reichstag in December 1906, the antisemites increased their seats from a combined total of thirteen to seventeen, one more than they had at the peak of their legislative power in the 1890s.[35] Although they never managed to bring antisemitic legislation to a vote during Dernburg's time, the antisemites did occasion discussions of the Jewish Question. Topics included Jewish immigration,

---

32. L. H. Gann and Peter Duignan, *The Rulers of German Africa, 1884–1914* (Stanford: Stanford University Press, 1977), 185.

33. Dernburg's ability to compromise on the issue of workers' rights helped him retain the support of the political right. In February 1909, he signaled a willingness to pressure Governor Rechenberg of German East Africa to use moderation when enforcing the new rules on worker wages, contracts, and recruitment (Schiefel, *Bernhard Dernburg*, 115).

34. *Sten. Ber.* XII/II/28, February 1, 1910, 989.

35. These numbers do not include representatives of the Agrarian League or individual antisemites in other parties, like Eduard von Liebert.

Jewish judges, and Jews in the army.[36] On several occasions, the antisemites even discussed in Dernburg's presence the immigration of Jews into German Southwest Africa. Despite their continued anti-Jewish agitation, however, the parliamentary antisemites did not try to obstruct Dernburg. To the contrary, the most ardent supporters of empire among them gave him their enthusiastic support, and no antisemitic deputy raised the fact of his Jewish ancestry while speaking in the Reichstag. The procolonial antisemites acknowledged the merits of Dernburg's vision of colonial development—with its emphasis on increasing revenue and creating an infrastructure—and appreciated the order and direction that he brought to the colonial bureaucracy.

The potential for a positive working relationship between Dernburg and the parliamentary antisemites became evident early on when the antisemites' point man on colonialism, Wilhelm Lattmann, congratulated him in November 1906 for a promising start. Dernburg's cancellation of the Tippelskirch and Woermann company contracts gratified colonial enthusiasts, as did his sharp rebuke of colonial critics during his first few appearances in parliament.[37] Lattmann praised Dernburg's actions and declared their accord with what the antisemites wished from the leadership of the colonial bureaucracy. Specifically, he compared Dernburg's grappling with the problem of colonial monopolies with his predecessor's "taciturnity" on the matter.[38] He also praised Dernburg's plans for a colonial infrastructure, noting with particular approval his intention to have the government, and not private investors, fund railroad development. In addition, Lattmann complimented Dernburg's handling of accusations of colonial atrocities from the Left and Center. Referring, no doubt, to Dernburg's assertion on November 28 that, while "guilty officials will be punished," the vast majority needed protection from "unjustified and malicious attacks,"[39] Lattmann praised Dernburg for taking a "clear and . . . healthy position" on "colonial officialdom."[40] He even joined Dernburg in refuting Georg Ledebour's accusation that the army planned to "hunt down" the remaining Nama rebels in Southwest Africa.[41] Lattmann lauded Dernburg overall for proposing "a system" of colonial development, as opposed to the

---

36. See for example the plenary debates of March 26 and 30, 1908.

37. By 1906, even colonial enthusiasts called for the cancellation of the Tippelskirch and Woermann company contracts.

38. *Sten. Ber.* XI/II/130, November 30, 1906, 4023.

39. *Sten. Ber.* XI/II/128, November 28, 1096, 3962.

40. *Sten. Ber.* XI/II/130, November 30, 1906, 4017.

41. Ibid., 4018.

"systemlessness" of his predecessors. He insisted that Dernburg "broke with everything that came before" by advocating financial independence for the colonies, and he declared that here, "finally," was a "clear and intelligible goal for our German colonial policy."[42]

Dernburg's indirect activity on behalf of procolonial parties during the election campaign seemed to reconcile other antisemitic deputies to his leadership of the Colonial Office. Before, however, deputies like Ludwig Werner and Oswald Zimmermann of the German Reform Party expressed skepticism of the new colonial director and even a muted hostility, Lattmann's early praise of him notwithstanding. In an article in September shortly before Dernburg's appointment, Zimmermann's party organ, the *Deutsche Reform,* lamented—in a clear reference to the incoming colonial director—"the advance of Jewified capitalism in the imperial government."[43] Several months later, Zimmermann declared his party's intention to maintain a "skeptical cautious attitude" toward Dernburg despite supporting his colonial budget.[44] For his part, Werner criticized Dernburg in December for painting too positive a picture of colonial conditions, and he insisted that dissolving the Tippelskirch contract was only to be expected.[45]

Praise from antisemitic deputies was more forthcoming the following year. On December 13, 1906, Chancellor Bülow dissolved the Reichstag after the Social Democratic and Center parties defeated the government's supplemental spending bills for Southwest Africa that were needed to continue the fight against Nama rebels in the colony. Over the following months, Dernburg lectured in public on the colonies, implicitly campaigning for the government-friendly procolonial parties. After this, the attitude of the antisemites in parliament began to noticeably thaw. On February 27, Max Liebermann von Sonnenberg of the German Socials declared his desire to give Dernburg "without any reservation full recognition for the energetic manner in which he has begun to redress the insalubrities in his office."[46] On February 28, Zimmermann stated that Dernburg's recent speeches "greatly elucidated the value of our colonies."[47] In March, fellow party member Friedrich Bindewald announced his confidence that colonial officialdom under Dernburg would encompass only men of good

42. Ibid., 4020.

43. "Excellenz Dernburg," in *Deutsche Reform (Deutsche Wacht): Wochenblatt für volkstümliche Politik* 2, no. 36 (September 1906).

44. *Sten. Ber.* XI/II/140, December 13, 1906, 4377.

45. *Sten. Ber.* XI/II/133, December 4, 1906, 4125.

46. *Sten. Ber.* XII/I/5, February 27, 1907, 96.

47. *Sten. Ber.* XII/I/6, February 28, 1907, 114.

character. "Thereby falls away another reason," Bindewald declared, "that might motivate some to be against colonialism."[48] Undoubtedly, Dernburg's procolonial speeches during the campaign were interpreted as a sign of his dedication to the colonial cause and, perhaps, a vindication of Lattmann's early praise. This must have been especially true for those who remembered Lattmann's insistence on November 30 that "winning the approval of the people" for colonialism was "the duty of all friends of the colonies."[49]

Outspoken appreciation for Dernburg and his policies by procolonial antisemites in parliament only increased with time. It quickly became clear to even skeptics like Werner that Dernburg was an ally dedicated to fulfilling many of their demands—like railroad construction, a reduction in the power of concession companies, a reorganization of the colonial bureaucracy, and an end to the seemingly endless colonial scandals. Although some grumbled at first that Dernburg was simply advancing their own colonial program, many soon recognized the gains to be made by strongly supporting the new energetic colonial director, soon to be state secretary.[50] This realization motivated the parliamentary antisemites to overlook his Jewish ancestry, at least while speaking in public, and moved them to form a common front with Dernburg in attacking the detractors of empire. This had unusual results. It led to the ironic situation of antisemites in parliament rallying to Dernburg's defense against the biting criticisms of colonial critics not just in the Catholic Center Party but also among the Social Democrats, where the staunchest ideological opponents of political antisemitism were found.

The irony was not lost on the critics of empire, who occasionally referred to the new director's Jewish heritage in order to embarrass him and his supporters on the political right. Soon after Dernburg's appointment, the Social Democratic satirical magazine *Der Wahre Jacob* printed a cartoon showing two men in conversation, one at the wheel of an automobile and the other standing next to the car. The caption read: ". . . Dernburg—this is the beginning of the end! Just you watch, Count, in two years' time

48. *Sten. Ber.* XII/I/11, March 6, 1907, 294.

49. *Sten. Ber.* XI/II/130, November 30, 1906, 4023.

50. Liebermann von Sonnenberg, for example, qualified his praise of February 27 by reminding the Reichstag that the German Socials had "long before . . . already demanded the colonial policies that the government now begins to follow" (*Sten. Ber.* XII/I/5, February 27, 1907, 96).

a baptized Jew will be sitting on the Prussian throne!"[51] Then, a day after Lattmann's initial praise of Dernburg in the Reichstag on November 30, the Social Democratic deputy August Bebel announced his happiness that "the savior of the German colonial calamity has again had to come, like so many other saviors, from Israel, from where we have already received so much that is good, and that this time, even the gentlemen of the antisemitic persuasion [*die Herren Antisemiten*] expect good from there, completely against their usual habits and beliefs."[52]

Catholic Center Party deputy Schaedler followed suit after the election, a time when critics accused Dernburg of having exaggerated the positive during his campaign speeches about the colonies. One statement that critics seized upon was his insistence before an audience of scientists and artists in January 1907 that "a box of dried dates . . . dropped on the road" in Southwest Africa had quickly produced "date palms three meters in height."[53] In an obvious reference to Dernburg's Jewish roots and, most likely, with this anecdote in mind, Schaedler accused Dernburg before the assembled Reichstag of having a "rampant, oriental imagination" with regard to the colonies.[54] Other deputies recognized the implicit antisemitism in Schaedler's comment; immediately afterward, the deputy Georg Gothein insisted that this "'subtle' remark" brought the antisemitism of the Center Party "clearly to light."[55]

The postelection attacks on Dernburg gave the antisemites their first real occasion to come to his defense against the critics of empire. The loudest critics were to be found among the Social Democrats, a fact that undoubtedly helped to promote the informal alliance between Dernburg and the antisemites. Unlike colonial critics in the Center Party who wished to improve the situation in the colonies, the Social Democrats opposed colonialism on principle. Both before and during Dernburg's tenure, they tried to derail colonial budgetary debates with revelations of wrongdoing in the colonies. They were not content with Dernburg's promises of reform or with the reforms themselves, and they continued to press the issue of colo-

---

51. *Der Wahre Jacob,* October 16, 1906.
52. *Sten. Ber.* XI/II/131, December 1, 1906, 4057.
53. Lecture Delivered at the Invitation of an Informal Gathering of Scientists and Artists on the 8th January 1907, RKA 6938, BAB.
54. *Sten. Ber.* XII/I/8, March 2, 1907, 178.
55. Ibid., 189.

nial violence long after important Center Party critics had signaled their satisfaction. The Social Democrats were also the most biting and sarcastic public critics of the antisemitic movement, and for this reason, antisemitic parliamentary deputies expressed a violent hatred of their Social Democratic counterparts. In the months after the 1907 election, which saw a dramatic reduction in Social Democratic seats, critical discussions of colonialism in parliament degenerated more than once into acerbic exchanges between Dernburg and the Social Democrats, and the Social Democrats and the antisemites. The Social Democrats criticized Dernburg and the procolonial antisemites as advocates of the same racist and exploitative colonial system, and Dernburg and the antisemitic deputies sometimes found themselves under attack by the same left-wing members of parliament.

This occurred repeatedly in March 1907, beginning when Social Democratic deputy Singer joined the chorus lampooning Dernburg's "box of dried dates" story by mocking the director's "fantasy-filled plans" for colonial development. In the same speech, Singer also attacked the antisemites, criticizing Lattmann for suggesting in the past that the German colonies be used to "threaten" British possessions in Africa.[56] Lattmann did not respond, but the antisemitic Eduard von Liebert—a member of the conservative Reichspartei and the procolonial Pan-German League—let loose invective against the Social Democrats. Liebert reported that a Social Democratic newspaper lampooned Germany's national flag as the "dirty-rag of the Hottentot-block," and he suggested that the responsible parties should suffer an American-style "lynch justice."[57]

Several days later, Social Democratic deputy Georg Ledebour accused antisemites and pan-Germans alike of viewing Southwest Africa as a launching point for an invasion of Britain's Cape Colony. Ledebour attacked what he called "the Lattmannish world-political strategy" and the "pan-German fantasist politicians." He also accused Dernburg in the same speech of overstating the value of German trade with the colonies.[58] Dernburg responded by suggesting to "tumultuous applause" that it was their rejection of empire that had recently cost the Social Democrats so many seats in the Reichstag.[59] These exchanges showed that, in addition to shar-

---

56. *Sten. Ber.* XII/I/7, March 1, 1907, 157.

57. Ibid., 171.

58. *Sten. Ber.* XII/I/11, March 6, 1907, 287.

59. Ibid., 296. The Social Democrats returned with forty-three seats from an original eighty-one.

ing some of the same goals, Dernburg and the antisemites shared some of the same political enemies.

Recognition of this fact likely motivated Lattmann to speak up against left-wing colonial critics on Dernburg's behalf after the election. Although Lattmann also criticized Dernburg for painting "slightly too rosy" a picture of colonial conditions during the election campaign (even advising him "as a friend of the colonies" to rein in his "fanciful imagination"), he argued that far too much was made of Dernburg's "box of dates" story.[60] To make his point, he read aloud from a pamphlet written by August Bebel where the Social Democrat compared Dernburg's anecdote to the Old Testament tale of Moses conjuring up a spring in the Egyptian desert. "Everyone who has lived off the land and has practiced horticulture knows the amazing way in which grains and seeds can often develop in amazing places," Lattmann stated.[61] He insisted that date palms grew throughout Southwest Africa, and he attacked Bebel for using the story to impugn Dernburg's credibility on colonial matters. In the same speech, Lattmann also praised the current colonial budget and stated his accord with "the opinion of the Colonial Director in the domain of the native question."[62] Perhaps as a way to reassure his constituency that all this did not entail a relaxation of his antisemitism, Lattmann concluded by briefly denouncing the immigration of "Capeland and Russian Jews" into Southwest Africa.[63] This prompted a follow-up by Bindewald who, likewise, concurred with Dernburg on several points of colonial policy before denouncing the presence of "this foreign-race element, the Jews" in the German colonies.[64]

The antisemites continued, however, to defend the new director against attacks from the Left. Lattmann and Werner were the only representatives of the antisemitic parties to speak during plenary debates on colonial matters during Dernburg's tenure after February 28, 1907, and they found ample opportunity to counter Social Democratic criticisms of his efforts and policies. After Dernburg's first trip to the colonies in 1907, for example, he was widely lampooned for the pomposity with which he

---

60. Ibid., 278.
61. Ibid., 277.
62. Ibid., 278.
63. Ibid., 279.
64. Ibid., 295. Lattmann also denounced Jewish immigration to German Southwest Africa in parliament on May 8, again in Dernburg's presence (*Sten. Ber.* XII/I/49, May 6, 1907, 1498).

had reportedly conducted himself while touring East Africa.[65] Upon his return, Social Democratic deputies also ridiculed his announced intention to improve the treatment of the colonized and to curtail colonial violence by noting that his own black porters had been whipped.[66] Werner came to Dernburg's defense. He pointed out that "interest" in colonialism "in the German people has been reawakened and invigorated" as a result of Dernburg's trip to East Africa. Werner compared Dernburg favorably with his predecessors who, with the exception of Paul Kayser, never visited the colonies. "Precisely this defective knowledge of the colonies was probably, essentially, the reason why many bad and inferior measures were issued by Berlin," he commented.[67]

Criticisms from the Left were also made upon Dernburg's return in August 1908 from a second trip, this time to German Southwest Africa. Social Democrats remarked in parliament that Dernburg's impressions of the colony's possibilities for development seemed overly optimistic. Deputy Eichhorn suggested that Dernburg had only seen "Potemkin villages" and, therefore, knew little of actual conditions in the colonies.[68] Once again, Werner came to Dernburg's defense, delivering perhaps the most complimentary speech in praise of Dernburg ever made by an antisemite in parliament. He insisted to "applause" that Dernburg had traveled to Africa for the explicit reason of forming "a general factual judgement of the colonies."[69] He thanked Dernburg for "not wanting to govern the colonies from an armchair" and for visiting Africa "annually." "The fault of the early colonial policies, was that the predecessors of the Herr State Secretary, the former Colonial Directors, with the exception of one, Herr Dr. Kayser, never saw the German colonies," Werner reiterated. "How can one correctly judge conditions in Africa if one never goes there!"[70]

Continued allegations of excessive colonial violence again united Dernburg and the antisemites against critics on the Left toward the end of

---

65. Following Dernburg's trip to German East Africa, articles and editorials complaining of a reported lack of modesty during his inspection tour appeared in the German press. For example, Maximilian Harden faulted Dernburg in *Die Zukunft* in March 1908 for sporting a "white uniform and epaulettes with gold tinsels" and wearing his medals prominently (Schiefel, *Bernhard Dernburg*, 68).

66. *Sten. Ber.* XII/I/125, March 18, 1908, 4063.

67. Ibid., 4086.

68. *Sten. Ber.* XII/I/215, February 27, 1909, 7204.

69. *Sten. Ber.* XII/I/216, March 1, 1909, 7228.

70. Ibid., 7230.

Dernburg's tenure. Although Dernburg had issued regulations in 1907 to limit and control the use of corporal punishment, recorded instances of whipping in German Africa nevertheless increased while he was in office. The Social Democrats' parliamentary expert on military and colonial affairs, deputy Gustav Noske, denounced this while speaking in parliament in January 1910. Noske argued that claims of progress in the treatment of the colonized were misleading: "Observing the present colonial policy with a careful eye, one finds that whenever something is actually given to the native people with one hand, just as much, if not more, is taken away with the other." Expanding on this theme, he argued that the Germans had brought peace to their African colonies only through extremely violent means: "with machine guns," he stated, "which often have more victims in a single battle than would have fallen during a hundred tribal feuds."[71] Dernburg and the antisemites responded by belittling this comment. Deputy Liebert suggested that the condemnation of machine guns reflected a dearth of real scandals, while Dernburg stated that the military could not shoot with "chocolate creams."[72] Lattmann weighed in several days later, arguing that machine guns actually benefited the colonized by making the work of "doctors and teachers" possible.[73] The Social Democrats should, he insisted, support the shipment of more machine guns to German Africa, for which provision was made by the contemporary colonial budget.

The antisemites in parliament also defended Dernburg from criticisms from the political right. Beginning in the summer of 1907 with the decrees regulating corporal punishment, supporters of settler colonialism complained of a notable shift in Dernburg's attitude toward the so-called native question, in particular, a greater concern with the rights of the colonized and with moderating colonial violence. This shift was not imagined. Over the years, Dernburg moved from defending whipping to opposing it, generally, and to advocating the substitution of monetary fines for corporal punishment.[74] He also shifted in his estimation of the capabilities of the colonized, eventually preferring indigenous over settler agricultural pro-

71. *Sten. Ber.* XII/II/27, January 31, 1910, 953.

72. *Sten. Ber.* XII/II/28, February 1, 1910, 995.

73. *Sten. Ber.* XII/II/29, February 3, 1910, 999.

74. *Sten. Ber.* XII/I/125, March 18, 1908, 4079; ibid., XII/I/214, February 26, 1909, 7177; ibid., XII/II/28, February 1, 1910, 995.

Fig. 5. A photograph of Dernburg in Zanzibar during his 1907 visit to German East Africa that reveals something of his personality. (Bundesarchiv, Bild 146-1984-041-10.)

Fig. 6. Dernburg conversing with the students of a missionary school in German East Africa in 1907. (Bundesarchiv, Bild 146-1982-170-31A.)

**Fig. 7. Dernburg on the march to Tabora in German East Africa in 1907.
(Bundesarchiv, Bild 146-1982-170-28A.)**

duction and even reversing his judgment on the truthfulness of blacks.[75]
Moreover, Dernburg began speaking in 1908—after his return from German East Africa—of both "ethical and economic reasons" for treating
blacks better and, by extension, for removing colonial officials who injured
German "standing" through their "injustice, brutality, and egoism."[76] In
1909, he openly condemned older colonial policies of "oppression, force,
and destruction." At the same time, he denounced predictions of the eventual extinction of blacks predicated on "Darwin's law of the survival of the
fittest," an idea that would, he believed, lead to a "war of extermination

75. Compare Dernburg's disparaging remarks about the reliability of black witnesses
made in the Reichstag on December 3 and 13, 1906, to his statements on March 2, 1909. In the
latter, he sharply attacked the practice of denying blacks the right to testify under oath in
colonial courts of law (*Sten. Ber.* XI/II/132, December 3, 1906, 4100; ibid., XI/II/140, December 13, 1906, 4363; ibid. XII/I/217, March 2, 1909, 7271). On another note, Dernburg spoke repeatedly in the Reichstag in 1907 of the need to educate blacks to work, but he stopped doing
so after returning from German East Africa.

76. *Sten. Ber.* XII/I/124, March 17, 1908, 4026, 4025.

against the Negroes" in the colonies.[77] He even insisted that black workers be treated "like human beings."[78] Lattmann and Werner defended Dernburg against the criticisms these statements engendered, even though in this instance, they came from the Right.

Their motive was purely practical. Unlike colonial critic Matthias Erzberger, whose opposition to excessive violence against the colonized stemmed from Christian principles, racial antisemites like Lattmann and Werner considered the well-being of indigenes only insofar as it affected the success of the colonies.[79] Excessive cruelties were to be avoided and indigenous populations preserved, but for practical reasons, like the need for a willing and pliable labor force, and not from a sense of shared humanity with the colonized. Lattmann articulated this viewpoint while speaking in September 1907 at a German Social Party conference. Responding to accusations from Social Democrats that Germany pursued policies of extermination in the colonies, Lattmann affirmed the necessity of preserving "the natives' necessary and precious manpower," but only "out of pure egoism. . . . we pursue this colonial policy not for the sake of the natives, but rather in the interest of the homeland."[80] In a similar vein, racial antisemites like Lattmann opposed colonial practices that hurt the cause of empire by making it appear shameful in the eyes of the German public, and so welcomed Dernburg's desire to control settler violence. They also rejected policies that, in their view, hindered the most effective use of indigenous populations for the maximum benefit of the German people back home. This was congruent with their belief that, in opposing Jews and big capital, the antisemitic movement fought special interests for the good of the entire German *Volk*.

In practice, this meant opposing the more radical actions and demands of German settlers, despite an ideological predilection for settler

---

77. *Sten. Ber.* XII/I/214, February 26, 1909, 7192, 7193.

78. Ibid., 7193.

79. Erzberger suffered widespread derision when he stated in March 1908 that "the native is also a human being possessing an immortal soul and a divinely appointed destiny identical to our own" (*Sten. Ber.* XII/I/126, March 19, 1908, 4098).

80. "Der Deutsch-Soziale Parteitag," *Staatsbürger-Zeitung,* September 10, 1907. Lattmann did not speak for all antisemites in this matter. Like colonial critics from the Center Party, Adolf Stöcker of the Christian Socials was a paternalist who argued that the cultural and moral improvement of colonized peoples was an important goal in itself, independent of practical considerations (*Sten. Ber.* 67, May 14, 1889, 1738). Stöcker's colonial paternalism was occasionally echoed in the pages of the antisemitic *Staatsbürger-Zeitung,* which printed a series of front-page articles in 1906 condemning what the authors deemed to be unnecessarily brutal colonial practices.

colonialism among the antisemites. For example, when colonial extremists argued for the removal of the entire Nama population from German Southwest Africa following the uprising of 1904, Lattmann voiced his opposition in parliament.[81] Likewise, Lattmann supported Dernburg in opposing the demands of white East African plantation owners that indigenous farmers be prohibited from growing competing cash crops. He cited the danger of another uprising, plus the success of indigenous agriculture in Togo and Cameroon.[82]

This type of thinking led both Lattmann and Werner to recognize the problems of uncontrolled settler violence and, consequently, to respond positively to Dernburg's calls in 1908 for improving the treatment of the colonized. To bolster Dernburg's position, Lattmann argued before parliament that "many have already held his opinion for a number of years."[83] He cited Bismarck as an example, insisting that the former chancellor had likewise opposed unnecessary cruelty to blacks with the reasoning of an animal trainer who rejects unnecessary violence. Lattmann expounded on this theme again in February 1910, two days after Dernburg reiterated his general opposition to whipping in the colonies.[84] In this speech, Lattmann discussed the practical drawbacks of what he called an unrestrained "*Herrenstandpunkt*" in colonial matters. Quoting from a colonial expert who faulted Spain and Portugal for creating "an unrestrained system of man-hunting and slavery" in their colonies, Lattmann insisted that such policies hurt colonizers because they led to "the extermination of the blacks." "From this," he quoted, "the motherland will later have a disadvantage." Lattmann quickly pointed out, however, that he rejected "the viewpoint that only marches under the pretty flag of humanism and perceives the natives' cultural and ethical elevation and economic furtherance as the reason for our colonial policy." He argued that a "reasonable humanitarianism" be paired with a "reasonable *Herrenstandpunkt*" to reduce colonial violence while maintaining the racial hierarchy.[85]

Certainly, Dernburg's own utilitarian rhetoric made it easier for the antisemites to continue to support him despite his shift to the left on the so-called native question. After his trip to German East Africa in 1907, Dernburg spoke in the Reichstag of ethical reasons for moderating colo-

---

81. *Sten. Ber.* XII/I/11, March 6, 1907, 278.

82. *Sten. Ber.* XII/I/125, March 18, 1908, 4082.

83. Ibid., 4081.

84. *Sten. Ber.* XII/II/28, February 1, 1910, 995.

85. *Sten. Ber.* XII/II/29, February 3, 1910, 999–1000.

nial violence. But he argued much more strongly that brutality was simply inefficient and hampered colonial development. It simply made more sense, Dernburg insisted, to treat "natives" well, because this would increase their productivity while winning them over to German colonialism. "Make the Negro into a well-treated, prosperous, and healthy charge," Dernburg stated in the Reichstag in March 1908, "and you will in the future be able to cut down on all sorts of expenses which today heavily burden, as unproductive, the imperial budget."[86] Dernburg eventually advocated the substitution of monetary fines for corporal punishment with similar logic, indicating that it made sense on utilitarian as well as ethical grounds. Responding to complaints from deputy Liebert in February 1909 over the introduction of what the former governor called "the broadest humanitarianism" into German East Africa, Dernburg offered the following explanation: "We punish people where we can with money instead of the whip because, on the one hand, money appears to us to be a better and more dignified punishment and, secondly, it helps fulfill somewhat the maintenance of the justice system in the colonies."[87] He pointed out that German East Africa experienced "twenty-five rebellions" under Liebert's governorship, but that for the past two and a half years, there were none.[88]

The fact that Dernburg insisted upon maintaining the racial hierarchy despite his desire to treat the colonized better also reassured the racial antisemites. In 1907, Dernburg allowed for new stiff penalties in Southwest Africa for Germans who violated the ban on mixed-race marriages, and his correspondence with the colony's governor in 1908 showed his continued support for the prohibition.[89] In addition, Dernburg continued to profess the stereotypical view that "abstract concepts" for blacks were "nearly inconceivable" even after his trip to East Africa convinced him that blacks were capable of "independent" and "orderly" agricultural production.[90] Racial equality, therefore, was out of the question. Even when advocating milder treatment, Dernburg insisted that "the respect, the authority, and the preponderance of the whites must be preserved."[91]

---

86. *Sten. Ber.* XII/I/124, March 17, 1908, 4026.

87. *Sten. Ber.* XII/I/214, February 26, 1909, 7172, 7177. Deputy Liebert complained that the substitution of "the broadest humanitarianism" for the "earlier peaceful impartial severity" was causing "rebelliousness" among blacks.

88. Ibid., 7198.

89. Dernburg to Governor Schuckmann, November 19, 1908, R151/FC 5181, BAB. In 1907, Dernburg allowed for the stripping away of the civic and voting rights of Germans who violated the ban.

90. *Sten. Ber.* XII/I/124, March 17, 1908, 4026.

91. *Sten. Ber.* XII/I/214, February 26, 1909, 7177.

While speaking before the Reichstag in March 1908, Dernburg also mentioned several times the idea of "racial justice." What he meant was not exactly clear; he used the term while justifying the continued use of corporal punishment for blacks, arguing that "whipping" was customary for "these people" and "justice is that which society perceives as such."[92] This seems to have been a cultural and not a racial argument for flogging, but procolonial antisemites—and Social Democrats—seized on Dernburg's words as a sign of his commitment to the racial status quo, meaning the continued treatment of indigenous people as racial inferiors. Lattmann gave a long delivery after Dernburg made this statement, defending him from the accusations of settler advocates that he concentrated too much on "the rights of blacks." Lattmann insisted that this criticism was "unjustified" because "the Herr State Secretary has stressed racial justice in addition to the legitimate humanity of the natives."[93] Dernburg's continued toleration of corporal punishment—although he was opposed to it in principle—mollified deputy Werner as well, who saw the African as "a man of slave instincts" who needed to be treated as such.[94]

Occasionally, the parliamentary antisemites publicly disagreed with Dernburg on matters of colonial policy. But disagreements never drove them during his tenure to the right-wing opposition that represented the disgruntled proponents of settler colonialism, who increasingly saw Dernburg as an opponent.[95] Instead, both Lattmann and Werner went out of their way to express their continued support for Dernburg even when they broke with him on specific matters.

One such issue concerned the existence of an Indian business class in German East Africa. Although vital to the colony's economic growth, Indian businessmen were reviled as "parasites" and "usurers" by the white settler community, which pressured the government to limit their commerce and restrict Indian immigration. Dernburg, however, repealed anti-

---

92. *Sten. Ber.* XII/I/125, March 18, 1908, 4079.

93. Ibid., 4083. Lattmann pointed out that a memorandum from the Colonial Office also used the idea of "racial justice" to legitimate corporal punishment. He quoted the following from page 4: "It lies in the nature of the Negro that the existing racial justice can not be changed for a long time, and that certain methods of corporal punishment . . . can also not be abolished."

94. Ibid., 4087.

95. In particular, settlers were annoyed by Dernburg's advocacy of indigenous agricultural production, a position he developed as a result of his positive estimations of the capabilities of black Africans during his trip to German East Africa. The antisemites tended to side with Dernburg on this issue, in line with their position that the colonies needed to be developed for the benefit of the entire German *Volk* and not for the advantage of a small number of white settlers.

Indian legislation upon coming to office, and he ultimately refused to restrict their economic activity through discriminatory laws.[96] Both
Lattmann and Werner criticized Dernburg for this in parliament, where
they insisted that he misconstrued the danger of the Indian presence that,
according to Werner, hindered the development of "healthy economic conditions" in the colony.[97] But each softened his criticism with compliments.
In the same speech where he attacked Indian traders, Lattmann reaffirmed
his party's general satisfaction with the government's colonial policies
"even if we disagree with Dernburg here and there."[98] Werner prefaced his
own critical remarks about Indian traders in March 1908 with praise for
Dernburg's trip to German East Africa. He also congratulated Dernburg
for initiating a "strong, defined colonial program."[99]

The antisemitic deputies maintained their general support for Dernburg throughout his last months in office, and they continued to defend
him even as their own concerns about specific policy positions mounted.
With the passage of time, Lattmann and Werner even seemed to move
closer to Dernburg's positions on certain matters. In his complimentary
speech of March 1909, Werner reiterated that "the native" is "a man with
slave instincts" and insisted that "one can hardly get on without whipping,
completely." He then added, "It is nevertheless, in any case, something to
welcome, that one has come to more humane opinions concerning the punishment of natives, and that one tries to substitute, when possible, fines for
corporal punishment." Werner echoed Dernburg's own rationale: "This is
indeed, also, more advantageous for the reason that income for the administration of justice is obtained in this way."[100]

For his part, Lattmann continued to give Dernburg the benefit of the
doubt concerning his commitment to maintaining the racial hierarchy in

---

96. In 1906, Dernburg repealed a recently enacted rule that had obstructed Indian
traders by mandating the keeping of financial records in either German or Kiswahili.

97. *Sten. Ber.* XII/I/125, March 18, 1908, 4087.

98. Ibid., 4084.

99. Ibid., 4087. Eduard von Liebert also expressed continued support for Dernburg despite disagreeing with his "native policies." Liebert began his speech of February 26, 1909—
where he criticized the introduction of the "broadest humanitarianism" into German East
Africa—by admitting that "our protectorates, without exception and everywhere, are making
progress in their development." He remarked upon the increase in white immigration, the
"elimination" of "colonial scandals," and the establishment of stricter control over colonial
finances. He concluded that "one can therefore sing a long song of praise for the present colonial administration" (*Sten. Ber.* XII/I/214, February 26, 1909, 7170–71).

100. *Sten. Ber.* XII/I/216, March 1, 1909, 7228.

German Africa. Speaking before the Reichstag on Februrary 3, 1910, Lattmann admitted that some of Dernburg's recent statements gave the worrisome impression that he had changed his mind on the importance of preserving white supremacy, as right-wing critics had claimed. As a case in point, Lattmann cited Dernburg's support for allowing indigenes the right to testify under oath in colonial courts of law.[101] Lattmann asserted his confidence, however, that Dernburg maintained the correct outlook on racial matters. He quoted from a recent London speech where Dernburg spoke of the shared interest among "white colonialists" in convincing colonized people of the white man's superior "power and knowledge."[102] "It is good," Lattmann stated, "that the Herr State Secretary expressed this racial-political viewpoint so forcefully." Lattmann added that "the question of whether or not a change in [Dernburg's] understanding occurred is pointless" as long as one continues to "take to heart" the opinions Dernburg had expressed in London.[103]

Even Dernburg's ardent disapproval of Lattmann's proposal in April 1910 of a one-time levy of 1 percent on landed wealth in Southwest Africa—intended to make investors share more of the financial burden of the wars with the Herero and Nama—did not induce the antisemites to publicly break with him before he left office. Dernburg's opposition came on top of revelations about a new treaty that he hoped to sign with the German Colonial Corporation over diamond mining rights in the colony.

---

101. See chap. 2.

102. A copy of this speech does not seem to exist in the Reichskolonialamt records in Berlin or the Bernhard Dernburg Papers in Koblenz. The Reichskolonialamt records do contain, however, an article from the *South African News* from late November 1909 detailing an interview given by Dernburg to the *Daily Chronicle.* This interview helps explain the confusion over Dernburg's exact position on racial matters. "In his opinion," states the *South African News,* "the majority of the coloured peopled of South Africa are quite 'unfit to be trusted with a vote,' but he views apparently with satisfaction the safeguarding of the coloured vote in this Colony." The article then quotes Dernburg as saying: "If I may sum up my observations in a sentence, I should say don't delude yourself by imagining that the black man is equal to the white one. He is not equal, and you will only make mischief by pretending that he is." But when asked if Dernburg would advocate restricting nonwhites to "a purely technical or industrial training," he replied: "God forbid . . . . When the aspiration is in the soul of the coloured man to acquire literary education, by all means let him have it." Dernburg also discussed race mixing in the interview: "He considers the coloured men with white blood in their veins as forming 'the leaven of discontent' in the Southern States of America and, presumably, also in this country. 'But,' he continues, very justly: 'They are also the element of progress'" (*South African News* vom 26-11-09, RKA 2086, BAB).

103. *Sten. Ber.* XII/II/29, February 3, 1910, 1001.

Those representing settler interests denounced the treaty, claiming it unfairly favored big capital, an argument that appealed to the antisemites.[104] Together, these events led both Lattmann and Werner to sharply criticize Dernburg in parliament. Lattmann accused him on April 30 of appearing to oppose a "middle-class" colonial program in favor of "an exaggerated one-sided capitalistic colonial policy."[105] Werner weighed in shortly after and, for a moment, appeared to drop the usual deference toward the state secretary. "Business magnates invest their money in the colonies in order to earn money, and not, perchance, on account of the Herr State Secretary's pretty blue eyes," he stated. "We permit gentlemen to 'make' money, but they should also pay appropriate taxes to the Reich. If gentlemen acquire large fortunes in a short time, which even they did not count on," he continued, "it is, indeed, not an unfair demand that they make a small one-off contribution to the cost of war."[106]

As previously, however, both men qualified their criticisms of Dernburg with compliments aimed at assuaging their constituency's concern regarding his real intentions. Werner noted that he was "firmly convinced" that "the welfare and continued development of our colonies are very close to the Herr State Secretary Dernburg's heart."[107] Lattmann went even further, taking pains to explain that his quarrel with Dernburg over the tax proposal for Southwest Africa was not motivated by antisemitism, despite allegations to the contrary, and that he continued to support Dernburg's general vision for the colonies. After reading aloud from an unnamed newspaper that characterized a similar tax proposal from Erzberger as an attempt to unseat Dernburg, Lattmann insisted that "it is just as deplorable and off the point when a certain press tries to see in me merely the antisemite in this battle and to place the antisemite Lattmann next to the Center Party deputy Erzberger and, in so doing, to deceive the general public about the fundamental importance of the whole question." Singling out the Jewish-owned *Berliner Tageblatt,* Lattmann noted that "those gentlemen who scornfully attack me because I oppose the Herr State Secretary in this instance have [previously] accused me of simply parroting the Herr State Secretary."[108] "I have, in all the years, tried to face him objectively,"

---

104. Dernburg rejected these concerns and asserted his right to decide the diamond matter on his own authority. He concluded the controversial treaty shortly before submitting his resignation in May, sparking outrage in the Reichstag.

105. *Sten. Ber.* XII/II/76, April 30, 1910, 2790.

106. Ibid., 2791.

107. Ibid., 2793.

108. Ibid., 2786. Dernburg's father, Friedrich, wrote for the *Berliner Tageblatt.*

Lattmann stated, pressing the point further. "I have happily and joyfully supported him. I declare again today that many of the attacks that have been leveled against him are not justified."[109] Lattmann then recounted some of Dernburg's policies he supported, like railroad construction. He concluded by acknowledging that "the interest of our people in colonialism has penetrated to the last cottage during recent years" and that "the national will stands everywhere behind an energetic colonial policy."[110]

At the end of Dernburg's career, then, a continued appreciation for many of his achievements led the antisemitic deputies to express their general support even as their disagreements with Dernburg mounted. This changed in a dramatic fashion, however, after Dernburg's exit in June 1910, principally as a result of his decision to conclude the controversial treaty with the German Colonial Corporation despite the objections of many in the procolonial camp. His onetime supporters among the antisemites were particularly outraged. Speaking on December 12, 1910, Lattmann articulated his extreme unhappiness, calling the conclusion of the treaty a "slap in the face" for the entire Reichstag. Lattmann also advised parliament to refrain from "an overestimation of this man" who, he pointed out, proved to be a "bureaucrat and autocrat" despite his initial moves against bureaucratism. Contradicting his earlier insistence that Dernburg had maintained the proper outlook on racial matters, Lattmann announced that "his policy lacked a regard for the racial question." And in an even more striking turnabout, he denied Dernburg any credit for elevating the public's colonial consciousness, attributing this instead to the outbreak of the Herero and Nama Wars. The ripening of the people "for colonial ideas" was something Dernburg "could take advantage of," Lattmann continued, "and he did so with success, according to many estimations."

Lattmann ended his attack on Dernburg with a final dig. For the first time, he used language that was unquestionably antisemitic, suggesting that Dernburg had a foreign understanding of German colonial policy. He declared that, "according to the *Kolonialen Rundschau* of November 21, 1907," Dernburg had made the following statement after returning from German East Africa: "Young people who can earn 2,000 marks in Tietz- or Wertheim are foolish if they migrate to our colonies." Lattmann read what he claimed was the *Rundschau*'s commentary.

---

109. Ibid., 2789.
110. Ibid., 2791.

Hopefully, there still lives in our people enough Viking blood, that we will not . . . shrink back from the difficulties and dangers that threaten the bearers of the German flag abroad. Herr Dernburg does not understand us. He represents what is to us a foreign outlook on life. He reckons only with money and does not know that there is still something else that is worth more than the highest-ranking stock on the Berlin stock market. And it would be sad if such principles are allowed to be even more standard for our colonial policy.

Although this antisemitic assessment of Dernburg's "outlook on life" was not Lattmann's own, it was clear that Lattmann identified with it. He added, "for this reason, we are happy to see the change in the Colonial Office."[111]

While Lattmann waited until after Dernburg's departure to attack him in the Reichstag with antisemitic language, the same did not hold true for the traditional opponents of the government's colonial policies. In March 1909, the Social Democratic deputy Georg Ledebour asked how opponents of mixed-race marriages like Dernburg could reconcile their opposition with their Christianity when Christians were involved. The vice president of the Reichstag recognized this as an antisemitic slight and accused Ledebour of "having spoken of the Christianity of the Herr State Secretary in an ironic way."[112] Deputy Erzberger took a more direct jab the following year. Like Lattmann, he also proposed a one-time property tax on landed wealth in Southwest Africa and was stung by the state secretary's ardent opposition. While defending his proposal on April 30, 1910, he noted that Dernburg had recently misquoted the Bible. "Certainly, there are extenuating circumstances for the Herr State Secretary if he is not so well-versed in the Holy Scriptures," Erzberger joked, to the "great amusement" of his fellow deputies.[113] As at the beginning of Dernburg's career, antisemitic slights in parliament came from deputies on the Left and Center toward the end. The Left and Center lost this monopoly, however, once Dernburg left office.

Many factors had constrained the antisemites from speaking about Dernburg in an antisemitic fashion while in parliament. Some deputies gen-

---

111. *Sten. Ber.* XII/II/99, December 12, 1910, 3589. This could not have been Vohsen's *Koloniale Rundschau,* because the *KR* began publication in 1909. Vohsen's *KR* was also very favorable to Dernburg.

112. *Sten. Ber.* XII/I/218, March 3, 1909, 7295.

113. *Sten. Ber.* XII/II/76, April 30, 1910, 2793.

uinely appreciated Dernburg's accomplishments. In addition, the state secretary's initial popularity with the procolonial public, and the traditional deference owed a representative of the emperor's government, necessitated a shelving of antisemitic sentiments during public interactions with Dernburg while he was in power. But the antisemitic press was a different story. Some newspapers openly evoked Dernburg's Jewish ancestry during his tenure in office and made it a focus of their criticisms of him. The antisemitic press, however, was not united in its outlook: an examination of four of the most important periodicals of the racist wing of the antisemitic movement—the *Hammer,* the *Deutsche Zeitung,* the *Staatsbürger-Zeitung,* and the *Deutsch-Soziale Blätter*—shows remarkable discord. While the *Deutsche Zeitung* and the *Staatsbürger-Zeitung* generally overlooked Dernburg's Jewish roots in light of his activities on behalf of colonial empire, the *Hammer* emphasized his Jewish heritage and interpreted all his plans and actions in an antisemitic light. The *Deutsch-Soziale Blätter,* on the other hand, had difficulty deciding its position, distrusting Dernburg at first, then expressing appreciation and, finally, disgust. The readership of individual newspapers reflected these divisions as well, revealing a degree of confusion over Dernburg within the antisemitic movement that was not evident among its elected deputies in the Reichstag. Much like the Emin Pasha phenomenon of the 1880s and early 1890s, the Dernburg phenomenon of 1906 to 1910 illustrates the extent to which even racial antisemites disagreed over whether an alleged Jew could surmount his Jewishness by possessing the right attitude toward national issues, like colonial empire.

Theodor Fritsch's *Hammer* magazine was Dernburg's harshest critic, consistently negative from the start. It identified Dernburg right away as coming from "the tribe of Juda" and quickly announced its animosity. "All experiences from ancient and recent times permit one to expect that a Jewish Colonial Director will probably pursue a skillful Jewish but not a German policy," it proclaimed in mid-September 1906. "He will probably govern his office with businesslike routines . . . he will perhaps clear away many bureaucratic old humdrum ways, he will turn out incapable officials and substitute others. On the surface, he will bring a fresh course to things, care for everything correctly, and will therefore win the rich praise of the popular press." But none of this would benefit the German people, the *Hammer* declared, because "the Hebrew—also the baptized—is too deeply rooted in his tribe for him to ever honestly protect anything other than Jewish interests." For the *Hammer,* Dernburg's appointment was part of the "gradual surrender of imperial power to the Jews," and, therefore, nothing good could come of it.[114]

The *Hammer* continued its attack after the Reichstag election, during the height of Dernburg's popularity. It printed an article in February dripping with sarcasm, lampooning the public's enthusiasm. Its author, Hans Wehleid, proclaimed Dernburg to be "the idol of the German people" and the "hero of the day," and remarked that "everything regarding the previously unknown bank director has suddenly become of significance. . . . It will probably not be long until we have a style of hat or tie after Dernburg, a 'Dernburg' cigarette or liqueur, and an enterprising author will write us a 'Dernburg as Educator.'"[115] While other nationalists congratulated Dernburg for taking on the Center Party, Wehleid gave him no credit. "It was easier for him to have courage than for many others," Wehleid wrote, because Dernburg had "a powerful international association" with an "almost unlimited influence" behind him.[116] Echoing complaints from parliamentary antisemites like Liebermann von Sonnenberg, Wehleid insisted that Dernburg had nothing original to say about the colonies. But his words were circulated "as if they were a revelation" because they came from "one belonging to the ancient association."[117]

Such sentiments did not accord with the feelings of all *Hammer* readers. In December 1906, shortly after Dernburg denounced the methods and motives of Social Democratic and Center Party colonial critics, he received several postcards published by the *Hammer* magazine replete with printed quotations on the fronts by Theodor Fritsch. In their notes on the back, the senders praised Dernburg's actions in parliament: "Hurrah Dernburg!," one wrote. "Finally the Blacks [the Center Party] have had the mask pulled from their hypocritical faces! Hurrah, cheers!"[118] A second postcard contained a hand-written poem wherein the author expressed his "grateful devotion" to the new colonial director.[119]

The *Hammer* magazine also reported in mid-October 1906 that some

---

114. "Der neue Kolonial-Direktor," *Hammer: Blätter für deutschen Sinn* 5 (1906): 555.

115. Wehleid was remarkably perceptive. Certainly unbeknownst to him, a cigarette company wrote Dernburg in December 1906 following his denunciation of deputy Roeren, asking if it could use his name and likeness to sell a type of cigarette (L. Wolff Cigarren-Fabriken to Dernburg, December 8, 1906, no. 14, BDP, BAK). In imagining a book titled *Dernburg as Educator,* Wehleid was alluding to the well-known work *Rembrandt as Educator* by the *völkisch* ideologue and antisemite Julius Langbehn.

116. Hans Wehleid, "Messias Dernburg," *Hammer: Blätter für deutschen Sinn* 6 (1907): 84.

117. Ibid., 87.

118. Anonymous to Bernhard Dernburg, December 4, 1906, no. 17, BDP, BAK.

119. Ewald Luedine to Bernhard Dernburg, December 4, 1906, no. 13, BDP, BAK.

readers took issue with its September article on Dernburg because it did not prove the director's Jewish origins. In response, the paper printed a short summary of Dernburg's family history, recounting how his grandfather converted to Christianity in the 1840s.[120] This, however, was still not enough for some. In March 1907, the *Hammer* printed a letter highly critical of the February article by Hans Wehleid that had attacked Dernburg. Written by a self-professed "old *Hammer* reader and *Hammer* friend," the author, Fritz Krone, accused Wehleid of letting "hatred and jealousy" blind him to Dernburg's "act of patriotism [*nationale Tat*]." "The *Hammer* paper is named the Paper for German Spirit," Krone declared, "and Dernburg showed German spirit when he defied the insolent disciples of Rome [*Römlingen*] and imparted to them a rebuff which every good German rejoiced in from their hearts." Although Krone admitted that Wehleid was probably correct in supposing that Dernburg enjoyed an unusual advantage, he insisted that Dernburg's "courageous act done in German spirit" didn't deserve disparagement. "As men of German spirit," he wrote, "we must be thankful to anyone, be he Christian or Jew, who contributes to a rousing of our people from their slumber." Krone asserted that "a whole string of *Hammer* friends" felt as he did on this matter.[121]

The editor and staff did not let this go unanswered. Immediately after, they printed Wehleid's lengthy response. In it, Wehleid suggested that answering the question why Dernburg could do what he did was essential to understanding the mysteries of contemporary politics. According to Wehleid, the reason for Dernburg's political success and his unprecedented popularity lay with "the sympathy of the Jews." Because of this, he found "everywhere sympathy and assistance, approval and aid; the public press chooses him as a leader" and the "blindly-believing masses" followed.[122] Wehleid argued that other bold men who acted without this sympathy become "economically endangered," finding their intentions distorted by a "public press" that "obstructs" their policies. Turning then to Krone's apparent willingness to forgive Dernburg his Jewish ancestry, Wehleid asked, "Can it not happen that a man of Jewish descent lay his Jewishness down, fully, and become a genuine valid German? Surely the possibility is not impossible," he answered, "but historical experiences speak against it." Wehleid wrote that "Jewry" was like a "blood-conspiracy out of which no

120. "Der Stammbaum Dernburg's," *Hammer: Blätter für deutschen Sinn* 5 (1906): 632.

121. Dr. Fritz Krone, "Zur Dernburg-Frage," *Hammer: Blätter für deutschen Sinn* 6 (1907): 153.

122. Hans Wehleid, "Antwort," *Hammer: Blätter für deutschen Sinn* 6 (1907): 154.

one once taken in is allowed to leave." Those who do, achieve in Jewry a "fanatical enemy." Accordingly, Wehleid reasoned that Dernburg must still be Jewish, because of the friendly attitudes of the Jewish press.[123] He argued that one could expect from Dernburg only "Jewish" policies.[124]

Contributions supporting Wehleid followed. In April, a reader wrote that Krone's views were "thirty years" behind the times and that their persistence "after a generation of almost unlimited dominion of Jewish blood" was "almost inconceivable." He delegitimated Krone's argument by insisting that "the accusation of jealousy" was a Jewish trait, "only raised from those of Jewish blood."[125] In May, a contributor identified as Phg. attacked the idea of the good or harmless Jew that seemed to gird Krone's protest. Pointing to the example of the German Jew Eduard Lasker who led the National Liberal Party during the speculative years of the early 1870s, Phg. wrote, "Already once has a Jew put 'good German men' into a true frenzy of enthusiasm by summoning up his oriental eloquence."[126] "Can a Jew produce a practical policy?" he asked. "Above all, does he have the correct understanding for a national policy? Those knowledgeable of the soul of the Jewish people answer in the negative, unconditionally."[127]

With the exception of an anti-Dernburg letter from a settler in 1909, the editors let this stand as the last word on the matter until Dernburg's retirement.[128] Afterward, they reprinted from elsewhere a short editorial accusing Dernburg of sparking through exaggerated statements an "unhealthy speculations-frenzy" in the colonies. They also noted that Matthias Erzberger estimated a loss of 140 million marks to the Reich through Dernburg's controversial treaty with the German Colonial Corporation of Southwest Africa. With clear satisfaction, the editors remarked that the *Hammer* "belonged to the few organs that did not join in the general rapture" when "the Hebrew Dernburg entered his office." They recalled that their "characterization of his personage . . . aroused even the displeasure of many old *Hammer* friends" and predicted that these would "now admit" their "injustice."[129]

Krone may have been a minority among *Hammer* readers in his sup-

---

123. Ibid., 155.
124. Ibid., 156.
125. K. H., "Zur Dernburg-Frage," *Hammer: Blätter für deutschen Sinn* 6 (1907): 251.
126. Phg., "Noch ein Wort zur Dernburg-Sache," *Hammer: Blätter für deutschen Sinn* 6 (1907): 284.
127. Ibid., 285.
128. Phg., "Die 'Aera Dernburg,'" *Hammer: Blätter für deutschen Sinn* 8 (1909): 712–13.
129. E. M., "Dernburg, der Sanierer," *Hammer: Blätter für deutschen Sinn* 9 (1910): 445.

port for Dernburg, but his was by no means an isolated voice within the wider antisemitic movement. While the *Hammer* was consistently negative toward Dernburg throughout his career, Friedrich Lange's *Deutsche Zeitung* backed him strongly. Like the *Hammer,* the *Deutsche Zeitung* acknowledged Dernburg's Jewish roots; it printed a report in mid-September 1906 detailing his parental lineage. Unlike the *Hammer,* however, it did not seem to hold it against him, even though the *Deutsche Zeitung* shared with Fritsch's newspaper a strong racial antisemitism.[130] The difference likely resulted from the different attitudes held by the two publishers toward the colonies. While the *Hammer* was decidedly cool toward the very idea of colonial empire, the *Deutsche Zeitung* was invested in colonialism's success, given Lange's involvement with the Society for German Colonization in the 1880s. Like other procolonial enthusiasts, Lange became increasingly critical of the colonial administration over the years, attacking the bureaucratic nature of the colonial office and denouncing concessionary policy.[131] He complained of the inability of individual colonies to fund their own administrative expenses, and he lamented the government's failure to develop a substantial railroad network. The energy, determination, and capability with which Dernburg attacked these problems won the *Deutsche Zeitung*'s admiration early on.

The *Deutsche Zeitung* displayed a remarkable open-mindedness toward Dernburg even before day one. On September 4, a day before Dernburg's appointment, it ran a short note stating its desire that the coming "bank master. . . build railroads and procure further capital" and avoid the mistakes of concessionary policy.[132] The *Deutsche Zeitung* then printed a front-page article the next day, criticizing the outgoing colonial director for a lack of accomplishments and introducing its readers to the new one. The *Deutsche Zeitung* identified Dernburg's father, Friedrich, as a former National Liberal deputy and a current editor of the *Berliner Tageblatt,* and it detailed Dernburg's financial career in Germany and abroad. It quoted a statement by Friedrich about the "full confidence" his son had in the colonies' "capacity for development," and about the large income reduction he assumed by accepting his new post in the colonial bureaucracy. The *Deutsche Zeitung* remarked that "one can read much that is promising in

---

130. Lange fulminated frequently against "Rassenschande" with Jews in the *Deutsche Zeitung*'s weekly edition, the *Deutsche Welt.* See F. L., "Rassenschande," *Deutsche Welt: Wochenschrift der Deutschen Zeitung,* November 17, 1904.

131. Friedrich Lange, *Reines Deutschtum: Gründzuge einer nationalen Weltanschauung* (Berlin: Verlag von Alexander Duncker, 1904), 282–84.

132. *Deutsche Zeitung,* September 4, 1906.

these words." It then printed a front-page article outlining "two initial important tasks for His Excellency Dernburg": changing colonial finances so
that the federal military budget subsumed defense costs, and building a
railroad system connecting German Southwest Africa to British territory.
The *Deutsche Zeitung* remarked that Dernburg's role "as a former bank
master" would serve him well in tackling the second project.[133]

The following weeks only saw the *Deutsche Zeitung*'s estimation of
Dernburg grow. The newspaper reported at length on the new director's
initial speeches, and it remarked upon the proximity of his ideas to its
own. For example, the *Deutsche Zeitung* printed a favorable review of the
newly published colonial novel *Peter Moore's Journey to Southwest Africa*
in late October, and it reported in the same issue that Dernburg had
praised the book for elevating interest in the colonies.[134] The *Deutsche
Zeitung* then printed an extremely positive review of Dernburg's initial
Reichstag speeches in late November, noting with particular approval his
emphasis on railroad building, plus his exclusion of military costs from
his memoranda on the colonies. Dernburg justified the latter by comparing colonial military expenses to those for Alsace-Lorraine, an integral
part of Germany. The *Deutsche Zeitung* noted with satisfaction and no
trace of jealousy that "by chance, we, ourselves, advanced a similar . . .
perspective twenty-four hours before Dernburg's speech." The newspaper
also reported with approval that Dernburg spoke of the "spiritual and
cultural" as well as "political" benefits to Germany of "a systematic colonial policy."[135]

Such praise reached new heights following Dernburg's action on December 3, when he accused deputy Roeren of political improprieties. In a
lead editorial titled "Finally, a man!," one contributor characterized Dernburg's appointment as proof of the government's commitment to real
change and lauded Dernburg profusely. "One no longer stands still, but instead goes forward," he wrote, and then called Dernburg "a man of work
and ability who has the courage of truth and a high moral sense of responsibility, who walked out into the hailstorm without an umbrella."[136]

---

133. "Zwei erste große Aufgaben für Exzellenz Dernburg. I.," *Deutsche Zeitung*, September 20, 1906.

134. "Peter Moors fahrt nach Südwest," *Deutsche Zeitung*, October 31, 1906; "Kolo-
nialexzellenz und Kolonialherzog," *Deutsche Zeitung*, October 31, 1906.

135. O. E., "Dernburgs Programm-Rede," *Deutsche Zeitung*, November 30, 1906.

136. O. E., "Endlich ein Mann!" *Deutsche Zeitung*, December 5, 1906. The *Deutsche
Zeitung* claimed that a "known conservative deputy" had cried out the words "finally a man"
during Dernburg's third parliamentary speech.

Editorials attacking Erzberger and Roeren followed, and in January, a contributor even protested an antisemitic jab at Dernburg by an organ of the Catholic Center Party. He also chastised ideological fellow travelers, like the antisemitic and procolonial *Deutsche Tageszeitung,* for failing to support Dernburg enthusiastically. The author insisted that Dernburg's electioneering speeches deserved tremendous praise because they "opened up the nearly impregnable fortresses" of "the indifferent and detached soul of the German professor and the purse of the Hanseatic merchant."[137]

The *Deutsche Zeitung* never explained how it maintained this support in light of its antisemitism. At times, the contradiction was glaring: in late September 1906 a front-page article appeared lamenting the large number of "ministers with Jewish blood" in state governments around the world, even though a separate piece on the same page objectively reported Dernburg's stated intention to visit the colonies.[138] What is more, the *Deutsche Zeitung's* weekly edition, the *Deutsche Welt,* harped on the perils of "race-mixing" between Jews and Germans, an outlook problematic in the extreme given that Dernburg was, himself, a product of just this type of union. An article that appeared in the *Deutsche Welt* in July 1908 provides the only possible solution to this quandary. Written by the antisemitic editor of the *Bayreuther Blätter,* Hans von Wolzogen, it characterizes "race" as an "aesthetic idea" and speaks of the possibility of an "individual personality" abandoning his own *Volksgeist* for another. Concerning Jews specifically, Wolzogen wrote that "the power of Christianity" could help certain "geniuses" in their "leap into Germanness." He claimed that such people were "extremely rare" and that he, himself, had "known only one." He also denied that race mixing facilitated this process.[139] Despite these important qualifications, Wolzogen's theory opened the door to a logical way out of the problem, although neither he nor the editors ever indicated that Dernburg belonged to the rare "personalities" capable of leaving their Jewish racial traits behind.

The *Deutsche Zeitung* became more critical of Dernburg as the years

---

137. A. Pz., "Dernburg," *Deutsche Zeitung,* January 25, 1907.

138. "Tagesfragen. Jetzt amtierende jüdische Minister aller Länder," *Deutsche Zeitung,* September 22, 1906.

139. Hans v. Wolzogen, "Gar nicht genug zu sagen!" *Deutsche Welt: Wochenschrift der Deutschen Zeitung,* July 5, 1908. As editor of the *Bayreuther Blätter,* Wolzogen enthusiastically supported Berhard Förster's attempt to establish a "Jew-free" German settlement in Paraguay in the 1880s. (Ben Macintyre, *Forgotten Fatherland: The Search for Elisabeth Nietzsche* [New York: Farrar Straus Giroux, 1992], 111). Wolzogen wrote repeatedly in the *DW* on the dangers of race mixing between Jews and Germans.

progressed, although it never stopped supporting him in general. The one issue that it attacked Dernburg on repeatedly was his stance on the so-called native question, in particular his eventual privileging of indigenous cultivation over white plantation agriculture and his push for a more humane treatment of colonized people. In 1908, the *Deutsche Zeitung* closely followed Dernburg's speeches promulgating his new views, and it printed five front-page critical responses from January through March. One lead writer identified only as O. E. insisted that a false understanding of "the characteristics of blacks" encouraged in Dernburg a "naive-optimistic and lighthearted Negrophilia." "European cultivation of the land with black helping labor extracts incomparably more value than the slower, and in the long run, less reliable native cultivation," he wrote. The same author complained that Dernburg saw in the black man "only a difference of degree," merely a "'diluted European,'" and ignored the "hundred-and-thousand-year difference between Aryan and Negro."[140] Unlike Dernburg, the *Deutsche Zeitung* also advocated forced labor. In addition, it denied that the state had a moral duty to "raise" black Africans, insisting that this was solely the task of missionaries. Furthermore, *Deutsche Zeitung* lead writers contested Dernburg's controversial statement that the colonies' "most important asset" was their native people.[141]

These differences, however, never led the *Deutsche Zeitung* to repudiate Dernburg. Even in 1908, lead writer O. E. registered his newspaper's agreement "with the large part of Dernburg's programmatic statements." He noted with satisfaction in March that reports of "foul deeds" no longer preoccupied parliament, and he lauded Dernburg's success in securing money for railroad development from the Reichstag. The fact that Dernburg used the term *racial justice* in parliament on March 18 when justifying corporal punishment also gratified him, and he reported a desire on Dernburg's part to see "racial domination . . . strictly maintained" in the colonies.[142] A mixture of criticism and praise characterized another article by O. E. in 1909. Here, he contested Dernburg's position on the Indian traders of German East Africa and criticized Dernburg's sharp tone toward critics in the Reichstag. He also attacked Dernburg's "somewhat one-

---

140. O. E., "Vor Beginn der großen Kolonialdebatten," *Deutsche Zeitung,* March 17, 1908.

141. Dernburg made this statement repeatedly in early 1908, and it became a catchphrase for both his supporters and opponents (Informationsreise Seiner Exzellenz des Staatssekretars Dernburg nach Südwestafrika im Jahren 1908, RKA 1463, BAB). The *Deutsche Zeitung* contested this characterization of "natives" in O. E., "Der sachliche Ertrag," *Deutsche Zeitung,* March 24, 1908.

142. O. E., "Der sachliche Ertrag," *Deutsche Zeitung,* March 24, 1908.

sided commercial-colonial point of view" on settlement colonialism. O. E. prefaced these criticisms, however, by reviewing Dernburg's positive achievements, which included an "undeniable" "new prosperity" in the colonies.[143] When O. E. penned the newspaper's report on Dernburg's departure in June 1910, he reconfirmed the *Deutsche Zeitung*'s generally positive outlook. "We stood by him so in his courageous cleansing work toward the Center Party's doings in the colonial administration, in his excellent colonial political propaganda, and in his laying of colonial economic foundations, that even he occasionally warned us, playfully, with a 'Ne nimis,'" O. E. wrote.[144] "The deeds and achievements of the departing State Secretary shine bright," he insisted, concluding that it was "exclusively" the "shady side of his temperament" that caused his departure.[145]

The *Deutsche Zeitung* was not alone among antisemitic newspapers supporting Dernburg's leadership. The *Staatsbürger-Zeitung* backed him as well, often enthusiastically. Run by the racial antisemite Wilhelm Bruhn and associated with Oswald Zimmermann's German Reform Party (renamed the German Social Reform Party from 1894 to 1903), the *Staatsbürger-Zeitung* was a strong advocate of colonial empire, much like the *Deutsche Zeitung*. Unlike the latter, however, it expressed discontent with Dernburg at first, arguing that his connections to "circles of big finance" made him a poor choice for the "pitiless battle against big capital" that was needed in the colonies.[146] But its attitude changed quickly, and the newspaper praised his early statements and proposed policies. In November, it referred approvingly to Dernburg's insistence upon an unpolitical approach to colonial matters. It also noted the financial sacrifices required of him to enter the colonial bureaucracy.[147] After his first Reichstag speeches, *Staatsbürger-Zeitung* lead writers applauded Dernburg's intention to finance railroad development through state funds (and not private capital), and they cheered his dissolution of the government's contracts with the Tippelskirch and Woermann companies.[148] One lead writer wrote in early

---

143. Ibid., "Das System Dernburg-Rechenberg," *Deutsche Zeitung*, March 2, 1909.

144. "Ne nimis" means "not too much."

145. O. E., "Staatssekretär Dernburg geht,"*Deutsche Zeitung*, June 8, 1910.

146. "Das Kolonial-Amt," *Staatsbürger-Zeitung*, September 5, 1906, morning edition.

147. Ulrich von Hassell, "Reichstag und Kolonien," *Staatsbürger-Zeitung*, November 12, 1906, evening edition; "Deutsches Reich. Der Gutsherr von Dallmin," *Staatsbürger-Zeitung*, November 15, 1906.

148. Monheim, "Kolonialkrisis—zur Gesundung," *Staatsbürger-Zeitung*, November 29, 1906, morning edition; ibid., "Innerpolitische Wochenrückschau," *Staatsbürger-Zeitung*, December 1, 1906, evening edition.

December that Dernburg awakened "trust throughout that he is the right man in the right position."[149]

While the *Deutsche Zeitung* supported Dernburg despite his so-called native policies, the *Staatsbürger-Zeitung* backed him in part because of them. Rejecting the utilitarian approach to the "native question" advocated by Lattmann and Werner in parliament, the *Staatsbürger-Zeitung* expressed a far more paternalistic outlook toward colonized people. This perspective was represented best among antisemites by Adolf Stöcker of the Christian Social Party. Stöcker employed paternalist rhetoric as a Reichstag deputy beginning in the 1880s, arguing for—among other things—an abolition of the colonial liquor trade because of its nefarious effects on local populations. The *Staatsbürger-Zeitung* echoed this paternalism in late 1906 and early 1907 when it printed a series of front-page articles condemning unnecessary colonial violence. One author argued for policies of "education" instead of "extermination" and insisted that Germans had a duty to bring indigenes "Christianity and legal certainty" and "economic improvement."[150] Another—possibly the same author—wrote critically of a tendency within "many colonial circles" to treat blacks as nothing more than "work animals."[151] A third rejected the idea of "white superhumanity" and argued for "a capable and, if necessary, strict, but above all just and humane government," one that "permits the natives to maintain their land and village order."[152] A fourth demanded an end to "the slavery-like handling of the coloreds."[153] Several of these authors called on Dernburg directly to improve the condition of the colonized.

Quite unlike the *Deutsche Zeitung*, then, the *Staatsbürger-Zeitung* approved of Dernburg's push in early 1908 for better treatment of native populations. It also applauded his intention to rely more on indigenous cultivation than white-owned plantations, something that set it apart again from the *Deutsche Zeitung*. In an anonymous front-page editorial printed in March, the newspaper argued that white plantation production in

149. R. M., "Die Waffen ruhn," *Staatsbürger-Zeitung*, December 5, 1906, morning edition.

150. M., "Deutschland in Afrika," *Staatsbürger-Zeitung*, November 28, 1906, morning edition.

151. Monheim, "Kolonialkrisis."

152. R. M., "Die Waffen ruhn," *Staatsbürger-Zeitung*, December 5, 1906, morning edition.

153. Ulrich von Hassell, "Die Bilanz der Kolonialpolitik für 1906," *Staatsbürger-Zeitung*, January 4, 1907, morning edition.

Africa was "of no consequence" while "independent Negro labor" produced goods valued at hundreds of millions of marks. It claimed that Dernburg had done a "service" in dispelling "the fairy tale of the 'lazy, workshy' Negro," and it repeated Dernburg's statement that "natives" were "the most important asset" of the German colonies. It also insisted on the necessity of raising "the Negro" in "sanitary and ethical regards" by limiting the importation of alcohol and by creating a colonial infrastructure.[154] On the same page, the author of one of the abovementioned editorials characterized the coming Reichstag debate over Dernburg's ideas as "a battle of *Weltanschauungen*" involving "the idea of humanity." "An agreement," he wrote, "between the mission on the one side and a General v. Liebert on the other" was "impossible."[155]

As with the *Deutsche Zeitung,* this support for Dernburg flew in the face of the *Staatsbürger-Zeitung*'s racial antisemitism, which the newspaper continued to express even while Dernburg was in office. Following the dissolution of the Reichstag in mid-December 1906, for example, the newspaper printed a long front-page article identifying the Jews as a race and discussing their power over politics and society. Without a trace of irony, it even lamented that "Jewish blood" was "probably also sufficiently represented in the ministries" in addition to the fields of business, medicine, and law.[156] Unlike the *Deutsche Zeitung,* the *Staatsbürger-Zeitung* also printed several antisemitic pieces aimed at Dernburg at this time. One appearing in December discusses the former director of the Prussian Mortgage Stock Bank, Eduard Sanden, who was accused of financial misconduct in or around 1900. The author suggested that Sanden was persecuted because his "was the only non-Jewified financial institution," and the author implicated Dernburg in the attacks upon him.[157] Another is a reprinted article from the Viennese *Deutsches Volksblatt* that complains of improper pressure by "Jewified progressives" on the German government to fill posts with "liberal men." The article mentions Dernburg and his

---

154. "Koloniale Landwirtschaft," *Staatsbürger-Zeitung,* March 17, 1908.

155. Monheim, "Kleine Pfeile," *Staatsbürger-Zeitung,* March 17, 1908.

156. "Vom 'staatserhaltenden' Judentum," *Staatsbürger-Zeitung,* December 15, 1906, morning edition.

157. "Eduard Sanden," *Staatsbürger-Zeitung,* December 11, 1906, morning edition. Dernburg, who had been a director of the German Trust Company, did, indeed, play a central role in reorganizing the Prussian Mortgage Stock Bank's finances (Schiefel, *Bernhard Dernburg,* 24).

"Jewish racial instincts" in this context.[158] Notably, the editors of the *Staatsbürger-Zeitung* did not partake in these attacks. For the *Deutsches Volksblatt* article, they simply remarked in a preface on the "justice" of its claim that Liberals wished to create a "backstairs government." What is more, they distanced themselves from the piece on Sanden with a footnote. "We do not want to restrain the recording of these words of a friend of the deceased," the editors wrote. "That which can be said with severity over Sanden has been said. So it is allowable that also a friendly word finds a place where there is a fresh grave."[159]

The *Staatsbürger-Zeitung* grew more critical of Dernburg with time. In January 1909, a contributor complained that the state secretary's "blood-rich fantasy-filled" speeches had fueled financial speculation in Southwest Africa by way of a misleading optimism.[160] The messy conclusion to Dernburg's career antagonized the *Staatsbürger-Zeitung* further, fueling a disenchantment that was reflected in its 1910 editorial on Dernburg's departure. The piece begins by admitting the newspaper's past support and listing the secretary's positive achievements; these included railroad development, an increase in exports, an enthusing of the masses, and improvements in the treatment of the colonized. It then criticizes Dernburg sharply, censuring his diamond policies and his rejection of Lattmann's proposal for a special tax on wealthy landowners in Southwest Africa. Reflecting, no doubt, the depth of the newspaper's disillusionment, the piece also comes close to attacking Dernburg from an antisemitic standpoint; after referring to the *Berliner Tageblatt* as the "'Jewish World Paper,'" its author noted that "the father of the Colonial Secretary, Friedrich Dernburg" edited its feuilletons. He also remarked that the state secretary was "thoroughly dazzled" by "progressive-Jewish" circles. Finally, he denied any regrets over Dernburg's retirement. "We are probably obliged to thank him," he wrote, "but we have no tears that we can shed over his departure."[161]

If the *Hammer* was irreconcilably hostile to Dernburg from the very beginning, and the *Deutsche Zeitung* and *Staatsbürger-Zeitung* were gener-

---

158. "Die Reichstagswahlen und die antisemitische Bewegung im Deutschen Reiche," *Staatsbürger-Zeitung*, December 18, 1906, morning edition. At the time, Dernburg was rumored to have connections with the left-liberal progressive Freisinnige Vereinigung party, a party of bankers and wealthy businessmen that had Jewish supporters (Schiefel, *Bernhard Dernburg*, 41).

159. "Eduard Sanden," *Staatsbürger-Zeitung*, December 11, 1906, morning edition.

160. Dr. Oestreicher, "Dernburg und die Börse," *Staatsbürger-Zeitung*, January 31, 1909.

161. Dr. O., "Staatsekretär Dernburgs Rücktritt," *Staatsbürger-Zeitung*, June 8, 1910.

ally favorable at the start, the procolonial *Deutsch-Soziale Blätter* had much greater difficulty deciding its position. Out of the four, the *Blätter* struggled the most visibly with the fact of Dernburg's Jewish ancestry, expressing an initial deep suspicion on anticapitalist and antisemitic grounds. Upon Dernburg's appointment, it complained of his connections to the world of high finance, noted his Jewish heritage, and insisted that "a good degree of mistrust is justified." The newspaper also claimed that it would wait for Dernburg's actions before supporting or opposing him, and that this would be determined by his attitude toward "the main evil of German colonial policy," "the large capitalist suction-pump land companies."[162] Unlike with the *Staatsbürger-Zeitung,* Dernburg's first appearance in the Reichstag did not resolve the *Blätter*'s suspicions; one editorialist complained that "a German ear finds annoying the many foreign words that he likes to conspicuously employ."[163] It was only after Dernburg attacked deputy Roeren of the Catholic Center Party on December 3 that the newspaper printed an extremely positive editorial on the new director, albeit by a member of the Pan-German League and not one of its own regular lead writers.[164] The *Deutsch-Soziale Blätter* maintained an essentially neutral outlook on Dernburg for approximately the next two years, avoiding excessive praise or criticism.

This changed in 1909. Dernburg's wish to improve the treatment of colonized people conflicted with the sensibilities of the *Blätter*'s leadership. Things came to a head when the state secretary publicly criticized the 1904 decimation of the Herero people under General von Trotha.[165] Although Dernburg insisted in March 1909 that he meant no disrespect to "the personal achievements of the General and the magnificent behavior of his troops," and that he only regretted the "economic and programmatic" ramifications of the destruction of "indispensable colored manpower," the *Blätter* condemned Dernburg's criticisms sharply.[166] A front-page editorial labels Dernburg's "native policy " as "radically wrong." Its author, H. Teut., printed von Trotha's written defense justifying his wartime actions, wherein the general argued for the necessary eventual disappearance of "natives" from the German colonies. H. Teut. concluded that this was the

162. Frisius, "Die neue Exzellenz," *Deutsch-Soziale Blätter,* September 8, 1906.

163. H. Teut., "Die beiden Bernharde," *Deutsch-Soziale Blätter,* December 1, 1906.

164. P. S., "Ein reinigendes Gewitter," *Deutsch-Soziale Blätter,* December 12, 1906.

165. Informationsreise Seiner Exzellenz des Staatssekretars Dernburg nach Südwestafrika im Jahren 1908, RKA 1463, BAB.

166. *Sten. Ber.* XII/I/217, March 2, 1909, 7269.

"bitter truth." He accused Dernburg of viewing colonial policy with the eyes of a "dividend scout."[167]

Early 1910 witnessed a further shift in the newspaper's attitude: it began emphasizing Dernburg's Jewish roots and expressing a hostility almost approximating that of Theodor Fritsch's *Hammer* magazine. Yet for a time, the paper showed a continued uncertainty as to whether Dernburg should be labeled as a Jew, unconditionally, and mistrusted as such. One lead writer admitted toward the end of January that "it is not easy to give a completely accurate judgement of Dernburg's work." He had a "bias toward large-scale capitalism," Frisius wrote, but had also "played the strong man toward some land companies," forcing them to renounce certain "advantages." The author argued that Dernburg stood closer in his outlook to the "Jewish liberal big bankers and men of finance" than to a "German-*völkisch*" perspective and that this reflected "the old opposition between Jewish nomadism and conservative settled-ness." But he then remarked on the surprising support Dernburg enjoyed across the political spectrum, including antisemites, and on the confusion this caused. "Precisely this last, that lies close to us, startles us," Frisius wrote of the antisemites' support, "and forces the question time and again: is our mistrust against His Excellency Dernburg justified? Does he truly stand before us as a laudable product of the mixing of Jew and German? Is he really one of the miraculously seldom exceptions?" Frisius gave no answer, although he noted that Dernburg enjoyed widespread support from Jewish organizations.[168]

This apparent uncertainty about Dernburg seemed to vanish, however, after the details of his proposed treaty with the German Colonial Corporation of Southwest Africa came to light. This occurred in late January. Soon after, the *Deutsch-Soziale Blätter* printed detailed information about the Jewish side of Dernburg's family for the very first time.[169] It also commented on Dernburg's "Jewish" traits in a short piece in May, insisting that a recent lack of composure by the state secretary in parliament demonstrated the inability of "baptism" to "expel" his "racial characteristics."[170] The newspaper then savaged Dernburg upon his retirement, arguing, among many other things, that he only saw the "numerical value" in

---

167. H. Teut., "Deutsche Kolonialpolitik," *Deutsch-Soziale Blätter*, February 6, 1909. Of indigenes, Trotha wrote, "We cannot do without them, especially in the beginning, but they must finally recede."

168. Frisius, "Deutsche Kolonialpolitik," *Deutsch-Soziale Blätter*, January 29, 1910.

169. "Dernburgs Diamanten," *Deutsch-Soziale Blätter*, February 2, 1910; "Dernburgs Vorfahren," *Deutsch-Soziale Blätter*, February 16, 1910.

170. "Rassen-Eigentümlichkeiten," *Deutsch-Soziale Blätter*, May 21, 1910.

men and had used false information to mislead the Reichstag. The author of this piece did give Dernburg some credit; he admitted that "his rise was German" and that his veins held "a few drops of German blood." But he argued that his departure displayed "the traits of the Jewish stock exchange," noting that colonial companies lost value when he left, while the stock of a company that Dernburg was rumored to soon direct rose in price.[171] The *Blätter* remarked upon Dernburg's "Jewish" traits in the following weeks when it recounted how the former state secretary elaborated on his bejeweled medals at a social gathering. "The inclination to diamonds and medals is indeed a so particular attribute of the Jewish race," the newspaper stated, "that one needs to wonder nothing more about the above-mentioned tendency."[172] Two years later, a contributor to the *Deutsch-Soziale Blätter* insisted that "the Jews had their minister" when Dernburg was state secretary.[173]

Participation in colonialism did not immunize Dernburg from antisemitism. As seen above, Dernburg's Jewish ancestry remained an indelible stain for some antisemites, and nothing he did could remove their suspicion that he was destined to betray German interests by virtue of his "Jewish" blood. But this appears to have been a minority position, as many antisemites forgave Dernburg's Jewish roots in light of what they perceived to be his service to colonialism and other national causes. Like Emin Pasha before him, Dernburg emerged as an example of what antisemitic ideologues like Theodor Fritsch believed was virtually impossible: the existence of a patriotic-minded Germanized "Jew" who overcame his Jewish ancestry to do what was right by the German people. In the eyes of his numerous supporters, both within and without the antisemitic movement, Dernburg was someone who championed the needs of the entire German *Volk* against inimical special interests, be they "internationalist" Catholics and "unpatriotic" Social Democrats at home or selfish settlers abroad. This image eventually faded, but it never disappeared completely, and, for a time, it was valid for a remarkably large segment of the German population.

The hundreds of congratulatory letters, postcards, and telegrams that flooded to Dernburg in 1906 and 1907 confirm the reality of this impression for ordinary Germans across the Reich. The missives show that Dernburg's

171. Frisius, "Der kleine Bernhard," *Deutsch-Soziale Blätter,* June 11, 1910.

172. "Ueber Dernburgs Abschied," *Deutsch-Soziale Blätter,* June 22, 1910. Upon his departure, Dernburg received a medal of the Roter-Adler-Orden from the Kaiser.

173. W. Städter, "Mit dem Musterkoffer," *Deutsch-Soziale Blätter,* June 15, 1912.

supporters included young and old, and also male and female, and that they came largely from those who opposed social democracy and political Catholicism. For these individuals, Dernburg's early actions in the Reichstag made him a model of "Germanness" and conjured up memories of both Luther and Bismarck. In the weeks and months after his attack on Center Party colonial critics, Dernburg's adherents thanked him for his "patriotic act," wrote poems about his "bravery," and even named their children after him. As one well-wisher wrote in a letter where he informed Dernburg that his newborn son now bore his name, "Bernhard" became synonymous for many with standing "strong as a bear . . . against everything un-German and all injustice."[174] "Thank God," declared another well-wisher, "that there still exist *German* men with the courage" to take on the Center Party.[175]

The press confirmed Dernburg's immense popularity at this time. One newspaper described the stir that Dernburg's presence caused at a public thoroughfare in mid-December 1906: people lifted their hats and took photographs, while ignoring the appearance of the state secretary of the Imperial Treasury.[176] Another newspaper noted that "the great colonial battle" in the Reichstag had moved "many" of its readers "to celebrate the momentous occasion in verse." It printed two poems as examples. One, titled "On Dernburg," classified the colonial director as a "valiant hero," and another, titled "Heil Dernburg," called him an "undaunted knight" to whom a grateful Germany gave its thanks.[177] The *Allgemeine Zeitung* reported in February 1907 that children in a town near Dresden had erected a monument to Dernburg out of snow.[178] Private companies tried to capitalize on his fame. In 1906 and 1907, a cigar, a postcard, and even a player piano company wrote to Dernburg, requesting the right to use his name or likeness on their products.[179]

---

174. Hans Stoltenhoff to Bernhard Dernburg, February 2, 1907, BDP, BAK. Dernburg's Jewish roots were well known by this time, as many newspapers had reported on them. See "Bernhard Dernburg," *Im deutschen Reich: Zeitschrift des Centralvereins deutscher Staatsbürger jüdischen Glaubens* 12 (1906): 594–96.

175. Lordes to Bernhard Dernburg, December 4, 1906, no. 12, BDP, BAK.

176. Clipping from the *Eisenacher Zeitung*, no. 44, BDP, BAK.

177. *Leipziger Neueste Nachrichten*, December 7, 1906.

178. Clipping from the *Allgemeine Zeitung*, February 13, 1907, no. 21, BDP, BAK. This is not the *Allgemeine Zeitung des Judentums*, as there is no February 13 issue for this newspaper for 1907.

179. K. Heilbrunn to Bernhard Dernburg, January 15, 1907, no. 15, BDP, BAK; Glass and Tuscher to Bernhard Dernburg, December 19, 1906, no. 14, BDP, BAK; L. Wolff to Bernhard Dernburg, December 8, 1906, no. 14, BDP, BAK.

Few well-wishers mentioned Dernburg's Jewish ancestry in their messages to him, but it was not forgotten. The anti-Catholic newspaper the *Sachsenschau* lauded Dernburg in December 1906 for his attack on "Rome" while declaring in the same article, "We have not opposed Dernburg, despite his Jewish heritage."[180] In April 1907, Dernburg received a lengthy printed pamphlet, written by Wilhelm Mannes, titled "From Lassalle to Dernburg. A Colonial-Social Contemplation." The author celebrated Dernburg as "a new Moses" who was leading "the German people toward Africa." He insisted that Dernburg's example proved "that Jewry is capable of producing dutiful nationally minded men," and that "we" should not dispense with the cooperation of "our nationally-minded Jewish fellow-citizens."[181]

Ironically, antisemites contributed to this impression. As seen above, men like Lattmann, Werner, and Friedrich Lange backed Dernburg strongly and in a public fashion, downplaying his Jewish heritage while emphasizing his accomplishments. They did so motivated by the perception that Dernburg acted in accordance with their own ideas about the proper comportment of a German colonialist and statesman—attacking the political Left and Center, strengthening popular enthusiasm for the colonies, limiting the power of the colonial concession companies, and maintaining the colonial racial hierarchy. Some of this support was precarious, to be sure, because it rested upon Dernburg's policy positions and perceived ideological orientation. Lattmann's resorting to antisemitic language in late 1910 demonstrated the fragility of antisemitic enthusiasm and the rapidity with which it could disintegrate under changed circumstances. Nevertheless, many dedicated antisemites seemed genuinely convinced of Dernburg's "German spirit," at least for a time. Their support undoubtedly contributed to Dernburg's elevation to the position of a model patriot in the eyes of the procolonial public. Only antisemites less committed to the colonial project—like Theodor Fritsch—condemned Dernburg throughout and seemed to understand the danger that his popularity posed to antisemitic ideology.

What did Dernburg think of all this? Did he have a sense of his own relevance to the ongoing debate on the Jewish Question in Germany at the time? And was he affected by the antisemitism directed at him, like Paul Kayser? Unfortunately, these questions cannot be answered, because most

---

180. "Dernburgs Griff ins Kuttennest," *Sachsenschau,* December 9, 1906.
181. Von Lassalle bis Dernburg: Eine kolonial-soziale Betrachtung by Wilhelm Mannes, April 1907, no. 24, BDP, BAK.

of Dernburg's private papers were destroyed during the Second World War.[182] Practically all that remains are his public speeches and official correspondence, along with a few private letters, plus an unfinished memoir composed in the 1930s—before his death in 1937—that says little about his time in the Colonial Office. This limited material only shows that he was aware of antisemitism and that he suffered it as a child.

In December 1907, for example, Dernburg received a request from his old Gymnasium that he proofread an address, presumably to check the accuracy of its information concerning its famous alumnus. In his reply, Dernburg remarked that he could recall "few happy moments" from his days at the school, and he gave the following rationale: "Especially during those times, the pupils and also, unfortunately, many teachers at the Gymnasium were contaminated, aggressively, with antisemitism, and I was in constant battle against an outlook directed against my lineage and even more against my humanistic philosophy of life."[183] Dernburg wrote of his childhood experiences with antisemitism in his memoir as well, wherein he expressed a sense of kinship with other victims of antisemitic prejudice.[184]

At the very least, then, we know that Dernburg was not unprepared for the antisemitism he faced as a public figure, since he knew from past experience that he was seen as "Jewish" by others. But we cannot know what he thought of the irony of his particular situation, where some of his strongest supporters in parliament came from the antisemitic political parties, and antisemitic jabs came from the antisemites' traditional political opponents. Also unknowable is his understanding of the potentially positive ramifications for Jews and Germans of Jewish descent of his presence on the national stage as the director of such a patriotic project.

One can also only conjecture how his experience with antisemitism affected his public posturing and colonial policies. Like Paul Kayser, Ernst Vohsen, and others, Dernburg eventually articulated a more liberal perspective on race than was popular with many colonialists at the time. To be sure, he believed in meaningful racial differences and white superiority, something that helped reconcile racial antisemites. But he often credited black Africans with greater capabilities and accorded them more rights.

---

182. Schiefel, *Bernhard Dernburg*, 8.
183. Bernhard Dernburg to Prof. Dr. Imelmann, December 20, 1907, no. 53, BDP, BAK.
184. Lebenserinnerungen Bernhard Dernburgs 1865–ca. 1906, no. 11, BDP, BAK.

Genuine moral considerations as well as practical ones motivated his concerns over the ramifications of the extreme racism gaining ground among colonialists and their supporters both at home and in the colonies. The possibility cannot be discounted that Dernburg's own experiences with racial hatred—in addition to his positive encounters with the colonized—influenced his thinking on racial matters.[185]

---

185. Dernburg continued to play a role in public life after he left the Colonial Office. In 1913, he became a member of the Prussian House of Lords. After the First World War, he served as the German minister of finance from April through June 1919. Dernburg then won a seat in the Reichstag as a member of the new left-wing liberal German Democratic Party, and he sat in parliament until 1930. Following his retirement from politics, Dernburg lived in Germany as a private citizen until his death in 1937. The National Socialist regime left him alone, aside from occasional attacks in *Der Stürmer* (Schiefel, *Bernhard Dernburg,* 143–80).

Conclusion

Modern antisemitism has been described, correctly, as a reaction to the loss of distinction between "Jewishness" and "Germanness" that resulted from the Jewish acculturation to German ways that began in the eighteenth century.[1] Antisemites attempted to substitute certainty for confusion about what separated "Jews" from "Germans" by asserting a binary (though not equal) opposition between the two. In the early and mid-nineteenth century, antisemites focused on character, contrasting "Jewish" with "German" notions of morality, among many other things. By the century's end, racial antisemites claimed that the oppositions were biologically determined, making Jewish characteristics an unchanging fact of nature. All of this roughly coincided with an expansion in how most Europeans imagined the communal self: as something more national than local by definition. As Helmut Walser Smith has convincingly argued, this reimagining of the community gave rise to a new antisemitic stereotype that had a particular potential for inciting violence: the idea that Jews were traitors to the nation.[2]

Colonialism during the *Kaiserreich* era worked against antisemitism by confusing the divide, breaking down the alleged divisions between "Jew" and "German." The newness of colonial empire meant the absence of an entrenched elite in the colonial bureaucracy, something that, if in existence, would have prevented full participation by individuals identified as Jewish by their peers. As it stood, men like Paul Kayser and Bernhard Dernburg were able to rise to the highest levels of administrative power in what became the most patriotic of nationalist projects: overseas colonialism. Other Germans of Jewish descent also distinguished themselves

---

1. Uffa Jensen, "Into the Spiral of Problematic Perceptions: Modern Anti-Semitism and *gebildetes Bürgertum* in Nineteenth-Century Germany," *German History* 25 (2007): 348–71.

2. Helmut Walser Smith, *The Continuities of German History: Nation, Religion, and Race across the Long Nineteenth Century* (Cambridge: Cambridge University Press, 2008).

through their service to the colonial cause. Bernhard Dernburg and Emin Pasha even became popular public heroes, something hitherto unheard of for men whose Jewish backgrounds brought the barbs of racial antisemitism.

An admiring procolonial public attributed Dernburg and Emin with exactly what the antisemites claimed that Jews could not possess, which supposedly distinguished them from right-thinking German Gentiles: true German patriotism. At the height of their popularity, Dernburg and Emin were perceived by many within the procolonial public as fighting champions of colonialism, as loyal defenders of German interests abroad, as honest patriots, and these sentiments even spread to large sections of the antisemitic movement. From this, it is clear that colonialism cannot only be seen as having encouraged more exclusive notions of Germanness in ways that furthered antisemitic aims. Rather, through the public examples of German-Jewish actors working on behalf of overseas empire, colonialism helped weaken the imagined racial divide within the German body politic that mattered most to antisemites, showing that certain "Jews" could act like "Germans" and that the two could work together for Germany's benefit. It did so even as it hardened racial attitudes toward colonized peoples, especially black Africans.

The positive public reception of Dernburg and Emin Pasha that came despite knowledge of their Jewish ancestry would seem to support the contention of some scholars that the success of antisemitism in imperial Germany has been overstated. Samuel Moyn argued in 1996 that historians of German-Jewish history need to stop "configuring as dusk everything prior to the night that eventually fell,"[3] while Till van Rahden contends that the historiography of German antisemitism neglects "dissenting voices and ambivalent positions."[4] The fact that the thousands of postcards, telegrams, and letters sent to Dernburg at the height of his popularity contained virtually nothing antisemitic and few references to his Jewish heritage testifies to the limits of Wilhelmian antisemitism. So too do the dissent and confusion that Dernburg and Emin Pasha caused within antisemitic ranks, where some defended them not just from the critics of colonial empire but also from fellow antisemites. All this provides perhaps

---

3. Samuel Moyn, "German Jewry and the Question of Identity: Historiography and Theory," *Leo Baeck Institute Yearbook* 41 (1996): 293.

4. Till van Rahden, *Jews and Other Germans: Civil Society, Religious Diversity, and Urban Politics in Breslau, 1860–1925,* trans. Marcus Brainard (Madison: University of Wisconsin Press, 2008), 15.

the strongest evidence yet that the antisemitic milieu of imperial Germany was not that of the Weimar era. It seems unlikely that a public that could enthusiastically embrace men like Dernburg and Emin Pasha—that, outside of antisemitic circles, made relatively little of their Jewish backgrounds—could have produced National Socialism as a genuine people's movement without an intervening national trauma, such as the First World War, to first radicalize public opinion on the so-called Jewish Question.[5] Uncovering this moves us toward what Gideon Reuveni has demanded of histories of German Jewry: "research beyond [the] rather sterile binary divisions that tend to oscillate between approaches stressing inclusion and those which highlight exclusion."[6]

The tremendous fury of a minority of racial antisemites who denounced Kayser, Dernburg, and Emin Pasha was undoubtedly due to a frustrated realization of just how far most Germans were—dedicated antisemites included—from an uncompromising racial antisemitism. Their insistence upon the "Jewishness" of German-Jewish colonial actors paralleled the repeated claims of Paul Kayser's subordinates in Cameroon that blacks were unsuited for a European education because their essence would never change. But it is important to note that while colonialism furnished public examples that "Jews" could be loyal "Germans"—which was itself a crucial defeat for racial antisemites, as it countered the dangerous accusation of an unavoidable predetermined national disloyalty—there is little evidence that Jewish participation in the colonial project changed German minds about what "Jewishness" meant. It did not force a general reevaluation of the premise that "Jewishness" was something negative. The closest thing to an exception found in non-Jewish sources is the review of Stanley's memoir in the antisemitic *Tägliche Rundschau,* where the author saw something Jewish in what he lauded as Emin Pasha's "administrative talents" and "diplomatic inclination."[7] Otherwise, only Jewish authors claimed that "Jewish" colonial actors revealed something positive about "Jewishness" itself. The magazine *Ost und West* asserted in 1903 that Emin

---

5. In *Holocaust: A History,* Deborah Dwórk and Robert Jan van Pelt quote the German-Jewish novelist Georg Hermann: "Antisemitism was present," he wrote in 1933 of the prewar era, "irritating as a gnat in a summer evening; but one frightened it away and found it quite pleasant out there, mild and warm. After 1914 this changed sharply" (quoted in *Holocaust: A History* [New York: W. W. Norton, 2002], 34).

6. Gideon Reuveni, "'Productivist' and 'Consumerist' Narratives of Jews in German History," in *German History from the Margins,* ed. Neil Gregor, Nils Roemer, and Mark Roseman (Bloomington: Indiana University Press, 2006), 179.

7. Dr. H. Pastenaci, "Stanley und Emin," *Tägliche Rundschau,* July 6, 1890.

Pasha had demonstrated his "Jewish heart" through his "deferential love" for his parents.[8] In 1937, the Jewish War Veterans Association claimed that Emin exemplified the "heroic spirit" that had infused Jewish history for three millennia.[9]

More indicative of the way in which colonialism might have affected public attitudes is Wilhelm Mannes's pamphlet, sent to Dernburg in 1907. According to Mannes, Dernburg "destroyed the error that Jewry is not capable of also bringing forward conscientious, nationally-minded men." Significantly, however, Mannes also wrote that "great distrust" had resulted in Germany by "the indifference of Jewry in national things."[10] Of additional interest is a biography of Carl Peters by Carl Baecker, published in 1934. Baecker insisted that "the danger-filled career" that Emin Pasha chose over a life of comfort spoke to the fact that "other currents must have dominated in his blood" besides the Jewish one.[11] It seems that the examples of Dernburg and Emin did not alter conventional views of "Jewishness," either during the colonial era or after. "Jewishness" retained its generally negative connotations, even if individual "Jews" were sometimes singled out as having overcome their Jewish heritage.

Colonialism challenged the idea that individual "Jews" could not be good German patriots, and it exposed the limits of antisemitism among the general public. It also divided the antisemitic movement between a procolonial majority and a vocal minority of colonial skeptics. But the relationship between colonialism and antisemitism was much more complex than this. Overseas empire helped the antisemitic movement in significant ways even as it hindered it. It gave antisemites new political life and relevancy after public enthusiasm for political antisemitism—which peaked in the early 1890s—had declined. In addition, Reichstag debates on colonial matters gave racial antisemites an alternative platform on which to propagate their racialist view of the world, one that the very existence of overseas colonial states seemed to legitimate. Even indirect participation in the creation of the colonies allowed antisemites to help shape and propel public discourses

---

8. Dr. Adolf Kohut, "Berühmte jüdische Weltreisende," *Ost und West: Illustrierte Monatsschrift für modernes Judentum* 12 (1903).

9. Reichsbund Jüdischer Frontsoldaten, *Heroische Gestalten Jüdischen Stammes* (Berlin: Erwin Löwe, 1937), vii.

10. Von Lassalle bis Dernburg: Eine kolonial-soziale Betrachtung by Wilhelm Mannes, April 1907, no. 24, BDP, BAK.

11. Paul Baecker, *Carl Peters: Der Wiking der deutschen Kolonialpolitik* (Berlin: De Vo Verlag, 1934), 89.

on the meaning of racial difference and the rectitude of racial domination long after political antisemitism was no longer viable.

Most important of all, colonialism propagated to the wider public a vocabulary of racial domination and notions of the morality of racial violence that mirrored the thinking on Jews of radical antisemites. Discourses on black Africans eventually came to approximate the rhetoric of the most extreme armchair advocates of antisemitic violence, especially with the outbreak of the Herero uprising. The radical perspective on black Africans depicted them as a kind of antirace, completely alien and pernicious and possessed of a burning hatred of whites. It was popular with extremists like Carl Peters all along, but beginning in 1904, it spread within colonial circles, becoming, to a certain extent, normalized. Colonialism, therefore, propagated a type of thinking and imagery that paralleled the most radical racial antisemitism, and some antisemites encouraged this through their engagement in colonial empire. Colonialism complemented the antisemitic movement at the same time that it partly undermined it.

The complex relationship between colonialism and antisemitism was also a reciprocal one. There was significant engagement in colonialism by dedicated antisemites of all stripes. From revolutionary ideologues like Friedrich Lange to the rank-and-file members of the important antisemitic political parties, a majority within the antisemitic movement acquired a colonial consciousness during the *Kaiserreich*. Colonialism attracted most as patriots, but also many as racists who saw in the overseas colonies the realization of their dreams of a legally enshrined racial hierarchy. Some movement members spoke among themselves of similarities between Jews and black Africans, even speculating on the applicability to the Jewish Question of colonial lessons of racial domination. But the relationship was not one-sided. The active participation in colonialism of individuals like Carl Peters, Friedrich Lange, Frieda von Bülow, and others, and the political investment in colonialism by the major antisemitic political parties, meant an important degree of reciprocity. Antisemites affected the course and character of Germany's colonizing project at certain moments in time, and antisemites—as well as antisemitic prejudices—helped shape discourses about the colonized. This occurred even as overseas colonialism influenced antisemitic thinking on the so-called Jewish problem.

The effects that colonialism had on what was "possible to think" in terms of race and racial domination in imperial Germany have been downplayed in historiography that denies an important link between colonialism and National Socialism.[12] Recently, the question of a link has turned in part on whether the same concerns that motivated National Socialist policy in Eastern Europe also drove important colonial developments during the *Kaiserreich*.[13] Isabel V. Hull argues that the destruction of the Herero in 1904 was not driven by racial ideology like Nazi massacres later on, but by a German military culture that tended toward extremes and predated the acquisition of the colonies.[14] Birthe Kundrus insists that fears of racial pollution did not motivate the condemnation of "miscegenation" in colonial contexts during the *Kaiserreich,* as they did during the Nazi period. Rather, colonialists feared that mixed marriages would lessen German prestige and threaten German political domination over indigenous populations that were biologically defined.[15] Likewise, Dieter Gosewinkel denies the centrality of biological racism to colonial violence.[16] The evidence presented in this study, however, shows that colonialism belongs to the important prehistory of National Socialism precisely because it encouraged, propagated, and helped introduce ideas about race that came into play later on. This remains true even if these ideas were initially expressed on the fringes of the colonial movement and only gained popularity in the final decade of overseas empire.

Central to the National Socialist worldview, for example, was the notion that "not every being with a human face is human."[17] This was an extremist position during the Wilhelminian era, but it existed, professed by those for whom the colonial experience either demonstrated or confirmed

---

12. In *Continuities,* H. Smith gives great weight to what he sees as a transformation in what was "possible to think, support, and enact" in modern Germany due to the combination of "nationalism, anti-Semitism," and "violent ideologies" that stemmed in part from colonialism (H. Smith, *Continuities,* 233).

13. Matthew P. Fitzpatrick, "The Pre-History of the Holocaust? The *Sonderweg* and *Historikerstreit* Debates and the Abject Colonial Past," *Central European History* 41 (2008): 477–503.

14. Isabel V. Hull, *Absolute Destruction: Military Culture and the Practices of War in Imperial Germany* (Ithaca: Cornell University Press), 2005.

15. Birthe Kundrus, *Moderne Imperialisten. Das Kaiserreich im Spiegel seiner Kolonien* (Vienna: Böhlau Verlag Wien, 2003).

16. Dieter Gosewinkel, "Rückwirkungen des kolonialen Rasserechts? Deutsche Staatsangehörigkeit zwischen Rassestaat und Rechtsstaat," in *Das Kaiserreich transnational. Deutschland in der Welt 1871–1914,* ed. Sebastian Conrad and Jürgen Osterhammel (Göttingen: Vandenhoeck und Ruprecht, 2004), 236–56.

17. Carl Schmitt, "Das gute Recht der deutschen Revolution," *Westdeutscher Beobachter,* May 12, 1933. Quoted in Claudia Koonz, *The Nazi Conscience* (Cambridge: Belknap Press of Harvard University Press, 2003), 2.

the nonhumanity of black Africans.[18] Fear of an antirace that was identified as a legitimate target for both preemptive and avenging German violence—due to an anti-German aggression that was biologically determined—was central to the National Socialist worldview as well. As is commonly understood, this is what made the Jews so unique in the imaginations of radical antisemites like the Nazis.[19] It is now clear that the colonialism of the *Kaiserreich* generated similar attitudes toward black Africans. Like the future perpetrators of the Holocaust, Carl Peters, Siegfried Passarge, Woldemar Schutze, and others imagined blacks as a type of antirace—with many "Jewish" qualities—and they projected their own brutal intentions upon them. What is more, individuals within the colonial movement who were known for their antisemitism often took the lead in this type of violent thinking, a fact that some contemporaries seemed attuned to.

In addition, it has long been noted that the concept of *Lebensraum* (living space) so important to the Nazis originated from the colonial experiences of the *Kaiserreich.*[20] Recent work by Benjamin Madley has expanded the list to include ideas like *Vernichtungskrieg,* a war of total destruction.[21] To this, we can now add the notion of an *Endkampf*—an uncompromising final battle—among the races. The *Endkampf* concept typified the thinking of the Nazi leadership over the eastern theaters of

---

18. Such sentiments were heard in public forums like the Reichstag during the Herero War. They were heard again at the time of the debate on colonial miscegenation in 1912, as when the *Deutsch-Soziale Blatter* bemoaned the "miserable idea of equality for all 'wingless bipeds'" (B. W., "Rassenbewußtsein," *Deutsch-Soziale Blätter,* May 25, 1912).

19. David Furber and Wendy Lower note that Nazi fears of Jews were predicated on their images of Jews as successful colonizers and of Germans as the victims of Jewish subjugation and penetration. (David Furber and Wendy Lower, "Colonialism and Genocide in Nazi-Occupied Poland and Ukraine," in *Empire, Colony, Genocide: Conquest, Occupation, and Subaltern Resistance in World History,* ed. A. Dirk Moses [New York: Berghahn Books, 2008], 372–400). This did not find a counterpart in the extreme representations of black Africans that emerged during the *Kaiserreich.* However, the idea that blacks were an aggressive force, brutally antagonistic to whites, that would one day unite in opposition, and the idea that this would lead to an *Endkampf,* did, however parallel the thinking about Jews by Nazis and other extreme racial antisemites.

20. Woodruff D. Smith, *The Ideological Origins of Nazi Imperialism* (New York: Oxford University Press, 1986).

21. Benjamin Madley, "From Africa to Auschwitz: How German South West Africa Incubated Ideas and Methods Adopted and Developed by the Nazis in Eastern Europe," *European History Quarterly* 35 (2005): 429–64.

war in the final years of their regime.[22] As seen here, it, too, had its earliest articulation in colonial circles, again, as part of the process of the radicalization of thinking about blacks. Extremists used the term to describe a coming apocalyptic war between blacks and whites in Africa, and it reached mainstream colonial circles through media like the staid *Zeitschrift für Kolonialpolitik, Kolonialrecht und Kolonialwirtschaft*. Combined with the radical racism of those who denied the existence of a civilizing mission, this reference to an Armageddon-type conflict amounted to an ideological turning point of significant moral dimensions. It expelled Africans from the moral universe of its purveyors, removing moral obligations from the relationship between the colonizer and the colonized. In another setting and under different circumstances—in a Germany fearful of communist revolution and traumatized by war and the loss of empire— such colonial ideas, redirected toward Jews, would make a Holocaust mentality possible.

Some of the same historians who minimize the significance of the colonial period in explaining what occurred under National Socialism further their argument by insisting that the Nazis gave different meanings to the ideas they inherited from the Wilhelminian era.[23] To this, it can be answered that it would be surprising, indeed, if changing times and circumstances did not generate new interpretations of, or give added or altered meanings to, older ideologies. This is not enough of a reason to limit the Third Reich's prehistory to the period of 1918 to 1933. To do so would imply that only the immediate past is useful in explaining later events: that a past one or two generations removed has little relevance.

Future research should examine whether the German experience in eastern Prussia had a similar reciprocal relationship with antisemitism as did the colonial experience abroad. There is a growing tendency to view Wilhelminian Germany as both a continental and overseas empire and to perceive the situation in Polish-majority German territories as a type of colonialism, with Poles treated much like colonized subjects.[24] The literary

---

22. Michael Geyer, "*Endkampf* 1918 and 1945: German Nationalism, Annihilation, and Self-Destruction," in *No Man's Land of Violence: Extreme Wars in the 20th Century*, ed. Alf Lüdtke and Bernd Weisbrod (Göttingen: Wallstein Verlag, 2006), 35–68.

23. Birthe Kundrus, "Continuities, Parallels, Receptions. Reflections on the 'Colonization' of National Socialism," *Journal of Namibian Studies* 4 (2008): 25–46.

24. Dieter Gosewinkel, *Einbürgern und Ausschließen: Die Nationalisierung der Staatsangehörigkeit vom deutschen Bund bis zur Bundesrepublik Deutschland* (Göttingen: Vanden-

genre of the *Ostmarkenroman* (novels of the eastern marches) that originated in the 1890s not only racializes Poles but warns German "settlers"
against the dangers of "going native," which speaks of a colonial mentality.[25] But it would be surprising if the "colonization" of eastern Prussia
captured the antisemitic imagination to the same extent as overseas colonialism. One reason why the latter so interested racial antisemites like
Friedrich Lange is that it appeared to confirm the reality and importance
of racial divides: in Africa, the fact of race seemed obvious, but it was less
so in Europe. The extension of citizenship rights to German Poles also
meant that the types of experimentations in racial rule that took place
overseas were simply not possible in Polish Prussia. For racial antisemites,
it was colonial Africa that showed most clearly what the future could look
like.

On a final note, the story of colonialism, antisemitism, and Germans of
Jewish descent raises the question: Should special condemnation be re-
served for Germans of Jewish descent who participated in the racist project of overseas empire? Their involvement gains significance with our understanding of how colonialism became harnessed to the antisemitic cause.
It gains significance as well with the revelation that men like Kayser and
Dernburg sided with antisemites against colonialism's critics, some of
whom, like the Social Democrats, numbered among the most vocal opponents of political antisemitism. In this light, the participation of Germans
of Jewish descent in colonialism is worrisome. It speaks, at best, of a depressing shortsightedness, and at worst, of troubling moral compromises.

In considering this matter, it should remembered that the most important Germans of Jewish descent examined here were forces of moderation in the colonial project. Dernburg publicly rejected the application of
Social Darwinist principles to the colonies and the waging of total war on
colonized people. He stood out as an important alternative voice to colo-

---

hoeck und Ruprecht, 2001); Philipp Ther, "Imperial instead of National History: Positioning
Modern German History on the Map of European Empires," in *Imperial Rule,* ed. Alexei
Miller and Alfred J. Rieber (Budapest: Central European University Press, 2004), 47–68; Se-
bastian Conrad, *Globalisierung und Nation im Deutschen Kaiserreich* (Munich: Beck, 2006);
Edward Ross Dickinson, "The German Empire: An Empire?", *History Workshop Journal* 66
(2008): 129–62.

25. Kristin Kopp, "Constructing Racial Difference in Colonial Poland," in *Germany's
Colonial Pasts,* ed. Eric Ames, Marcia Klotz, and Lora Wildenthal (Lincoln: University of
Nebraska Press, 2005), 76–96.

nial extremists at a time of increasing radicalization, notwithstanding his own racial prejudices and oversight of racial violence. For his part, Kayser worked quietly to educate young Africans in Germany. To do so he had to reject the hard-nosed racism of his subordinates in Africa who claimed that the racial inferiority of blacks rendered a European education ineffectual. Although their efforts did not have the desired results, Kayser and Dernburg—and others like Ernst Vohsen and Moritz J. Bonn—also acted at specific times to limit colonial violence. Even Emin Pasha helped advance a more moderate colonizing vision, albeit inadvertently: his reputation as a "gentle" colonizer gave ammunition to those who argued for a more peaceful type of colonialism. Although Germans of Jewish descent cooperated with antisemites who often advanced the extremist agenda on matters of race and violence, they can be seen, on the whole, as a moderating presence in German colonialism, notwithstanding men like Otto Arendt and Julius Scharlach.

But the problematic nature of the participation of Germans of Jewish descent remains, despite these qualifications. Like everyone who had a hand in the building and maintenance of the overseas colonies, Dernburg, Kayser, and the other figures examined here bolstered a colonial project that had dangerous potential domestic ramifications, despite their attempts to temper the harsh consequences of the colonial racial hierarchy. As seen here, overseas colonialism gave rise to a way of thinking conducive to racial antisemitism and spread it beyond the confines of the antisemitic movement. The colonial project confirmed the significance of race for racial antisemites and, certainly, for members of the wider public. It showed antisemitic observers what was possible in terms of racial domination, moving some to identify Jews with the colonized and advocate a similar subjugation. For individual antisemitic actors, it opened up possibilities for the acting-out of violent fantasies of racial rule unavailable in Europe.

Some procolonial antisemites understood all this. Men like Friedrich Lange and Otto Böckler saw colonialism as an edifying experience, both for themselves and the nation. The proximity and occasional mixing in antisemitic rhetoric of discussions of Jews and the colonies shows that whenever colonial topics arose, the Jewish Question was never far from an antisemite's mind. This held true for the antisemitic critics of colonialism as well as its supporters: the former's fears of racial contamination through contact with colonial blacks and Asians was an extension of their fears of Jewish-Gentile intermixing. Despite the real problems that the involvement of Germans of Jewish descent in colonialism caused for the antisemitic movement, the inevitable conclusion is that colonialism had the capacity to strengthen antisemitism in the long run. Germans of Jewish descent who were colonial actors helped generate forces that would contribute to Europe's nightmarish future, even if colonialism did not point to any one path with certainty or predestine what was to come.

Bibliography

ARCHIVED SOURCES

See notes for the location numbers of individual files used from each archived collection.

Bundesarchiv Berlin (BAB)
    Bestand Alldeutscher Verband (ADV)
    Bestand Deutsche Kolonialgesellschaft (DKG)
    Bestand Reichskolonialamt (RKA)
    Carl Peters Papers
    Emin Pascha Papers
    Max Liebermann von Sonnenberg Papers
Bundesarchiv Koblenz (BAK)
    Bernhard Dernburg Papers (BDP)
    Chlodwig Fürst zu Hohenlohe-Schillingsfürst Papers, Kleine Erwerbungen
    Paul Kayser Papers
    Philipp Fürst zu Eulenburg und Hertefeld Papers
    Walter Frank Papers (WFP)

NEWSPAPERS AND MAGAZINES

Alldeutsch Blätter
Allgemeine Zeitung des Judenthums
Antisemitisches Volksblatt
Berliner Tageblatt
Deutsche Kolonialzeitung
Deutsche Tageszeitung
Deutsche Wacht
Deutsche Welt: Wochenschrift der Deutschen Zeitung
Deutsche Zeitung: Unabhängiges Tageblatt für nationale Politik
Deutscher Reichsanzeiger
Deutsch-Südwestafrikanische Zeitung
Deutsches Wochenblatt

Deutsch-Ostafrikanische Zeitung
Deutsch-Soziale Blätter
Familienblatt: Tägliche Unterhaltungsbeilage zur "Berliner Morgen-Zeitung"
Frankfürter Zeitung
Die Gartenlaube: Illustriertes Familienblatt
Hammer: Blätter für deutschen Sinn
Im deutschen Reich: Zeitschrift des Centralvereins deutscher Staatsbürger jüdischen Glaubens
Kladderadatsch
Das Kleine Journal: Zeitung für alle Gesellschaftsklassen
Kölnische Zeitung
Kolonial-Politische Correspondenz
Koloniale Rundschau: Monatsschrift für die Interessen unserer Schutzgebiete und ihrer Bewohner
Koloniales Jahrbuch
Kolonie und Heimat
Magdeburgische Zeitung
Militärwochenblatt
Mittheilungen aus dem Verein zur Abwehr des Antisemitismus
Der Moderne Völkergeist: Organ des Socialitären Bundes
National-Zeitung
Neue Preußische Zeitung (Kreuzzeitung)
Ost und West: Illustrierte Monatsschrift für modernes Judentum
Der Reichsbote
Reichsgeldmonopol.
St. James's Gazette
Staatsbürger-Zeitung
Tägliche Rundschau
Times (London)
Vorwärts: Berliner Volksblatt
Vossische Zeitung
Windhuker Nachrichten: Unabhängige Zeitung für Deutsch-Südwestafrika
Der Zeitgeist: Beiblatt zum "Berliner Tageblatt"
Zeitschrift für Kolonialpolitik, Kolonialrecht und Kolonialwirtschaft (Koloniale Monatsblätter)
Die Zukunft

GOVERNMENT DOCUMENTS

Department I of the Military Section of the General Staff, *Der Hottentottenkrieg: Ausbruch des Aufstandes; die Kämpfe am Auob und in den Karrasbergen*, book 4 of *Die Kämpfe der deutschen Truppen in Südwestafrika. Auf Grund amtlichen Materialsbearbeitet von Kriegsgeschichtlichen Abteilung I des Großen Generalstabes.* Berlin: Ernst Siegfried Mittler und Sohn, 1907.
Stenographische Berichte über die Verhandlungen des Reichstags. Berlin, 1871–1918.

PUBLISHED PRIMARY SOURCES

Baecker, Paul. *Carl Peters: Der Wiking der deutschen Kolonialpolitik.* Berlin: De Vo Verlag, 1934.

Bebel, August. *Sozialdemokratie und Antisemitismus: Rede auf dem sozialdemokratischen Parteitage in Berlin.* Berlin: Buchhandlung Vorwärts, 1906.

Bericht über die Sitzung des Vorstandes der Deutschen Kolonialgesellschaft am 4. Oktober 1905 im Reichstagsgebäude zu Berlin. Berlin: Deutsche Kolonialgesellschaft, 1905.

Blanck, E., and S. Passarge. *Die Chemische Verwitterung in der Ägyptischen Wüste.* Hamburg: Kommissionsverlag L. Friederichsen, 1925.

Bley, Fritz. *Am Grabe des deutschen Volkes: Zur Vorgeschichte der Revolution.* Berlin: August Scherl G.m.b.h., 1919.

Bley, Fritz. *Die Buren im Dienste der Menschheit.* Vienna: F. Schalk, 1900.

Bley, Fritz. *Deutsche Pionierarbeit in Ostafrika.* Berlin: Paul Parey, 1891.

Bley, Fritz. *Südafrika niederdeutsch!* Munich: J. F. Lehmann, 1898.

Bley, Fritz. *Wie kam es doch?* Leipzig: Erich Matthes, 1918.

Bonn, Moritz J. *Wandering Scholar.* London: Cohen & West LTD, 1949.

Bourne, H. R. Fox. *The Other Side of the Emin Pasha Relief Expedition.* London: Chatto & Windus, 1891.

Bülow, Bernhard Fürst von. *Memoirs of Prince von Bülow.* Trans. F. A. Voigt. Boston: Little, Brown, and Company, 1931–32.

Bülow, Frieda von. *Im Land der Verheissung.* 6th ed. Dresden: Carl Reissner, 1914.

Bülow, Frieda von. *Der Konsol: Väterlandischer Roman aus unseren Tagen.* Dresden: Carl Reissner, 1891.

Bülow, Frieda von. *Tropenkoller: Episode aus dem deutschen Kolonialleben.* Berlin: F. Fontane, 1896.

Class, Heinrich [Daniel Frymann, pseud.]. *Wenn ich der Kaiser wär-Politische Wahrheiten und Notwendigkeiten.* Leipzig: Dieterich, 1913.

Dühring, Eugen. *Die Judenfrage als Frage des Racencharakters und seiner Schädlichkeiten für Völkerexistenz, Sitte und Cultur: Mit einer denkerisch freiheitlichen und praktisch abschliessenden Antwort.* Nowawes-Neuendorf bei Berlin: Ulrich Dühring, 1901.

Emin Pasha. *Emin Pasha, His Life and Work Compiled from his Journals, Letters, Scientific Notes and Official Documents by Georg Schweitzer with an Introduction by R. W. Felkin.* Vol. 1. New York: Negro Universities Press, 1969.

Emin Pasha. *Emin-Pascha: Eine Sammlung von Reisebriefen und Berichten Dr. Emin-Pascha's aus den ehemals ägyptischen Aequatorialprovinzen und deren Grenzländern.* Compiled by Dr. Georg Schweinfurth and Dr. Friedrich Ratzel. Leipzig: F. A. Brockhaus, 1888.

Förster, Bernhard. *Deutsche Colonien in dem oberen Laplata-Gebiete mit besonderer Berücksichtigung von Paraguay. Ergebnisse eingehender Prüfungen, praktischer Arbeiten und Reisen, 1883–1885.* Naumberg: Bernhard Förster, 1886.

Götzen, Gustav Adolf von. *Deutsch-Ostafrika im Aufstand 1905/06.* Berlin: D. Reimer, 1909.

Hassan, Vita. *Die Wahrheit über Emin Pascha, die ägyptische Aequatorialprovinz und den Ssudan.* Berlin: Dietrich Reimer, 1893.

Kandt, Richard. *Caput Nili: Eine empfindsame Reise zu den Quellen des Nils.* Berlin: Dietrich Reimer, 1904.

Kayser, Alwine. *Aus den Anfängen unserer Kolonien. Meine Erlebnisse als Begleiterin meines Gatten, des ersten Kolonialdirektors, Wirkl. Geh. Legationsrats Dr. Kayser auf seiner Inspektionsreise nach Deutsch-Ostafrika 1892.* Berlin: Dietrich Reimer (Ernst Vohsen), 1912.

Knox, Robert. *The Races of Men: A Fragment.* Philadelphia: Lea and Blanchard, 1850.

Lagarde, Paul de. *Ausgewählte Schriften.* 2nd ed. Edited by Paul Fischer. Munich: J. F. Lehmann, 1934.

Lange, Friedrich. *Reines Deutschtum: Grundzüge einer nationalen Weltanschauung.* Berlin: Verlag von Alexander Duncker, 1904.

Liebert, Eduard von. *Aus einem bewegten Leben: Erinnerungen.* Munich: J. F. Lehmann, 1925.

Lion, Alexander. *Die Kulturfähigkeit des Negers und die Erziehungsaufgaben der Kulturnationen.* Berlin: Verlag Wilhelm Süsserott, 1908.

May, Karl. *Die Sklavenkarawane.* Bamberg: Karl-May-Verlag, 1949.

Merensky, Alexander. *Erinnerungen aus dem Missionsleben in Transvaal (Südafrika) 1859 bis 1882.* Ed. Ulrich van der Heyden. Berlin: edition ost, 1996.

Mounteney-Jephson, A. J. *Emin Pasha and the Rebellion at the Equator: A Story of Nine Months' Experiences in the Last of the Soudan Provinces.* New York: Charles Schribner's Sons, 1891.

Oetker, Karl. *Die Neger-Seele und die Deutschen in Afrika: Ein Kampf gegen Missionen Sittlichkeits-Fanatismus und Bürokratie vom Standpunkt moderner Psychologie.* Munich: J. F. Lehmann, 1907.

Paasch, Carl. *Eine jüdisch-deutsch Gesandtschaft und ihre Helfer. Geheimes Judenthum, Nebenregierungen und jüdische Weltherrschaft.* Leipzig: Carl Paasch, 1891.

Passarge, Siegfried. *Adamaua: Bericht über die Expedition des Deutschen-Kamerun Komitees in den Jahren 1893/94.* Berlin: Dietrich Reimer, 1895.

Passarge, Siegfried. *Die Buschmänner der Kalahari.* Berlin: Dieter Reimer, 1907.

Passarge, Siegfried. *Die Erde und ihr Wirtschaftsleben, eine Allgemein verständliche Darstellung für Kaufleute, Volkswirte, Lehrer, Studierende der Handelshochschulen und Universitäten.* Hamburg: Hanseatische Verlagsanstalt, 1926.

Passarge, Siegfried. *Das Judentum als landschaftskundlich-ethnologisches Problem.* Munich: J. F. Lehmann, 1929.

Peters, Carl. *Das Deutsch-Ostafrikanische Schutzgebiet: Im amtlichen Auftrage.* Munich: R. Oldenbourg, 1895.

Peters, Carl. *Gesammelte Schriften.* 3 vols. Edited by Walter Frank. Munich: Beck, 1943–44.

Peters, Carl. *New Light on Dark Africa: Being the Narrative of the German Emin Pasha Expedition.* Trans. H. W. Dulcken. London: Ward, Lock, 1891.

Pudor, Heinrich. *Deutschland für die Deutschen. Vorarbeiten zu Gesetzen gegen die jüdische Ansiedlung in Deutschland.* Munich: H. Sachs, 1912.

Raschdau, Ludwig. *In Weimar als preussischer Gesandter.* Berlin: E. S. Mittler, 1939.

Reichard, Paul. *Dr. Emin Pascha. Ein Vorkämpfer der Kultur im Innern Afrikas.* Leipzig: Verlag Otto Spamer, 1891.

Reichsbund Jüdischer Frontsoldaten. *Heroische Gestalten Jüdischen Stammes.* Berlin: Erwin Löwe, 1937.

Richthofen, Ferdinand Freiherr von. *Schantung und seine Eingangspforte Kiautschou.* Berlin: Dietrich Reimer, Ernst Vohsen 1898.

Ropes, Edward D., Jr. *The Zanzibar Letters of Edward D. Ropes, Jr., 1882–1892.* Ed. Norman Robert Bennett. Boston: African Studies Center, Boston University, 1973.

Schütze, Woldemar. *Schwarz gegen Weiss: Die Eingeborenenfrage als Kernpunkt unsere Kolonialpolitik in Afrika.* Berlin: C. A. Schwetschke und Sohn, 1908.

Sombart, Werner. *The Jews and Modern Capitalism.* Trans. M. Epstein. New York: B. Franklin, 1969.

Sombart, Werner, Friedr. Naumann, Matth. Erzberger, Prof. Weber, Frank Wedekind, Hanns Heinz Ewers, Heinrich Mann, Prof. Josef Kohler, Fritz Mauthner, Max Nordau, Prof Ludwig Geiger, Hermann Bahr, Richard Dehmel, Prof. Maybaum, Franz Oppenheimer. *Judentaufen.* Munich: Georg Müller, 1912.

Stairs, William G. *Victorian Explorer: The African Diaries of Captain William G. Stairs, 1887–1892.* Edited by Janina M. Konczacki. Halifax, NS: Nimbus Publishing, 1994.

Stanley, Henry M. *In Darkest Africa or the Quest, Rescue, and Retreat of Emin, Governor of Equatoria.* 2 vols. London: Sampson Low, Marston, Searle and Rivington, 1890–91.

Stuhlmann, Franz. *Mit Emin Pascha ins Herz von Afrika.* Berlin: Geographische Verlagsbuchhandlung von Dietrich Reimer, 1894.

Vietor, Johann Karl. *Geschichtliche und Kulturelle Entwickelung unserer Schutzgebiete.* Berlin: D. Reimer, 1913.

Wagner, Johannes. *Deutsch-Ostafrika. Geschichte der Gesellschaft für deutsche Kolonisation und der Deutsch-Ostafrikanische Gesellschaft nach den amtlichen Quellen.* Berlin: Engelhardt, 1886.

SECONDARY SOURCES

Books

Adas, Michael. *Machines as the Measure of Men: Science, Technology, and Ideologies of Western Dominance.* Ithaca: Cornell University Press, 1989.

Ames, Eric, Marcia Klotz, and Lora Wildenthal, eds. *Germany's Colonial Pasts.* Lincoln: University of Nebraska Press, 2005.

Arendt, Hannah. *The Origins of Totalitarianism.* New ed. San Diego: Harcourt Brace, 1979.

Austen, Ralph A., and Jonathan Derrick. *Middlemen of the Cameroons Rivers: The Duala and Their Hinterland, c. 1600–c. 1960.* Cambridge: Cambridge University Press, 1999.

Bartov, Omer. *Hitler's Army: Soldiers, Nazis, and War in the Third Reich.* Oxford: Oxford University Press, 1991.

Bartov, Omer. *Murder in Our Midst: The Holocaust, Industrial Killing, and Representation.* Oxford: Oxford University Press, 1996.

Berman, Russell A. *Enlightenment or Empire: Colonial Discourse in German Culture.* Lincoln: University of Nebraska Press, 1998.

Bley, Helmut. *Namibia under German Rule.* Trans. Hugh Ridley. Hamburg: LIT Verlag, 1996.

Burleigh, Michael, and Wolfgang Wippermann. *The Racial State: Germany, 1933–1945.* Cambridge: Cambridge University Press, 1991.

Burrin, Philippe. *Nazi Anti-Semitism: From Prejudice to the Holocaust.* Trans. Janet Lloyd. New York: New Press, 2005.

Chickering, Roger. *We Men Who Feel Most German: A Cultural Study of the Pan-German League, 1886–1914.* Boston: George Allen and Unwin, 1984.

Cocker, Mark. *Rivers of Blood, Rivers of Gold: Europe's Conquest of Indigenous People.* New York: Grove Press, 1998.

Coetzee, Marilyn Shevin. *The German Army League: Popular Nationalism in Wilhelmine Germany.* Oxford: Oxford University Press, 1990.

Conklin, Alice L. *A Mission to Civilize: The Republican Idea of Empire in France and West Africa, 1895–1930.* Stanford: Stanford University Press, 1997.

Conrad, Sebastian. *Globalisierung und Nation im Deutschen Kaiserreich.* Munich: C. H. Beck, 2006.

Cooper, Frederick, and Ann Laura Stoler, eds. *Tensions of Empire: Colonial Cultures in a Bourgeois World.* Berkeley: University of California Press, 1997.

Craig, Gordon A. *Germany, 1866–1945.* New York: Oxford University Press, 1980.

Curtin, Philip D. *The Image of Africa: British Ideas and Action, 1780–1850.* Madison: University of Wisconsin Press, 1964.

Debrunner, Hans Werner. *Presence and Prestige: Africans in Europe; A History of Africans in Europe before 1918.* Basel: Basler Afrika Bibliographien, 1979.

Deutscher, Isaac. *The Non-Jewish Jew and Other Essays.* London: Oxford University Press, 1968.

Drechsler, Horst. *"Let Us Die Fighting": The Struggle of the Herero and Nama against German Imperialism, 1884–1915.* Trans. Bernd Zöllner. London: Zed Press, 1980.

Dwork, Debórah, and Robert Jan Van Pelt. *Holocaust: A History.* New York: W. W. Norton, 2002.

Efron, John M. *Defenders of the Race: Jewish Doctors and Race Science in Fin-de-Siècle Europe.* New Haven: Yale University Press, 1994.

El-Tayeb, Fatima. *Schwarze Deutsche: Der Diskurs um "Rasse" und nationale Identität 1890–1933.* Frankfurt am Main: Campus, 2001.

Fischer, Klaus P. *The History of an Obsession: German Judeophobia and the Holocaust.* New York: Continuum, 2001.

Fischer, Lars. *The Socialist Response to Antisemitism in Imperial Germany.* Cambridge: Cambridge University Press, 2007.

Fischer-Tiné, Harald, and Michael Mann, eds. *Colonialism as Civilizing Mission: Cultural Ideology in British India.* London: Anthem Press, 2004.

Fredrickson, George M. *Racism: A Short History.* Princeton: Princeton University Press, 2002.

Friedrichsmeyer, Sara, Sara Lennox, and Susanne Zantop, eds. *The Imperialist Imagination: German Colonialism and Its Legacy.* Ann Arbor: University of Michigan Press, 1998.

Fritzsche, Peter. *Reading Berlin 1900.* Cambridge: Harvard University Press, 1996.

Gann, L. H., and Peter Duignan, eds. *African Proconsuls: European Governors in Africa.* New York: Free Press, 1978.

Gann, L. H., and Peter Duignan. *The Rulers of German Africa, 1884–1914.* Stanford: Stanford University Press, 1977.

Gerhson, Stuart Weinberg. *Kol Nidrei: Its Origins, Developments, and Significance.* Northvale, NJ: Jason Aronson, 1994.

Gilman, Sander L. *The Case of Sigmund Freud: Medicine and Identity at the Fin de Siècle.* Baltimore: Johns Hopkins University Press, 1994.

Gilman, Sander L. *The Jew's Body.* New York: Routledge, 1991.

Gilman, Sander L. *On Blackness without Blacks: Essays on the Image of the Black in Germany.* Boston: G. K. Hall, 1982.

Glassman, Jonathon. *Feasts and Riots: Revelry, Rebellion, and Popular Consciousness on the Swahili Coast, 1856–1888.* Portsmouth: Heinemann, 1995.

Gordon, Robert J., and Stuart Sholto Douglas. *The Bushman Myth: The Making of a Namibian Underclass.* 2nd ed. Boulder: Westview Press, 2000.

Gosewinkel, Dieter. *Einbürgern und Ausschliessen: Die Nationalisierung der Staatsangehörigkeit vom Deutschen Bund bis zur Bundesrepublik Deutschland.* Göttingen: Vandenhoeck und Ruprecht, 2001.

Gould, Stephan Jay. *The Mismeasure of Man.* New York: W. W. Norton, 1996.

Graml, Hermann. *Antisemitism in the Third Reich.* Trans. Tim Kirk. Oxford: Basil Blackwood, 1992.

Grosse, Pascal. *Kolonialismus, Eugenik und bürgerliche Gesellschaft in Deutschland, 1850–1918.* Frankfurt am Main: Campus Verlag, 2000.

Hamann, Brigitte. *Hitler's Vienna: A Dictator's Apprenticeship.* Trans. Thomas Thornton. New York: Oxford University Press, 1999.

Harding, Leonhard, ed. *Mpundu Akwa: Der Fall des Prinzen von Kamerun. Das neuentdeckte Plädoyer von Dr. M. Levi.* Munster: LIT, 2000.

Hartston, Barnet. *Sensationalizing the Jewish Question: Anti-Semitic Trials and the Press in the Early German Empire.* Leiden: Brill, 2005.

Herf, Jeffrey. *Reactionary Modernism: Technology, Culture, and Politics in Weimar and the Third Reich.* Cambridge: Cambridge University Press, 1984.

Hertz, Deborah. *How Jews Became Germans: The History of Conversion and Assimilation in Berlin.* New Haven: Yale University Press, 2007.

Hess, Jonathan M. *Germans, Jews, and the Claims of Modernity.* New Haven: Yale University Press, 2002.

Hoffmann, Christhard, Werner Bergmann, and Helmut Walser Smith, eds. *Exclusionary Violence: Antisemitic Riots in Modern German History.* Ann Arbor: University of Michigan Press, 2002.

Holborn, Hajo. *A History of Modern Germany, 1840–1945.* Princeton: Princeton University Press, 1982.

Hull, Isabel V. *Absolute Destruction: Military Culture and the Practices of War in Imperial Germany.* Ithaca: Cornell University Press, 2005.

Hull, Isabel V. *The Entourage of Kaiser Wilhelm II, 1888–1918.* Cambridge: Cambridge University Press, 1982.

Iliffe, John. *A Modern History of Tanganyika.* Cambridge: Cambridge University Press, 1979.

Iliffe, John. *Tanganyika under German Rule, 1905–1912.* Cambridge: Cambridge University Press, 1969.

Jeal, Tim. *Stanley: The Impossible Life of Africa's Greatest Explorer.* New Haven: Yale University Press, 2008.

Kalmar, Ivan Davidson, and Derek J. Penslar, eds. *Orientalism and the Jews.* Hanover: Brandeis University Press, 2005.

Katz, Jacob. *From Prejudice to Destruction: Anti-Semitism, 1700–1933.* Cambridge: Harvard University Press, 1980.

King, Richard H., and Dan Stone, eds. *Hannah Arendt and the Uses of History: Imperialism, Nation, Race, and Genocide.* New York: Berghahn Books, 2007.

Klein, Thoralf, and Frank Schumacher, eds. *Kolonialkriege: Militärische Gewalt im Zeichen des Imperialismus.* Hamburg: Hamburger Edition HIS Verlag, 2006.

Knoll, Arthur J. *Togo under Imperial Germany, 1884–1914. A Case Study in Colonial Rule.* Stanford: Hoover Institution Press, 1978.

Knoll, Arthur J., and Lewis H. Gann, eds. *Germans in the Tropics: Essays in German Colonial History.* New York: Greenwood Press, 1987.

Koonz, Claudia. *The Nazi Conscience.* Cambridge: Belknap Press of Harvard University Press, 2003.

Koponen, Juhani. *Development for Exploitation: German Colonial Policies in Mainland Tanzania, 1884–1914.* Helsinki: Finnish Historical Society, 1995.

Koszyk, Kurt. *Deutsche Presse im 19. Jahrhundert: Geschichte der deutschen Presse.* Vol. 2. Berlin: Colloquium Verlag, 1966.

Kundrus, Birthe. *Moderne Imperialisten. Das Kaiserreich im Spiegel seiner Kolonien.* Vienna: Böhlau Verlag Wien, 2003.

Kundrus, Birthe, ed. *Phantasiereiche: Zur Kulturgeschichte des deutschen Kolonialismus.* Frankfurt am Main: Campus Verlag, 2003.

Kurlander, Eric. *The Price of Exclusion: Ethnicity, National Identity, and the Decline of German Liberalism, 1898–1933.* New York: Berghahn Books, 2006.

Lahme, Rainer. *Deutsche Außenpolitik, 1890–1894. Von der Gleichgewichtspolitik Bismarcks zur Allianzstrategie Caprivis.* Göttingen: Vandenhoeck & Ruprecht, 1990.

Langbehn, Volker, ed. *German Colonialism, Visual Culture, and Modern Memory.* New York: Routledge, 2009.

Lehmstedt, Mark, and Andreas Herzog, eds. *Das bewegte Buch. Buchwesen und soziale, nationale und kulturelle Bewegungen um 1900.* Wiesbaden: Harrassowitz Verlag, 1999.

Levy, Richard S. *The Downfall of the Anti-Semitic Political Parties in Imperial Germany.* New Haven: Yale University Press, 1975.

Liebowitz, Daniel, and Charles Pearson. *The Last Expedition: Stanley's Mad Journey through the Congo.* New York: W. W. Norton, 2005.

Lindemann, Albert S. *Esau's Tears: Modern Anti-Semitism and the Rise of the Jews.* Cambridge: Cambridge University Press, 1997.

Lindqvist, Sven. *"Exterminate all the Brutes:" One Man's Odyssey into the Heart of Darkness and the Origins of European Genocide.* Trans. Joan Tate. New York: New Press, 1996.

Macintyre, Ben. *Forgotten Fatherland: The Search for Elisabeth Nietzsche.* New York: Farrar Straus Giroux, 1992.

Mahler, Karl. *Die Programme der politischen Parteien in Deutschland.* Leipzig: O. Gracklauer, 1911.

Maß, Sandra. *Weiße Helden, schwarze Krieger: Zur Geschichte kolonialer Männlichkeit in Deutschland, 1918–1964.* Cologne: Böhlau, 2006.

Massing, Paul W. *Rehearsal for Destruction: A Study of Political Anti-Semitism in Imperial Germany.* New York: Harper & Brothers, 1949.

Mazón, Patricia, and Reinhild Steingröver, eds. *Not So Plain as Black and White: Afro-German Culture and History, 1890–2000.* Rochester: University of Rochester Press, 2005.

McCulloch, Jock. *Black Peril, White Virtue: Sexual Crime in Southern Rhodesia, 1902–1935.* Bloomington: Indiana University Press, 2000.

Mendes-Flohr, Paul. *German Jews: A Dual Identity.* New Haven: Yale University Press, 1999.

Merkl, Peter H. *Political Violence under the Swastika: 581 Early Nazis.* Princeton: Princeton University Press, 1975.

Mommsen, Wolfgang J. *Imperial Germany, 1867–1918: Politics, Culture, and Society in an Authoritarian State.* Trans. Richard Deveson. London: Arnold, 1995.

Moses, Dirk A., ed. *Empire, Colony, Genocide: Conquest, Occupation, and Subaltern Resistance in World History.* New York: Berghahn Books, 2008.

Moses, Dirk A., ed. *Genocide and Settler Society: Frontier Violence and Stolen Indigenous Children in Australian History.* New York: Berghahn Books, 2004.

Moses, John A., and Paul M. Kennedy, eds. *Germany in the Pacific and Far East, 1870–1914.* St. Lucia: University of Queensland Press, 1977.

Mosse, George L. *German Jews Beyond Judaism.* Bloomington: Indiana University Press, 1985.

Mosse, George L. *Toward the Final Solution: A History of European Racism.* New York: Howard Fertig, 1978.

Müller, Fritz F. *Deutschland—Zanzibar—Ostafrika: Geschichte einer deutschen Kolonialeroberung, 1884–1890.* Berlin: Rütten und Loening, 1959.

Müller, Fritz F. *Kolonien unter der Peitsche.* Berlin: Rütten und Loening, 1962.

Nochlin, Linda, and Tamar Garb, eds. *The Jew in the Text: Modernity and the Construction of Identity.* London: Thames and Hudson, 1995.

Nwezeh, E. C. *Africa in French and German Fiction, (1911–1913).* Ile-Ife: University of Ife Press, 1978.

Oguntoye, Katharina. *Eine afro-deutsche Geschichte: Zur Lebenssituation von Afrikanern und Afro-Deutschen in Deutschland von 1884 bis 1950.* Berlin: Hoho Verlag Christine Hoffmann, 1997.

Oschilewski, Walther G. *Zeitungen in Berlin: Im Spiegel der Jahrhunderte.* Berlin: Haude & Spener, 1975.

Pakenham, Thomas. *The Scramble for Africa: White Man's Conquest of the Dark Continent from 1876 to 1912.* New York: Avon Books, 1991.

Perras, Arne. *Carl Peters and German Imperialism, 1856–1918: A Political Biography.* Oxford: Oxford University Press, 2004.

Perraudin, Michael, and Jürgen Zimmerer, eds. *German Colonialism and National Identity.* New York: Routledge, 2009.

Poliakov, Léon. *The Aryan Myth: A History of Racist and Nationalist Ideas in Europe.* Trans. Edmund Howard. New York: Basic Books, 1974.

Pulzer, Peter. *The Rise of Political Anti-Semitism in Germany and Austria.* New York: John Wiley and Sons, 1964.

Puschner, Uwe. *Die völkische Bewegung im wilhelminischen Kaiserreich: Sprache, Rasse, Religion.* Darmstadt: Wissenschaftliche Buchgesellschaft, 2001.

Ragins, Sanford. *Jewish Responses to Anti-Semitism in Germany, 1870–1914.* Cincinnati: Hebrew Union College Press, 1980.

Rahden, Till van. *Jews and Other Germans: Civil Society, Religious Diversity, and Urban Politics in Breslau, 1860–1925.* Trans. Marcus Brainard. Madison: University of Wisconsin Press, 2008.

Reinharz, Jehuda, and Walter Schatzberg, eds. *The Jewish Response to German Culture: From the Enlightenment to the Second World War.* Hanover: University Press of New England, 1985.

Ridley, Hugh. *Images of Imperial Rule.* New York: Croom Helm, 1983.

Robertson, Ritchie. *The "Jewish Question" in German Literature, 1749–1939.* Oxford: Oxford University Press, 1999.

Rosenbaum, Ron. *Explaining Hitler: The Search for the Origins of His Evil.* New York: Random House, 1998.

Rudin, Harry R. *Germans in the Cameroons, 1884–1914: A Case Study in Modern Imperialism.* New Haven: Yale University Press, 1938.

Said, Edward W. *Culture and Imperialism.* New York: Knopf, 1993.

Said, Edward W. *Orientalism.* New York: Vintage Books, 1979.

Scheil, Stefan. *Die Entwicklung des politischen Antisemitismus in Deutschland zwischen 1881 und 1912. Eine wahlgeschichtliche Untersuchung.* Berlin: Duncker & Humblot, 1999.

Schiefel, Werner. *Bernhard Dernburg, 1865–1937: Kolonialpolitiker und Bankier im wilhelminischen Deutschland.* Zurich: Atlantis Verlag, 1974.

Seligmann, Matthew S. *Rivalry in Southern Africa, 1893–99: The Transformation of German Colonial Policy.* Houndmills: Macmillan, 1998.

Smith, Helmut Walser. *The Butcher's Tale: Murder and Anti-Semitism in a German Town.* New York: W. W. Norton, 2002.

Smith, Helmut Walser. *The Continuities of German History: Nation, Religion, and Race across the Long Nineteenth Century.* Cambridge: Cambridge University Press, 2008.

Smith, Helmut Walser, ed. *Protestants, Catholics, and Jews in Germany, 1800–1914.* New York: Berg, 2001.

Smith, Woodruff D. *The German Colonial Empire.* Chapel Hill: University of North Carolina Press, 1978.

Smith, Woodruff D. *The Ideological Origins of Nazi Imperialism.* Oxford: Oxford University Press, 1986.

Soggot, David. *Namibia: The Violent Heritage.* New York: St. Martin's Press, 1986.

Spitzer, Leo. *Lives in Between: Assimilation and Marginality in Austria, Brazil, West Africa, 1780–1945.* Cambridge: Cambridge University Press, 1989.

Spöttel, Michael. *Hamiten: Völkerkunde und Antisemitismus.* Frankfurt am Main: Peter Lang, 1996.

Steinmetz, George. *The Devil's Handwriting: Precoloniality and the German Colonial State in Qingdao, Samoa, and Southwest Africa.* Chicago: University of Chicago Press, 2007.

Stern, Fritz. *Gold and Iron: Bismarck, Bleichröder, and the Building of the German Empire.* New York: Vintage Books, 1979.

Stern, Fritz. *The Politics of Cultural Despair: A Study in the Rise of the Germanic Ideology.* Berkeley: University of California Press, 1974.

Stöber, Rudolf. *Deutsche Pressegeschichte: Einführung, Systematik, Glossar.* Constance: UVK Medien, 2000.

Stoecker, Helmut, ed. *German Imperialism in Africa.* London: C. Hurst, 1986.

Transverso, Enzo. *The Origins of Nazi Violence.* Trans. Janet Lloyd. New York: New Press, 2003.

Vital, David. *A People Apart: The Jews in Europe, 1789–1945.* Oxford: Oxford University Press, 1999.

Volkov, Shulamit. *Germans, Jews, and Antisemites: Trials in Emancipation.* Cambridge: Cambridge University Press, 2006.

Wagner, Wilfried, ed. *Rassendiskriminierung, Kolonialpolitik und ethnisch-nationale Identität.* Münster: LIT Verlag, 1992.

Warmbold, Joachim. *Germania in Africa: Germany's Colonial Literature.* New York: Peter Lang, 1989.

Wehler, Hans Ulrich. *Bismarck und der Imperialismus.* Cologne: Kiepenheuer und Witsch, 1969.

Weiss, John. *Ideology of Death: Why the Holocaust Happened in Germany.* Chicago: Elephant Paperbacks, 1996.

Wertheimer, Jack. *Unwelcome Strangers: East European Jews in Imperial Germany.* New York: Oxford University Press, 1987.

Wertheimer, Mildred S. *The Pan-German League, 1890–1914.* New York: Columbia University, 1924.

Wildenthal, Lora. *German Women for Empire, 1884–1945.* Durham: Duke University Press, 2001.

Wistrich, Robert S. *Antisemitism: The Longest Hatred.* New York: Schocken Books, 1991.

Wistrich, Robert S. *Socialism and the Jews: The Dilemmas of Assimilation in Germany and Austria-Hungary.* Rutherford: Fairleigh Dickinson University Press, 1982.

Zantop, Susanne. *Colonial Fantasies: Conquest, Family, and Nation in Precolonial Germany, 1770–1870.* Durham: Duke University Press, 1997.

Zimmerer, Jürgen. *Deutsche Herrschaft über Afrikaner: Staatlicher Machtanspruch und Wirklichkeit im kolonialen Namibia.* Münster: Lit Verlag, 2002.

Zimmerer, Jürgen, and Joachim Zeller, eds. *Genocide in German South-West Africa: The Colonial War of 1904–1908 and Its Aftermath.* Trans. E. J. Neather. Monmouth, Wales: Merlin Press, 2008.

Zimmerman, Andrew, *Anthropology and Antihumanism in Imperial Germany.* Chicago: University of Chicago Press, 2001.

Articles and Book Chapters

Amos, Alcione M. "Afro-Brazilians in Togo: The Case of the Olympio Family, 1882–1924." *Cahier D'Études Africaines* 41 (2001): 293–314.

Bartov, Omer. "Defining Enemies, Making Victims: Germans, Jews, and the Holocaust." *American Historical Review* 103 (1998): 771–816.

Bonnell, Andrew G. "Discussion: Was German Social Democracy before 1914 Antisemitic?" *German History* 27 (2009): 259–69.

Cohen, Cynthia. "'The Natives Must First Become Good Workmen': Formal Educational Provision in German South West and East Africa Compared." *Journal of Southern African Studies* 19 (1993): 115–34.

Davis, Christian Stuart. "'Coddling' Africans Abroad: Colonial Director Paul Kayser and the Education of Africans in Germany, 1891–96." *Journal of Colonialism and Colonial History* 9, no. 1 (2008).

Davis, Christian Stuart. "Colonialism and Antisemitism during the *Kaiserreich:* Bernhard Dernburg and the Antisemites." *Leo Baeck Institute Yearbook* 53 (2008): 31–56.

Dickinson, Edward Ross. "The German Empire: An Empire?" *History Workshop Journal* 66 (2008): 129–62.

Epstein, Klaus. "Erzberger and the German Colonial Scandals, 1905–1910." *English Historical Review* 74 (1959): 637–63.

Essner, Corneila. "Zwischen Vernuft und Gefühl: Die Reichstagsdebatten von 1912 um koloniale 'Rassenmischehe' und 'Sexualität.'" *Zeitschrift für Geschichtswissenschaft* 45, no. 6 (1997): 503–19.

Feuser, Willfried. "Slave to Proletarian: Images of the Black in German Literature." *German Life and Letters* 32 (1979): 122–33.

Field, Geoffrey G. "Nordic Racism." *Journal of the History of Ideas* 38 (1977): 523–40.

Firth, S. G. "The New Guinea Company, 1885–1899: A Case of Unprofitable Imperialism." *Historical Studies* 15 (1972): 361–77.

Fitzpatrick, Matthew. "Narrating Empire: *Die Gartenlaube* and Germany's Nineteenth-Century Liberal Expansionism." *German Studies Review* 30 (2007): 97–120.

Fitzpatrick, Matthew P. "The Pre-History of the Holocaust? The *Sonderweg* and *Historikerstreit* Debates and the Abject Colonial Past." *Central European History* 41 (2008): 477–503.

Frank, Walter. "Der Geheime Rat Paul Kayser: Neues Material aus seinem Nachlaß." *Historische Zeitschrift* 168 (1943): 302–35, 541–63.

Furber, David, and Wendy Lower. "Colonialism and Genocide in Nazi-Occupied Poland and Ukraine." In *Empire, Colony, Genocide: Conquest, Occupation, and Subaltern Resistance in World History,* edited by Dirk A. Moses, 372–402. New York: Berghahn Books, 2008.

Gerwarth, Robert, and Stephan Malinowski. "Hannah Arendt's Ghosts: Reflections on the Disputable Path from Windhoeck to Auschwitz." *Central European History* 42 (2009): 279–300.

Geyer, Michael. *"Endkampf* 1918 and 1945: German Nationalism, Annihilation, and Self-Destruction." In *No Man's Land of Violence: Extreme Wars in the 20th Century,* edited by Alf Lüdtke and Bernd Weisbrod, 35–68. Göttingen: Wallstein Verlag, 2006.

Gilman, Sander L. "The Figure of the Black in German Aesthetic Theory." *Eighteenth-Century Studies* 8 (1975): 373–91.

Gordon, Robert J. "The Making of the 'Bushmen.'" *Anthropologica* 34 (1992): 183–202.

Gosewinkel, Dieter. "Rückwirkungen des kolonialen Rasserechts? Deutsche Staatsangehörigkeit zwischen Rassestaat und Rechtsstaat." In *Das Kaiserreich transnational. Deutschland in der Welt 1871–1914,* edited by Sebastian Conrad and Jürgen Osterhammel, 236–56. Göttingen: Vandenhoeck und Ruprecht, 2004.

Grimmer-Solem, Erik. "Every True Friend of the Fatherland": Gustav Schmoller and the 'Jewish Question,' 1916–1917." *Leo Baeck Institute Yearbook* 52 (2007): 149–63.

Grimmer-Solem, Erik. "The Professors' Africa: Economists, the Elections of 1907, and the Legitimation of German Imperialism." *German History* 25 (2007): 313–47.

Grosse, Pascal. "What Does German Colonialism Have to Do with National Socialism? A Conceptual Framework." In *Germany's Colonial Pasts,* edited by Eric Ames, Marcia Klotz, and Lora Wildenthal, 115–34. Lincoln: University of Nebraska Press, 2005.

Jensen, Uffa. "Into the Spiral of Problematic Perceptions: Modern Anti-Semitism and *gebildetes Bürgertum* in Nineteenth-Century Germany." *German History* 25 (2007): 348–71.

Kopp, Kristin. "Constructing Racial Difference in Colonial Poland." In *Germany's Colonial Pasts,* edited by Eric Ames, Marcia Klotz, and Lora Wildenthal, 76–96. Lincoln: University of Nebraska Press, 2005.

Kundrus, Birthe. "Continuities, Parallels, Receptions: Reflections on the 'Colonization' of National Socialism." *Journal of Namibian Studies* 4 (2008): 25–46.

Levenson, Alan. "Philosemitic Discourse in Imperial Germany." *Jewish Social Studies* 2 (1996): 25–53.

Madley, Benjamin. "From Africa to Auschwitz: How German South West Africa Incubated Ideas and Methods Adopted and Developed by the Nazis in Eastern Europe." *European History Quarterly* 35 (2005): 429–64.

Marks, Sally. "Black Watch on the Rhine: A Study in Propaganda, Prejudice, and Prurience." *European Studies Review* 13 (1983): 297–334.

Moyn, Samuel. "German Jewry and the Question of Identity Historiography and Theory." *Leo Baeck Institute Yearbook* 41 (1996): 291–308.

Naranch, Bradley D. "'Colonized Body,' 'Oriental Machine': Debating Race, Railroads, and the Politics of Reconstruction in Germany and East Africa, 1906–1910." *Central European History* 33 (2000): 299–338.

Phelps, Reginald H. "'Before Hitler Came': Thule Society and Germanen Orden." *Journal of Modern History* 35 (1963): 245–61.

Poiger, Uta G. "Imperialism and Empire in Twentieth-Century Germany." *History & Memory* 17 (2005): 117–43.

Rahden, Till van. "Words and Actions: Rethinking the Social History of German Antisemitism, Breslau, 1870–1914." *German History* 18 (2000): 413–38.

Reuss, Martin. "The Disgrace and Fall of Carl Peters: Morality, Politics, and *Staatsräson* in the Time of Wilhelm II." *Central European History* 14 (1981): 110–41.

Reuveni, Gideon. "'Productivist' and 'Consumerist' Narratives of Jews in German History." In *German History from the Margins,* edited by Neil Gregor, Nils Roemer, and Mark Roseman, 165–84. Bloomington: Indiana University Press, 2006.

Ridley, Hugh. "Colonial Society and European Totalitarianism." *Journal of European Studies* 3 (1973): 147–59.

Ridley, Hugh. "Germany in the Mirror of Its Colonial Literature." *German Life and Letters* 28 (1975): 375–86.

Seligmann, Matthew S. "The Pfeil Family and the Development of German Colonial Ambitions in Southern Africa: A Study of Diplomacy and Colonial Trends." *German History* 12 (1994): 27–38.

Short, John Phillip. "Everyman's Colonial Library: Imperialism and Working-Class Readers in Leipzig, 1890–1914." *German History* 21 (2003): 445–75.

Smith, Helmut Walser. "The Learned and the Popular Discourse of Anti-Semitism in the Catholic Milieu of the Kaiserreich." *Central European History* 27 (1994): 315–28.

Smith, Helmut Walser. "The Talk of Genocide, the Rhetoric of Miscegenation: Notes on Debates in the German Reichstag Concerning Southwest Africa, 1904–1914." In *The Imperialist Imagination: German Colonialism and Its Legacy,* ed. Sara Friedrichsmeyer, Sara Lennox, and Susanne Zantop, 107–23. Ann Arbor: University of Michigan Press, 1998.

Sunseri, Thaddeus. "The *Baumwollfrage:* Cotton Colonialism in German East Africa." *Central European History* 34 (2001): 31–51.

Telman, D. A. Jeremy. "Adolf Stoecker: Anti-Semite with a Christian Mission." *Jewish History* 9 (1995): 93–112.

Walther, Daniel. "Creating Germans Abroad: White Education in German Southwest Africa, 1894–1914." *German Studies Review* 24 (2001): 325–51.

Warmbold, Joachim. "If Only She Didn't Have Negro Blood in Her Veins: The Concept of *Métissage* in German Colonial Literature." *Journal of Black Studies* 23 (1992): 200–209.

Weiss, Yfaat. "Identity and Essentialism: Race, Racism, and the Jews at the Fin de Siècle." In *German History from the Margins,* edited by Neil Gregor, Nils Roemer, and Mark Roseman, 49–68. Bloomington: Indiana University Press, 2006.

Wildenthal, Lora. "'When Men Are Weak': The Imperial Feminism of Frieda von Bülow." *Gender and History* 10 (1998): 53–77.

Wilke, Sabine. "'Verrottet, verkommen, von fremder Rasse durchsetzt': The Colonial Trope as Subtext of the Nazi 'Kulturfilm' *Ewiger Wald* (1936)." *German Studies Review* 24 (2001): 353–76.

Zimmerer, Jürgen. "The Birth of the *Ostland* out of the Spirit of Colonialism: A Postcolonial Perspective on the Nazi Policy of Conquest and Extermination." *Patterns of Prejudice* 39 (2005): 197–219.

Zimmerer, Jürgen. "Colonialism and the Holocaust: Towards an Archeology of Genocide." In *Genocide and Settler Society: Frontier Violence and Stolen Indigenous Children in Australian History,* edited by A. Dirk Moses, 49–76. New York: Berghahn Books, 2004.

Zimmerer, Jürgen. "War, Concentration Camps, and Genocide in South-West Africa: The First German Genocide." In *Genocide in German South-West Africa: The Colonial War of 1904–1908 and Its Aftermath,* edited by Jürgen Zimmerer and Joachim Zeller, 41–63. Trans. by E. J. Neather. Monmouth: Merlin Press, 2008.

Zimmerman, Andrew. "Anti-Semitism as Skill: Rudolf Virchow's *Schulstatistik* and the Racial Composition of Germany." *Central European History* 32 (1999): 409–29.

Theses and Dissertations

Bernstein, George. "Anti-Semitism in Imperial Germany, 1871–1914: Selected Documents." EdD diss., Teachers College, Columbia University, 1973.

Crothers, George Dunlap. "The German Elections of 1907." PhD diss., Columbia University, 1941.

Haunss, Jürgen. "Weiß und Schwarz, und Mann und Frau: Die Diskussion um die sog. Mischehen in den deutschen Kolonien unter besonderer Berücksichtigung des 'Schutzgebietes' Deutsch-Südwestafrika. Ein Beispiel für die Konstruktion von Geschlechterdifferenz als Mittel zur Legitimation von Herrschaft im wilhelminischen Deutschland." Wissenschaftliche Hausarbeit zur Erlangung des akademischen Grades eines Magister Artium der Universität Hamburg, 1997.

Pierard, Richard Victor. "The German Colonial Society, 1882–1914." PhD diss., Graduate College of the State University of Iowa, 1964.

Volland, Alexander. "Theodor Fritsch (1852–1933) und die Zeitschrift '*Hammer.*'" PhD diss., Johannes Gutenberg-Universität, 1993.

Index

Adolf Woermann (shipping company), 58, 202, 208, 208n37, 235
Agrarian League, 60–61, 102n92, 120n154, 173, 207n35
Ahasuerus, 91–92
Ahmad, Muhammad, 138, 138n10
Allgemeine Zeitung des Judenthums, 59, 126, 193, 194, 242
American Indians, 89, 130
American South, 116–17
anti-Catholicism, 58, 197–99, 228
Antisemites' Petition, 27n5, 45, 106
Antisemitic People's Party, 26, 29
Antisemitische Correspondenz, 153, 159, 160
Antisemitisches Volksblatt (and *Reichs-geldmonopol*), 147, 108
Arabs, 59, 59n94, 60, 60n95, 80, 89, 93, 139, 177, 177n175, 188, 191n225
Arendt, Hannah, 2, 2n3, 3, 16, 16n42, 17
Arendt, Otto, 63, 135, 144, 144n26, 173n157, 194, 255
  and C. Peters, 62, 71n141, 142, 172–73
  and colonial violence, 71n141, 143
  as a target of antisemitism, 191
Arnim-Muskau, Hermann Graf von, 65, 172–73, 172n155

Baecker, Carl, 249
Bagamoyo, 154, 156n87
Bamberger, Ludwig, 146
Bartels, Adolf, 90, 90n44, 115–17
Bayreuther Blätter, 233, 233n139
Bebel, August, 1, 13, 65n117, 69, 120–21, 121n155, 172, 197, 211, 213
beheadings, 206n29
Bendix, Josef, 137n8
Berliner Tageblatt, 152–53, 192, 201,

224, 224n108, 231, 238
Berthold, H., 105, 105n106
Bible (Christian New Testament), 139, 157, 226
Bielefeld Mission Society, 188
Bindewald, Friedrich, 146, 209–10, 213
Bismarck, Herbert, 164
Bismarck, Otto von, 25, 42, 164–65, 165n116, 169, 169n138, 170, 219, 242
black Africans
  denied the right to testify in colonial courts of law (*see* testifying under oath)
  living in Germany, 180–81
  racist fantasies of, 69–70, 72–73, 78–132
  violence against (*see under* German Southwest Africa: Herero and Nama uprisings)
  See also beheadings; corporal punishment
Bley, Fritz, 59–61, 60n96, 61n98, 68, 71–72
Bley, Helmut, 17
Böckel, Otto, 29, 29n11, 33n23, 60n96, 157, 157n90, 168
Böckler, Otto, 121, 132, 255
Boer War, 13
Boers, 63, 96, 120
Book of the Kahal, 67
Bruhn, Wilhelm, 25n1, 235
Bülow, Bernhard von, 38n39, 164, 196, 197n4, 198n7, 201–2, 202n16, 207, 209
Bülow, Frieda von, 62, 144n26
  antisemitism of, 63–64, 191
  and colonial violence, 71, 84
Büttner, Carl Gotthilf, 188–89